Religion and Politics
in the Middle East

Religion and Politics in the Middle East

Identity, Ideology, Institutions, and Attitudes

Robert D. Lee

Colorado College

Westview PRESS

A MEMBER OF THE PERSEUS BOOKS GROUP

Copyright © 2010 by Westview Press

Published by Westview Press,
A Member of the Perseus Books Group

Every effort has been made to secure required permissions to use all images, maps, and other art included in this volume.

Westview Press books are available at special discounts for bulk purchases in the United States by corporations, institutions, and other organizations. For more information, please contact the Special Markets Department at the Perseus Books Group, 2300 Chestnut Street, Suite 200, Philadelphia, PA 19103, or call (800) 810-4145, ext. 5000, or e-mail special.markets@perseusbooks.com.

A CIP catalog record for this book is available from the Library of Congress.
ISBN: 978-08133-4420-1
10 9 8 7 6 5 4 3 2 1

Contents

Preface

I emerged from graduate school in an epoch of great hope for the discipline of comparative politics. David Easton's definition of the political system offered a basis for analyzing both democratic and authoritarian, developed and underdeveloped countries. Structural-functionalism dominated the academy. Modernization theory garnered nearly unanimous support. We argued about whether the concept of "political culture" paved the way toward more useful comparison or only served to emphasize those elements of a system that are unique, but we thought we knew where we were going.

As I finished a dissertation and began to teach, I saw that those ideas and schemes, however provocative, constituted a set of lenses colored differently than the older, institutional lenses but nonetheless colored. The hope for quantification contained in some of the structural-functional thinking never proved practical, at least not in the Middle East and North Africa, the area of my special interest. Detailed comparisons of structures and functions produced description more than analysis. So what if a particular political structure does not perform a particular function that it performs in another political system? Methods, approaches, and paradigms began to proliferate.

Some of the most persuasive and influential work on the Middle East and North Africa continued to focus on a single society at a time. However much inspired by theory, and even though their authors often referred to them as "case studies," they described a unique set of institutions functioning in a specific context. Even volumes in the Little, Brown series in comparative politics, while similar in theoretical interests, were not exercises in genuine comparison.

Alternatively, those who turned to rational choice models or political economy for theoretical inspiration neglected the unique for the general. Ronald Inglehart, who took political surveys to Europe (Eurobarometer) and then to the world as a whole (World Values Survey), claimed to show that political cultures remain unique even though his model of "human development" includes only universal propositions. According to Inglehart, all societies are headed in the same direction, though along somewhat different paths and at different speeds. The uniqueness of individual cultures gets lost in the wide-reaching comparisons.

In trying to teach comparative politics for more than thirty-five years I have struggled with a dilemma. I believe students, like scholars, must understand some political systems in depth before they can make broad comparisons. To introduce all the countries of the Middle East and North Africa and suggest that the cultures are all similar is not satisfactory, in my view. But books on the politics of individual countries—and I have always used four countries as my base: Egypt, Israel, Turkey, and Iran—provide some depth for students but differ so much in perspective and approach that comparison is difficult. Some monographs are too complicated for beginning students. Journalistic studies, however readable, lack systematic analysis. Historical studies, however useful, do not emphasize the political dimension I want to be the center of my course.

I have yearned for materials that would examine a subset of countries with regard to a single set of issues. In recent years, I have focused my course on the relationship between religion and politics, and I began to think about writing a book that would approach that domain and that domain alone. I yearned for a modern rendition of Donald Eugene Smith's *Religion and Political Development*, an enormously ambitious volume that set no geographical or cultural limits for itself. I admire his boldness, but the conclusions do not stand up in the wake of the religious revival that has occurred since it was written.

Would it not be possible to (1) examine the propositions Smith and others have advanced against a more modest range of examples in genuinely comparative fashion and at the same time (2) ground those examples in sufficient cultural detail so that the unique qualities of political systems do not get lost in the comparison? In other words, might it be possible to combine some of the merits of single-country monographs with an effort at comparison limited to a single issue area, religion? Might it be possible to generate some useful comparative generalizations at a regional level? This study pursues that possibility.

It also seeks middle ground in another respect. D. E. Smith's book was exceptional in its time, because it focused on a topic that was largely neglected: religion and politics. The infatuation of our discipline with modernization theory and the secularization hypothesis that lurked near the center of that theory caused most scholars to downplay the importance of religion. Then came the Iranian revolution, which brought a great turnaround. Suddenly there was an outpouring of studies on Islam and politics. From the supply of books now available on the subject, one could easily conclude that religion is the most important factor in explaining politics in the Middle East and North Africa. With its underlying contention that politics has shaped religion as much as or more than religion has shaped politics, this study seeks to pull back from that idea without dismissing the religious revival as a passing phenomenon of little consequence.

Acknowledgments

When a work is long in gestation, it is difficult to reconstruct all of one's debts. I delivered an early version of chapter 3 as a paper at the annual meeting of the Middle East Studies Association a few years ago. I don't remember that it stirred much discussion, but I do remember that Bill Ochsenwald encouraged me to think about writing a textbook. I am grateful for his encouragement.

I began work on this manuscript while on sabbatical leave from Colorado College, and later I received a second leave of absence that permitted me to accelerate the project. The college, where I have been happily employed since 1971, also provided research funds on several occasions to help defray travel expenses. Departmental colleagues listened with patience to elements of my argument and tolerated my occasional absence.

I am especially grateful to a friend from graduate school, Ann Lesch, currently dean of arts and sciences at the American University in Cairo, for reading the whole of the manuscript and providing excellent suggestions. Several anonymous readers also provided useful advice, much of which I have tried to follow. Libby Rittenberg, an economist who has worked in Turkey, read the Turkey chapter and provided comments and encouragement.

I did some of this work in Florence, Italy, where I shared many thoughts about religion and politics with Jean Blondel on long walks along the Arno. When he came to Colorado College in Colorado Springs as a visiting professor, we had to settle for sorties along Monument Creek. It is easy to be inspired by a friend of such accomplishment and energy.

To several scholars I have debts not fully reflected in the notes and bibliography. From Mohammed Arkoun, Mustapha Tlili, and Hamadi Redissi I have learned much about the matters I discuss in this book. Similarly, in the course of working on this manuscript I profited from conversations with Leonard Binder, Robert Bianchi, Eric Davis, Najib Ghadbian, Ellen Lust-Okar, and the late Iliya Harik, among others, in multiple sessions of a workshop on the *turath* (heritage) organized by Professor Binder at the University of California–Los Angeles.

Two students at Colorado College, both now alumni, made important concrete contributions to this manuscript. Elias Cohen helped with the research and drafting of the chapter on Israel, and Colin Johnson used a sharp pencil to help with both the prose and the substance of the manuscript. Other students too numerous to name have influenced my thinking by way of discussion in my classes.

At Westview, Karl Yambert showed early interest in this manuscript and offered helpful encouragement. Laura Stine, senior project editor, and Antoinette Smith, copyeditor, provided invaluable help in bringing the project to fruition and in achieving greater consistency in the text.

None of these persons bears responsibility, of course, for the errors of fact and judgment that I have surely committed despite their help, or for the inconsistencies that remain.

It is to my wife of forty-one years, Susan Ashley, professor of history and dean of the faculty at Colorado College, that I owe the most. In Colorado and Oregon, in France and Italy, we have shared a life marked by a combination of tranquility and stimulation, teaching and research, work and play. Her energy keeps me moving both physically and mentally. I run to keep up.

Transliteration

Three of the countries included in this study speak languages written in non-Western alphabets. The fourth country, Turkey, switched to the Western alphabet in the early twentieth century but uses diacritical marks to indicate pronunciation of letters with multiple uses. Turkish and Persian both include many words of Arabic origin, which are nonetheless pronounced and/or written differently than in Arabic. These problems create difficulty for every Western writer, who must decide how to spell words and proper names coming from these languages. Writers must decide how to transliterate terms; readers must adapt to those decisions.

I have opted to use spellings that are common in the press, largely shorn of diacritical marks. For words that appear frequently in texts on Middle Eastern affairs, I will not use diacriticals or set them off with italics. Where a word is less common and might be mistaken for other terms, I will use italics and indicate, in the case of Arabic, the presence of the *ayn* (') and the *hamza* ('). Thus I will write ulama (rather than ulema or *'ulama'*). "Ulema" and "ulama" are both common spellings of the plural noun meaning "learned men, scholars of Islam." I will write Quran, rather than Koran or Coran, because Quran has become the preferred spelling in this country. And I will write Quran rather than Qur'an or Qur'ān in the name of simplicity. I will write Shia rather than Shiah or Shi'a, and Shii rather than Shiite. For the concept of law in Islam, I will write sharia rather than shariah or shari'a. I will write halakha rather than halakha or halakhah for the concept of Jewish religious law. I will not italicize or capitalize either sharia or halakha on the grounds that these concepts are commonly invoked in English and capitalization should be minimized.

When words such as these appear in quotations, I will honor the spellings used in the original source.

In general, I will use Arabic versions of words rather than Persian or Turkish derivatives. Thus I will write Muhammad Ali rather than Mehmet Ali (or Muhammad 'Ali), and *tariqat* rather than *tarikat*, for Sufi orders; madrasas rather than medrese for institutions of higher religious learning. But I will violate that rule in some cases, such as "ayatollah," which is the Persian title for a high-ranking member of the ulama, meaning "sign of God." The Arabic would be *ayatallah*. And I will violate it with Persian and Turkish names, such as Khomeini.

For similar reasons I will drop the use of even *ayn* and *hamza* from proper names. Thus, the cousin and son-in-law of the Prophet, 'Ali ibn abi Talib, will be simply Ali. And the radical Islamist, 'Ali Shari'ati, will be Ali Shariati. Of course, such policies still involve choice. I will write Gamal abd al-Nasir rather than Gamal Abdel Nasser—both versions of that name seem broadly accepted—or Jamal 'abd al-Nasir or Jamal 'abd an-Nasir, which some Arabists might prefer.

I will write Turkish words and names as the Turks write them, diacriticals included, for the same reason one uses accent marks in writing French. The turks use "ş" to indicate the "sh" sound. They normally pronounce "c" as English speakers pronounce "j", but "ç" indicates a "ch" sound as in "child." The "ğ" (as in Prime Minister Erdoğan's name, for example) serves to lubricate the linkage of two vowels. Dots over vowels (as in Atatürk) have roughly the same effect on pronunciation in Turkish as they do in German.

Experienced readers will have little difficulty with these matters but may well disagree with my choices. My hope is that readers who are inexperienced in reading texts on the Middle East will be intrigued but not confused by these problems of transliteration. My objective is a policy that permits readers to focus on the substance of my argument.

COLORADO SPRINGS
APRIL 7, 2009

1

The Political Determinants of Religion

Presidential candidates in the United States routinely field probing questions about religious beliefs. Shared religious convictions may have brought George W. Bush and Tony Blair together in attacking Iraq. The Chinese government clamped down on the Falun Gong movement. The European Union struggled with the question of making reference to the continent's Christian heritage in its constitution. Despite explicit references to Islam in its fundamental document, Iran seems immobilized by conflict within the clerical class over the exercise of supreme power. Turkey edges toward renewing its ties with a religious past even as it negotiates to enter Europe. One is unlikely to read about current events in any country of the world without encountering some reference to the interplay of the religious and the political.

This is scarcely surprising. It is hard to think of any moment in the history of the inhabited space that emerged in the Mediterranean area in classical times and gave birth to three great interrelated religious traditions, Judaism, Christianity, and Islam, when this would not have been so. Only in the past two or three centuries have people begun to argue that there is something inherently wrong about entangling religion and politics and to suggest that they should be utterly separate spheres. Both Western scholars of Middle Eastern languages and cultures (Orientalists) and champions of modernization theory, such as the German sociologist Max Weber, argued that there were two contrasting possibilities: a "traditional," religiously based state and a modern, secular state. But politics and religion have seldom been so thoroughly fused as the "traditional" model suggests or quite so separate as modern secularists might wish.

Five centuries before the beginning of the common era, Socrates challenged his fellow citizens to think rationally about political matters; he challenged the notion that the state should depend for its notions of justice

1

upon the inscrutable actions and pronouncements of the gods. Accused of attacking the religion of the city, he responded obliquely that he believed in things "divine," and hence in gods, but that defense did not save him from conviction by his fellow citizens. Yet rather than run away from his death sentence, he chose to obey the laws of Athens, proclaiming that the state is "dearer than one's mother or father," because only within the confines of a state can one live under the law, and without law the good life is not possible. How could he be sure of these things?[1] The little demon, his divine inspiration, did not stop him in his course of action. He opposed the conventional religion of the city in the name of a belief in a logic itself sustained by divine inspiration.

About 1,000 years later, Muhammad emerged in Arabia with a fresh religious vision and the requisite political skills to fashion a state. For many Westerners, and for many modern Islamists, Muhammad's success illustrates the ultimate oneness of religion and politics in the Islamic tradition. In twentieth-century Egypt, Islamists following Sayyid Qutb would seek to re-create that oneness by invoking the revolutionary methods of Muhammad in an effort to overcome what he called the new age of ignorance, a modern *jahiliyya*.[2] Some Westerners, reacting in part to Islamist claims, have suggested that Islam necessarily implies a politics of authoritarianism and aggressiveness. Yet Muhammad, even if he incarnated some perfect fusion of religion and politics, lived only ten years beyond the *hijra* (migration) from Mecca to Yathrib, a town that became known as Medina, the city of the Prophet. From the year 732, the new Islamic community faced the future without a prophet to guide it. The office of successor (caliph) was neither entirely religious in responsibility nor entirely political. The first caliph, Abu Bakr, told his fellow Muslims to follow him only so long as he remained faithful to God and the Prophet. "If I do well, help me, and if I do ill, correct me." He claimed no divine powers.[3] Ever since, the Islamic world has struggled to balance the religious and the political.

About eight hundred years after Muhammad's death in 732, Sir Thomas More died a martyr in England for his principled stand against the king. A deeply pious man, More accepted appointment by Henry VIII as lord chancellor of England but could not bring himself to bend religious conviction on behalf of his king, who wanted to divorce his wife and marry his mistress, Anne Boleyn, without papal sanction. Henry believed he could not go forward without the moral legitimacy that More's support would convey, but More saw the legitimacy of the British Crown as anchored in the law, and the law as dependent on righteousness and morality. To break with the Roman

Catholic Church as the king wanted was simply wrong in More's view. Neither he nor Henry sought to separate religion from politics; it was precisely their interdependence that drove Henry to execute More.

Five hundred years later, in a political system proclaiming the separation of church and state, Martin Luther King Jr. used religious conviction as the foundation of his campaign for civil rights. Like Socrates and Sir Thomas More, he proclaimed his allegiance to absolute standards of truth and justice, which were for him a part of the Christian faith. He appealed to fellow Christians to recognize the injustice of discriminatory laws in the name of a political system founded, in his view, on the Christian precepts of truth and justice. It is hard to imagine that a secular MLK could have won such support in the black community, and it is hard to imagine the success of the civil rights movement without the support of white liberals, many of them acting from religious conviction.

Of the three religions so tightly related by Abrahamic revelation that they are often called the "religions of the book," Judaism seemed most disengaged from politics. In the Diaspora of Europe, Jews moved toward assimilation in nation-states dominated by Christians, keeping religion in the private sphere. Then, in the midst of the nationalist fervor of the nineteenth century, Theodor Herzl and others began to dream of a Jewish state, creating a movement that came to be known as Zionism. Although the leadership of the Zionist movement was predominantly secular, Zionism without reference to Judaism is inconceivable, and the notion of a Jewish ethnicity independent of religion—a concept embraced by the Israeli left—does not withstand close scrutiny. However, to equate Judaism with Israel and to label Israel a "religious state" oversimplifies a complicated matter. A purely religious state is a phenomenon just as difficult to imagine as a purely secular state.

Secular state, secularism, *état laic*, *laïcité*, *laïcisme*, separation of church and state, religious state, Islamic state—all these terms tend to be used in ideological fashion to indicate what proponents deem a proper balance between the political and religious spheres. "The separation of church and state is a construct of political theory rather than a description of governing reality."[4] The terms continue to be used even though they do not accurately describe historical realities. On the one hand, French writers attempt to reinterpret laïcité to accommodate the modern reality of state involvement in religious organizations and education. The French government's recent creation of a council to represent French Muslims illustrates a lack of clarity quite inconsistent with the theoretical formulation of the secular state, the état laic. On the other hand, although Iranians have declared that theirs is an Islamic state, their constitution contains few elements that correspond directly to Islamic concepts or practice. Debate rages inside Iran about what sorts of liberties and changes can be permitted without jeopardizing the regime's Islamic character.

All states combine religion and politics in some fashion. "Every set of political institutions is linked to a certain treatment of the religious fact."[5] When strong in organization, the religious sphere always constitutes a potential threat to the political domain because it appeals to the moral sensibilities of the nation. The political sphere, with the powers of coercion and incentive at its disposal, can make life difficult if not impossible for autonomous religious organizations; yet few states have managed to subjugate all manifestations of religion for long periods of time. Political stability requires "an appropriate harmony between religion and politics."[6] We might define harmony or balance as a condition in which neither the religious sphere nor the political sphere seeks radical redress in the relationship. That does not imply that the power of the two spheres is equal. The power resources of a religious establishment and a political regime are too different to be measured in terms of quantity or even quality. "Balance" merely suggests a condition, necessarily impermanent, in which neither side is explicitly seeking major change. "Settlement" would suggest the maintenance of a long-term condition of balance in a given country.

Any sort of balance depends upon the will of major actors in the two spheres, but it also depends upon the social environment in which these actors must function. Social change affects the two spheres differentially. For example, rising literacy rates increase the ability of the public to read scriptures and political propaganda, including that of religious groups. Believers who study religion in church and in school, and who learn about religions other than their own, come to think of religion as something chosen rather than given, as an object with a given set of characteristics that differentiates itself from other religions. Educated believers open the way toward change in the religious sphere; they enable, but do not necessarily force, religious elites to make new sorts of appeals to followers and demands upon them and the state. The political sphere, still dependent on old elites, may find these demands repugnant, even though by fostering education it may have triggered a transformation in the nature of religious activity. By promoting education and other welfare activities, the religious sphere may itself be able to change society in ways that threaten the power of dominant elites.

Hence, any balance between the religious and the political spheres depends upon a specific set of environmental circumstances over which each sphere has only marginal control. A relatively poor, isolated community governed by elites nominally responsible to an outside power may achieve balance by virtue of its distance from the forces of modernization and globalization. If that community comes to be absorbed into a larger one, or if indigenous forces take full control, or if the outside power introduces schools and teachers, stability may give way to instability in the relationship between religion and politics. To push social change, the state may seek to augment its autonomy from "traditionalizing forces," such as religion, and the balance may tip away from the religious. In other moments, the religious sphere may adapt and become aggressive in its efforts to redress the balance and curb the ability of political elites to act without religious support.

Historic Moments

Four historical developments have had particularly heavy consequences for the relationship between religion and politics. The first is the advent of the state itself. Gauchet hypothesizes a prehistoric domain in which religion holds a monopoly on the regulation of society.[7] The foundation of the state constitutes "the first religious revolution in history," he says, because it divides the locus of social control.[8] With the state there emerges a hierarchy that requires explanation and justification. "All subsequent major spiritual and intellectual developments will arise from the contradictions between the inherited representations of the foundation, in whose name sovereignty is wielded, and the historical forms clothing its practice."[9] The state creates movement, whereas the object of religion is to "ward off movement and everything in the society that is likely to engender it. . . . The essence of religion is to be against history and against that which it imposes on us as destiny."[10]

The second historical development is the shift from oral to written traditions, which gave rise to scholarship and the development of law and theology in the "religions of the book," Judaism, Christianity, and Islam. The religious sphere augmented its capacity to function in support of politics, or in opposition to it, over vast geographic spaces and even across cultures. The law (canon law in Catholicism, the sharia in Islam, the halakha in Judaism) became a standard for right conduct and rightful rule; usually a beneficiary, the state nonetheless felt constrained. The interpreters of the law constituted a group of intellectuals capable of exercising political influence.

The third great development, the invention of the printing press, made scholarship, scripture, and law accessible to much larger numbers of people. It was no longer just a few who were in a position to compare the standards of political activity with reality. As literacy rates began to rise, there emerged new religious sects and fresh political demands. The increasingly autonomous individual demanded liberty of religion and other freedoms. The printing press made its debut in Europe about the year 1500, stimulating a push for literacy and contributing to the spread of Protestantism, but it found its way to the Middle East only in the nineteenth century. That fact probably helps explain why the religious ferment linked to the diffusion of the printed text in Europe came later in the Middle East and North Africa.

Finally, as many have observed, the printing of materials in vernacular European languages after 1500 contributed to the growth of sentiments that have come to be identified as nationalism. Groups of people, divided by historical experience or united in vast empires with other groups, came to imagine themselves as communities.[11] These communities coincided in only a few cases with existing political boundaries and in still fewer cases with the limits of religious affiliation. As the new phenomenon of the nation-state took shape in Europe and America, the old relationships between religion and politics—for example, a relationship between a multinational empire, such as the Ottoman, and a multinational religion, such as Islam—faced nationalist threat. Italy is an example among late-developing European nations of a place where nationalism challenged religion. Far from achieving immediate congruence between religion and state after unification in 1870, the new Italian Republic found itself at odds with the central institution of Christianity, the papacy. The Ottoman Empire faced nationalist challenges in Serbia, Greece, Egypt, and elsewhere in the Balkans. When the empire finally succumbed to European defeat in World War I, Turkish nationalists sought to build a new state without the Ottoman dynasty or its legitimating prop, the religious establishment.

Nationalism in the Middle East

As the first new nation in the Middle East, one cut from the heart of a great empire, Turkey was the first to face the need to construct a new relationship between religion and politics. Having decided to accept the Anatolian peninsula as the geography of the new Turkey, the Turkish military, led by Mustafa Kemal (later called Atatürk, Father of the Turks), had little choice but to eliminate the imperial institutions that sustained the old order. And that meant attacking the Ottoman sultanate-caliphate, which had from the beginning pictured itself as a champion of mainstream (Sunni) Islam. While Mustafa Kemal invoked Islam in the name of the new Turkey, especially as he sought to rally non–Turkish speakers such as the Kurds to support the war for independence, politics dictated a revision of the relationship between Islam and the state.

Nationalism in the Middle East nonetheless differed from the European model, because new nations appeared without the widespread literacy that marked Europe in the nineteenth century. Whereas in Europe the development of national literatures had contributed to the growth of nationalism, the push toward mass literacy in the Middle East followed the development of nationalism.[12] It was result rather than cause. Thus, when Mustafa Kemal decided Turkish should no longer be written in the Arabic script but in the Western alphabet, he discombobulated the literate few but not the illiterate many. Similarly, when he acted against the religious elites (the *ulama* and the dervish orders), compromised by their ties to the landed and military classes of the old regime, he could do so with relative impunity. However, Saudi Arabia began its national history at the opposite end of the spectrum. There, as in other states of the Middle East, such as Jordan, Morocco, and the shaykhdoms of the Persian Gulf, the political irrelevance of the masses made it relatively easy to create or sustain relationships with religious elites. Limited literacy permitted radical "secularism" in Turkey, and unabashed "traditionalism" in Saudi Arabia, to capture nationalist impulses and minimize at least temporarily the new tensions between religious and political life.[13]

One place where widespread literacy conditioned nationalism from the outset was the state of Israel. And, not surprisingly given the history of Judaism, a fog enveloped the relationship between religion and politics in that country from the start. Most Jewish immigrants to Palestine before World War II came from Eastern Europe and had the benefit of schooling within the Jewish community. Once the immigrants were in Palestine, the Zionist leadership pushed them to learn Hebrew, which solidified national identity and underscored the relationship between Zionism and scriptures. The proliferation of secular and religious groups, each with somewhat different attitudes about the proper relationship between religion and politics in a Jewish community, made it impossible to govern in the name of religion and impossible to govern without the support of deeply religious people. Mass politics as a fundamental characteristic of Zionism, as it had been of European nationalism, conditioned the relationship between religion and politics from the outset.

The invention of the printing press, mass literacy, and the new mass media— radio, television, cassette recorders, the Internet—all have transformed religion and politics. When the dissident religious leader Ayatollah Khomeini succeeded in reaching the Iranian masses via taped sermons in the months before the 1979 revolution brought him to power, he effectively transformed the structure of Islam in that state. In Cairo, taxi drivers listening to sermons on cassette engage in a modern version of an age-old exercise, but sermons on cassette also help create a system of preacher-stars and, since it is more diffi-cult to control the production and dissemination of cassettes than it is to monitor who is preaching in a mosque, they hinder state efforts to control re-ligious discourse.[14] That the Saudi opposition finds itself reduced to using fax machines and the Internet to spread its ideas speaks both to the effectiveness and the ineffectiveness of the Saudi regime in its efforts to monopolize the re-ligious sphere. When any Muslim with a few skills and a little money can cre-ate a Web site to "explain" Islam, the power once exercised by clergy is diminished as a result.

A Changing Environment

Technology conditions the context in which both religion and politics func-tion, but geography, the structure of the economy, and the distribution of power and influence in a society also constitute formidable aspects of the en-vironment. Karl Marx saw religion and politics as mere superstructure, de-pendent on the class makeup of a society, which in turn depends on the ownership of the means of production. As technology brought changes in the means of production, requiring new forms of ownership and provoking new class relationships, religion itself would necessarily change. Emile Durkheim's notion that religion emerges from society's need for solidarity likewise posits religion as a dependent variable. As a society evolves, so must its effort to dis-tinguish between the sacred and the profane.

Marxist analysis helps explain aspects of both Christianity and Islam. For ex-ample, Wuthnow argues that a newly emerging class of prosperous merchants—an emerging capitalism—carried Protestantism from Germany into most of the towns and cities of Europe.[15] Similarly, Islam carried the day in Arabia be-cause it responded to the needs of towns such as Mecca, where a rising mer-chant class longed for a "rational" religion with great territorial respect, one that would provide an atmosphere of trust and protection that would extend well beyond the no-fight zone already established around Mecca.[16] Muham-mad himself was a businessman who had traveled north with caravans and understood the problems of trade, and Shaban has argued that the Islamic conquests themselves derived from an economic imperative: the search for booty.[17]

Economic circumstances and social class continue to condition religion in the modern era. The revolution in Iran depended on the long-term relationship between clergy and the *bazaaris*, the traditional merchant class in Iran, who suffered from the shah's efforts to encourage large-scale businesses. But Khomeini also pitched his appeal to the "dispossessed"—to the urban masses left out of the economic boom and to a rural population unaroused by Marxist and nationalist ideology. Kepel has argued that the Islamist movement succeeded in Iran because it appealed to both the lowest, most miserable sectors of society and to the "pious bourgeoisie."[18] Islamists elsewhere, as in Egypt, have been effective with one of those segments but not the other. Ibrahim demonstrated the impact of social class on the shape of the Islamist movement in Egypt.[19] Small businessmen from the Anatolian heartland have been the driving force of the Islamist movement in Turkey.[20] In Malaysia the government embraced Islamism in an effort to energize Malay entrepreneurs.[21] Class thus helps explain why Islamism has been reformist rather than revolutionary in these countries.

Geography may be as important as economic and social circumstances in shaping religious organization, belief, and practice. Distance from Rome probably helped governments in England, Denmark, and Sweden to jump toward Protestantism while southern Europe remained more thoroughly Catholic.[22] France and all of Europe might have become Muslim in the eighth century, if the capital of the Umayyad caliphate in Damascus, Syria, had not been so far away. The relative isolation of Saudi Arabia, by water and by sand, surely helps explain why the Wahhabi version of Islam, which defines the religion in particularly severe and peculiar ways, is prevalent there. Muslim trade routes explain why Islam gained a foothold along the coast of East Africa and all the way east to Indonesia. The Islamist movement in contemporary Egypt may be in some measure a new form of old grievances in the country's south and central regions against the dominance of Cairo.[23]

These factors—geography, economics, and social structure—shape both politics and religion. The two interlocking domains undergo the effects of social change, but both may also cultivate, solicit, and carry out change. States try to stimulate economic growth by providing incentives, infrastructure, and education. Religious organizations seek to soften the effects of social displacement under the impact of change and/or to promote further change—say, in educational programs—to solidify support among rising social groups and to shape social policy.

A Dependent Variable

In the long run, religion appears to be a dependent variable. It is not just a result of geography, economics, and social structure but also a product of political influence and decision. "Despite religion's prominence as a source of political legitimacy and campaign rhetoric, it is rarely a dominant factor in the affairs of state."[24] In a shorter-term perspective, however, religion is an independent variable of some significance in explaining why a given political system veers in one direction or another.

Such an argument may seem strange for several reasons. First, the great religions are relatively enduring phenomena. Many writers take religion to be a primordial, unchanging aspect of individuals and even of states. Thus, at first blush it is difficult to regard religion as a dependent variable. Yet it is quite possible to write histories of these three religions. They have all assumed different forms and characteristics with the passage of time and change of circumstance. They have all adapted to geographic, social, economic, and political conditions. There is not a single Judaism, a single Christianity, or a single Islam— not in time and not in space. Max Weber argued that the advent of Protestantism contributed to the spirit of the new capitalism, but the emergence of Protestantism itself constituted a notable change in Christianity. Wuthnow insists that the success of Protestantism in certain parts of Europe and failure in others can in turn be explained by environmental and especially political factors.[25] What appears fixed in the case of most individuals is anything but stable and unchanging from the perspective of societies across time.

Second, to identify religion as a short-term factor suggests that it does not have long-term importance, which seems both counterintuitive and counterfactual. (Have not American politics been shaped by Protestantism? How can one understand Ireland or Italy without Catholicism? What are Turkish politics without Islam? How can one understand Israel without taking account of the religious parties?) But seeing religion as a short-term factor is both consistent with findings that it does not account for differences in political development among nations and also consistent with the fact that politics everywhere bears traces of religious influence. That short-term forces disappear as significant factors in long-term explanation does not mean they are unimportant. It may mean, instead, that virtually everywhere religion has served positive and negative roles in political development and that those roles are much more similar than different from one country to another..

Religion threatens political stability when it channels dissent against a political regime, as it did in sixteenth-and seventeenth-century England, or as it did in the overthrow of the monarchy in Iran. In other times and places it enhances stability by spurring reform, as it did with the civil rights movement in the United States. Although the long-term influence of religion may be neutral, the short-term impact may be of critical importance to a single state's history, even though religion may not be a useful variable in explaining why a state advances more or less quickly toward bureaucratic-constitutional government.[26]

Third, it may seem strange to regard religion as a short-term variable, because survey research usually assumes that a respondent's answers to questions about religion reflect long-term proclivities, in contrast with fleeting political opinions. Cause necessarily precedes effect, so the assumption is that religious beliefs condition political attitudes, but respondents face questions put to them at a particular moment. Even when surveys seek out the same respondents at later moments in time in an effort to separate cause from effect, the questions do not necessarily have the same meaning at a distance of five or ten years. Hence, if a single individual's responses to questions about religion change significantly over a lifetime, the evolution might be as much a product of political attitudes as a cause of them. Questions about religious preferences, belief in God, and frequency of religious observance prove useful in predicting political attitudes in some contexts, irrelevant in others. In short, there is scarcely a clear pattern of short-term impact, much less proof that religion constitutes a long-term cause of political attitudes.

In the short run, religion may influence the course of political development, but in the long run the shape and character of religion in a single country seems to depend more on political events and decisions than the character of the political sphere depends on religion. Near term, religion and politics appear to be mutually determining. They may evolve together in a relatively balanced relationship, neither domain anxious for revision, but once the balance tips sharply one way or the other, as a result of environmental change or changes in proclivity on either side, the search begins for a new "set of regularities" to replace the old.[27] Now religion thrusts, and politics parries, and then the momentum is reversed. The state becomes aggressive in seeking to revise the balance. In fact, the state enjoys long-term advantages in each of the domains where politics and religion interact, but that does not mean that church and state necessarily separate or that "secularization" adequately describes the interaction. Religious and political actors fashion a new balance that is path-dependent, reflecting previous iterations of the dialectical process by which it is created, but there can never be a guarantee of permanence. One would have to know the future to be able to offer such a guarantee.

Identity

Every political entity—clan, tribe, shaykhdom, kingdom, city, empire, nation-state—proposes some sort of identity to its members. As the parts of the world have shifted from one to another of these levels of political organization, the leaders have often invoked religion to solidify that identity or blamed religion for their troubles in creating or preserving unity. Some Romans blamed the Christians for the breakdown of order in the empire. St. Augustine sought to refute the charge even as he helped remold Christian doctrine to accommodate a new set of circumstances in which Christians would be called upon to wield power. He argued that Christians could support and even fight for a government, however imperfect, in the cause of a peace that all human beings desire. Order trumped morality. Similarly, an Islam initially averse to power based on lineage rather than morality came to support kingship under the Umayyads (650–750) and then the Abbasids (750–1250).[28] Before the conversion of Roman Emperor Constantine, the Christian community offered a parallel and alternative, apolitical identity, the City of God—an island in a sea of iniquity, a permanent community residing momentarily in a transient world. In the Christian world, religious and political identities probably coincided more closely under the early Byzantines than at any other moment in history. In the Islamic world, coincidental political and religious identity ended with the fall of the Umayyads in Damascus, because the Abbasids never took Spain, and soon they began to lose control of eastern territories as well. The *umma*, or community of believers, extended beyond the boundaries of the political kingdom the Abbasids established.

The lack of congruence between religious and political identity may have weakened certain states, and congruity may have strengthened others, such as the Safavid state in Iran, which converted the country to Shiism after 1500, but the problem was not severe because most premodern forms of political organization depended upon the sovereignty of the one or the few, established not by social contract but by the forceful seizure of power. Dynasties bore the names of rulers, who created states. Peoples emerged from states, not states from peoples, until the nineteenth and twentieth centuries.

The modern doctrine of social contract proposes that states should be the creation of peoples who already have a common identity and reach agreement with each other to form a government. The French nation makes revolution. The American nation revolts against the British and adopts a constitution. What the new nations showed was an incredible vigor produced by the loyalty and energy of the citizens who identified with them. Identity powers the nation-state. The question, then, of what constitutes identity with the nation becomes a much more critical issue than ever it was in the age of empire. In fact, the Ottoman Empire, which housed a panoply of religious and ethnic identities, came under pressure to acknowledge the rights and legitimacy of ethnic and religious minorities, who were increasingly hostile to an empire they began to see as outmoded.

The triumph of the nation-state, thanks largely to imperialism in the Middle East, has disrupted the relationship between religious identity and political identity everywhere—or virtually everywhere. There is not, and never was, any perfect correspondence between religious and political identity in the area, but it scarcely mattered in an earlier era. Now it does matter, because the new nation-states lack legitimacy. To pretend that all Syrians gathered together to make Syria a state would be preposterous. Modern Syria emerged from Ottoman control after World War I as a result of French and British decisions rather than Syrian self-determination. But the leaders of the new Turkey, like leaders in Egypt, Morocco, Iraq, Syria, and elsewhere, know that any hope of making strong, effective political entities means building an identity within the body politic. That is the foundation of any nation-state. Religious identities, on the other hand, divide states within their borders and create allegiances across borders, weakening fragile nation-states.

Politics has already reshaped religion in this sense, because the triumph of the nation-state shapes the question of identity. It creates an issue where there was none. One response of the political elites has been to nationalize religion, harnessing it to the purposes of the nation-state.[29] Autonomous religious elites (the ulama in Muslim states) initially resisted without much success, but Islamist movements have arisen to challenge this new political domination of religion. They see nationalism as a vehicle for secularization and Westernization, a vehicle in the grips of Western ideologies that is losing touch with indigenous identities, rather than representing them. The call is for "authenticity," which comes out of the romanticism of the individual, as does nationalism itself. It calls for a search for a truth beyond and behind traditional truths, an identity that lies deeper than the more superficial identities, even religious, of the modern age. Authenticity, in its extreme forms, is a call for revolt against both tradition—understood as the whole history of Islam since 622—and modernity, understood as Westernization and the secularization brought by nationalism, liberalism, and socialism.[30] And for the proponents of authenticity in the modern Middle East, the search for authenticity leads back to Islamic roots. Self-determination means understanding oneself as a Muslim and using that understanding to construct an Islamic state.

Everywhere in the Muslim world, Islamists have forced political elites to rethink the question of identity. On one hand, the Islamist notions of self-determination, anchored as they are in the same European philosophy as the doctrine of nationalism itself, reflect the conventional political wisdom. States must mirror the fundamental identities of their people. All rulers of the modern era, even the most dictatorial, claim to represent their "nations." On the other hand, Islamists propose a narrow definition of what it means to be a Muslim, a definition that conflicts with the realities of religious pluralism and with state efforts to manage religious identification through state-controlled institutions. Political elites scramble to respond to these conflicting pressures with a combination of accommodation and repression.

Islamists (with the possible exception of Osama bin Laden) do not seek the destruction of the nation-state itself. In that sense, their victory (as in Iran) would perhaps be the ultimate legitimation of political modernity. It would mean a nationalization of Islam, different from the nationalization formula political elites have previously sought to achieve. However, no Muslim state in the Middle East can afford to neglect Islam as a primary component of identity. The much-criticized monarchies in the Arabian peninsula, together with the kingdoms of Jordan and Morocco, have always understood that point but have not averted the rise of Islamist protest movements.

The advantage of politics over religion in the realm of identity is that the state constitutes the prize to be captured. Imposed by imperialism or carved by bedouin armies, the Middle Eastern state exists as an entity that does not coincide with religion but rather reflects international realities of the twenty-first century. One may regret the disappearance of the Ottoman Empire, with its capacity to tolerate ethnic and religious diversity, but it is gone and unlikely to reappear.[31] One may yearn for the Islamic umma, but the armies that would carry it to victory as they did in the early days of Islam are lacking. The nation-state is a given of modern life; religion, on the other hand, has become a matter of choice. Islamists say the nation must choose to identify itself with Islam, because that is the "authentic" choice, and that means that Muslims must choose to be something other than what they already are, for they are already Muslims. Now they must choose to be "authentic" Muslims—activist Muslims, Egyptian Muslims, "true" Muslims—and, therefore, they can also choose not to be any of those things, either individually or collectively. But the context in which they must choose is the nation-state, the creation of which forces the choice and conditions the answer. With its monopoly on the use of force, the state is unlikely to tolerate a response that is inconsistent with national identity.

The doctrine of secularization suggests that there is only one possible solution: complete separation of religious and national identity. That solution lies at one end of the spectrum. At the other lies the creation of a national religious identity, a national church, in the British style. The Saudis have pursued this option, working with the idiosyncrasies of Wahhabism and the relative isolation provided by the Arabian peninsula (which the Arabs call an island). A sense of superiority based in their control of Mecca and Medina help them claim that Saudi Islam, conditioned by the needs of Saudi national identity and the Saudi monarchy, is thus both national and universal. Wahhabi zealots helped create the Saudi state, and the state cultivates Wahhabi particularism as a national religion while portraying itself as the champion of universal Islam.[32] The overwhelming domination of Twelver Shiism in Iran has made it easy for the Islamic Republic of Iran to claim that Shiism is the national religion, despite the existence of a significant Sunni minority. The Iranian constitution proclaims tolerance of minorities, though not members of the Bahai faith. The Saudi–Wahhabi alliance in Saudi Arabia still holds to an invariant version of Islam that seems inconsistent with toleration. Of course, it took the British centuries to develop toleration of Catholics, and then atheists, without abandoning the national church.

For most states in the Middle East, it is both difficult to deny religion a place in national identity and difficult to define what a national church would be. That is also the case of the United States, where some scholars have identified a "religious establishment," even though the Constitution forbids a national church. Mainstream Protestants, Catholics, and Jews lend full support to American institutions and enjoy the right to participate in the articulation of policy, to preside over ceremonies, and to condition the language of politics. Defined as inclusive of these groups, the religious establishment links a highly devout public with a political system that is ostensibly rigid in separating church and state.[33] Currently it seems difficult to imagine a Middle Eastern state such as Lebanon, Syria, Iraq, or Egypt supported by a religious establishment that includes Muslims, Christians, and Jews.

The Israeli formula constitutes a different sort of compromise. Zionism constitutes the core of national identity, and Judaism is a fundamental element of Zionism, but many Israelis (perhaps a majority) oppose giving Judaism a formal place in the constitution. Hence, there is no constitution. Israel is a Jewish state and yet it is not a religiously Jewish state in the eyes of many of its citizens, who think of themselves as secular Jews. It is the universal Jewish state, because there is no other and because it is the product of Zionism, which is nationalism, not Judaism. It is not a state that encompasses all Jews or satisfies either the most or least observant Jews. The reconciliation of national and religious identity is scarcely perfect, but it would be hard to deny that the power of Israeli nationalism derives in part from linking religious and political identities. That linkage also renders more difficult the problem of religious minorities in Israel and the place of Palestinian Arabs, who are Muslim and Christian, in particular.

The identity problem for most Middle Eastern states is how to achieve some sort of congruence between religious and national identities. If there is such a thing as a religious establishment in the United States, it emerged from idiosyncratic developments. Likewise, the Israeli compromise appears unique, a product of Zionism rather than a result of constitutional construction. In both cases the solution emerged in a relatively liberal, democratic atmosphere in which Jews of deep religious conviction decided to become players rather than protesters (as with most Orthodox and some ultraorthodox groups in Israel). A national identity framed the parameters, and both religious and non-religious actors found ways to understand that identity in terms of religion. A few groups on the two ends of the religious-secular scale nonetheless remained disaffected.

Ideology

To describe the authority of God, human beings must find analogy in the only world in which they have direct experience, this one, and the image that comes most easily to mind is that God governs the universe. To describe the ways in which God governs the universe, one must think about what it means to govern: to exercise sovereign authority, to prescribe rules for behavior, to enforce the law, to adjudicate disputes, to keep the peace, to promote the well-being of human beings. These ideas come to mind by virtue of what governments (or virtuous human beings) do on earth. Father, master, lord, judge, caretaker, healer, good shepherd—all these terms have been applied to God as well as to rulers.[34] If kings reign but do not rule, then God might also reign and merely let his laws of nature do the work of governing. If human beings can discover the laws of physics, they may also be able to know the other laws of God, the laws of nature. To reason about the authority of God, one must start from the nature of authority on earth, but earthly authorities then portray themselves in God's image.

It is not surprising that religious ideas about authority tend to follow from political ideas and that political ideas often seek to ground themselves in religious thought. "In Georgian England, as much as in the seventeenth century, politics was a branch of theology," writes Gibson.[35] One might say something similar about the Middle East in the twenty-first century. The political ideologies most hostile to religious authority—Marxism, especially in the Soviet interpretation, and French radicalism at the end of the nineteenth century—have not fared well. The Soviet Union collapsed without having eradicated religion, the French infatuation with laïcité diminished with the fall of the Third Republic and the rise of a Christian democratic party in that country, and Turkey backed away from its laïcisme when it moved to multiparty democracy after World War II. The flow of ideologies and analogies has been from politics to religion, not vice versa, but religion has successfully resisted ideas, such as Marxism, that threatened the existence of the religious sphere. Politics cannot dictate religious ideology, but religious actors have historically been creative in adapting religious ideas of authority to political circumstances.[36]

Modern religions have all faced the challenge of adapting to the democratic surge of the nineteenth and twentieth centuries. Burgat echoes what many have said: "There is a fundamental antipathy between all religious dogma and the democratic idea."[37] Dogma depends upon certainty, which is anchored in revelation for all peoples of the book. Dogma does not depend on democratic decision-making to give it the stamp of truth. In their dogmatic forms and over long spans of history, Christianity, Judaism, and Islam have all been illiberal and undemocratic in their basic message. Many thousands of pages have been written to show how one or the other of these religions is or is not propitious for the emergence of modern liberalism, socialism, or democracy, but since human beings constructed the dogmas of all religions when they knew nothing of modern liberalism, socialism, or democracy, any hint of these ideas must be regarded as purely accidental. Fortunately, all three of these religions do contain elements that can and do serve in the contemporary era as tools for legitimating the evolution of religious thought in liberal and democratic directions.

Protestants embraced liberal and eventually democratic thought more quickly than Catholics, but even Catholicism, which Smith rated as the most authoritarian (in structure and dogma) of the great religions, has found means to embrace democracy and even revolution, in the case of liberation theology.[38] The reason is political necessity. Similarly, many elements of ultraorthodox Judaism have made an uneasy peace with democratic practice in Israel by utilizing political parties to influence events.[39] Ayatollah Khomeini, the great pioneer of contemporary Islamism, asserted the absolute authority of the jurisprudent (*faqih*) but also accepted a constitution rich in liberal and democratic ideas.

Whether Islam can or will permit democracy depends upon whether states push it in that direction. Turkey is pushing, but most states in the Middle East use religious opposition as one excuse, among others, not to liberalize or democratize. Some states, such as Saudi Arabia, suppress fundamental liberties under the guise of protecting Islam (and the monarchy), and others, such as Egypt, restrict liberties and rig elections out of fear of the opposition, some of it Islamist. The Algerian government triggered a civil war in 1992 when it suppressed the second round of elections out of fear that Islamists would win, subverting democracy. The government used force against the Islamists, and the Islamists responded in kind. The result was a civil war that lasted almost a decade and killed tens of thousands.

The question of liberalization and democratization, however interesting and relevant to countries such as Turkey and Iran, remains secondary to the question of law in most countries of the Middle East. The reason lies in the centrality of law in the political ideology of historical Islam—a centrality tied to the Quran, which orthodoxy came to argue is the "uncreated" word of God, hence coeternal with God. In that capacity, like the brief appearance for Christians of God on earth, the Quran brings God closer to human beings without putting him, her, or it entirely within the world. All three religions of the book, by virtue of their monotheism, deny the possibility that a ruler could be divine, even though Christian and Muslim rulers have often claimed aspects of divinity.[40] The existence of revelation means, however, that God is not entirely indifferent to the course of human affairs. Either the immanence of a God who rules, or the transcendence of a God who merely reigns, would leave human beings defenseless against absolutism.

The law of Islam emerged as a tool of the Abbasid caliphate to implement uniform justice over a wide area under the supervision of the ulama. It would not have emerged without the support of the political sphere, but it became, especially when Abbasid rule began to crumble, a platform for the potential critique of abusive power. Sunnis argue that the law was complete by the ninth century. The Shia acknowledge the need for the sharia to adapt to contemporary conditions. But both Sunni and Shii Islamists maintain that the great distinction between a genuine Islamic state and one that is simply a state where Muslims are a majority is application of the sharia. The problem is defining the sharia and how it fits into the law of the state.

The Ottoman Empire, the principal Islamic state of its era, implemented positive law. Sultan Suleyman the Magnificent was known as Kanun-name, the lawgiver. In the nineteenth century the Ottomans began to import aspects of European law, as did the Egyptians. The French imposed their law in Algeria, and to a lesser extent in Morocco and Tunisia. Then came independent regimes in Turkey and Iran, Egypt, Iraq, and Syria, all of which used European legal models and made law to serve local needs. As the sharia courts became protectors of personal and family law, there emerged an ideological gap between religious thought, still attached to the notion of sharia, and the state, protagonist of secular law. Islamists have made this ideological gap the center of their campaign against existing states, and the states have responded by arguing that state law in fact includes the sharia.

Debates rage about whether the sharia has ever been (or could ever be) fully implemented anywhere; whether it constitutes a rather simple set of rules and penalties or represents a complex, ever-changing legal tradition; whether it should be seen as a product of Islamic history or, by virtue of its basis in the Quran and in hadith (accounts of what Muhammad said and did), it is lifted to a status approaching that of the Quran itself. The disjuncture between man-made and divine law turns on the question of what these terms mean and, in particular, what the word "sharia" means. The Islamist movement has launched a great debate about this matter and has drawn governments into the discussion. Courts implementing the sharia cannot function without state enforcement, and state efforts to modify and enforce positive law cannot ignore arguments about coincidence (or lack of it) with the sharia. In Egypt, the sharia was at first recognized as one source of legislation (Basic Law of 1971) and then as the principal source of legislation by amendment to the constitution in 1980, but this does not signify achievement of a new ideological equilibrium, as shown by the continuing debates over implementing the sharia.[41]

For Egyptian secularists, the full implementation of the sharia means the ignorance and abuses of the Taliban, or the excesses of the Sudan, but for Islamists it constitutes the sine qua non of an Islamic state, the key to justice and legitimacy. It evokes both hopes and fears, and the result is instability in the relationship of the religious and political spheres. This is the ideological dilemma that most threatens the contemporary relationship between religion and politics in the Middle East. The question of religion and democracy may become vital, as regimes begin to take steps toward democracy, but the question of positive versus religious law is already central. And behind that question lurks a more important one being confronted most directly in Iran: Is the state ultimately dependent on its religious credentials or on popular sovereignty for its legitimacy? The constitution of the Islamic Republic suggests dual foundations.

Ultimately there must be some common understanding of the relationship between religion and politics. Where that understanding has been disrupted, as in the postcolonial Middle East and North Africa, it must be rebuilt on the basis of a new reality: a plurality of ideologies. Some religious groups claim religion and secularism face each other in a deadly duel. In fact, the Muslim world resembles the Christian world of the sixteenth and seventeenth centuries; suddenly there is de facto pluralism of ideological positions, and secularists also differ among themselves. Some secularists object to any implementation of the sharia, while others argue for the implementation of the sharia for Muslims, so long as Christians are not forced to comply.[42] But many secularists remain intolerant of direct religious involvement in the body politic, and many religious spokesmen (ideologues), including reformists, claim theirs is the only proper reading of Islam.

Religious groups have demonstrated intolerance, as have governments. The Algerian case is the most notable. Burgat argues convincingly that government bears more than half the responsibility for the degradation of a clash of ideology and culture into violent confrontation during that country's civil war.[43] Tunisia has managed to keep militant Islamists in jail for two decades, demonstrating an intolerance toward the expression of religious ideology that seems likely to bear fruit as reciprocal intolerance if ever Islamists were to win power. Authoritarian governments do not want criticism from any quarter, including the religious domain; they often speak the language of liberty and democracy but their actions contradict their declarations. Meanwhile, religious leaders, official and unofficial, often speak the language of truth and certainty, which conflicts with the plurality of ideological positions that characterizes Islam. Only a state committed to tolerance, openness, liberalism, and representation is likely to elicit the sort of religious response required for a new equilibrium between religion and politics. Only a state able to assert its commitment to protecting religion and religious principles seems likely to get that sort of response. Neither authoritarian secularism nor an authoritarian Islamic state is a winning formula.

Institutions

Separation of church and state remains fundamental to liberal ideology, just as the fusion of religion and politics remains an objective of Islamists. But neither fusion nor separation of religious and political institutions has proved workable. Islamists look to the Medina state, founded by Muhammad in 622 and destroyed by the first civil war (656–660) within the Islamic community, as an example of the fusion they admire. Even then a struggle over compiling the Quran under the third caliph, Uthman, suggests potential if not real divergence between the organization of religion and the organization of the state. Similarly, it may be possible to speak of John Calvin's efforts to make the city of Geneva into "one great church," but, like the Medina state, the arrangements depended largely on the presence of a single man. Muhammad's Medina and Calvin's Geneva constitute but tiny segments of Muslim and Christian history. They are scarcely typical of either tradition.

The complete separation of religious and political institutions has been fleeting and illusory, because religious institutions cannot exist apart from sovereign authority. Even if they are not explicitly a part of the state but rather constitute a part of civil society, the authority of the state creates the shell in which civil society can function. The state may decide to tolerate autonomous religious organizations or even favor them with tax benefits in exchange for support of the existing political order. It may choose not to favor any one organization over another. It may choose to treat members of all religious organizations as equal in importance to each other and to atheists and agnostics. But no more than corporations chartered by the state or benevolent associations founded in conformity with the law can religious organizations be entirely separate from the state.

The case of France shows why complete separation is not possible. The French conception of secularism (laïcité) responded to a precise set of political circumstances.[44] Champions of republican institutions at the end of the nineteenth century regarded the Roman Catholic Church, bulwark of the nobility and the monarchy in the ancien régime, as a reactionary force, hostile to liberal, democratic ways. (At the same time the French state undertook a colonial *mission civilisatrice*, which was heavy in religious overtones.) Republicans sought to separate church and state and, especially, to take education out of "enemy" hands. A century later, after almost fifty years of the Fifth Republic, with the Church no longer an enemy, the state helps support private (Catholic) schools, permits tax deductions for religious donations, and funds cultural activities linked to religious causes. For example, it has supported museums located in churches, infrastructure for a papal visit to France, and Islamic cultural centers, which include mosques. This is the new version of laïcité. France may require more separation of political and religious institutions than do other European states, but the difference between France and the others is diminishing. (One French writer puts the other European states into three categories: (1) "absence of laïcité": Great Britain, Denmark, Greece; (2) "semi-laïcité": Germany, Belgium, Netherlands and Luxembourg; and (3) "quasi-laïcité": Portugal, Spain, and Italy.[45]) Very attached to the concept of laïcité, the French would rather redefine it than simply acknowledge its inadequacy.

Genuinely "separate" religious organizations functioning within the territory of a state constitute a potential threat to authority. Anabaptists in Protestant Germany, dissenters in seventeenth-century England, the Orthodox

Church in the Soviet Union, the Branch Davidians in the United States, and Islamic Jihad in contemporary Egypt are examples of religious organizations without protection from state authorities. The logic of state power is to repress such organizations, especially but not only when they take up arms against authority, but repression is costly and often unsuccessful. Even without taking up arms, religious groups that proclaim themselves subject only to the laws of God constitute a menace to legitimacy that few states can afford to ignore. Even though the threat of coercion lies at the foundation of state power, any resort to actual coercion constitutes failure of authority. Therefore, states usually try to prevent separation by keeping religious organizations within the purview of state authority. In Malaysia, Prime Minister Mahathir Mohammed decided to co-opt the Islamist movement and to engage in Islamization to promote economic development.

> Mahathir wanted to define Islamism as a moderate ideology that would accommodate pluralism, capitalism, globalization and Malaysia's foreign policy. It would provide Malays with positive work ethics and social values, but would not insist on rejecting modernity and sequestering Malays from the pursuit of wealth.[46]

In Pakistan, President Muhammad Zia ul-Haq concluded, like Mahathir, that "a state that is construed as a legitimate Islamic actor can both ride the tiger of Islamism and harness its energies in the service of the state."[47] In particular, he used Islamization as a means to subjugate the judiciary, which had offered resistance to military rule. Nasr sums up his study of Islamization in these two countries: "In the final analysis, Islamization [in Malaysia and Pakistan] was not so much about Islam as it was about the state."[48]

State takeover of religious institutions constitutes a response to separatism but not a long-term solution, because (1) complete takeover is impossible and (2) state control effectively deprives the state of a vital organizational and ideological support. The Egyptian state under Muhammad Ali and his heirs sought to subjugate the loosely structured religious sphere to curb the financial autonomy of the ulama.[49] Gamal abd al-Nasir was still pursuing similar policies a hundred years later, when he made al-Azhar University a state institution, but research suggests that the contemporary Egyptian state does not have full control even over ulama ostensibly on the state payroll, much less over independent preachers, the Muslim Brotherhood, and Sufis (Muslim mystics).[50] To suppress separatist groups, the state has had to accord freedom of speech and action to others; it needs and benefits from the services provided by nongovernmental organizations linked to the Muslim Brotherhood, and it needs the voluntary support of autonomous religious leaders to rally the population against the radical separatists. Complete government control is neither practical nor desirable.

States have historically depended on religious organizations for a number of services vital to political development. In Europe the early development of state bureaucracies depended upon the literate class, composed mostly of clerics, who became clerks. The Church helped supply local leadership, community solidarity, schools, and welfare services long before states began to think about supplying these things. Effectively, the Roman Catholic Church, and eventually Protestant churches, gave the state greater capacity to provide for the needs of subjects than it would otherwise have had. Mosques, religious foundations, Sufi orders, and lay Islamic organizations perform some of these same services in the Islamic world. State takeover requires an increase in the state's bureaucratic, managerial capacities; in the absence of that capacity, takeover diminishes innovation, reduces service, and increases public dissatisfaction.

Religious organizations also structure support of a state, in which political parties do not exist. Before the era of mass communication, the church reached more people than any other institution. Dissident groups used religion to oppose the state, and the state did not hesitate to ask the established church for its support against these groups, or for war against heretic foreigners. In his study of Lindau, Germany, Wolfart argues that the breakup of Christianity into multiple confessions contributed to state-building in early modern Europe.[51] The Catholic Church, closely tied to the French nobility, structured rural support of the monarchy in the ancien régime. The Church of England, reaching across class barriers, structured the social stability of eighteenth-century England.[52] Alexis de Tocqueville saw the churches of America as the great organizational underpinning of democracy at a time when parties were just beginning to take root. Meeting with friends and neighbors, talking about the issues of the day, committing oneself to God and country, and participating in the new democracy were all possible through the churches. The role of churches in fostering political interest and activity may still hold. Recent studies show that churchgoing among African-Americans correlates positively with political involvement.[53]

Religious organizations can structure opposition as well as support, and thus every state must decide how much autonomy it dares grant. Granting little autonomy to religion, a state deprives itself of voluntary adhesion. Support from an organization that has no freedom to oppose has less political value than support from a group that inspires genuine enthusiasm from its members. Ulama who preach support for government programs, at the cost of contradicting themselves and ignoring elements of the tradition, do not generate the same enthusiasm as autonomous preachers who denounce a weak government for its corruption, hypocrisy, and inadequacy. Granting much autonomy, the state risks finding itself faced with a mobilized opposition it is unprepared to accommodate.

Political development means not just bureaucratization and institutionalization but the eventual incorporation of all citizens into a single constitutional structure. The proponents of civil society have argued that this occurs once there exists an associational life outside the state, which can then be incorporated into the body politic. The growth of civil society will promote democratic development, and the cultivation of autonomous religious organizations can help foster such a civil society, or so the argument goes. But civil society cannot emerge until the state decides to tolerate relatively autonomous organizations, including religious groups, rather than to dominate them. And the state must eventually take that course, for it cannot enjoy full constitutional/liberal/democratic legitimacy until it has the voluntary adhesion of relatively autonomous group actors.

For the state to move in the direction of tolerance, it must be persuaded that group autonomy will not undermine stability. Religious groups, in particular, must be prepared to tolerate each other and therefore to accept less than the state of their dreams. They must play the democratic game in return for the autonomy they need and want. In undemocratic states, entrenched elites, who risk loss of power by democratization, postpone liberalization with the excuse that religious groups, if democratically empowered, would not behave democratically. Opposition groups, seeing governments acting in "bad faith," sharpen their tone to advocate precisely the solutions (full implementation of the sharia) that scare incumbent elites and minority groups.

Religious organizations depend upon the state's goodwill and authority. The state needs the support of religious organizations to supplement its own capacities and to mobilize support for its projects. Hence, the problem is not one of separating the religious and political spheres but rather one of achieving a mode of collaboration that includes a measure of autonomy in return for a measure of support, and tolerance of religious organizations for each other. The evidence from Europe is that such collaboration between the religious and political spheres emerged not from the idealism of political elites or the forbearance and goodwill of religious organizations but rather from particularistic political bargaining—different in the Netherlands than in England, different in France than in Italy—designed to avoid violence and chaos. As political processes became increasingly liberal and democratic, religious groups found themselves driven to participate in order to defend themselves and their interests. To remain opposed to the state and intolerant of all other groups proved impractical. States needed the support of religious groups to ensure stability; religious groups needed the protection and cooperation of the state. Participation and mutual tolerance resulted from pursuit of these needs.

Bargaining between states and religious groups goes on today in both Europe and the Middle East as social change and political circumstances disrupt the former balance between religion and politics. In Europe, the immigration of millions of Muslims, together with the push for political integration of the European Union, has upset delicate balances between religion and politics. The accommodations made with Christian churches do not necessarily fit the case of Islam in Europe. Far from wishing to isolate and ignore, at the risk of reinforcing a condition of apartheid, governments have sought contact with Islamic leaders and associations in the hope of pulling them toward the body politic. In doing so, they risk charges of violating existing arrangements and commitments, such as the separation and neutrality required by the classic understanding of laïcité in France. Special accords specific to each religious denomination appear to be the emerging pattern in France and elsewhere. For now, the question of religion remains a matter for individual states of the European Union to negotiate and regulate, but the free flow of labor will surely generate pressure for somewhat greater uniformity in this regard. What is common to the European states is freedom of religious expression and government neutrality toward religions.

Internal migration in the Muslim states, mainly from the rural areas toward the cities, has been one factor in the growth of Islamist organizations, which has undercut the old relationship between religion and politics. The success of Islamist groups in providing services where governments have been slow to respond to substandard living conditions explains their ability to recruit in these strata. But education is an even more important source of social change for explaining the emergence of these organizations. Lay religious leaders with modern education started by entreating the educated classes to reflect upon their circumstances and to think about Islamic action as an appropriate response. For example, the Muslim Brotherhood in Egypt found its earliest adherents among Egyptian civil servants. The educational advances that have facilitated the state's transformation thus transformed the religious sphere from one dominated by a narrowly trained scholarly elite and some mystical figures, using mosques and brotherhoods, to one that is much more differentiated, pluralistic, diverse, and politicized. The old formulas for balance no longer work, and neither complete separation of religion and politics nor complete domination of one by the other is a realistic option. A balance must be renegotiated.

Political Culture

Religion can contribute to personal and national identity. It offers ideological perspectives on the relationship of human beings to authority. It brings people together in organizations with potential and actual political influence. But above all, it constitutes a social "fact" in every country of the world. People pray. They attend services in churches, synagogues, and mosques. They participate in religious organizations. Most important, they see religion as a guide to behavior, promoting the good and enjoining evil. When people everywhere invoke God in happiness and in despair, in gratefulness and in resentment, the expressions may be more automatic than calculated. The instinct to do right may lie much deeper than the commandments people remember and invoke. People who do not profess religious commitments do not behave much differently than those who do, but the actions of those without explicit commitment may reflect religious upbringing or exposure. The religious "fact" is a powerful element of every national culture, and governments ignore it at their peril.

In some circumstances, political culture may change more quickly than political institutions, and the result may be political instability. The U.S. antislavery movement in the middle of the nineteenth century was an example. A groundswell of public opinion against slavery propelled in part by religious belief and religious organizations transformed the public mind-set about slavery before political institutions could move against it. In other circumstances, political institutions seek to change political culture. The French and Russian revolutions produced governments bent upon transforming the way citizens understood their relationship to political authority. With propaganda and education they sought to create a new citizenry. In postrevolutionary circumstances, the training of subjects and citizens becomes a critical issue. What are future generations to be taught about private versus public good, legitimate political authority, the relationship between law and morality, the place of religion in society, and the social mores they have come to take as defining elements of their lives? Such education must start from a notion of current attitudes, and in every country those attitudes reflect aspects of religious heritage.

Religion appears more important as a defining element of culture in some societies than in others. The stereotypical Orientalist portrayed the East as bound up in religion and the West as liberated from it, and it may be that the proportion of people in Egypt or Turkey or Iran who see religion as important to their daily lives is higher than it is in Europe. Survey data now offer support for that proposition.[54] But is there any society in which religion can be ignored as a factor in shaping mass attitudes toward morality and authority? If political development means movement toward greater participation and inclusiveness, then political stability will be increasingly dependent on congruence between state policies and political culture.[55]

Religion and politics are both embedded in culture. Islam arose in a context of a transition from bedouin to commercial society. It absorbed and reflected values and practices of nomadic and urban elements of Arab culture, and it has subsequently absorbed particularistic values of non-Arab societies wherever it has been transported and implanted. Of course, it has also shaped local cultures in the light of universal messages carried in its scriptural core, and by virtue of cultural appendages transmitted from Arabia. White has argued that the Islamist movement in Turkey has been successful not so much because it is religious as because it has succeeded in couching its appeals in ways that coincide with the mores of nonelitist Turks.[56] The faint evocation of the Ottoman memory, long repressed by the Kemalists; the appeal to morality, community, and mutual assistance; and the promise of group and individual promotion through a return to moral action—all do more to explain success than heightened religiosity or religious ideology.

The Islamists have practiced what White terms vernacular politics: "Vernacular politics brings a hybrid population together around a political and ideological agenda, but this agenda is personalized and popularized by situating it within a context of shared norms, idioms, and interpersonal trust."[57] The norms, idioms, and interpersonal trust reflect Turkey's long experience with Islam, but they are not so much products of the Islamist movement as they are the contextual condition for the success of its efforts. The vernacular style of politics, linking masses and elites, opens the way for the further development of Turkish constitutionalism. But if Turkey moves to a new level of liberal-democratic development, the credit will go not to Islam per se but to the skill of Islamist political organizations and their knowledge of Turkish culture. Turkey will not be democratic because it is Muslim but because some

Muslims have responded to political opportunities afforded by a Muslim political culture and an evolving set of political institutions.

To perpetuate themselves, modern states seek to train inhabitants as subjects or citizens. Similarly religious groups, whether majoritarian or minoritarian, must socialize their young, if they are to survive as distinct entities. For much of European and Middle Eastern history, religious organizations provided the only education available in society, training both secular and religious leadership, usually from the noble classes. In modern times some states have taken over all responsibilities for education including the preparation of clergy. Turkey in its first forty years of independence is an example. The idea was to teach an Islam that accepted the removal of religion from direct participation in the political sphere and distanced itself from the mystical sorts of religion that had great popular appeal, especially in the rural, less modernized areas. The British pushed such policies in Egypt, and the French did the same thing in Algeria to meet colonial subjects on their own turf and to move them closer to European thought and institutions.[58] But by adopting that policy, the colonial states, in fact, cut subjects away from the Ottoman tradition and the existing political culture, as the Turks themselves later did under Mustafa Kemal Atatürk.

In the nation-state era, there may not be a single country where all instruction lies within the religious sphere, but there are also few states that do not participate in teaching religion. In the Middle East, religious schools at the most elementary level (*quttab*) tended to emphasize memorization of the Quran and little more. At more advanced levels (*madrasas*), the emphasis was on training judges, preachers, and scholars of the tradition. Modern scientific education, introduced by the French in Egypt, developed separately from religious schooling in the beginning, and integration came later. In most countries, dual or even multiple educational tracks developed after the arrival of European influence in the nineteenth century. At independence, the state of Israel supported three varieties of state schools, one of them religious, and permitted independent schools run by the ultraorthodox as well.[59] Most Western states also provide for multiple educational tracks, one or more of them under religious direction.

Religious groups cannot perpetuate their beliefs, rituals, and lifestyles without schools to socialize the young into their worlds. To force all children into state schools, teaching little or nothing about religion or teaching religion in a relativist, comparative framework, is to determine the fate of religious particularism. The example of the ultraorthodox in Israel illustrates the case. Their yeshivas, which devote themselves almost exclusively to teaching the oral tradition and barely touch the basics of modern education, are the key to preserving the ultraorthodox sects, isolated from Israeli society in lifestyle as well as in geography. The augmentation of political influence achieved after the "earthquake" election of 1977, which brought the nationalist Right to power in Israel for the first time since independence, resulted in copious funding of their schools and institutions, and the ultraorthodox communities have continued to grow and prosper as a result.[60] Of course, the state pays a price in the lack of common citizenship training. The yeshivas can be counted upon to teach the dangers and evils of modern society and to instill at least doubts about, if not outright hostility toward, many institutions of the Israeli state. Israel has chosen to permit ultraorthodox particularism at the expense of a common Israeli political culture.

In France, the question is most frequently posed in the opposite way: Can the republic survive without an educational system that is laïc? When three Muslim girls were expelled from high school for wearing head scarves, the government asked the Conseil d'État, a high administrative court, to rule on whether laïcité had been violated. The court responded that the mere wearing of head scarves did not compromise the integrity of education, if there was no effort to proselytize or otherwise disrupt the classroom, but that response, far from settling the issue, touched off controversy and an outpouring of books defending laïcité. Most of these books note that laïcité nonetheless means something quite different now than it did at the end of the nineteenth century, when republicans deemed that they could solidify loyalty to the republic only by taking over the educational responsibilities exercised by the Catholic Church. Teachers became—and remain—apostles of republican unity, alert to any hint of religious particularism. But the Catholic Church no longer constitutes a threat to republican unity, and the state has even subsidized private (mostly Catholic) schools since 1958. Private schools must hire teachers with credentials approved by the state and include programs of instruction approved by the state, but they may also offer additional courses and activities. Socialist efforts in the 1980s to redress the balance in favor of purer secularism failed, as did rightist efforts to move the marker in the other direction, with the authorization of charter schools, in the following decade. The explosion of the head-scarf controversy shows the continued centrality of schools to the relationship between religion and political culture in France.[61]

Schools have also been at the center of the culture wars in the United States. On the one hand, if the Founders intended that separation of church and state would guarantee the autonomy of religion but not free the state from religious standards of right and wrong, public schools would not necessarily avoid teaching about religion, and government might reasonably encourage and even support religious schools. On the other hand, it is not obvious how state-funded schools should treat religion. Religious groups have protested the elimination of prayer from schools and the failure of schools to teach morality. Critics accuse schools of teaching an antireligious philosophy they call secular humanism. Teachers and school boards are afraid to include courses on comparative religion or the history of religions, which might well offend those groups most intent on promoting spirituality in the schools. Permitting and subsidizing religious schools, subject to conditions and cooperation, goes partway toward solving the problem at the risk of perpetuating discrete, autonomous religious communities, indifferent to the logic of public discourse, but it does nothing to expose the public-school student to religious history and doctrine. Surely the Founders did not imagine that the separation of church and state would mean the separation of citizens from knowledge of religion, but many contemporary Americans arrive in college without any knowledge of Judaism or Christianity, Protestantism or Catholicism, much less Islam.

Religion is part of the political culture everywhere, but it is not an immutable part anywhere. The Soviet effort to stamp out religion, unsuccessful though it was, does nonetheless seem the best explanation for the relatively secular attitudes among East Europeans. Education shapes and reshapes political culture, and therefore culture wars necessarily turn on the question of schools. Head scarves, school prayer, crucifixes in the classroom, the teaching of values, religion in the curriculum, compulsion (or not) for orthodox religious groups to attend public schools, the ability of orthodox groups to maintain their own school systems, exemptions of religious students from military service, the teaching of intelligent design as part of science, the celebration of religious holidays, the tolerance of religious minorities within the schools—such are a few of the issues. Long-term balance between the religious and political spheres requires an understanding on these matters. Who will be taught what about religion by whom and in what context? No formula including "separation of church and state" or "religion is a private matter" provides an adequate response to that question.

Culture is a product of human beings, and religion is both a producer and a product of culture. Culture changes in response to social, economic, and political forces, but it changes more slowly than political regimes, personnel, and policies. Thus it is possible to argue that the attitudes produced by the Reformation contributed to the industrialization and the democratization of Europe. But one proponent of that view—who also argues for the distinctiveness of national political cultures in Europe—contends that European political culture is now shifting toward postmodern, postbourgeois values: The political culture is changing, a product (rather than cause) of the economic prosperity Europe has enjoyed since World War II.[62] The political culture of Germany, still highly authoritarian when *The Civic Culture* was written, subsequently changed to become highly democratic.[63] Thus religion, as a part of culture, is a variable, not a constant, and any equilibrium of religion and politics must take into account both its enduring and changeable aspects: Both the religious and the political spheres must start from an understanding of prevailing attitudes, but they must ultimately come to some agreement about how attitudes will be shaped in the future. It is possible to imagine trade-offs between these dimensions of political culture, present and future. Pfaff concludes a study of Europe and America: "Both state intrusion into the religious sphere and the temptation to use state power to promote public piety have driven cycles of secularization and revival through history and may do so again."[64]

Conclusion

The complicated pattern of interaction between the religious and political spheres precludes broad generalizations about religion as either an independent or a dependent variable. As an independent variable, religion appears to have contributed to political development as much as hindered it, but rare have been cases where religious identity has contributed to the solidification of national identity, where religious ideology has contributed systematically to the development of bureaucratic and liberal-democratic development, where religious organizations have unambiguously favored pluralist, tolerant, constitutionalist tendencies, and where religion as a component of political culture has been favorable to these changes. To see England as such a case—and there would appear to be few other possibilities—would require overlooking moments in English history when religious conflict appeared to be a major obstacle to constitutional development. It is equally difficult to think of cases where religion has been an insuperable obstacle in each of the four domains: identity, ideology, institutions, and political culture. And the reason is not far to seek: Politics reshapes religion even as religion conditions political life.

Yet determined political efforts to eliminate the influence of religion or to subject religious identity, ideology, and organization to state control have been unsuccessful. The coercion required to enforce such policies may carry a country toward bureaucratic development, as in the Soviet Union, but run counter to the other component of political development, constitutionalism. Even coercion cannot obliterate religious instincts from the political culture as a component of the norms and idioms of daily life. Once coercion disappears or diminishes, religious activity springs back.

The shift toward multiparty politics in Turkey since 1950 demonstrates this principle. To abolish the sharia courts, as Atatürk did, does not necessarily make the concept of the sharia disappear. The state shapes religious life to such an extent that one cannot speak of the relationship between religion and politics except in the context of a specific state. With its control of the educational establishment, the state can attempt to alter the foundation of religious power, which lies in popular beliefs and attitudes. But a state that moves toward constitutionalism cannot, without contradiction, adopt arbitrary, absolutist educational policies designed to undercut all religious understandings of the world. Rather, a state inching its way toward liberal democracy must seek its foundation in the existing political culture. It must work from existing notions of what constitutes a good person, a good society, and a good government. To change the country it must win the support of doubters by persuading them that the values propounded in the schools and in the media are merely new versions of the values embraced in the existing political culture. Islamist movements in several countries have succeeded in pitching their proposals for the reformation of society in such terms. The problem of the state is not just to contain, absorb, or coalesce with Islamist movements but to respond as effectively as the Islamists to the political culture of the masses, their practices, and their norms. States find themselves resorting to the language of religion to compete with the Islamists for the allegiance of the masses, thereby giving religion even greater apparent importance in political life than it might otherwise have. They must teach religion in the public schools, because the public demands it and because refining the notion of citizenship means refining a political culture steeped in the language of religion. States have unwittingly contributed to the Islamic resurgence by virtue of policies designed to increase the power of the state.[65]

State schools all over the Middle East have helped make religion a matter of choice, as the Protestant Reformation made religion a matter of choice in Europe. What was given as a birthright comes to be a matter for reaffirmation, rejection, or reinterpretation. Islamism constitutes a set of choices, different in every time and place: a choice to run a business by certain principles, to dress in a way deemed appropriate for a believer, to adhere to a moral code that others seem to have abandoned, to associate primarily with those who have made similar choices, to participate in political life on behalf of those who are disadvantaged, to educate oneself about Islam, to rethink the meaning of basic scriptures, to work for the betterment of one's local community as a concrete way of implementing one's moral choices, to stay at home to tend one's children in deference to husband and patriarchal ways, to go into the workplace boldly, shielded by the protection of clothing that signifies commitment and virtue, or to undertake violent acts of political opposition. White emphasizes that Turkish Islamists embrace one or more such choices, even contradictory ones.[66] In exercising such choice, Turks engage in a process typical of the marketplace and of the liberal-democratic political arena, both grounded in personal choice. The expansion of the realm of choice is one way to define political development.[67]

In the contemporary Middle Eastern context, the expansion of choice has come in the realm of religion, but the reasons are not so much religious as political, economic, and social. More than any other factor, it is the nation-state with its need for identity and legitimacy that has created this set of choices. By using religion for its own purposes, and especially by teaching religion in its schools, it has demanded and enabled choice. The trials and tribulations of global ideologies such as Marxism and liberalism have constrained the definitions of choice in negative ways. Many choices bear burdens of foreign origin and influence. Modern technologies of communication have empowered choice by exposing options to people who thought they had none. Economic development has pulled people toward choices as both workers and consumers. Education and income continue to be primary constraints on choice.[68] All these factors vary from country to country, as does the coercive will of the state. The range of choices available at a given level of economic prosperity appears much greater in Turkey than in Saudi Arabia, for example, where a decision to oppose state religious teachings means prison.

The religious choices now available emerge from an evolving set of political and social circumstances that probably contribute more to understanding the choices than the study of religious scripture.[69] Religious identities, ideologies, and organizations have responded creatively to these national circumstances. Despite international ties among religious groups and a pattern of religious activity that seems similar in a number of countries, Islamist activity is probably most accurately seen as a broad set of responses to parallel (but not identical) political and social circumstances. Religion is much more a dependent than an independent variable, but that is not to say that it will not leave its mark or that any contemporary statesman can afford to ignore it.

Notes

1. See Plato's "Crito." Thomas G. West and Grace Starry West, trans., *Four Texts on Socrates: Plato's Euthyphro, Apology, and Crito, and Aristophanes' Clouds/Plato and Aristophanes* (Ithaca, NY: Cornell University Press, 1998).

2. Sayyid Qutb, *Milestones*, rev. trans. (Indianapolis: American Trust Publications, 1990), chapter 3. See also William E. Shepard, "Sayyid Qutb's Doctrine of Jāhiliyya," *International Journal of Middle East Studies* 35, no. 4 (November 2003): 521–545.

3. "The Accession Speech of Abu Bakr (632)," in Bernard Lewis, ed. and trans., *Islam from the Prophet Muhammad to the Capture of Constantinople*, vol. 1 (New York: Harper, 1974), 6.

4. N. J. Demerath III, "Religious Capital and Capital Religions: Cross-Cultural and Non-Legal Factors in the Separation of Church and State," *Daedalus* 120, no. 3 (Summer 1991): 22.

5. Jean-Paul Willaime, "Unification européene et religions," in Jean Baudoin and Philippe Portier, eds., *La laïcité, une valeur d'aujourd'hui? Contestations et negotiations du modèle français* (Paris: Presses universitaires de France, 2001), 134.

6. Robert Audi, *Religious Commitment and Secular Reason* (Cambridge, UK: Cambridge University Press, 2000), 3.

7. Marcel Gauchet, *The Disenchantment of the World: A Political History of Religion*, trans. Oscar Burge (Princeton, NJ: Princeton University Press, 1997), chapter 1.

8. Ibid., 13.

9. Ibid., 14.

10. Marcel Gauchet, *La démocratie contre elle-même* (Paris: Gallimard, 2002), 35.

11. Benedict Anderson, *Imagined Communities: Reflections on the Origin and Spread of Nationalism*, rev. ed. (London: Verso, 1991).

12. In several Arab states (Algeria, Syria, Egypt, Iraq, Morocco, Sudan, and Yemen), adult literacy remained at or below 60 percent in 1997. Clement M. Henry and Robert Springborg, *Globalization and the Politics of Development in the Middle East* (Cambridge, UK: Cambridge University Press, 2001), 3.

13. Parthe Chatterjee, *Nationalist Thought and the Colonial World* (London: Zed, 1986), suggests that nationalism has been appropriated for a variety of purposes by postcolonial movements and states.

14. See, for example, Charles Hirschkind, "The Ethics of Listening: Cassette-sermon Audition in Contemporary Egypt," *American Ethnologist* 28, no. 3 (August 2001): 623–649.

15. Robert Wuthnow, *Communities of Discourse: Ideology and Social Structure in the Enlightenment, and European Socialism* (Cambridge, MA: Harvard University Press, 1989), part I.

16. See, for example, Maxime Rodinson, *Mohammed*, trans. Anne Carter (New York: Viking, 1974), 37.

17. M. A. Shaban, *Islamic History: A New Interpretation,* 2 vols. (Cambridge, UK: Cambridge University Press, 1976).

18. Gilles Kepel, *Jihad: Expansion et déclin de l'islamisme* (Paris: Gallimard, 2000), chapter 6, for a discussion of Khomeini, but Kepel carries the argument throughout the book.

19. Saad Eddin Ibrahim, *Egypt, Islam and Democracy: Critical Essays* (Cairo: The American University in Cairo, 1996), chapter 4.

20. Haldun Gülalp, "Globalization and Political Islam: the Social Bases of Turkey's Welfare Party," *International Journal of Middle East Studies* 33, no. 3 (August 2001): 433–448.

21. Seyyed Vali Reza Nasr, *Islamic Leviathan: Islam and the Making of State Power* (Oxford, UK: Oxford University Press, 2001), 115.

22. Wuthnow, *Communities of Discourse*, part I.

23. See Mamoun Fandy, "Egypt's Islamic Group: Regional Revenge?" *Middle East Journal* 48, no. 4 (Autumn 1994): 611–625.

24. Demerath III, "Religious Capital," 38. Thomas Ertman's careful analysis of the European state-building supports that conclusion. See his *Birth of the Leviathan: Building State and Regimes in Medieval and Early Modern Europe* (Cambridge, UK: Cambridge University Press, 1997).

25. Wuthnow, *Communities of Discourse*, part I.

26. The reference is to Ertman, *Birth of the Leviathan.*

27. Leonard Binder, "The Crisis of Political Development," in Binder, James S. Coleman, Joseph LaPalombara, Lucien W. Pye, Sidney Verba, and Myron Weiner, *Crises and Sequences in Political Development* (Princeton, NJ: Princeton University Press, 1971), 16. On page 17, Binder writes, "The study of political development requires a theory of how the patterns of political life change from one set of regularities to another set of regularities."

28. Aziz al-Azmeh, *Muslim Kingship: Power and the Sacred in Muslim, Christian and Pagan Polities* (London: I. B. Tauris, 1995).

29. Daniel Crecelius, "The Course of Secularization in Modern Egypt," in John L. Esposito, ed., *Islam and Development* (Syracuse, NY: Syracuse University Press, 1980), 69.

30. Robert D. Lee, *Overcoming Tradition and Modernity: The Search for Islamic Authenticity* (Boulder, CO: Westview Press, 1997), Introduction.

31. Elie Kedourie denounced nationalism as a destructive force unleashed by Europe and expressed his nostalgia for the form of political organization represented by the multi-ethnic, multireligious Ottoman Empire. See his *Nationalism* (London: Hutchinson, 1960) and his *Democracy and Arab Political Culture* (Washington, DC: Washington Institute for Near East Policy, 1991).

32. Hamadi Redissi, *Le pacte de Nadjd: ou comment l'islam sectaire est devenu l'islam* (Paris: Seuil, 2007).

33. Eldon J. Eisenach, *The Next Religious Establishment: National Identity and Political Theology in Post-Protestant America* (Lanham, MD: Rowman & Littlefield, 2000).

34. Al-Azmeh, *Muslim Kingship*, chapter 2.

35. William Gibson, *The Church of England, 1688–1832: Unity and Accord* (London: Routledge, 2001), 5.

36. St. Augustine demonstrated the flexibility of Christianity. "If we want to learn how the decomposition and recomposition of Christian sociolatry was related to political crisis, the place to start is the monumental *City of God*, which is still Christianity's most influential treatment of piety and politics." Peter Iver Kaufman, *Redeeming Politics* (Princeton, NJ: Princeton University Press, 1990), 130.

37. François Burgat, *Face to Face with Political Islam* (London: I. B. Tauris, 2003), trans. from the French, *Islamisme en face* (Paris: Editions La Découverte, 1996), 124.

38. Donald E. Smith, *Religion and Political Development* (Boston: Little, Brown, 1970), 176.

39. See Ilan Greilsammer, *Israël: les hommes en noir* (Paris: Presses de la Fondation Nationale des Sciences, 1991), for a superb treatment of the ultraorthodox in Israeli politics. Also Ira Sharkansky, *Rituals of Conflict: Religion, Politics, and Public Policy in Israel* (Boulder, CO: Lynne Rienner, 1996).

40. al-Azmeh, *Muslim Kingship*, makes this point emphatically.

41. See, for example, the excellent piece by Nathan J. Brown, "Shari'a and State in the Modern Muslim Middle East," *International Journal of Middle East Studies* 29, no. 3 (August 1997): 359–376, which emphasizes the conflict between those who see the sharia as a process and those who see it is as a fixed legal code.

42. Nadje Al-Ali, *Secularism, Gender and the State in the Middle East* (Cambridge, UK: Cambridge University Press, 2000), chapter 4.

43. Burgat, *Face to Face with Political Islam*. Luis Martinez, *La guerre civile en Algérie, 1990–1998* (Paris: Editions Karthala, 1998), 23, distributes blame among a number of parties who came to see war as a source of "riches and prestige." See also Martin Evans and John Phillips, *Algeria: Anger of the Dispossessed* (New Haven, CT: Yale University Press, 2007), which tends to put greatest blame on the Algerian government.

44. René Rémond, "Les mutations contemporaines de la laïcité française," in Jean Baudoin and Philippe Portier, eds., *La laïcité, une valeur d'aujourd'hui? Contestations et negotiations du modèle français* (Paris: Presses universitaires de France, 2001), 347–350. Other articles in the same collection affirm that point.

45. Maurice Barbier, *La Laïcité* (Paris: Editions L'Harmattan, 1995), 173ff. The recent outpouring of literature on laïcité includes: Abderrahim Lamchichi, *Islam et musulmans de France* (Paris: L'Harmattan, 1999); Saheif Bencheikh, *Marianne et le prophète: l'Islam dans la France laïque* (Paris: Bernard Grasset, 1998); Greg Bedouelle and Jean-Paul Costa, "Les laïcités à la française (Paris: Presses universitaires de France, 1998); Bruno Etienne, *La France et l'islam* (Paris: Hachette, 1989); Guy Coq, *Laïcité et République: Le lien nécessaire* (Paris: Editions du Félin, 1995); Jocelyne Cesari, *Musulmans et républicains; les jeunes, l'islam, et la France* (Paris: Editions Complexe, 1998); and Baudouin and Portier, *La laïcité, une valeur d'aujourd'hui*.

46. Seyyed Vali Reza Nasr, *Islamic Leviathan: Islam and the Making of State Power* (Oxford, UK: Oxford University Press, 2001), 115.

47. Ibid., 136.

48. Ibid., 159.

49. Crecelius, "The Course of Secularization."

50. Malika Zeghal, *Gardiens de l'Islam: Les oulémas d'Alzhar dans l'Egypte contemporaine* (Paris: Fondation Nationale des Sciences politiques, 1996); Jakob Skovgaard-Petersen, *Defining Islam for the Egyptian State: Muftis and Fatwas of the Dār al-Iftā* (Leiden: Brill, 1997).

51. Johannes C. Wolfart, *Religion, Government and Political Culture in Early Modern Germany: Lindau, 1520–1628* (New York: Palgrave, 2002), 172.

52. Gibson, *The Church of England*, 176.

53. See Frederick C. Harris, "Something Within: Religion as a Mobilizer of African-American Political Activism," *Journal of Politics* 56, no. 1 (February 1994): 42–68.

54. Pippa Norris and Ronald Inglehart, *Sacred and Secular: Religion and Politics Worldwide* (Cambridge, UK: Cambridge University Press, 2004.)

55. Olivier Roy argues that all religions come out of specific cultural settings. Those with universal aspirations must necessarily adapt to alien cultures or, alternatively, engage in radical challenge to those cultures. The effort of universal religions to divorce themselves from culture helps explain the turmoil of the modern era. Roy, *La Sainte Ignorance: Le Temps de la Religion Sans Culture* (Paris: Seuil, 2008).

56. Jenny White, *Islamist Mobilization in Turkey: A Study in Vernacular Politics* (Seattle: University of Washington Press, 2002).

57. Ibid., 266.

58. See Gregory Starrett, *Putting Islam to Work: Education, Politics and Religious Transformation in Egypt* (Berkeley: University of California Press, 1998), chapter 2, and Véronique Dimier, "La laïcité: un produit d'exportation? Le cas du rapport Combes (1892) sur l'enseignement primaire indigène en Algérie," in Baudouin and Portier, *La laïcité, une valeur d'aujourd'hui*, 76.

59. Greilsammer, *Israël: les hommes en noir*, 74.

60. Ibid., chapter 4.

61. See René Rémond, "Les mutations," 347–350.

62. Ronald Inglehart, *Modernization and Postmodernization: Cultural Economic and Political Change in 43 Societies* (Princeton, NJ: Princeton University Press, 1997), chapter 9.

63. Gabriel A. Almond and Sidney Verba, *The Civic Culture: Political Attitudes and Democracy in Five Nations* (Princeton, NJ: Princeton University Press, 1963).

64. Steven Pfaff, "The Religious Divide: Why Religion Seems to Be Thriving in the United States and Waning in Europe," in Jeffrey Kopstein and Sven Steinmo, eds., *Growing Apart: America and Europe in the Twenty-First Century* (Cambridge, UK: Cambridge University Press, 2008), 52.

65. Robert W. Hefner, *Civil Islam: Muslims and Democratization in Indonesia* (Princeton, NJ: Princeton University Press, 2000), 17, makes this point about Indonesia, but it applies to many other Muslim states.

66. White, *Islamist Mobilization in Turkey*.

67. Gabriel A. Almond and Sidney Verba, eds., *The Civic Culture Revisited* (Newbury Park, CA: Sage Publications, 1989).

68. Jenny White makes that point effectively in her *Islamist Mobilization in Turkey*.

69. Spinner-Halev, *Surviving Diversity*, 60, argues that culture is an "enabling constraint: it enables us to have choices just as it restricts the choices we have."

2

Religion as a Causal Force

We do not yet have a very good conceptual model, much less a theory, to account for the tumultuous entanglement of religion in politics all around the globe.[1]

Modernization theory as it was articulated in the 1950s and 1960s identified political development with secularizing the polity. A fusion of religious and political systems was said to mark "traditional society," the term used to characterize third-world cultures prior to European intervention. The bureaucratization of the polity required the separation of religion and politics, and the creation of participatory institutions depended upon the rationalization of political culture. Religion might condition responses to modernity, but political development meant the progressive relegation of religion to the realms of civil society and private belief.

Modernization theory collapsed in the 1970s and 1980s under a withering barrage of critiques for its reification of two categories, "traditional society" and "modern society," for its insistence on development as a linear process, for its transparent embrace of Western ideals under the guise of scientific objectivity, and for its failure to account for important aspects of both Western and non-Western history—to name a few of its most notable weaknesses. The secularization hypothesis, central to the whole body of theory, proved especially vulnerable to counterfactual critique. Religion began to reemerge as a dynamic, vital force in the politics of most Muslim countries, and the civil rights movement in the United States, liberation theology in Latin America, the clash between Protestants and Catholics in Ireland, and the prominence of Christian democratic parties in several European states cast doubt on the notion that religion no longer counted in the politics of the West. The defenders of modernization theory found themselves trying to account for aberrations in implausible ways. "Yes, religion remains important in the United States, but American religion is more social than religious." Or "the Islamic revival is a mere blip on the screen, a short-term deviation from the pattern."

Modernization theory relegated religion to the dustbin of history—Marx had already put capitalism there—but like capitalism, religion did not go quietly. Religion and politics seem as thoroughly intertwined as ever, perhaps more thoroughly in some parts of the world than others, but the difference is one of degree rather than kind. Religion shapes politics, and vice versa. Under what circumstances, if any, can religion play a positive role in political development? How and in what way can the state negotiate a relationship with organized religion that serves the interests of political stability and of religious integrity? What are the possibilities for "settlement" of this relationship in a relatively durable way? Can one discern multiple versions of secularism or multiple roles for religion in political life?

Comparative politics necessarily presupposes a normative perspective. Aristotle founded the discipline with his effort to discern the advantages and disadvantages of different types of government. Machiavelli fashioned his notion of the ideal prince on the basis of a conviction that a strong government capable of maintaining political order is better than a weak government and that peace is a requisite of civilized life. Thomas Hobbes and John Locke both sought to construct models of good government capable of producing not just peace but a modicum of political liberty as well. Comparisons done in the name of structural-functionalism, Marxism, civil society, political economy—all presume judgment about desirable versus undesirable outcomes. Any comparative treatment of religion and politics must ask how interaction of religious and political spheres affects the possibility of realizing desirable outcomes.

The notion of political development, although it emerged from modernization theory, remains useful as a shorthand for desirable political outcomes. Following Huntington and others, Thomas Ertman defines political development to include two components: the institutionalization (bureaucratization) of the state and the expansion of inclusiveness through the implementation of constitutionalism.[2] A state that is increasingly staffed by professionals, chosen on the basis of merit, will be capable of providing higher-quality services—defense, economic regulation, infrastructure, health, education; it will be increasingly capable of responding to emerging needs and using resources efficiently. A state based on broad participation and the guarantee of individual rights will command greater loyalty from its citizens and be capable of extracting the resources required to provide high-quality services. A state based in patrimonialism and authoritarianism will be incapable of competing with a bureaucratic, constitutional state in waging war and providing the good life for its citizens. As Ertman shows in the case of Europe, neither aspect of political development is sufficient without the other.

A study of religion and politics undertaken with political development as the norm must ask how the interaction of religion and politics affects the possibilities for bureaucratization and constitutionalism. Can organized religion, understood in the broadest sense as a set of beliefs, identities, organizations, and practices, contribute under specific conditions to political development? Does religion under some (or all) circumstances retard political development? Why is it that religion serves to reinforce the strength and stability of the state under some circumstances and to undermine it in others? Why under some circumstances does it devolve into sectarianism while in other contexts it becomes a foundation for compromise and construction? Under what circumstances does religion tend to disappear from the public arena and under what conditions does it reappear?

Is there a relationship between the political and religious domains that is more conducive than others to the emergence and maintenance of a bureaucratic-constitutional state? The secularization hypothesis suggests that such a relationship is some form of political secularism. Or are there several models of religious-political equilibrium that may be conducive at one or more stages of political development? What might be the advantages of an official state religion?

Most efforts to analyze the relationship of religion and politics have focused on religion as an independent variable and politics as a dependent variable. For example, scholars have asked whether Protestantism or Catholicism is more conducive to democratic development,[3] whether Christianity or Islam poses greater obstacles to modernization,[4] and whether citizens with strong religious beliefs are more or less inclined to vote for certain parties or policies. Religion appears to be a fixed, primordial aspect of a person's psyche and a long-term influence over the politics of a country. It is usually treated as having existed prior to the formation of political institutions and policies, a cause of politics rather than an effect. I propose to examine a list of propositions offered in this vein.

Religion can also be seen as a product of political actions.[5] Gauchet argues that the appearance of the state apparatus in history transformed primitive religion.[6] Whereas religion is the domain that unites human beings with one another and with nature, the state creates another pole of identity, loyalty, and regulation. As a result, religion must necessarily be transformed by the emergence of the nation-state, which calls for much more direct identification of citizen and state. Religions, especially universal religions, must find ways to reconcile their universalizing tendencies with parochial loyalties. And insofar as the state encourages, funds, and promotes the general education of its citizens, it changes the character of a scripture-based religion, where a scholarly community enjoys a monopoly on interpreting revelation. By seeking religious legitimation, states necessarily reshape the ideology of the religious sphere. By opposing religious organizations and pushing them to the margins, the state alters the structure of religion.

Both religion and politics themselves depend upon the direction of social change. One does not have to accept modernization theory in its most deterministic form to recognize that changing technologies and changing societies affect both domains. For example, the invention of the printing press proved fundamental if not indispensable to the Protestant Reformation, just as it was critical to the emergence of nationalism in Europe. That innovation permanently transformed both the political and the religious spheres. When combined with increasing literacy rates and the development of radio, television, cassette recorders, and the Internet, the printed word has changed the character of political and religious discussion. Social mobilization in the form of urbanization, industrialization, and improved transportation have further transformed the structure and function of religion, just as it has redefined the task and capacities of the state.

Huntington has argued that rapid modernization can undermine political development, as institutions are overwhelmed by the new demands being made on them. In particular, social mobilization has produced political participation (strikes, demonstrations, demands) that the institutions may not be able to satisfy.[7] Both European history and recent events in the Middle East suggest that religion, transformed by social mobilization, may also become a force in promoting change, complicating the task of the state in maintaining order; yet the state may see religion as a useful tool in coping with the destabilizing effects of social mobilization. Politics, religion, and social mobilization should thus be seen as interactive variables, sometimes independent, sometimes dependent. At some moments of European history, religion appears dominant as a factor in political development, and at other moments it disappears. The secularization hypothesis emerged at the end of the nineteenth century, a moment when religion seemed an ever-diminishing force in Europe.

Ertman and others have found timing to be an important variable in explaining political development. He has argued that European states where institutional development came early (England, for example) found themselves competing with states that had not yet been able to establish a reliable bureaucratic apparatus; these states, such as France, depended on patrimonial appointments for performing critical political tasks, and the inefficiencies of the system cost them dearly. Latecomers to political development, such as Germany, learned from French mistakes and proceeded to build bureaucracies before they came under serious challenge.[8] Latecomers to economic development, such as states of the third world, have suffered first from the colonial environment they endured and then from an international arena dominated by a cold war that spared them the need to defend themselves militarily in the pattern of early modern European states.[9] Dependent on foreign aid and investment, without the incentive of military need to drive the creation of a strong national economy, these countries have floundered. Timing is everything.

For this reason, religion and politics might interact differently in two countries at the same moment, and differently in the same country at different moments, under the impact of social change. Even the international environment may condition the relationship. In each country one would expect to find periods in which there was relative equilibrium between the religious and political spheres and periods in which, for one reason or another, that equilibrium is disrupted. A semblance of equilibrium—defined crudely as a situation in which the state is not seeking to undermine religious institutions and attitudes and most religiously motivated actors are not seeking to undermine the state—may be restored, only to be disrupted again at a further stage of development. There is no reason to imagine that any permanent state of equilibrium can be achieved or that equilibria are necessarily similar across time or space. It may be that "equilibrium" simply means a condition in which continuous change and shifting occurs so slowly that the relationship seems to stand still.

The question is whether there are certain forms of equilibrium—regularities in the relationship between the religious and the political—that are conducive to political development, and whether those forms vary with time as well as local culture. It may be that religion is in the long run a relatively unimportant variable. That is, states may eventually move toward political development whether religion is relatively hierarchical or organic in structure, whether their citizens are relatively devout or largely indifferent to religion, whether state law is deeply influenced by religious law, and whether religious doctrine is highly authoritarian or relatively egalitarian. But close comparison suggests that religion facilitates or hinders political development in some places at different moments in time. Certainly contemporaries in many eras including our own have regarded religion as an important factor in political development. Imagine trying to tell American colonists, Germans of the sixteenth century, or Englishmen of the seventeenth and eighteenth centuries that religion was not a factor in political development! Contemporary Israelis, Saudis, and Iranians, to take just three examples, would also take issue with such a statement, as would those who have argued that militant Islam represents a threat to the stability of many modern states.

That does not mean that the arguments of religious ideologues can be accepted at face value. Proponents of religion tend to overestimate the contributions of religion to law, public morality, civil society, and political legitimacy. Similarly, many proponents of secularism exaggerate the dangers of religion and the negative impact of religion on political development. One must beware both of those who claim from conviction that religion has no place in political life and those who claim that there can be no separation between religion and politics. Comparative political investigation must seek to distinguish ideology from behavior, but it must also be careful not to discount the views of contemporary witnesses who, with or without deep ideological commitment, see an intimate relationship between religion and politics.

Careful investigation of national histories shows religion and politics intertwined in so many ways, some cooperative and some conflictual, that it is impossible to make any single judgment about the impact of religion on politics or the impact of politics on religion. Perhaps further research and analysis will show that religion matters at every stage of development but does not prove to be decisive in the long run. Even if this were so, it would still be useful to analyze the relationship between religion and politics for its relationship to the development process.

From the abundant literature on religion and politics produced by sociologists and political scientists, anthropologists and historians, philosophers and students of comparative religion, not to mention journalists and casual observers, I have compiled a set of hypotheses and put them in three categories: (1) those that regard religion as an obstacle to political development; (2) those that embrace religion as helpful in promoting political development; and (3) those that deny any importance to religion in explaining political development. I have further arranged these hypotheses according to the domains of primary relevance: political culture, institutions, ideology, or identity.

Religion Obstructs Political Development

Political Culture

Hypothesis #1: A culture steeped in religion—committed to myth, to magic, to faith in God rather than faith in human effort—will be unable to produce subjects, much less citizens, of a modern state. Such a culture must be "secularized"—that is, "rationalized"—if genuine political development is to occur.

In the introduction to his book on Spinoza, Steven Smith writes: "The aim of the work as a whole is the liberation of the individual from bondage to superstition and ecclesiastical authority. Spinoza's ideal is the free or autonomous individual who uses reason to achieve mastery over the passions."[10] Political development depends upon autonomous, rational individuals.

That seems to be what Weber meant by the "disenchantment of the world," a phrase that appears as the title of a recent book by Gauchet, who writes: "For Weber this expression specifically meant 'the elimination of magic as a salvation technique.' I do not believe that broadening it to mean the impoverishment of the reign of the invisible distorts this meaning."[11] Gauchet sees the very birth of scriptural religion as the beginning of a relentless process of secularization. The logic of secularization lies within all the religions of the book—Judaism, Christianity, and Islam—and secularization means declining influence of religion (and the supernatural) on culture. In *Religion and Political Development*, D. E. Smith writes:

> Underlying the secularization of political culture is the decline of explicitly religious values, generally throughout the society. Religiosity and piety are no longer highly valued socially. Material values rank higher than otherworldly values. . . . There is growing scepticism concerning the truth or validity of traditional religious doctrine. . . . Religious values no longer motivate importantly. . . . People do not think about religion much; it occupies a diminishing part of their consciousness. There is growing tolerance of religious values foreign to one's own culture and a growing relativism based on scepticism of all religious truth claims.[12]

Like Weber and Parsons, D. E. Smith regards secularization as fundamental to political development, a description of what has occurred in the West and a prescription for the third world. He describes not just a decline in the influence of organized religions but, with his reference to consciousness, to individual religiosity as well. Berger, who later had second thoughts about these matters, says much the same thing in *The Sacred Canopy*:

> [Secularization] affects the totality of cultural life and of ideation, and may
> be observed in the decline of religious contents in the arts, in philosophy, in
> literature, and most important of all, in the rise of science as an autonomous,
> thoroughly secular perspective on the world. And as there is a secularization
> of society and culture, so is there a secularization of consciousness.[13]

Echoes of logical positivism, a philosophical movement that began in nineteenth-century Europe and gained momentum in the twentieth century, reverberate in this and other statements of secularizing necessity. Logical positivism insists that only the empirical verification of testable hypotheses can generate truth. Science and rationality produce a truth that drives out magic and eventually every attachment to something that lies beyond empirical confirmation ("the reign of the invisible"). The ostensible objective of logical positivism is merely description, and description of the particular (as in the analysis of the secularization of Europe) becomes universal by virtue of theory. Political development, understood as the growth of bureaucracy and constitutionalism, requires secularization.

Most proponents of this perspective, from Spinoza through Weber, Durkheim, and Parsons, welcome or at least accept secularization as a positive outcome, and only a few, such as Marcel Gauchet and Ernest Fortin, deplore it. For example, Gauchet worries that the disenchantment of the liberal state leaves it without the capacity to assert itself on behalf of the common good. Without any magic to lift it above the fray, the state becomes a mere container for the multitude of ideas and interests that percolate within it.[14] Fortin deplores secularization, and the role of churches in that process, for its impact on the loss of spirituality. Not even the separation of church and state has saved spirituality from the mundane, because churches have been more preoccupied, in his view, with membership and material standing than with the welfare of souls.

> Contrary to its stated aim, liberal democracy does breed a specific type of
> human being, one that is defined by an unprecedented openness to all human possibilities. What this leads to most of the time is neither Nietzschean

creativity nor a noble dedication to some pregiven ideal, not a deeper religious life, nor a rich and diversified society, but easygoing indifference and mindless conformism.

No one takes religion seriously, and the culprit, in Fortin's opinion, is liberal democracy.[15]

Hypothesis #2: Because political development depends upon training subjects and then citizens, it ultimately depends upon education. The state must take from religious institutions the task of educating citizens; it has no responsibility for religious education and must avoid any involvement in particular sorts of religious education.

This hypothesis stems from the first. The construction of rational political institutions depends upon a rational citizenry. Socrates found himself accused of trying to subvert the state by teaching his brand of rationalism. The republic emphasizes the need to train leaders in the best possible way, but Jean-Jacques Rousseau, one of the pioneers of the shift toward democratic politics, laid out a plan for the rational education of every man—and to a lesser extent, every woman. By the late nineteenth century, champions of the Third French Republic had come to believe that only the *école laïque* could secure the future of democracy in that country.[16] The battle for the republic played itself out village by village, as the local schoolteacher, a missionary of secularism, took on the local priest in an effort to create citizens no longer beholden to the old ways and, more especially, to the old order.

In other parts of Europe and especially in the United States, the spread of public education seldom took on the antireligious overtones it did in France.[17] In England the threat of Catholicism disappeared with James II; the state allied itself with the Church of England to train subjects and citizens, and in the United States religion allied itself with both progress and progressive education. Still, the French notion of laïcité made its mark on the French colonial empire and on the military elite of the Ottoman Empire in the last decades of its existence. The reforms of Mustafa Kemal Atatürk, himself a product of European-style schools and an admirer of the French Revolution and French ideas, reflected a philosophy of laïcité.[18] The Turkish republic sought to combat not just religious institutions (as it did with the abolition of the sultanate-caliphate) but also the mentality of tradition anchored in religion. New schools would make new citizens.

Institutions

Hypothesis #3: Organized religion, where it takes hierarchical form, may obstruct political development by resisting state efforts to develop state authority and provide directly for the general welfare of citizens.

Machiavelli pronounced Christianity the worst of religions for sustaining political stability, because it was not identical in scope with any state. As a power outside the state, the papacy had followers and opponents in every community, dividing where it ought to have united. It did not hesitate to invite foreign intervention in the Italian peninsula, if it served the interests of the Church. Venice earned the enmity of Rome for treating the papacy as just another state, driven by interest rather than principle. The Venetian refusal to accept papal appointments led to the imposition of sanctions against one of the most advanced polities of its day.

Roman Catholicism is more hierarchical than Islam by virtue of the priesthood and centralized management. It was the alliance of the Catholic Church with the ancien régime and its opposition to the French Republic through the late nineteenth century that embittered the debate in France about public schools. The papacy set itself against the Italian Republic in the first half century of its existence, forbidding Catholics to vote or hold office. D. E. Smith treats Islam as an "organic" religion, lacking in a distinct religious hierarchy, but the Ottoman sultans of the Tanzimat period came to see the corps of ulama, with its prerogatives and privileges, as separate from the will of the sovereign and as an obstacle to reform.[19] In Egypt Muhammad Ali sought to subjugate the ulama, perhaps because of their standing as an indigenous elite sustained by significant economic resources. To do so he sought to create hierarchy by elevating the shaykh al-Azhar to preeminence over other ulama.[20] Thus Islam became hierarchical in some times and places.

Hypothesis #4: Only a state in which religion and politics are thoroughly separated can provide political development.

This is one possible corollary of the previous proposition. Another would be that the thorough fusion of church and state can prevent religion from becoming an obstacle, but this proposition tips toward the conclusion that religion can, under certain circumstances, reinforce political development. The separation hypothesis presumes that organized religion must move from the public realm to the private and become a matter of individual conscience.

The theory claims that government combined with an official church limits the freedom of citizens to practice religions of their choice. Effective, rational government requires the services of all citizens, religious or not. Since moral claims cannot be verified, the claims of religious organizations deserve no more weight than the interests and claims of groups lacking the authority of God. Constitutional, bureaucratic government depends upon the will of men, not the will of God. As Berger puts it: "Religion mystifies institutions by explaining them as *given* over and beyond their empirical existence in the history of society."[21] Modern government seeks to demystify itself and its processes.

Therefore, governments such as those of Israel and Iran cannot provide long-term political development. The fusion of religious and political institutions limits the capacity of these states to include those who are non-Jews or non-Muslims (or non-practicing Jews, non-practicing Muslims, and atheists). Even if non-Jews can accede to citizenship and to positions of political power, they can never be fully equal, if Judaism defines the nature of the state. It could certainly be argued (and will be argued below) that religious cohesion has contributed to the development of these states, but the separation hypothesis holds that their development as fully constitutional states will be blocked, other examples notwithstanding.

On behalf of the separation hypothesis, it is easy to cite examples where the fusion of religion and politics has imposed heavy costs on the development of the state. (The Marxist regimes of Russia and central Europe might be the outstanding examples, even though they were, in the main, quite antireligious. Marxism became the religion of the state.) The rule of the Taliban in Afghanistan deprived women of social and political opportunities, damaged education, disrupted the fledgling bureaucracy, and, in general, set back political development. In the Sudan and in Pakistan, even in Egypt, as religion gained a more prominent position, ideology became more and more prominent in public discourse. Discussing the possible linkage of Islam and state in Indonesia, Hefner writes:

> The markets, media, and migrations of our age make any enduring institutionalization of such a statist Islam difficult. It may be attempted, but again and again it will fail. Virtue will give way to hypocrisy and abuse, and religion itself will be threatened.[22]

Many who argue for separation, whether in Iran or the United States, make that same point. The integrity of religious institutions requires it.

Vaclav Havel, the Czech leader, revived the idea that democratic political development must proceed from a strong civil society. Organizations beyond the confines of the state give citizens the capacity to shape, criticize, and sustain constitutional government. The Catholic Church in Poland boosted spirits and eventually contributed to the overthrow of Soviet rule. Many have argued that Islamist groups in the Middle East, active in creating schools, clinics, and other welfare services, are contributing to the construction of civil societies in their countries.[23] Carter insists that sound liberal-democratic government depends upon the autonomy of religious organizations, capable of injecting fresh perspectives from the outside.[24] He echoes Spinoza, who argued that "true religion" could bow only to the secular and never the religious authority of the state. True religion must be a part of the civil society.[25]

That religion and politics should be separate matters applies more easily to the realm of institutions than to political culture, ideology, or identity. No one has suggested that Martin Luther King should have abandoned the language of religion, or the mobilization of churches, to pursue civil rights. Separation of church and state surely does not prevent Catholics from voting against candidates who oppose abortion. Nor does the separation of church and state prevent the use of religion to sustain constitutional legitimacy. Even though Turkey has attempted to separate the religious and political domains, it has not hesitated to identify itself as a Muslim state. Separation of church and state therefore does not necessarily constitute a separation of religion and politics.

Hypothesis #5: Religious organizations and parties formed by groups intent upon imposing their version of God's will threaten the stability of any proto-democratic regime. To ensure its own development, a state must block the progress of such groups.

Manfred Halpern raised the specter of neo-Islamic totalitarianism in *The Politics of Social Change in the Middle East and North Africa.*[26] The Muslim Brotherhood in Egypt served as his primary example of a group seemingly bent on thwarting the political modernization of which Halpern was an advocate. The founder of the Brotherhood, Hasan al-Banna, had initially forsworn politics in favor of creating an association dedicated to cultural revival in the name of Islam and Egyptian nationalism. By the 1940s the organization had, through its success at the local level, acquired a potential for political influence that outweighed the only Egyptian political party, the Wafd, with aspirations to a popular following. When the Wafd betrayed its nationalist principles by condoning British reentry into Egypt during World War II, the Brotherhood began to veer toward direct political intervention, and the government responded by outlawing the organization. The Brotherhood's "secret apparatus" nonetheless succeeded in assassinating a prime minister and provoking the government to arrange the assassination of Banna. Recovering legal status, the Brotherhood supported the 1952 coup d'état, which brought to power Gamal abd al-Nasir and the Free Officers, a group of military officers who opposed the Egyptian monarchy and British influence. It then quarreled with Nasir and ostensibly tried to assassinate him, whereupon he outlawed the organization and sent its leadership to prison.

It would be difficult to identify the Brotherhood with any political ideology other than nationalism in the first thirty years of its existence. Banna, himself a layman, held sway over his followers by appealing to the values of traditional Islam (which Egypt seemed to be abandoning), to a spiritualism and mysticism that transcended the rational Islam dear to reformers of the period, and to a thoroughly modern conception of social action. Nationalism is itself, of course, a modern concept. Banna called his creation a "a Salafiyya message, a Sunni way, a Sufi truth, a political organization, an athletic group, a cultural-educational union, an economy [sic] company and a social idea."[27]

The Brotherhood's lack of an explicit ideology before Sayyid Qutb constructed one from his prison cell in the 1950s and 1960s makes it hard to sustain Halpern's argument about "totalitarian" tendencies. Even Qutb's ideas, emphasizing the absolute sovereignty of God and the illegitimacy of all human sovereignty, lend themselves to both authoritarian and antiauthoritarian interpretations. The organization itself, especially after Banna's death, was scarcely democratic, but neither was it totalitarian in its hold on its membership, which was dominated by the educated middle class. Mitchell describes a Brotherhood meeting attended by 330 people, composed of students, civil servants, teachers, clerks, and professionals, mostly dressed in Western fashion.[28]

The threat of the Brotherhood in Egypt was its organizational strength rather than its ideology. From the perspective of Halpern, convinced that the military represented a new middle class dedicated to modernizing the Middle East, and from the perspective of military leaders such as Gamal abd al-Nasir, such an organization threatened progress toward political and social development in the name of religion and the values of the past. Nasir sought to suppress all opposition to his regime, and so did similar "modernizing" regimes in Syria, Iraq, and Algeria—all places where the military played a heavy role in politics after World War II. Islamist organizations on the model of the

Brotherhood, whatever their objectives, found broad popular support and came to threaten the stability of illegitimate (by definition) military regimes. In Turkey, where democratization had begun in 1950, and in Tunisia, where the military had not initially been directly involved in politics, commitments to secularization served as justification for military suppression of the threat from organizations couching their appeal in religion.

Ideology

Hypothesis #6: Some religions, such as Roman Catholicism and Islam, are undemocratic in tendency. Others (varieties of Protestantism) seem to be linked to the growth of democratic institutions. Hence, some types of religion must give way or engage in reform if political development is to occur.

Nicholls argues that images of God necessarily derive from human experience. Insofar as human beings imagine God as authoritative and powerful, they invoke political analogies to describe those roles—ruler, Lord, king, master, sovereign, judge. God rules the heavens as kings and presidents rule on earth.[29] By the same token, religious understandings of God necessarily come to influence political ideology. For example, a notion of a transcendent God far removed from human affairs, oblivious to the disputes of mankind, unavailable to the prayers and entreaties of mere individuals, prime mover and final judge of human behavior becomes one model for political authoritarianism. However, the image of a God present in the world to alleviate the suffering of mankind and guide it to better pastures, a God to be discovered in the actions of some and absent from the actions of others, may lend itself to exploitation by political authorities claiming to represent God on earth. "A God who is unambiguously immanent may too easily be used to sanctify a current political system, while a merely transcendent being, ruling over an alien world, readily provides a model, and thus a potential legitimation, for arbitrary political rule."[30]

Radically transcendent and thoroughly immanent concepts of God sustain authoritarianism, but neither mainstream Christianity nor mainstream Islam takes an extreme position on this matter. In the case of Christianity, God appeared on earth. In the case of Islam, God sent down the Quran to shepherd human beings toward a better life. Saint cultures emerged in both religions to soften the dichotomy between heaven and earth. D. E. Smith rates Islam and Roman Catholicism equal in "dogmatic authority" and "directive authority" (three points each on a three-point scale) but ultimately judges Catholicism more authoritarian not because of ideology but because of organization (a hierarchical as opposed to an organic religion).[31]

Rulers in both traditions have found ample ammunition to claim divine origin, divine guidance, and divine status for their own versions of authoritarianism. Scholars have argued that the Catholic countries of Europe struggled longer and harder against authoritarian rule than the Protestant states. Inglehart has reiterated the Weberian contention that Protestantism triggered the growth of materialism and entrepreneurship in northern Europe, and this shift in values ultimately contributed to the growth of liberal constitutional regimes in these countries. Attitudes in Catholic Europe remain somewhat more "traditional" and authoritarian in the survey data he analyzes.[32] Ideology slows political development by retarding the shift in values toward greater citizen confidence and competency.

The reform movement in Islam launched by Jamal al-Din al-Afghani and carried forward by Muhammad Abdu in Egypt proceeded from similar assumptions. Abdu believed that political and economic development in the Muslim world depended upon revising Islamic theology. The prevailing Sunni view held that truth came only through revelation, and Islamic law, as compiled by the great authorities of the ninth and tenth centuries, followed directly from revelation. Religious authority aligned itself to support an authoritarian ruler committed to upholding Islam and to opposing any "innovation," deemed heretical because one man cannot change what God has fixed. Abdu argued that revelation itself affirmed reason, and thus modern scientific discoveries based in reason could not contradict revelation; they could not be deemed heretical innovation. For Afghani, Abdu, Rashid Rida, and others of reformist inclination, the capacity of Muslim societies to modernize depended first upon change in the ideology of Islam. They looked for inspiration to the pious ancestors (*salafi*).

Westerners joined these salafi reformers in blaming the backwardness of Muslim societies—economic, social, and political—on the dogmatic character of Islamic thought. Describing the victory of theology over philosophy in the medieval Islamic world, Orientalists portrayed a society convinced it had established the truth and insulated itself against fresh ideas in any realm. The late representatives of the Islamic philosophical tradition, Ibn Rushd (Averroes) and Ibn Khaldun, however influential in the West, exercised little or no influence on Islamic thought. More advanced in military and bureaucratic techniques than its European contemporaries of the fourteenth and fifteenth centuries, the Ottoman Empire could not keep pace with Europe as

the scientific, technological, philosophical, social, and political revolutions
unfolded there. The Ottomans disdained innovation in deference to an ideology of unchanging truth founded in revelation. Such is the argument that religious ideology can obstruct political development.

Hypothesis #7: Religious ideology has no place in the public forum.
Reasoned argument susceptible to challenge must be the basis for the le-
gitimacy of regimes and policies in a liberal-democratic setting, whereas
arguments based in religious doctrine and conviction cannot be debated.
Thus, one might argue against abortion on the grounds that a fetus is
already a person worthy of defense, but one cannot simply say, "I am
against abortion because God says it is wrong."

It might be difficult to find someone who puts it quite so baldly. Voye stops
just a bit short when she writes:

> The process of secularization is still advancing, but . . . the religious field and
> religious actors have regained the right to express themselves legitimately on
> the public scene, insofar as they abandon any dogmatism and as far as they
> serve interests outside their own field.[33]

Apparently "religious field and religious actors" have no intrinsic rights to intervene in the public forum. They have re-earned the right only by adhering
to guidelines. Carter says our rhetoric "refuses to accept the notion that rational, public spirited people can take religion seriously."[34] Liberalism accepts religion as long as "God is a hobby"—purely private and spiritual—and not a
force in daily life, shaping personal, social, and political attitudes.

Hypothesis #8: The transformation of religious doctrine into contem-
porary political ideology cannot serve the purposes of political develop-
ment (or the purposes of religion, for that matter). D. E. Smith calls
the politicization of religion a "short-lived process characteristic of the
politics of transitional societies."[35] Inglehart refers to the Islamic revival
in the Middle East as a short-term exception to the pattern of secular-
ization characteristic of modernization.[36]

This proposition presumes the truth of Hypothesis #6, that religious ideology
is necessarily authoritarian. Abul ala Mawdudi of Pakistan and Qutb of Egypt,
who are the best-known ideologues of radical Sunni Islam, do argue against

human sovereignty. They see God as utterly transcendent, distant, dominant, authoritarian, one who has provided a set of rules and guidelines for mankind that permit the creation of an orderly world consistent with divine sovereignty. Other Sunni Islamists of somewhat lesser stature, such as Rachid Ghannouchi in Tunisia and Hasan al-Turabi in the Sudan, have spun out democratic theories of Islam to power their movements. But even with Turabi himself in a critical position to guide affairs, Islamization in the Sudan did not advance the causes of liberalism and democracy. In fact, it undermined them. Islamists in Egypt and elsewhere have claimed the right to attack the state and assassinate its leaders in the name of undisputable higher truth.

In Pakistan and Malaysia the state promoted the politicization of Islam "to establish hegemony over society and expand its powers and control."[37] In his study of those two states, Nasr argues that "Islamism is not a threat to the state per se, only to the secularism of the state." And he writes: "The Islamist ideology implies that the state has a right to be intrusive and interventionist."[38] By this line of argument, the politicization of Islam may thus serve one aspect of political development, the creation and maintenance of strong bureaucratic institutions capable of encouraging economic and social development, but it does not necessarily contribute to the liberal, democratic, constitutional dimension of development.

The politicization of Shii Islam in Iran, a process that began in the nineteenth century and reached fruition in the writings of Ayatollah Khomeini in the 1960s and 1970s, proposed to replace one version of authoritarianism with another: the *velayat-e faqih*, or the task of governing the community in the absence of the hidden imam, which according to Khomeini fell to the most qualified student of holy law, the faqih. His theory avoided the extremes of immanence and transcendence. When he himself assumed power in the role of the faqih, he let himself be called imam, but he never claimed to possess the divine powers of one of the twelve designated imams of Shii history, much less the powers of Ali or the Prophet, which would have been a sharp move toward immanence. The theory of velayat-e faqih put divine resources at the disposal of an earthly government no longer (seemingly) neglected by a transcendent God. The Scylla and Charybdis of Islamic authoritarianism thus avoided, Khomeini went on to approve a constitution of the Islamic Republic of Iran that included elected officials. That fact appeared to further undercut any basis for authoritarianism, but authoritarianism has nonetheless flourished without legitimate foundation in either religious or political theory.

For Muslim liberals the politicization of Islam threatens the tolerance they wish to nurture. Arkoun associates the politicization of Islam with the efforts of nation-states to exploit Islam for their own purposes, to bludgeon intellectual acceptance of ideas built on dubious scholarship, to cultivate allegiance and narrow-mindedness rather than enlightenment and tolerance of Islamic diversity. Politicization has proceeded on the assumption that one can identify authentic Islamic foundations and build an authentic Islamic state on top of them. But Arkoun argues that the choice of any one version of Islam as the authentic version is necessarily arbitrary and can be defended only by dogmatic assertion, not by scholarship meeting international standards. Hence, politicization serves to divide the community of believers and push it farther away from reconciliation with the totality of its past.[39]

Identity

Hypothesis #9: Religious identities, when not congruent with a state's boundaries, may prevent the formation of strong polities capable of ensuring peace and liberty for its citizens.

The champions of this hypothesis tend to see religious (and ethnic) identity as primordial, anchored deep within the human consciousness, hence enduring and nonnegotiable. Examples to support that notion abound: India, Northern Ireland, Belgium, Lebanon, Iraq, Sudan, Nigeria, and others. Hobbes, who saw the divisive effect of religion in seventeenth-century England, thought the leviathan required a single religious identity focused upon the sovereign. Locke built a case for toleration, but not of Catholics or atheists, groups deemed incapable of collaborating in the construction of a liberal state. Arend Lijphart's consociational or consensus model, liberal and somewhat democratic, seemed to promise political development in states deeply divided by religion, but the collapse of Lebanon, and the tribulations of Belgium, have weakened the case for consociationalism.[40] Of course, there are also examples of modern states where multiple religious identities have not prevented the development of a strong constitutional state.

The hypothesis gains strength from being sharpened. An increased emphasis on religious identity as a tool for mobilizing political action may divide a state and compromise its ability to ensure peace and liberty. It may lead to sectarianism rather than to "sectorialism," by which Margalit means that a group retains an "overriding commitment to keeping a shared framework."[41] The mobilization of the Shia in Lebanon in the early 1970s under Imam Musa al-Sadr to fight for social justice and a fair share of political influence in that country triggered resistance from the dominant Maronite Christian group. While the subsequent civil war can scarcely be regarded as a struggle between Christians and Muslims over religious doctrine, the appeal to religious identity in the Shii community elicited an analogous appeal on the part of others. Similarly, the rise of Islamism in Egypt in the 1970s and 1980s led to attacks on the Christian minority, who, suddenly embattled, began to rally as a group to fight for their place in politics. The creation of an Islamic republic in Iran jeopardized the already precarious position of minorities such as the Bahais.

Hypothesis #10: Strong religious identities tend to spill over boundaries and cause groups to identify with religious cohorts elsewhere. Conflicts grounded in economic inequality, social injustice, or political struggle come to be regarded as religious confrontations and even elevated into a clash of civilizations.

Osama bin Laden has attempted to subsume a variety of complaints about Middle Eastern governments and U.S. foreign policy into a single religious question. He calls upon all Muslims to unite and throw off their internal and external oppressors. His followers, and others in the Middle East and North Africa, are quick to lump Europeans and Americans together as Christians (Crusaders) bent upon spreading the faith or at least spreading materialism, pornography, and corruption of all decency. The fact that Israel identifies itself as a Jewish state fosters religious response, whether from fundamentalist Christians who cite biblical support for the enterprise, or opposition from fundamentalist Muslims, bent upon its destruction. The proclamation of the Islamic Republic of Iran as the modern bearer of the Islamic standard initially alarmed much of the Middle East and especially its neighbor, the relatively secular state of Iraq. Ayatollah Khomeini goaded Saddam Hussein into launching a disastrous eight-year war with Iran.

Huntington projects a clash of civilizations on the assumption that religion constitutes the glue of civilization and that civilizations persist over millennia. With the cold war ended, world conflicts tend to pit civilization against civilization, the Christian West against Confucianism or the Islamic East. The identification of individual states with a single religion aligns them on one side or the other and makes it more likely that intrastate and interstate disputes will also assume religious or civilizational significance. Religion thus seems to threaten not just political development but world peace—unless civilizational unity is to be regarded as a source of order. The cold war brought order even though it seemed to promise Armageddon. Huntington suggests that civilization can be a stable source of order, if the West hangs together and prepares to defend itself against "the rest." Religion seems to end up on the positive side of his ledger, even though he once predicted demise for those religion-dependent monarchies trying to straddle tradition and modernity in the Middle East.[42]

These ten hypotheses surely do not exhaust the case to be made against religion as a force for political development, but they at least suggest the breadth and diversity of arguments that have been made. With its foundation in modernization theory, and backed by D. E. Smith in the only book written explicitly on religion and political development—albeit one that is now more than thirty years old—the negative position has long enjoyed the upper hand.[43] But the contrary proposition, that religion can promote political development, also enjoys considerable plausibility and rising support.

Religion Promotes Political Development

Political Culture

Hypothesis #11: Political development means weaning people from magic and superstition, but it also means winning the support of the rural masses for the political system. Religion constitutes the point of contact. Hence, the state must use religion to reach the masses and wean them from magic and superstition. It must foster a version of religion that is friendly to state authority, liberalism, tolerance, and democracy.

The Iranian revolution offers dramatic proof of the power of religion to rally support for the state. Liberal and Marxist opposition to the shah had little capacity to rally support in the villages, or even in the slums of south Tehran. The revolution used the language and symbols of Islam, including the more particularistic discourse of Shii Islam, to portray the old regime as evil and to recommend an alternative. Of course, the new regime soon found itself confronting popular elements of religion—such as amulets to ward off evil spirits—which imposed limits on change.[44] Armies of young cadres marched to the villages to teach "Islam" to those caught up in magic and superstition! The new regime set out to teach "good Islam" as its vehicle for promoting political and social development.

The British set out to do much the same after they took control of Egypt in 1881. The only existing elementary schools, the Quranic schools, had been weakened in the nineteenth century by state seizure of religious resources.

Run by clerics and based upon memorizing the Quran, they failed to provide a foundation in arithmetic, history, or modern science. The British and their collaborators among the Egyptian elite believed they had to provide an alternative in the form of modern schools teaching a "good" version of Islam, together with secular subjects.[45] The British-run Egyptian government wanted schools to furnish staffing for the civil service, to spread literacy in the countryside, and to create a "thrifty peasantry and an artisan class skilled in European manufactures."[46]

Egyptian public schools have never ceased to teach Islam, and even the hierarchy of religious schools culminating in al-Azhar University has come under state control. Gamal abd al-Nasir sought to further identify public instruction in Islam with loyalty to the state and its programs: A good Muslim practices good personal hygiene and fulfills his duties as a citizen. Later Nasir sought to show that socialism corresponded with the commands of the Prophet. "The ruling officers [were] faced with a paradox: the need to appeal to the 'Islamic myth' of communal and cultural identity in order to work for the achievement of a new formula to supersede it."[47]

These examples come from the Middle East, but the British took the idea of using religion to mold citizens from their own experience. A good Christian is a good citizen, a point St. Augustine had made. Calvinism turned citizenship into an obligation for Christians. In many of the German mini-states of the early modern era, loyalty to the prince and loyalty to his sect were nearly indistinguishable. Teaching the faith was synonymous with cultivating citizenship. In the American colonies, most of them founded by religious dissenters, religious belief constituted the foundation of allegiance to the state.

Hypothesis #12: "Rational" types of religion may trigger individual initiative, encourage the spread of education, and spur economic growth. Economic prosperity will in turn make available resources vital to the construction of a modern nation-state, and an increasingly educated, rational political culture will support liberalization and democratization.

In *The Protestant Ethic and the Spirit of Capitalism*, Weber argued that the peculiar propensities of Calvinism as a kind of worldly asceticism had triggered the development of capitalism in Western Europe. The Calvinist belief in predestination seemed to deprive human beings of even the slightest control over their eternal fate. An inaccessible, omniscient God preordained the destiny of every human being, but this transcendent God also left human beings free to read the Bible and think about what one who merited salvation ought to do.

Calvinists found themselves driven by inner ethical impulses to make this world and their place within it better. Success made them confident of their selection by God, and the certainty of selection gave them the confidence to be pioneers of the Industrial Revolution in Europe.

Inglehart found support in modern survey data for an updated version of the Weberian hypothesis. Protestantism instilled a drive for achievement and a desire for education that fostered economic growth in the West. Constructing an index of "achievement motivation" from interviews conducted in forty-three countries, Inglehart discovered a high correlation between the mean index for each country and the mean economic growth rate for that country between 1960 and 1990. He reasons that countries ranking high in achievement motivation tend to save and invest for the future and to act with determination to obtain their goals. "In short, growth rates are best understood as a consequence of both economic and cultural factors."[48]

Inglehart takes this argument one step further by confirming that economic development correlates positively with the emergence of liberal democracy. But he goes beyond that to assert that cultural factors, such as the level of education, push a society toward more liberal, participatory values that are, for him, a second major axis of modernity. "Rational religion," which Weber defined as religion shorn of most of its magical and mystical properties and anchored in an ethical code, thus promotes political development.

In a study of Canada and the United States, Smidt concludes: "The data reveal that religious tradition is moderately related to both social trust and civic engagement, though somewhat more strongly so in terms of civic engagement than social trust." The study shows a particularly strong relationship between religiosity and civic engagement among black Protestants in the United States. "This pattern is consistent with the findings of previous research that religious involvement, particularly among those who lack the resource of money, imparts civic skills and engenders civic involvement."[49]

Hypothesis #13: A state united in religious belief may enjoy higher levels of mutual trust among citizens and rulers. Rulers may come to identify their own well-being with the state's strength and prosperity, and subjects may be willing to sacrifice short-term well-being for the long-term strength of public institutions.

Mutual trust has long been regarded as a key to the development of a political community. Banfield found that a lack of trust in fellow citizens deprived a southern Italian town of the capacity to respond collectively to its backwardness.[50] Almond and Verba argue that higher levels of mutual trust help explain the participant political culture to be found in Britain and the United States; they say lower levels of mutual trust in Germany and France, and especially in Mexico, account in some measure for the lack of a civic culture in those countries.[51] Spinner-Halev writes: "If liberal citizens are not willing to discuss, cooperate and compromise, then politics is in danger of becoming bloody. If liberal citizens do not trust one another, then the societal cohesion needed to discuss and cooperate is absent."[52]

Religions can generate mutual trust of two sorts, one more particular and the other more general. Members of a single religious congregation or organization, such as the Tijaniyya Brotherhood of Senegal, trust one another enough to engage in economic enterprise far from home, selling on European beaches and cities, and sending home much of the profit. Mutual trust within the European Jewish community probably contributed to the success of some of its members in the banking business and financial community, or perhaps this mutual trust stemmed instead from a second, broader source: adherence to a common religious ethic. It is commonplace to argue that Islam, with its radical monotheism and its proclamation of a set of ethics for war and peace, commerce and husbandry, served the interests of a new trading class from the start. The development of the sharia and its acceptance across Muslim lands otherwise divided into competing dynasties helped produce a commonality of culture that permitted the broad circulation of people and goods.

Gibson has argued that the Church of England helped solidify British society from the 1688 Glorious Revolution into the early nineteenth century, linking rural and urban society, rich and poor, mainstream Christianity and moderate forms of dissent. Far from being weakened by the Enlightenment, the church helped hold society together despite the breakaway of the American colonies and the onset of the Industrial Revolution. The anti-Catholicism of the Church of England reflected the sentiments of the population at large and gave meaning to foreign policy. The liturgy, the Book of Common Prayer, and the services and facilities of the church provided a shared national experience, and the church stood with the monarchy in a posture of moderation. That moderation "militated against extremism and radicalism in both politics and wider society."[53] Religious solidarity helped the English accept the unwelcome effects of the American Revolution.

Tocqueville found the various forms of American Protestantism remarkably similar in cultivating a sense of equality, competence, and trust in the nineteenth century. By some ways of thinking, religion remains a unifying factor in America as Jews and Catholics have been pulled into what is an ever-changing religious establishment.[54] In 1960 the candidacy of John F. Kennedy, a Roman Catholic, generated a fear of papal control and the possibility of religious division in political matters. However, in the 2000 election, a vice presidential candidate's adherence to Jewish tradition seemed to make him more, not less, appealing to the religiously observant American electorate.

Inglehart's data suggest a link between high levels of religiosity in a society and national pride. Turkey, Poland, and the United States figure among the examples of countries that rank high on both scales.[55] After World War II, patriotic groups insisted on adding the words "under God" to the American Pledge of Allegiance. In establishing an independent Turkey, Atatürk abolished both sultanate and caliphate, and he sought to subordinate religious institutions to state direction, but he did not hesitate to invoke Islam to rally groups, especially the Kurds, to the new republic. In Poland the Catholic Church helped sustain a notion of national identity even under conditions of Soviet occupation. While religious issues divide Israel along many lines, Judaism provides the glue for Zionism.

Ideology

Hypothesis #14: At a basic level, religion and state are inseparable. Every state reflects a moral (or immoral) purpose, whether that be mere personal aggrandizement of the rulers, the rather modest objective of keeping the peace, or some combination of more ambitious objectives, such as justice and liberty. To enjoy any semblance of legitimacy, the state must champion objectives grounded in the predominant understanding of morality.

While religion is scarcely identical with morality, religious ideas help to define morality in most societies; what is deemed right and moral is often defended in religious terms. Most societies value honesty. Many Christians think of honesty as particularly incumbent on Christians; in fact, the ethics of Judaism, Christianity, and Islam all sustain honesty. Although many governments are thoroughly corrupt, rare is the government that embraces dishonesty as its guiding principle. It cannot be entirely indifferent to morality, or to the religion that helps sustain it—a point George Washington made in his farewell address.

In the areas dominated by religions of the book, moral purpose comes from God, and the state's authority therefore derives from God. Some rulers claim the ability to know God's purposes directly. Others have sought to identify their actions with the moral purposes defined by God and contained in scripture and law. In the modern period, as God became more identified with nature, government came to be seen as a product of human nature and the reason that God had imparted to every human being rather than a direct result of divine action. Yet government identifies itself with virtue, and if religion represents virtue, then the two cannot ever be entirely separate.

Hypothesis #15: The progressive exclusion of religion from the body politic would undermine the state's legitimacy. The most fundamental principles of liberal-democratic government cannot be reduced to empirical propositions. It is impossible to show empirically that people are equal. That proposition, like others, requires a leap of faith or a normative judgment. Religion can help nurture faith in democracy.

Liberalism in Europe came from political thought deeply influenced by both classical and Christian writers, and religious dissenters were among those who pushed first and hardest for liberty. "In Western Europe the ultimate claim of the liberal was religious. Liberal faith rested in origin upon the religious dissenter."[56] To be free to practice religion meant freedom to speak on other matters. When dissenters formed colonies in North America, they did so to be free to worship and free to establish ethical governments. In the Great Awakening of the eighteenth century, Jonathan Edwards and his followers invoked a new, benevolent, rational God. Fewer were the references to God as king. Instead, "biblical ideas of covenant were combined with Lockean ideas of political obligation."[57] Religion supported the new politics and the new Constitution. "The constitution was viewed by many Americans as an earthly reflection of that divine constitution according to which God rules the universe."[58]

Can a liberal polity sustain itself and its authority in the long run without reference to any standards external to its own decision-making processes? Those processes depend upon some form of majority rule to lend rightness and moral purpose to the actions of the state. A majority authorizes a constitution, which authorizes a majority to decide what is right. Yet many would insist, with Martin Luther King, that laws approved by the majority can be unjust. For him, there was little question that the legitimacy of American government depended upon notions of justice generated in the Western tradition of political thought, itself conditioned by Christianity. To sever the link between religion and politics would deprive the political system of a critical source of its claim to do what is right.

Some have argued that liberalism faces a crisis of legitimacy precisely because it has sought to separate itself from its religious origins. The state has come to represent individual interests, whose only legitimacy lies in the wills of its citizens. Descended from its pedestal, the state must follow what its members decide is the path of virtue; it has lost the ability to chart that path.[59] The liberal state, condemned by modernism to defend itself in secular terms, looks to philosophy for new foundations, but philosophy still seems more bent on destroying than on creating foundations. "Civil society depends for its stability and well-being on the attachment of its citizens to a set of laws and a corresponding way of life that are never completely rational, but that attachment is undermined by the philosopher's unswerving dedication to reason."[60]

The nation-state itself is an artificial entity. It has no intrinsic legitimacy. Whereas the early nation-states of Europe found plausibility in common language, they also looked in many cases to religion as a legitimating force. Newer states, many contrived on the drawing boards of Europe and constructed on the European model by imperial powers, struggle to establish legitimate credentials. It is not surprising that they, too, seek to cover themselves with religious symbols and rhetoric. They seek a grounding that secular liberalism cannot provide.

Hypothesis #16: The separation of religion and politics deprives the state of a moral critique vital for its renewal. To exclude religious language from the public place and to insist on the complete assimilation of conservative religious groups is to weaken the state by alienating citizens for whom religion necessarily defines every political project.

Huntington identifies historical periods in which America, seized by idealism, tries to reduce the gap between the American Creed and the realities of American life. He labels them creedal passion periods. The campaign to eliminate slavery in the mid-nineteenth century constituted one such moment. The Age of Reform was another, and the 1960s and 1970s, dominated by the rights movements, a third. Religious revival stoked the fires of discontent in all three periods.[61] Although Huntington suggests that these moments call the foundations of government into question, most Americans would retrospectively acknowledge that the republic emerged stronger from each such period of renewal. Separation of church and state means religion remains free to support but also free to protest the state's actions. And, of course, the protests run from those of Martin Luther King in Birmingham to right-to-lifers at abortion clinics. At least initially, the majority is almost always hostile to moral dissent.

The temper of the times makes it difficult to invoke religion in political debate. Whether in Europe or the Americas, Africa or Asia, religious language tends to be divisive. Its use also tends to stifle argument: "Abortion is wrong because my faith tells me this is so." But there are other phrases that also stop debate: "We hold these truths to be self-evident." "It is a violation of the Universal Declaration of Human Rights that . . ." In fact, all those assertions stir further possible questions: Why does your faith hold to that position? What is self-evident about these truths? What is authoritative about the UDHR? Carter points out that all political arguments can be pushed back, through reasoned argument, to sets of assumptions that may be beyond the realm of possible discussion. The broader and more inclusive the political debate, the more likely policy is to command support, or at least loyal dissent. He writes that liberalism must learn to listen "not because the speaker has the right voice but because the speaker has the right to speak. Moreover, the willingness to listen must hold out the possibility that the speaker is saying something worth listening to; to do less is to trivialize the forces that shape the moral convictions of tens of millions of Americans." Citizens must try to understand and evaluate one another's arguments wherever and however they are grounded.[62]

A state may also be stronger if it tolerates conservative religious groups that wish to live distinctive lifestyles and educate their young in such a way that permits the perpetuation of their groups. Schools are one of the critical issues. Should religious schools be subsidized? Both Carter and Spinner-Halev argue that they should. Parents should be free to educate their children in the way they wish; if they cannot, then groups cannot maintain their religious autonomy, and religious traditions cannot sustain themselves. But according to Spinner-Halev, the state should use its leverage to ensure a general education for students, one that permits them to think for themselves and enables them to survive outside the group, if that is what they choose to do.[63] Such a policy pulls these groups toward the system rather than alienating them; for Carter, it helps ensure that strong, autonomous religious groups will remain a conscience for the nation.

The hypothesis takes on even greater strength in the Islamic context. Religion has become the language of politics. Media dominated by religion and government-controlled media alike discuss the merits of many major policy proposals in the light of the sharia. Health care, foreign policy, regulation of the media, rules governing elections, and especially education come under intense scrutiny in the light of what varying groups deem to be religious principles. Some countries exclude religious groups from participating directly in the formation of political parties, but it is virtually impossible to exclude religion and religious reasoning from the public forum. A political system that did so would be weaker rather than stronger.

Institutions

Hypothesis #17: Religious organizations engaged in projects promoting the common welfare—education, medical care, child care, etc.— can help generate a set of nongovernmental institutions that train citizens and open the way to a stronger, more inclusive state. They can contribute to the construction of civil society.

Durkheim posits that religions inherently reflect society. They grow from people's needs for social solidarity, and therefore they inevitably produce "churches"—communities of believers or disciples, who profess common beliefs and follow common rites. Serving social needs is thus a primary rather than a secondary goal.[64] Religious institutions in many parts of the world have been major providers of clerical and educational services. Tocqueville noted the extent to which the churches of America helped draw people together and prepare them for full participation in democratic political life.

Vaclav Havel has done more to revive the theory of civil society than any other statesman. For him civil society comes as a response to a state that tries to dominate every aspect of social interaction so that citizens forget that they themselves can be the protagonists and animators, that they can, independently of the state, provide for many of their own needs and from that experience learn that the state, too, is their instrument, not their tutor. Political scientists have seized upon this notion and examined the extent to which various contemporary states nourish civil societies capable of carrying them eventually toward more liberal and democratic institutions. A pair of volumes on the Middle East reflect that perspective.[65]

Islamist organizations such as the Muslim Brotherhood in Egypt and Jordan have created or reinvented a set of associations and organizations that enhance civil society.[66] The Brotherhood got its start as a community organization in Ismailia, an Egyptian city in the Sinai peninsula. As the Brotherhood spread to other cities, it sought to engage its members in constructing facilities such as mosques, schools, sports centers, or parks. It provided services, including education, to its members. With roots in the literate, modernizing, lower middle class, it created elements of a civil society that eventually became a political force. The state has nonetheless regulated, channeled, controlled, limited, and otherwise dominated the civil society.[67] Religion has strengthened civil society, and if civil society has thus far been unable to take control of the state in which it functions, it nonetheless represents a force for democracy. Hefner calls it civil-democratic Islam as opposed to statist Islam.[68]

Hypothesis #18: Harnessing the organizational power of religion can enhance the state's reach, giving it the strength to push ahead with economic and social development. Alternatively, the organizational capacity of religion can overturn a state otherwise incapable of galvanizing the support of the masses, as in Iran.

A recent study shows how regimes in Pakistan and Malaysia have exploited the organizational power of Islamism to spur economic development.[69] In Malaysia between 1981 and 1997, Mahathir Mohammed incorporated Islam into Malay nationalism to win support for greater state intervention in the economy and to push Malays forward as entrepreneurs. One result was spectacular economic growth. In Pakistan from 1977 to 1988, Muhammad Zia ul-Haq brought an Islamist party into government and invoked Islamic law to reinforce state power and legitimacy, which Islamist challenge in the 1970s had eroded. He came to the same conclusion as Mahathir: "Namely, a state that is construed as a legitimate Islamic actor can both ride the tiger of Islamism and harness its energies in the service of the state."[70] Nasr goes on to argue that Islamization of the state served the interests of these two postcolonial states at critical junctures.[71]

In the nineteenth century, rulers of both Egypt and the Ottoman Empire came to similar conclusions. No sooner had Muhammad Ali taken power in Egypt than he began to reduce the ulama's autonomy by undercutting their financial independence and by creating a hierarchy among them that was subordinate to the state, because he apparently feared the ulama's ability to thwart the program of modernization he was undertaking. He started a campaign to control and exploit Islam for state purposes. In theory, the Ottomans (nominally sovereign over Egypt) had always enjoyed such control, in Egypt as in Anatolia and elsewhere, but in fact nineteenth-century sultans, determined to modernize the empire, found themselves struggling to reassert state control of Islam. They wanted to shore up wavering Ottoman legitimacy with an official nationalism anchored in Islamic identity. "Where the Tanzimat had stressed the equality of all subjects, Abdülhamid realigned the basis of the state on a more Islamic foundation."[72] He was trying to bring a society back together and to enhance the power of the state.

Hypothesis #19: Politicization of religion produces a pluralization of religious groups that may eventually contribute to pluralism in the political arena.

In Renaissance Italy the politicization of religion set Guelphs against Ghibellines in every city-state. The Reformation sought to bring Christianity out of the church and into the world, and the world it created was ever more divided. As religion became a vehicle of protest in seventeenth-century England, the number of groups multiplied exponentially. In the New World, every colony had its own religious orientation, and eventually there emerged a plurality of sects within each.

In most Muslim countries, the politicization of Islam in the nineteenth and twentieth centuries began with laymen who criticized the ulama for their blanket support of backward, authoritarian, foreign-supported regimes. In Iran, part of the clerical class began to involve itself in the politics of dissidence during the protest against that country's economic concessions to foreigners at the end of the nineteenth century. A part of that class involved itself in the Constitutional Revolution of 1906 and in the accession of Mussadiq to the prime ministership in the early 1950s. This was also true in Algeria, where Abd al-Hamid Ben Badis led the Association of Reformist Ulama. But for the most part, laymen such as Hasan al-Banna, founder of the Muslim Brotherhood in Egypt, championed Islam as a remedy for the ills of their countries. In the first instance, there emerged differences among the clergy that are apparent in Iran to this day. In the second instance, the lay challenge to the ulama opened up new public space for debate about religious issues and action.

As Eickelman and Piscatori argue, it is increasingly difficult to identify Islam with a single voice and a single organization in Muslim-dominated countries.[73] Even in Saudi Arabia, where the state uses its power to maintain a unified front, dissident voices from within the ulama have made themselves heard. In the more liberal atmosphere of Egypt, a cacophony of voices claims to speak for Islam: militants demanding revolution, secularists demanding a rethinking of the sharia, ulama attempting to support/influence state decisions, the Brotherhood and its multiple offshoots seeking to steer government action by undercutting the interpretations and authority of the ulama, and the state itself trying its best to flood the market with religious propaganda designed to legitimate its policies and actions. That list leaves out Coptic Christians, who have become more politicized in an effort to stave off Islamist legislation, and Muslim Sufis, who seemingly remain less politicized. Eickelman and Piscatori, among others, speculate that the de facto pluralization of Islamic institutions in Egypt and elsewhere bodes well for democratization.[74] Pluralism coupled with tolerance produces political competition.

Hypothesis #20: When organized religion decides to enter the democratic fray by sponsoring (or tolerating) political parties bearing the name of religion, the result is often tantamount to accepting democratic rule. Incorporating religious groups strengthens the state and constitutes a step toward political development.

The strength of democratic regimes depends upon their ability to include the widest possible array of opinion. By appeasing groups who might otherwise take up arms against the state or who engage in verbal attacks on political legitimacy, the state secures its stability in return for concessions on policy and possible cession of offices. Kalyvas argues that the Roman Catholic Church came to support the liberal-democratic game in Belgium purely for tactical, pragmatic political reasons, not for any abstract support of democratic theory. It abandoned ultraorthodox elements and supported secular conservative political forces to protect its manifold political interests. With the church inside the system rather than hostile, the political system itself acquired legitimacy and stability.[75]

In Italy, where the Church had initially opposed the republic with all the tools at its disposal, the Christian Democratic Party emerged from the ashes of fascism as the fulcrum of liberal democracy. Itself discredited by its relationship to fascism but also distrustful of the menace of communism, the Church found itself dragged forward by laymen and laywomen in an organization called Catholic Action and in the Christian Democratic Party. It was the collaboration between Catholics and communists, marked by hostility at one level and recognition of common needs at another, that resurrected a liberal-democratic regime in Italy after World War II. Yet neither the Church nor international communism was noted for its liberal-democratic attitudes.

In the Middle East, several states have declared their intent to democratize but resisted including explicitly religious parties, such as the Muslim Brotherhood in Egypt, the National Salvation Party (subsequently the Welfare Party and then the Virtue Party) in Turkey, the Islamic Tendency in Tunisia, or the

Islamic Salvation Front (FIS) in Algeria. When in 1991–1992 the FIS won municipal elections in Algeria and then showed even greater strength in the first round of legislative elections, the government canceled the second round and sought to suppress the Islamist movement. The result was civil war. In defending themselves against the possibility that Islamist parties would take full power and subvert any possibility for democracy, these states have reduced the inclusive capacities and legitimacy of their systems. Of course, it is impossible to demonstrate that inclusion of these parties would have contributed to liberal-democratic development, or that the historic association of Islam with authoritarianism would have proved irrelevant, as have the similarly authoritarian patterns of Catholicism and communism in the development of Western European democracy.

Identity

Hypothesis #21: Modernization has generated the problem of identity by pulling people closer together, making them aware of differences, causing them to think about others and therefore about themselves. The spread of literacy enabled people to read for themselves the texts that defined their faith and to think about religion as a separable aspect of self. Identity then becomes a question, rather than an unreflected given. Political development requires an answer to that question, and religion can help provide such an answer.

If religious identity were primordial—ingrained in human beings at the moment of birth and insensitive to social, economic, and political change—it would threaten political development. In most cases, religious identity would not coincide with national identity. In the cases of Christianity, Islam, and Judaism, it would be much too broad for any single nation-state. In the religious minorities of the Fertile Crescent, such as the Druze or the Yazidis, it would be too narrow. Religious identity would undermine political loyalties, as it did in Italy during the Renaissance.

Modern research suggests that religious identity is malleable, not primordial. The Safavids drew upon Twelver Shiism and turned it into a badge of national identity in Persia after 1500, an identity perhaps intended to stave off Ottoman absorption. The predominance of Catholicism in all of Western Europe does not in and of itself explain why religion remains vital to the identity of countries such as Ireland and Poland but is much less important in other Catholic countries. In the contemporary era, the awakening of Islamic identities has occurred in specific sets of social, economic, and political circumstances: imperialism obliterated existing identities, education created a group of believers prepared to read scripture for themselves and to choose to identify themselves with Islam, and urbanization produced a new underclass prepared to identify with Islamist groups promising and delivering social services.

The Iranian Revolution acquired its religious character not because Iranians felt a more intense religious identity than other Muslims but because dissidents such as Ali Shariati and Ayatollah Ruhollah Khomeini found receptive audiences for their messages. They proposed Islamic identity as an authentically Iranian response to rapid Westernization, increasing economic inequality, and political authoritarianism. Islamic identity contributed to political development by attracting support for the revolution among city-dwellers and villagers, farmers and businessmen, Marxists and nationalists. Khomeini acquired political legitimacy by virtue of his identification with Islam, and he managed to transmit some of that legitimacy to the new institutions, themselves partially derivative of Western experience.

Hypothesis #22: A state built upon religious identity and reflecting major elements of national history may be able to construct institutions seen as indigenous in origin, capable of generating a loyalty among subjects and citizens that other governments do not enjoy.

While similar to the previous hypothesis, this one suggests that a state that shapes its institutions to reflect religious tradition may appear more authentic and genuine than a state that keeps religion at arm's length. The Saudi and Iranian states enjoy an aura of legitimacy that comes from identifying with Islam. Whether their institutions reflect foreign influences, as well, or whether their policies always adhere to Islamic law, as they say they do, is another matter. Though surely not invulnerable, both states have survived difficult times and avoided the political instability characteristic of more secular states. The Moroccan and Jordanian monarchies have also clothed themselves in Islam and have managed to survive despite what Huntington defines as "the king's dilemma": To modernize is to undercut the tradition upon which the regime depends, but not to modernize society and economy is to invite revolt from a people that sees others benefitting from better lifestyles.[76]

In the Middle East, Israel is perhaps the state that has used religion most successfully as a badge of its uniqueness and authenticity. While Judaism does not figure in the constitution, because there is no constitution, it constitutes an essential aspect of state institutions. The government honors the Sabbath, leaders let themselves be photographed participating in religious ceremonies, Yeshiva students enjoy military exemptions, and, most important, the state bases its case for legitimacy on Jewish history. The Shoa (Hebrew for the Holocaust) constitutes the most critical aspect of that history; the Vad Vashem, a memorial to the Holocaust, is where foreign leaders go first when they make official visits. It is difficult to imagine a state capable of incorporating Jewish immigrants from all over the world that does not have Judaism built into its institutions.

States of relatively recent origin, such as those of the Middle East, may have particular need to mitigate religion and politics. Durkheim argued that religion had its origins in the human need for society. All societies come together to assert common values and in that process they create a distinction between the sacred and the profane. Religion necessarily evolves as societies expand and contract and the elements of commonality evolve. No community can be without religion, in his view. To integrate church and state, extending tolerance toward minority traditions makes for a stronger community in newly created societies. Separation of church and state relativizes all religion and diminishes the value of the religious bond.[77]

The case for religion as a positive force in political development could be extended beyond these twelve hypotheses, just as the ten propositions offered to sustain the contrary position can scarcely be understood as exhaustive. All twenty-two of these propositions share one characteristic: They take some aspect of religion as an independent variable useful in explaining political development or decay. But the "independence" of the religious variable is itself open to question. Any given state of religious identity, ideology, organization, or culture may be more a product of politics than a factor in political development. Or it may be that religion does not have any significant impact on politics in the long run.

Religion Is Irrelevant

Hypothesis #23: Building a strong state means developing a strong resource base, and to do that a state must grant productive forces sufficient autonomy and liberty to generate wealth. Once a state achieves a certain level of prosperity, the new, prosperous middle class will demand inclusion in the political system. Neither element of political development (institutional strength, inclusiveness) depends on religion.

Bates asks why some rulers have sought fame and fortune by seeking to develop the wealth of their states, while others have been content to use the public treasury as their own bank account and to steal resources from their subjects.[78] In Europe, many studies have suggested that the need to prepare for war was a key factor.[79] Rulers needed help to finance their armies and turned to the nobility and eventually even to the commercial classes for resources. In England, consistent application of the law and a realm of relative liberty created an atmosphere conducive to economic growth, which then provided the wherewithal to pay for military strength as well as royal palaces. In France, where the ancien régime used the sale of offices rather than taxes (it could not collect) as a primary source of revenue, the French state could not compete with England in its ability to finance war. The English Parliament made a key difference by insisting upon bureaucratic development rather than patronage as a way of conducting business.[80] Religion appears irrelevant to the explanation.

Third-world states in the modern era have not faced the challenge of war, and when they have, they have sought external support—something that was rarely forthcoming on a large scale in Europe. The availability of external aid and the lack of war have permitted contemporary rulers to enrich themselves without building strong states. They have not been driven by necessity to construct a legal structure and a set of guarantees that would enhance productivity and generate enough wealth to ensure autonomy.[81] Sometimes they have felt pressures to expand participation before generating sufficient wealth to pay for the welfare services demanded in a more inclusive regime. Waldner says premature expansion of political participation handicapped economic development in Turkey and Syria by comparison with that of Korea and Taiwan. Religion does not appear as a significant variable in Waldner's study.[82]

Inglehart asserts that culture is vital to an understanding of economic and political development, yet his own findings may not support that conclusion. By examining national averages of responses on two scales, from traditional to modern, and from materialistic to postmaterialistic, Inglehart places countries on a grid that suggests cultural groupings.[83] Huntington has referred to that grid to support his view that there are differences among civilizations. But these geographical and cultural groupings are scarcely compact. In fact, the Inglehart grid suggests that increasing prosperity pushes countries upward on both scales toward the position of the most prosperous and secular of states, the Scandinavian countries. There is no suggestion that religion is a vital factor in the direction or outcome of development. Quite to the contrary, Inglehart asserts that contemporary religious movements are but momentary deviations from long-term patterns of secularization. The fact that the United States appears much too religious for its income, or that former Soviet satellites in Eastern European (but not Poland) appear much too secular for their relative poverty, does indeed demonstrate cultural diversity in patterns of development. But culture does not emerge decisive in the Inglehart analysis.

For Inglehart, secularization would appear to be an integral aspect of modernization, a necessary ingredient if not a cause, but secularization might also be understood as the simple disappearance of religion, once but no longer a factor in political development. Gauchet takes that position. "Religion can only historically express itself formally and materially by having a clearly defined function. Not only does this function no longer exist, it has been turned into its opposite through a transformation that has integrated its component parts into the collective operation."[84] Its function—and here Gauchet seems to follow Durkheim—was to maintain the cohesion of society, but the emergence of the state, which inevitably pretended to represent the sacred, damaged forever the integrative capacity of religion, and from that point forward religion has been on the way out and down until it no longer matters. Dobbelaere, writing principally of Europe, says religion can no longer block change, nor can it any longer provide the integration required of a community.[85] These observations serve to reinforce Asad's argument that there are many varieties of secularism.[86]

Hypothesis #24: Politics shapes religion much more than religion shapes politics. Religion should thus be understood as a dependent variable, not a causative factor for political development.

In the grand scheme of human history, religion has been a variable. Insofar as it is a product of society, as Durkheim argued, then it is logical to see that it must change as the definition of society itself evolves with the ages. Berger says, "Religion is the human enterprise by which a sacred cosmos is established."[87] Since all human enterprises change, religion must necessarily change. If religion is a search for meaning in life, in nature, and in the cosmos, then the effort has no logical end, because the object of the search is not fixed. Most religions seek to establish foundational truths that can resist the erosion of history. God is portrayed as an author of historical change who is unaffected by it, yet religions are produced by human beings whose experience and knowledge of God have necessarily occurred within history, not outside of it.

Each of the major religious traditions prominent today emerged out of previous traditions and practices, combining, reworking, and inventing elements of belief and ritual and unifying human beings who had been disparate in their practices. Each of these traditions evolved in ways that make them different today from what they were at the foundings. Religion in the early kingdoms of ancient Egypt was quite different from what it later became. Judaism in exile became something quite different than it was in the ancient commonwealths. Christianity in Jesus's lifetime surely did not resemble what it became by virtue of Paul's work or Constantine's conversion. The Islam of the Abbasid caliphate did not resemble the Islam of the Medina state with Muhammad still alive, much less the Islam of the early Meccan period.

Political turbulence and change, probably more than any other factor, probably explain this historical evolution. Gauchet insists that the creation of the state—one should probably speak rather of the gradual appearance of statelike bodies—"can be regarded as the first religious revolution in history."[88] Before the state, religion alone drew the line between sacred and profane and pulled the society together, but then the state usurped the dominant place and created human beings who incarnated invisible forces. "All subsequent major spiritual and intellectual developments will arise from the contradictions between the inherited representations of the foundation, in whose name sovereignty is wielded and the historical forms clothing its practice."[89]

The historical forms change with the size of the state, the character of the state, and its place in the world. As states merge into larger ones, belief systems must themselves be integrated. If states splinter, each piece may develop systems of ritual and belief to help solidify the new entity, or scriptural, scholarly legal systems may serve to cement a group that becomes geographically dispersed. States conquer or confront defeat, and religious loyalties usually follow the will of the victor. Rulers themselves seek to enhance their personal power and solidify their regimes by invoking new beliefs and practices. They promote state religions by funding a friendly priesthood and repressing dissenters. Every religious organization must respond to the incentives and disincentives offered by the political circumstances in which it exists.

Hypothesis #25: Where there is sharp competition among religious sects and groups, religious organizations will tend to be stronger than in countries where a state-sponsored church dominates religious life.

This is a corollary of Hypothesis #24. It is the so-called supply-side argument first articulated by Adam Smith, a strong believer in the benefits of competition. Pfaff argues that this hypothesis helps explain why church membership and participation run much higher in the United States than in European countries, even though the "demand" for religion, represented by belief in God and the importance of religion, do not differ significantly.

In Europe, secularization occurred largely from the bottom up. Elites created and defended religious establishments that widening sectors of the population simply ignored or abandoned. By the end of the twentieth century, these churches became so anemic that the political elites no longer relied on them for purposes of legitimacy or popular mobilization, and disestablishment was even discussed. The situation was very different in the United States, with its decentralized and plural religious culture.[90]

More than half of Americans say they belong to a church organization, and 95 percent say they believe in God, whereas about one in ten Europeans (EU countries) belong to church organizations and 70 percent say they believe in God.[91] Not surprisingly, Americans worry less than Europeans about political involvement of religious leaders. "Precisely because religion is an important focus of public life and interest group politics, there is a weaker consensus in the United States favoring political secularism."[92] Political arrangements that set the environment in which religious organizations function turn out to be the critical, independent variable.

The argument for the primacy of politics sketched here and developed in subsequent chapters does not negate the possibility that religion also affects political development. If in the long run political events seem to account for much of the history of religions, it may also be that religion has affected politics in shorter-term perspectives. One could hold to this hypothesis and still find truth in at least some of the first twenty-two hypotheses, all of which speak to the impact of religion on politics. The question becomes one of deciding when and under what conditions the primary flow of influence runs in one direction or the other. One might ask about the dialectic of religion and politics, the balance or lack of balance between these two spheres of human activity, and how this dialectic affects or is affected by the process of political development.

Notes

1. Jeffrey K. Hadden, "Desacralizing Secularization Theory," in Hadden and Anson Shupe, eds., *Secularization and Fundamentalism Reconsidered: Religion and the Political Order, vol. III* (New York: Paragon House, 1986), 22.

2. Thomas Ertman, *Birth of the Leviathan: Building States and Regimes in Medieval and Early Modern Europe* (Cambridge, UK: Cambridge University Press, 1997).

3. David Martin, *A General Theory of Secularization* (Oxford, UK: Blackwell, 1978), for example.

4. D. E. Smith, *Religion and Political Development*, (Boston: Little, Brown, 1970) chapter 8, for example.

5. David C. Leege, "Toward a Mental Measure of Religiosity in Research on Religion and Politics," in Ted G. Jelen, ed., *Religion and Political Behavior in the United States* (New York: Praeger, 1989), begins by making that point.

6. Marcel Gauchet, *The Disenchantment of the World: A Political History of Religion*, trans. Oscar Burge (Princeton, NJ: Princeton University Press, 1997), chapter 2.

7. Samuel P. Huntington, *Political Order in Changing Societies* (New Haven, CT: Yale University Press, 1967), chapter 1.

8. Ertman, *Birth of the Leviathan*, 34.

9. Robert H. Bates, *Prosperity and Violence: The Political Economy of Development* (New York: Norton, 2001).

10. Steven B. Smith, *Spinoza, Liberalism, and the Question of Jewish Identity* (New Haven, CT: Yale University Press, 1997), 17.

11. Gauchet, *The Disenchantment of the World*, 3.

12. D. E. Smith, *Religion and Political Development*, 114.

13. Peter Berger, *The Sacred Canopy: Elements of a Sociological Theory of Religion* (Garden City, NY: Doubleday, 1967), 107.

14. Marcel Gauchet, *La religion dans la démocratie* (Paris: Gallimard, 1998),159 and elsewhere in the book.

15. Ernest L. Fortin, *Human Rights, Virtue and the Common Good: Untimely Meditations on Religion and Politics*, ed. J. Brian Benested (Lanham, MD: Rowman & Littlefield, 1996), 11.

16. The current discussion of laïcité in France still focuses on education. The question of permitting Muslim girls, and now Muslim teachers, to wear head scarves in the classroom has touched off a reconsideration of laïcité.

17. Hurd distinguishes between Judeo-Christian secularism (the English-American tradition) and laicism, the French tradition. Elizabeth Shakman Hurd, *The Politics of Secularism in International Relations* (Princeton, NJ: Princeton University Press, 2008), chapter 2.

18. See Mohammed Arkoun, "Positivisme et tradition dans une perspective islamique: Le cas du kémalisme," *Diogène* 127 (July–September 1984) for careful analysis of the Turkish effort to impose laïcité.

19. D. E. Smith, *Religion and Political Development*, 7, defines the organic model as one where religious and political functions are fused. For further discussion, see 266–267.

20. See Daniel Crecelius, "The Ulama and the State in Modern Egypt" (PhD dissertation, Princeton University, May 1967), 112 ff.

21. Berger, *Canopy*, 90.

22. Robert W. Hefner, *Civil Islam: Muslims and Democratization in Indonesia* (Princeton, NJ: Princeton University Press, 2000), 220.

23. Denis J. Sullivan and Sana Abed-Kotob, *Islam in Contemporary Egypt: Civil Society vs. the State* (Boulder, CO: Lynne Rienner, 1999), takes this position.

24. Stephen L. Carter, *The Culture of Disbelief* (New York: Basic Books, 1993).

25. S. B. Smith, *Spinoza*,114.

26. Princeton, NJ: Princeton University Press, 1963.

27. Richard P. Mitchell, *The Society of Muslim Brothers* (New York: Oxford University Press, 1993, originally published in 1969), 14.

28. Ibid., 329–330.

29. David Nicholls, *Deity and Domination: Images of God and the State in the Nineteenth and Twentieth Centuries* (London: Routledge, 1989).

30. Ibid, 240.

31. D. E. Smith, *Religion and Political Development*, chapter 6.

32. Ronald Inglehart, *Modernization and Postmodernization: Cultural, Economic, and Political Change in 43 Countries* (Princeton, NJ: Princeton University Press, 1997), 93.

33. Liliane Voye, "Secularization in a Context of Advanced Modernity," *Sociology of Religion* 60, no. 3 (Fall 1999): 275–288.

34. Carter, *The Culture of Disbelief*, 6.

35. D. E. Smith, *Religion and Political Development*, 125.

36. Inglehart, *Modernization and Postmodernization*, 106; Inglehart and Christian Welzel, *Cultural Change and Democracy: The Human Development Syndrome* (Cambridge, UK: Cambridge University Press, 2005), 45 and 156; and Pippa Norris and Inglehart, *Sacred and Secular: Religion and Politics Worldwide* (Cambridge, UK: Cambridge University Press, 2004), chapter 10.

37. Seyyed Vali Reza Nasr, *Islamic Leviathan: Islam and the Making of State Power* (Oxford, UK: Oxford University Press, 2001), 4.

38. Nasr, *Islamic Leviathan*, 17.

39. See Mohammed Arkoun, *Rethinking Islam* (Boulder, CO: Westview, 1994), chapter 16; Arkoun, *Humanisme et islam: combats et propositions* (Paris: Vrin, 2005), chapter 1; or other works.

40. Arend Lijphart, *Democracy in Plural Societies* (New Haven, CT: Yale University Press, 1977).

41. Avishai Margalit, "Sectarianism," *Dissent* 55, no. 1 (Winter 2008): 37–46.

42. Samuel P. Huntington, *The Clash of Civilizations and the Remaking of World Culture* (New York: Simon & Schuster, 1996), and Huntington, *Political Order in Changing Societies* (New Haven, CT: Yale, 1968), 168.

43. D. E. Smith, *Religion and Political Development*.

44. See Erika Friedl, *Children of Deh Koh* (Syracuse, NY: Syracuse University Press, 1997).

45. See Gregory Starrett, *Putting Islam to Work: Education, Politics and Religious Transformation in Egypt* (Berkeley: University of California Press, 1998), chapter 2.

46. Starrett, *Putting Islam to Work*, 31.

47. Guenter Levy, "Nasserism and Islam: A Revolution in Search of Ideology," in D. E. Smith, ed., *Religion and Political Modernization* (New Haven, CT: Yale University Press, 1974), 280, quoting from P. J. Vatkiotis.

48. Inglehart, *Modernization and Postmodernization*, 231.

49. Corwin Smidt, "Religion and Civic Engagement: A Comparative Analysis," *Annals of the American Academy of Political and Social Science* (September 1999): 176–192.

50. Edward C. Banfield, *The Moral Basis of a Backward Society* (New York: Free Press, 1958).

51. Gabriel A. Almond and Sidney Verba, *The Civic Culture: Political Attitudes and Democracy in Five Nations* (Princeton, NJ: Princeton University Press, 1963).

52. Jeff Spinner-Halev, *Surviving Diversity: Religion and Democratic Citizenship* (Baltimore: Johns Hopkins University Press, 2000), 88.

53. William Gibson, *The Church of England 1688–1832: Unity and Accord (London: Routledge, 2001)*, 236 and chapter 7, more generally.

54. Eldon Eisenbach, *The Next Religious Establishment* (Lanham, MD: Rowman & Littlefield, 2000).

55. Inglehart, *Modernization and Postmodernization*, 85.

56. Owen Chadwick, *The Secularization of the European Mind in the Nineteenth Century* (Cambridge, UK: Cambridge University Press, 1975), 26.

57. David Nicholls, *God and Government in an 'Age of Reason'* (London: Routledge, 1995),119.

58. Nicholls, *God and Government*, 105.

59. Gauchet, *La religion dans la démocratie*, 155–159.

60. Fortin, *Human Rights,* 2.

61. Samuel P. Huntington, *American Politics: The Promise of Disharmony* (Cambridge, MA: Belknap Press, 1981), chapter 3.

62. Carter, *The Culture of Disbelief,* 230–231.

63. Spinner-Halev, *Surviving Diversity*, chapter 5.

64. Emile Durkheim, "The Elementary Forms of Religious Life," in W. S. F. Pickering, ed., *Durkheim on Religion* (Atlanta: Scholars Press, 1994).

65. Augustus Richard Norton, ed., *Civil Society in the Middle East,* 2 vols. (Leiden, Netherlands: Brill, 1995–1996). Not all chapters in the two volumes take that point of view.

66. See, for example, Sana Abed-Kotob, "The Accommodationists Speak: Goals and Strategies of the Muslim Brotherhood of Egypt," *International Journal of Middle East Studies* 27 (1995): 321–339.

67. Sullivan and Abed-Kotob, *Islam in Contemporary Egypt*, 135.

68. Hefner, *Civil Islam*, 218.

69. Nasr, *Islamic Leviathan.*

70. Ibid., 136.

71. Ibid., 160.

72. Selim Deringil, "The Invention of Tradition as Public Image in the Late Ottoman Empire, 1808 to 1908," *Comparative Studies in Society and History* 35, no. 3 (January 1993): 3–30.

73. Dale F. Eickelman and James Piscatori, *Muslim Politics* (Princeton, NJ: Princeton University Press, 1996).

74. Eickelman and Piscatori, *Muslim Politics*, 159.

75. Stathis N. Kalyvas, "Democracy and Religious Politics," *Comparative Political Studies* 31, no. 3 (June 1998): 292–330.

76. Huntington, *Political Order*, chapter 2.

77. Fortin, *Human Rights*, 11–15.

78. Bates, *Prosperity and Violence.*

79. See Ertman, *Birth of the Leviathan*, chapter 1, for a list of such studies.

80. Ertman, *Birth of the Leviathan.*

81. Bates, *Prosperity and Violence.*

82. David Waldner, *State Building and Late Development* (Ithaca, NY: Cornell University Press, 1998).

83. Inglehart, *Modernization and Postmodernization*, 93. See also Inglehart and Welzel, *Cultural Change and Democracy*, and Norris and Inglehart, *Sacred and Secular*.

84. Gauchet, *The Disenchantment of the World*, 163.

85. Karel Dobbelaere, "The Secularization of Society? Some Methodological Suggestions," in Jeffrey K. Hadden and Anson Shupe, eds., *Secularization and Fundamentalism Reconsidered: Religion and the Political Order, vol. III* (New York: Paragon House, 1986), 41.

86. Talal Asad, *Formations of the Secular: Christianity, Islam, Modernity* (Stanford, CA: Stanford University Press, 2003).

87. Berger, *Sacred Canopy*, 26.

88. Gauchet, *The Disenchantment of the World*, 13.

89. Ibid., 14.

90. Steven Pfaff, "The Religious Divide: Why Religion Seems to Be Thriving in the United States and Waning in Europe," in Jeffrey Kopstein and Sven Steinmo, eds., *Growing Apart? America and Europe in the Twenty-First Century* (Cambridge, UK: Cambridge University Press, 2008), 43–44.

91. Ibid., 32.

92. Ibid., 47.

3

The Taming of Islam in Egypt

*From that time [1800] to this, the secularization of the polity
has been the most fundamental structural and ideological
change in the process of political development.*

—D. E. SMITH, 1970[1]

The term "secularization" seems inappropriate to describe what has happened
in Egypt or in most of the Middle East in the past thirty years. The modernization of Middle Eastern polities has not rendered these countries secular;
quite to the contrary, religion and politics have become ever more thoroughly
intertwined. Politics permeates virtually every aspect of religion, and religion
permeates almost every aspect of politics.[2]

One explanation commonly offered in the 1970s and still echoed in some
quarters today is Islam. It is the nature of Islam (structure, doctrine)—its tendency to fuse religion and politics—that would, from this perspective, explain
developments in Egypt and elsewhere. That explanation fails, however, to
take account of the fact that Islam was a force in all these countries long before 1970 and that Muslim countries have not evolved in a single pattern.
Moreover, such a perspective does not account for the case of Israel.

A second explanation is that a continuation of poverty in third-world
countries such as Egypt has produced deviations from the long-term pattern
of secularization. Secular ideologies have failed to remedy poverty and to generate genuinely liberal institutions. Instead, Islamizing movements have
forced authoritarian governments to depend heavily on religion for legitimacy.[3] The advanced, postindustrial countries with low birthrates continue to
become more secular, but poor countries with high birthrates resist secularization and make it appear as if the world as a whole were becoming more religious. "The net effect is that the religious population is growing fast, while

the secular number is shrinking, despite the fact that the secularization process is progressing steadily in rich nations."[4]

Indeed, Egypt is a place where nationalism, liberalism, and socialism have not lived up to their promise, where an Islamic movement has won increasing support, and where an authoritarian regime has come to identify itself with religion. Like the United States, where religiosity registers at higher levels than the secularization model predicts, Egypt appears to be an aberration.[5] Or perhaps Egypt should be seen as the norm among poor countries with high birthrates. In the long run, as Egypt and other countries achieve higher per capita income, the secularization hypothesis may eventually be validated.[6]

For now a contrary trend appears to prevail. The immixture of religion and politics has been a primary characteristic of political development in Egypt since 1800. At every moment the state has been the driving force toward fusion. It has consistently sought to subjugate Islam to its purposes—the modernization of the country, the strengthening of state power, the sharpening of identity, the legitimation of state authority—and in this effort at subjugation it has empowered and politicized the religious sphere. It is the neediness of the state, not the character of Islam or the contingencies of the moment, that best explains the politicization of religion and the intermixture of religion and politics in Egypt.

The aggressiveness of the state in undermining, dominating, and reforming—hence politicizing—the religious establishment in Egypt spurred reactions from within and without. Elements of the religious establishment responded to the political opportunities afforded them by the state in its need for identity, authority, and legitimacy. Even those who might have wished to erect a wall between religion and politics found political struggle the only means of defense. Ultimately assaulted by Islamists seeking to subordinate the state to their agenda, the state found itself ever more deeply involved in seeking to manipulate religion to its own advantage. The result is a spiral in the politicization of religion and the sanctification of politics that contradicts the predictions of secularization theory.

D. E. Smith proposed that religion and politics had been fused in "traditional societies."[7] Moreover, he hypothesized that religion and politics would undergo radical separation under the impact of external forces. Smith then suggested that interaction between separate political and religious spheres results in an equilibrium consistent with autonomous, secular political development. Neither of these hypotheses fits Egypt. Under the Ottomans (after 1517), Egypt was a traditional society in that it was largely unscathed by Western influence before the French invasion of 1798. The country was marked by visible separation of the religious and the political. Muhammad Ali, who seized power after the French left, sought to attack the autonomy of the indigenous ulama in the early nineteenth century, asserting political control over religion. There was progressive expansion of the state and its intrusion into religious affairs; overlap and tension between the religious and political that tended to increase over time; and increased penetration of society by politicized religion and the sacralized state.

Tensions between the religious and the political did not begin in 1800, nor are they likely to end at some precise moment, but in any society there are periods when tension between religion and politics becomes more acute and periods when it subsides. One might define moments of low tension, or relative equilibrium, as moments when neither the religious nor the political seeks major modification of the relationship. At other moments, one side or the other seeks revision. In Egypt, the state assumed the revisionist role in the nineteenth century. Religion has struck back effectively in the twentieth century with the exception of the Nasirist period (1952–1970).

One result is that Islam in Egypt no longer resembles what it was a century ago. It has transformed itself and been transformed by the actions of the state, and the Egyptian state is likewise being reshaped by the activities of the religious sphere. While there may still be those who imagine an outcome in which religion becomes utterly pliant and secondary to a triumphant secular state, as Smith predicts, or who imagine a scenario in which politics becomes subordinate to religious direction, as the Muslim Brotherhood once hoped it would, neither outcome now seems plausible. The question to be asked is how, after two centuries of intensified rivalry and even violent conflict, the two spheres may build an enduring, collaborative arrangement out of the unstable, conflictual relationship that continues to prevail.

Stabilizing the relationship between religion and politics in Egypt would require consensus about the place of Islam in Egyptian identity. On the one hand, the monuments left by the pharaohs remind all Egyptians that their country does not owe its existence to Islam. The presence of a Coptic Christian minority (about 15 percent of the population) also predates Islam. On the other hand, Egypt was the seat of the Fatimid caliphate in the tenth and eleventh centuries. The Fatimids, builders of Islamic Cairo, were the first Islamic dynasty to arise from Shii Islam. Egypt happily claims Arab precedence in Islam and Egyptian dominance among the Arabs.

Moreover, stabilization would require further agreement about the place of Islam in the country's political ideology. The Egyptian constitution of 1971, as amended in 1980, makes the sharia the primary source of legislation. What does this mean? Stabilization would require not separation of church and state—whatever that would mean in this context—but some regularization of the relationship among political decision-makers, unauthorized preachers, the Muslim Brotherhood, Sufi orders, and Islamist dissidents. Finally, stabilization would require a common understanding of the appropriate role of the state in maintaining the country's moral climate. In an era of expanding literacy and seemingly infinite demand for education in Egypt, the question is what sort of education the state should provide, what sort of moral guidance it should impose on the political culture. Islam calls upon the state to "promote the good and fight evil." Is there any political system that does not try to do that? The problem is defining good and evil.

Identity

Islam has been an aspect of Egyptian identity since the Arab conquest of the seventh century, but it has never been the only binding force in the society. Napoleon Bonaparte regarded Islam as the cement of Egyptian society, which he sought to destroy with proclamations posted on doors all over Cairo proclaiming that he would save Egyptian Muslims from the predations of those false Muslims, the Turks.[8] The ulama provided the leadership for Egyptian resistance, such as it was. But once Muhammad Ali seized power in 1803, he did not hesitate to attack the religious establishment in his effort to solidify Egyptian military and economic strength against European threats and Ottoman rule. Islam served to distinguish Egyptians from the French, who were allies, but not from the Ottomans, who became unwelcome masters, rivals, and then enemies. In the eyes of Muhammad Ali and his successors, impressed by all things European, Islam was a drag on change and modernization. He began a campaign to nationalize *waqf* land, set aside in perpetuity for the support of religious institutions, and to reduce the autonomy of the ulama.[9] In one form or another, successive Egyptian governments continued his policies for 150 years. The 1952 Egyptian Revolution, which ended the dynasty established by Muhammad Ali, "carried to a conclusion the secularization trend begun in the nineteenth century."[10]

Egyptians constituted a society before the advent of Islam. As inhabitants of the Nile Valley, modern Egyptians live with monuments that testify to a long history together under the pharaohs. They also live with the knowledge that Alexandria was once a center of Greek learning. The Romans later conquered the country along with most of the Mediterranean region, and early Christianity both flourished and suffered there. Christian monasticism originated in Egypt. The Arabs followed the Romans as conquerors, and the country became Arabized and Islamized over the course of several centuries. "Slave soldiers" (Mamluks) of Turkish origin won control of the country in the thirteenth century, and then the Ottoman Empire, itself a Sunni Muslim state governed by Turks, imposed itself on the Mamluks in the sixteenth century. When Napoleon entered the country in 1898, he found a tiny Ottoman administrative class governing by virtue of a Mamluk military class and a native Egyptian religious class, the ulama. Egyptians thus had reason to think of themselves in many ways—primarily as subjects of foreign rule. Even Muhammad Ali, liberator of Egypt from the Ottomans, was a foreigner, a Turkish-speaking Albanian.

In the nineteenth century, Egyptians began to think of Egypt as a nation in the modern sense.[11] The French and American revolutions had demonstrated the potency of the idea that a group of people united by language, religion, and history might act to establish and control a geographical state. The era of empires began to wane as the new concept of the nation-state gained traction. In Egypt, Muhammad Ali and his heirs, though still theoretically subject to the Ottoman Empire and governed from Istanbul, embarked on a program of autonomous economic, military, and political development that finally led them to challenge the Ottoman dynasty for control of the empire itself. In the process they depended on French and then British support, which entangled them in another form of external dependence. Financial dependence on Europe became political dependence after Great Britain seized control of Egypt in 1882. Thus, in subsequent decades, with liberation from the Ottomans largely achieved, Egyptian nationalism focused on freedom from British imperialism.

Arabism

It was an epoch in which Arabs, principally intellectuals in the cities of Damascus, Beirut, and Cairo, were beginning to assert that they constituted a single nation.[12] Language was the foundation of that idea, as it had been the foundation in Europe, but some of these intellectuals emphasized religion as the primary glue. For example, Jamal al-Din al-Afghani, who was actually of Persian rather than Afghan origin, flitted from capital to capital propounding his notion that only a union of Muslims could be effective in opposing European power.[13] Most European nationalists of the era saw Arabism and Islamism as mutually reinforcing principles. The Arabs were, after all, the first Muslims, and even non-Muslim Arabs acknowledged the impact of Islam on Arab culture. Egyptians helped generate some of these ideas without necessarily seeing a contradiction between them and the concept of the Egyptian fatherland.[14]

The first concrete proposal for an Arab state did not include Egypt or any other part of North Africa. Sharif Husayn, an Ottoman official entrusted with the care of the holy places in Mecca and Medina, made contact with the British government during World War I. He proposed to mount an Arab revolt against the Turkish-dominated Ottoman Empire, which had joined Germany and Austria in the war against France, Britain, and Russia. In return, he asked the British to support the creation of an Arab state after the defeat of the Ottomans and even to support the idea of an Arab caliphate for Islam. The state he proposed included the Arabian peninsula and the modern states of Syria, Lebanon, Iraq, Israel-Palestine, and Jordan—but not Egypt or any Arab country west of Egypt. Presumably he thought the British would object to the inclusion of Egypt in such a state. Who knows how he thought a Christian power could create an Arab caliphate for Islam. The whole episode testifies to the relative weakness of both Arabism and Islamism, or rather the weakness of the groups promoting both of those ideas.

Egyptians faced the practical problem of gaining liberation from a British occupation that, though defined as temporary in 1882, showed no signs of disappearing some twenty years later. The British converted their unofficial tenure in the country into "protectorate" status during World War I and refused the demands of a delegation (wafd) of Egyptians, led by Saad Zaghlul, which traveled to Paris and asked for independence at the end of the war. Instead, Britain imposed "independence" on Egypt in 1923 with a set of conditions that the newly created Wafd party and its leader, Zaghlul, found unacceptable. The party stood for Egyptian independence from European domination, but it affirmed Egyptian identity in a thoroughly modern, European way. Nationalism was simply another step in the process of economic, social, and political modernization initiated by Muhammad Ali.

The creation of the Muslim Brotherhood after 1928 challenged the European model and reemphasized the identification of Egypt with Islam. The founder of the Brotherhood, Hasan al-Banna, who was a schoolteacher in Ismailia, set out to promote an Islamic society as the basis for an Islamic state and eventually an Islamic world. He saw the first step as one of bringing Egyptians together through education, social activities, sports, and public meetings—all to promote morality and good citizenship as defined by Islam. In religion, Egyptians could find a common identity and the organizational strength to permit genuine independence.[15]

However, it was the idea of Arabism that took precedence over Islamism in the 1930s once Egyptian governments and intellectuals became more attuned to developments elsewhere in the Middle East. The Wafd party became interested in Arab issues in the late 1930s, especially after the Arab general strike of 1936 began to create turmoil in Palestine. In and out of the premiership in the 1930s, the Wafd came back to power in 1942 as part of a deal that smacked of selling out to the British and the Egyptian king. The deal, which brought Egypt squarely into the war on the British side, damaged beyond repair the reputations of the Wafd and King Faruq. In an effort to recover credibility, the Wafd subsequently took the lead in sponsoring the creation of the League of Arab States. Although the Arab states joined the league as autonomous entities, the initial headquarters was in Cairo, and the first secretary general an Egyptian who had championed the project. "The new Arab League was thus an Egyptian triumph, and marked a new era of Egyptian ascendancy within inter-Arab politics."[16] Egypt elbowed its way past Iraq to become the leader of the Arab world.

The focus on Islam proposed by Afghani and reinvoked by the Muslim Brotherhood in the interwar period served the purposes of political elites seeking the liberation of Egypt and the rest of the Arab world from European domination. Gamal abd al-Nasir welcomed the support of the Brotherhood for the 1952 revolution, which swept away King Faruq and the dynasty established by Muhammad Ali. Nasir made Islam the country's official religion in 1964, even though he had dissolved the Brotherhood and imprisoned its leaders. By subjugating the religious establishment to his political purposes and maintaining the place of Islam in the public schools, he sought to show that he was not indifferent to Islam as a source of national identity. Pious or not, he behaved as the conventional wisdom said he should: keeping his wife out of sight, drinking no alcohol in public, and playing the role of an authentic Muslim uncorrupted by European decadence. But President Nasir nonetheless made Arabism, rather than Islamism, the focus of his presidency.

It was probably more accident than design that caused Nasir and Egypt to claim supranational obligations toward the Arab world. The failure of five Arab states to defeat a fledgling Israel in the war of 1948–1949 created one backdrop for the new Arabism. Another was the efforts of the United States and Great Britain to defend the Middle East against the Soviet Union by focusing on so-called northern-tier countries (Turkey, Iran, Iraq) rather than Egypt. The United States turned down Egyptian requests for arms and for funding of a new, high dam on the Nile at Aswan. In response, President Nasir nationalized the Suez Canal. The owners of the canal (the British and the French) fussed and fumed and finally conspired with Israel to invade Egypt with the aim of overthrowing Nasir, whom the British called a "new Hitler."[17] The failure of the invasion, thanks to British and French bungling and to American expressions of outrage, made Nasir into an Arab hero. Suddenly he was an icon who could lead the Arabs out of the shadow of imperialism into an age of prosperity and unity. Egypt became an Arab state, while the leaders of the Muslim Brotherhood, champions of Islamism, went to prison for allegedly trying to assassinate Nasir in 1954.

Arabism led not to unity but to conflict. In 1958, Nasir led Egypt into union with Syria, forming the United Arab Republic, which was supposed to draw in other Arab states. Jordan and Lebanon trembled as Nasir flexed his muscles and the Iraqi monarchy fell to revolutionaries. But rather than following instructions from the Voice of the Arabs, Nasir's radio station, the other Arab states fell to quarreling with each other and with Egypt. Syria withdrew from the union, and Nasir himself stumbled into a war with Israel he could not win. The war of June 1967, in which Israel defeated three Arab states in six days, tarnished both Nasirism and Arabism. Egypt's effort to unite the Arabs under Egyptian leadership had led to military and economic disaster.[18]

Islamism

When in the fall of 1970 Nasir succumbed to a heart attack, his fellow collaborator in the 1952 coup d'état, Anwar al-Sadat, ascended to the presidency of Egypt. Instantly he freed political prisoners of the Nasirist era, including members of the Muslim Brotherhood, who promised loyalty to the regime in return for freedom. Sadat cultivated a religious image, spoke frequently at Friday mosque, and became known as "the believer president." A new constitution (1971) proclaimed the sharia one source of legislation, and amendment in 1980 made it the "principal source." Meanwhile, Sadat sought to extract Egypt from the Arab–Israeli conflict for the sake of his own country. The other Arab states expelled Egypt from the Arab League after Sadat concluded a peace treaty with Israel in 1979. Egypt's Arabism receded in favor of a rekindled loyalty to Islam and a rediscovered enthusiasm for capitalism, liberalism, and the West.

The identification of Islam with the Egyptian state has always generated two sorts of problems. The appeal to Islam as a source of identity invokes an identification much broader than Egypt, on the one hand, and narrower than Egypt on the other. To identify Egypt with Islam exposes the Egyptian state to criticism not just by its own citizens but by foreign groups and states claiming to represent the universal principles of Islam. Before World War II, with encouragement from the Egyptian religious establishment, King Faruq considered advancing a claim to be the new caliph, successor to the Ottoman sultan/caliph deposed by Mustafa Kemal Atatürk in 1923. Other Muslim states, including Saudi Arabia and Turkey, made it clear they would not support such a claim.[19] Internal political forces also made their objections known.

Internally, the identification between Islam and the Egyptian state tends to separate Coptic Christians, treated as *dhimmis*—a group protected as a religious minority under Islamic law—from full identification with the state. Should Islam take precedence over identification with ancient Egypt, Christian Egypt, or the Arab world in Egyptian politics? Coptic Christians tend to see these as pieces of a single puzzle, whereas Muslims see the pharaonic age as part of the jahiliyya.[20] A state that embraced all these and other dimensions of Egyptian history would be more inclusive, but its secularism would make it suspect in the eyes of Islamist groups. The Muslim Brotherhood and groups spun off from it have succeeded in evoking a positive response among millions of Egyptians with a plea that spiritual renewal and societal renovation depend upon a fresh commitment to Islam. But they have also alienated many Egyptians, who regard their projects as suspect and divisive.[21] "Islam limits what is perceived as permitted in Egyptian society and politics, and fundamentalists today are further narrowing the limits of the possible. A radical reinterpretation of the *dhimmi* concept in favor of non-Muslim equality is at present unlikely."[22]

Under the Ottoman Empire, Christians, Jews, and some other religious minorities had enjoyed protected (*dhimmi*) status as "peoples of the book," those that honor scriptures from the Abrahamic tradition. In return for acknowledgment of subordinate positions and payment of a special tax, these communities enjoyed the right to regulate many of their own affairs. They organized their own religious communities, selected their leaders, and applied religious law to matters that concerned only their community—all within the limits established by the Ottoman authorities. As Coptic Christians acquired greater access to European education in the late nineteenth and early twentieth centuries, they sought reform and began to think of themselves as a community with its own heritage and church. They "rediscovered a glorious past and sought to revive it."[23]

The Coptic community took on a new militancy after the Egyptian government under Sadat's presidency sought to accommodate the Islamist "awakening" triggered by the 1967 defeat. When Nazir Gayyid became patriarch of the Coptic church in 1971, taking the title of Pope Shenouda, he broke the "millet partnership" that his predecessor had established with President Nasir, built on the notion of Copts' accepting their role as a minority in a Muslim state. Pope Shenouda initiated educational and social programs to help middle-class Copts and propel them into mainstream posts, even at a moment of economic contraction. He ruffled feathers, as did Islamist extremists on the other side. Arrested by the government before Sadat's assassination in 1981, Shenouda pulled back toward a more traditional stance of cooperation with the regime. Such a policy pleased Coptic business elites, content to sacrifice political influence for the sake of economic interests. Shenouda consolidated his position as the unique intermediary between Christians and the government. "There exists no secular leadership of the Coptic community untainted by complicity with the government—no independent voice willing and able to voice Copts' grievances."[24]

A survey taken in 2000 reported that some 80 percent of Egyptian respondents identified themselves first as Muslims and only secondarily as Egyptians (10 percent) or Arabs (1 percent).[25] The percentage of Egyptians saying that they are best described by a religious term (Muslim in this case) exceeds comparable numbers for Turkey (29 percent), Israel (44 percent), and Iran (61 percent). Although no direct comparison with past surveys is available, the magnitude of that number seems to confirm what many have observed: that Egyptians seem to be more religious than ever before. "More people are praying, more people are reading about Islam and listening to its preachers, more people are discovering consciously the salience of religious ideas and practices to their private and public lives, than did a generation ago."[26] More women and more men appear in the streets dressed in ways that suggest religious commitment. More women wear the *hijab* (head scarf) or even the *niqab* (long, concealing form of modest dress that usually includes a facial veil) than in the past. Religious publications have multiplied, and the market for sermons on cassette, authorized and unauthorized, is brisk.[27] Sadat welcomed and encouraged an upsurge of religious feeling, apparently believing it useful in strengthening citizen identification with the state and support for him as president, but this upsurge in religiosity appears to complicate the question of identity.

At a popular level, common sense may soften the importance of the identity issue. Religious belief and practice do not necessarily equate with an exclusivist version of Egyptian identity. Personal "religiosity" does not necessarily translate into political attitudes. Al-Ali interviewed "secularist" women who, though often religious, were able to differentiate between personal observance and the political sphere. Some women explicitly saw secularism as a way of including Muslims, Christians, and Jews in a single discourse and a single society. While Islamists tend to equate secularism with atheism, many of the women Al-Ali interviewed saw secularism as a nondogmatic view of religion, an attitude perfectly consistent with being a Muslim, a Christian, or a Jew.[28]

At an intellectual level, many have sought to broaden the Egyptian sense of identity. A group of Egyptian intellectuals whom Raymond William Baker calls "New Islamists" have crafted a doctrine of "civilizational" Islam that is inclusive rather than exclusive. They are highly critical of the narrow-mindedness of many Islamists, especially the extremists, but also critical of the government for its unwillingness or inability to support full equality for all citizens, freedom of the press, the right of artists to be creative, and the right of women to play public roles in society. While the New Islamists insist that every society must establish limits to freedom based on underlying values, they insist that those rules are as much civilizational as religious. They want reform of Egyptian education to make possible the emergence of a society based on Islamic values. They are skeptical of the notions of authenticity and cultural specificity, dear to both Islamism and Coptism. They portray an Egypt open to the world, ready to adapt and create but conscious nonetheless of fundamental values anchored in a nonexclusive Islam. Some Copts joined members of the Muslim Brotherhood to form the Wasat (Center) Party in 1995, but the state's Party Formation Committee denied them status as a political party in 1996, 1998, and 2004.[29] Centrist efforts to expand Egypt's political identity thus have not had visible effect.[30]

The fundamental illegitimacy of the Egyptian state, committed to democratic principles it does not observe, enhances regime incentives for cultivating Muslim religiosity rather than seeking a long-term equilibrium solution to the problem of identity. Identification with all religions, or with a Muslim-Christian religious establishment that reflects underlying Egyptian morality, seems more promising than the pursuit of radical separation between the political and religious identities. But such a reformulation may require more strength and courage than the current regime can muster. Democratization might conceivably open the way for a solution, but democratization requires a regime with sufficient strength and confidence to permit the transition. Lacking these attributes, political elites have an interest in strengthening the state by emphasizing its Islamic identity. Islamist groups seeking democratization and full participation share that interest. But more secular-minded

Muslims and Coptic Christians regard that coincidence of interests as a threat to democratization.

The meaning of Islamic identity and the needs of the state change with every iteration of religious-political conflict. For Muhammad Ali, Islam meant dependence on the Ottomans and dependence on an entrenched indigenous elite out of touch with what he believed were new global imperatives. As much as Muhammad Abdu sought to alter that image of Islam by reworking its substance, the early nationalist movement did not see Islam as a defining feature of Egyptian identity. In a third period, after "independence" from the British, the emergence of the Muslim Brotherhood once again transformed Islam into a primary symbol of Egyptian resistance to British imperialism and internal moral degradation. And finally, in the most recent period, which has followed the war of 1967 and the Iranian Revolution, the meaning of identity with Islam has acquired yet another nuance. Those events, together with Nasir's death, pushed the Egyptian state toward a more fulsome (though hesitant) embrace of Islamic identity as a defense against enemies of the left and the right, internal and external.

Ideology

Political ideology is an invention of revolutionary politics. The Ottoman Empire identified with Islam from its modest beginnings on the fringes of the Byzantine Empire about 1300. Adhering to a Sunni model inherited from the Abbasid caliphate, the Ottoman sultans empowered religiously trained judges to implement the sharia. But Ottoman rule did not depend on a political ideology any more than did the French monarchy under Louis XIV or any other premodern political system. Political ideologies, elements of philosophy combined with recipes for action, emerged from the French, American, and Russian revolutions. Only in the nineteenth century did governments come to see any advantage in committing themselves to programmatic objectives such as liberalism, constitutionalism, or nationalism. Drawn to these ideas, Egyptian intellectuals began to regard Islam as an obstacle to economic, social, and political modernization. They began to think that Islam itself needed to change to accommodate modern needs. Far from thinking that Islam should dictate political change, they thought the needs of the polity required reform of Islamic doctrine.

Not all ideologies invoke religion, and religions do not necessarily produce political ideologies, but all religions propose notions of what is good. Because government must try (or at least pretend) to put itself on the side of "the good," it cannot be indifferent to religious conceptions of authority and general welfare. Political ideologies, such as Marxism, have often assumed an almost theological character, and theology has sometimes become ideological in a political sense.

> Every effective religious establishment . . . must have some theology defining, directing, and binding it together. Every effective political order, whether relatively open and democratic or relatively hierarchic, closed and authoritarian, must have some ideology performing these same integrative and directing functions.[31]

Both theology and ideology became more important as literacy increased and politics came to require some element of popular participation. Although they need not conflict, a theology that proclaims that God's law is all inclusive, fixed, and unchanging will necessarily clash with a political ideology that says constitutions and positive law take precedence over God's law. The advocates of reform in nineteenth-century Egypt came to see organized Islam, represented by the ulama, as an obstacle to change. Some of them tackled the problem as one of theology.

The leader of Egyptian religious reformers was Muhammad Abdu, a man trained in traditional religious schools but with an exposure to European education. Abdu studied at Azhar and began a teaching career before the British invasion of Egypt. After the invasion, exiled for supporting a revolt against the monarchy, he spent six years in Lebanon and in France collaborating with intellectuals such as Jamal al-Din al-Afghani before returning to Egypt and undertaking a legal career that culminated in his appointment as the mufti of Egypt in 1899. From that high pulpit he propounded a doctrine of return to the Islam of the ancestors (salafi), peeling away layers and layers of traditional Quranic exegesis to identify what he saw as the fundamental impulses of the religion. The Quran brought truth, and Muslims ever since have been striving to build upon that truth with all the intellectual powers at their disposal. In the modern era, scientists have carried the search for truth into new domains and brought it to new levels. In Abdu's view, the Muslim view of truth is that it is one, absolute, and complete. Scientific truths cannot possibly conflict, therefore, with revealed religious truth. A proper understanding of Islamic law must accommodate the new realities, and theology needs to adapt to modern politics.[32]

The significance of Abdu's work may lie more in this revived interest in Islamic theology than in his own conclusions. His student, Rashid Rida, built on Abdu's work and edited a journal called *al-Manar,* dedicated to rethinking the relationship between Islam and modernity. Rida came to believe that his mentor, Abdu, had given away too much ground by making Islam into a supple, reactive, adaptive agent and undermining its qualities as an unchanging moral foundation for society. He and others contributed to the rising sense that Islam could not be ignored as an essential part of Egyptian identity, but no one, not even Hasan al-Banna, founder of the Muslim Brotherhood, turned Islam into a modern political ideology.

Banna acknowledged his debt to Abdu, Rida, and the salafiyya movement, which had created a discourse about Islam's relevance to the condition of Egypt. But Banna insisted he was first and foremost interested in creating a moral, Muslim society. From a Muslim society might follow a Muslim state, and from a set of Muslim states might follow a Muslim world. Banna set out to generate discussion of Islam among educated Egyptians, to create schools and sports teams, to engender trust and a commitment to moral behavior among his fellow citizens. "Banna was steeped in both the theological and Sufi traditions, and from both he absorbed, and in his teachings demonstrated, the nonrationalist, even nonintellectual quality which has been observed to be an aspect of Muslim thought."[33] For him the problem was not the theological one identified by the salafiyya movement but the practical one of renewing Egyptian society through the spiritual transformation of individuals.

The transformation of Islam into a modern political ideology followed World War II, and it came not only from the renewed interest in Islam but from efforts to articulate a secularist ideology. Between the wars, liberal secularism had taken the ideological offensive against a condition of theoretical ambiguity created by a century of modernization, state aggression against the religious establishment, and the renewed interest in Islam.[34] A government employee and member of the religious establishment, Ali Abd al-Raziq published a book in 1925 in which he advocated separation of religion and state. Islam, as a religion, had "no application to temporal governance," he wrote. The ulama of Azhar reacted by getting him fired as a judge (*cadi*) in the religious (sharia) court system. In this same moment in Turkey, Mustafa Kemal Atatürk, having abolished the caliphate claimed by the last of the Ottoman sultans, implemented his interpretation of secularism, which was heavily influenced by the French notion of secularism (laïcité*).

In the 1930s, one Egyptian intellectual, Khalid Muhammad Khalid, renewed the secularist attack on the tenuous, unstable, ill-defined position of the Egyptian state by saying that a prophet outranks a ruler. The Prophet did not want to be a ruler and did not, as a result, establish a model for government. Khalid equated religious government with tyrannical government. Religion must speak to the religious needs of the individual, not to the questions of governance and public policy. The government permitted the book's publication but not without acknowledging objections from Azhar and thus accepting state responsibility for religion. The state had "continuing need for religious legitimacy in order to neutralize its political Islamist rival, the Brotherhood, and promote its essentially secular policies."[35]

Sayyid Qutb

The Islamist response to this ideological challenge came from Sayyid Qutb, who joined the Muslim Brotherhood about the time Banna met his death in 1949, presumably at the hands of the state in retaliation for the Brotherhood's 1948 assassination of the Egyptian prime minister. Qutb has left an account of a rather idyllic childhood in Upper Egypt.[36] His prodigious intelligence propelled him to Cairo in pursuit of modern education. He became a writer and a literary critic but was then drawn to social issues and to the Brotherhood's vision of nationalism and social justice. A visit to the United States convinced him that the Western version of modernity had produced rampant materialism and moral degradation. He returned to Egypt, acceded to an important post with the Brotherhood, and then went to prison with other Brotherhood leaders in 1954, after the attempt on President Nasir's life. In prison, Qutb wrote volumes, most of them part of a commentary on the Quran, in which he articulated an Islamic political ideology.

Banna had created an organization that effectively acquired great power in Egypt and had talked about the need for an Islamic state. Qutb offered reasons why the creation of an Islamic state was imperative and explained how the first generation of Muslims had created a revolutionary model by which it could be achieved. He asserted that Muhammad had encountered the same sort of problems that confront modern Muslims: social inequities, flagrant immorality, and human beings who exercise political authority over fellow human beings. Perhaps following a line of argument already advanced by Pakistani activist Mowlana Abul ala Mawdudi, Qutb said the condition of ignorance (jahiliyya) that marked the pre-Islamic age again afflicts mankind. Modern Muslims must therefore fight the modern jahiliyya with the same methods and weapons as the first Muslims. They first took counsel with themselves and strove through individual jihad to perfect their faith in God, then they retreated from Mecca's hostility to strengthen their community in Medina, and finally they launched violent jihad against Mecca's illegitimate power structure. The new Muslim community recognized no final authority except God. All human claims to sovereignty, ancient or modern, are necessarily illegitimate because they defy God's sovereignty. All existing governments, including Egypt's, were therefore seen as illegitimate and targets for revolution, according to Qutb, even though the leadership might claim to be Muslim. The president of Egypt, Gamal abd al-Nasir, did not mistake the message contained in Qutb's little volume, translated as *Signposts on the Road* or *Milestones*.[37] Qutb was hanged in 1966.

Banna had called for spiritual revival, but Qutb argued that it was unrealistic to ask Muslims to lead virtuous lives in a corrupted society, where material and sexual temptation was too great. While Banna had seen society's renewal as a precondition for political change, Qutb thought that Islamic government based on the sovereignty of God and the laws formulated in the sharia was a prerequisite for moral behavior. Like Marx, who thought human beings could overcome alienation only when they came to have collective ownership of the means of production, Qutb posited that Muslims would finally be free only when liberated from the domination of other human beings and the pressures of a degraded social situation. The laws of God would guide Muslims toward virtue and righteousness. He thought the entire world would eventually become Muslim in the sense of "submitting to God," whether within the established Islamic tradition or beyond it.

The ideological battle between Islamists and secularists has raged ever since. Because Qutb portrayed the modern jahiliyya as thoroughly entrenched and unlikely to give up power voluntarily, he seemed to suggest the necessity of violence against a state that had, after all, used violence to oppose the Muslim Brotherhood. Qutb lauded Muhammad's use of military force against Mecca and therefore the notion of violent jihad as well as that of jihad as the internal effort of every Muslim to know and follow God's will. Unlike the several radical groups that subsequently took inspiration from his writings in Egypt— Takfir wal Hijra, Islamic Jihad, and the Islamic Group, for example—he did not explicitly urge the use of violence or condone the use of terrorism to undermine the Egyptian regime. Abdassalem al-Faraj, who collaborated in the assassination of President Sadat in 1981, published a book justifying the action in which many of Qutb's ideas are visible. In addition, he argued that a medieval Muslim scholar, Ibn Taymiyya, had endorsed the legitimacy of Muslim violence against other Muslims who had abandoned the path of God.[38] Ibn Taymiyya's question was whether Muslims had the right to revolt against Mongol rulers, who were converts to Islam. The radicals built on Qutb's distinction between Muslims and "true Muslims." A true Muslim must do more than believe and wait for eternal salvation. He must act with other Muslims to make this world better. Islam supplies the goals and it supplies the methodology. Qutb created the basis for a revolutionary political ideology.

The leadership of the Muslim Brotherhood broke with this sort of radical analysis when they emerged from prison soon after Sadat succeeded Nasir in the presidency in 1970. The group retained its ambitions of making Egypt an Islamic state but committed itself to advancing its cause within the confines of Egyptian law. Radical groups nonetheless launched a series of attacks in the 1970s and managed to assassinate Sadat in 1981. A second spurt of radicalism in the 1990s, marked especially by attacks on Egyptian police and foreign tourists, constituted a severe test for the regime. At one point radicals established full control over two impoverished suburbs of greater Cairo. The government used military force to regain control. The radicals functioned most easily in Upper Egypt, where they launched a spectacular assault at Luxor in 1997. Some fifty-eight Western tourists and four Egyptians died at the hands of the Islamic Group in an incident that outraged ordinary Egyptians and constituted a turning point in sentiment against the radicals.[39] The government prevailed. Within a year, one of the most prominent radicals was recanting, proclaiming the "mistakes" of the Islamic Group. The most radical version of Qutbian ideology may continue to flourish underground but it does not figure in contemporary Egyptian debates.

The Sharia

Those debates turn, instead, on the place of the sharia in Egyptian politics. With passage of the democratizing constitution of 1971, Sadat opened the way for ulama to join Islamists in pushing for the application of the sharia. Abd al-Halim Mahmud, who acceded to the role of shaykh of Azhar in 1973, seized upon that opportunity to challenge the regime by advancing a proposal to codify the sharia, which bore fruit in 1978, when the People's Assembly created a committee that brought together ten members of the assembly with six ulama from Azhar.

> The ulama as a group were united on the principle of applying Islamic law. Whether members of Sufi brotherhoods or close to the Muslim Brotherhood, the ulama were together in demanding the *tatbiq* [application] of the sharia. It was a question of returning to Islamic law, which would be applied once codification had been completed.[40]

Mahmud also associated himself and Azhar with an effort of the Academy of Islamic Research to draft a generic Islamic constitution. Under these pressures from Islamists and Azhar, the regime agreed to modify the Egyptian constitution in 1980 to make the sharia the principal source of legislation.

Faraj Ali Fuda, founder of the new Wafd party, renewed and augmented the arguments of Ali Abd al-Raziq and Khalid Muhammad Khalid, saying the sharia is not holy (because it was fashioned by human beings) and not relevant, although positive (man-made) law in Egypt is in fact consistent with the spirit of the sharia. He agreed that Islam is a part of Egyptian identity, that something called Egyptian Islam exists, and that religion could be a part of the public sphere, but he argued that religious governments are tyrannical "because they hold to a single absolute truth, denying the possibility of multiplicity."[41] He was murdered in 1992. Such is the intensity of the debates about the sharia.

The sentence from the constitution "Islamic jurisprudence is the principal source of legislation" does not satisfy radical Islamists, determined secularists, or even Azhar, but it has served to turn debate toward a more manageable question: whether existing Egyptian law reflects the sharia. It is this debate that preoccupies much of the flourishing religious press in Egypt, and the government has responded with its own set of religious publications to argue its point of view. At its core, the debate inevitably depends upon an understanding of what the sharia is and how the sharia relates to the process of legal science (fiqh). For a secular jurist and writer such as Muhammad Said al-Ashmawi, it is a set of principles anchored in the Quran that must be interpreted by every generation. Egyptian law conforms to that standard.[42]

The constitutional language has opened the way for vigorous public debate about the relevance of the sharia to particular matters of public policy. Azhar, though a participant in the debate about the sharia, cannot afford to challenge the legitimacy of the regime from the inside; instead it has defended the state against the radical perspective that defines the political leadership as kufr, unbelievers. The Muslim Brotherhood cannot reopen those issues without risking its position as a major actor in the debate about the sharia, and the radical Islamists, through attacks on secularists such as Nobel Prize winner Naguib Mahfouz and Fuda, make it clear that they will not tolerate a reopening of the broader issues from a perspective hostile to the mainstream of Islamic thought.

The centrists whom Baker calls the New Islamists argue that fiqh is a necessarily a human process open to continuous revision. Any and all Muslims, whether members of the ulama or laymen, can and must engage in the process of ijtihad, by which general principles are applied and interpreted. In that view the sharia is an abstraction, a set of foundational concepts derived principally from the Quran and to a much lesser extent from the sunna of the

Prophet. The early legal authorities, creators of the four legal traditions within Sunni Islam, all worked from the relatively small amount of legal material in the Quran and from the sunna, known primarily through collections of hadith, reports on what the Prophet said or did in his lifetime. Although early lawyers winnowed and compiled the hadith in an effort to eliminate the fraudulent, many hadith reports are contradictory, and modern scholars tend to be skeptical about the reliability of many of them. Hence, a notion of sharia that depends on a fiqh anchored in hadith does not inspire confidence among the New Islamists. For many Islamists and ulama, however, the sharia, though constructed after Muhammad's death and well after the compilation of the Quran, constitutes a complete set of instructions good for all ages, a set of instructions that should guide and take precedence over all positive law. Egyptian legislation and judicial procedures, deeply influenced by European law and jurisprudence, do not measure up, in their view.

All parties functioning within the legally permissible spectrum voice support for democracy. By one line of thinking, opening the doors to full democracy in Egypt and permitting all forces including the Brotherhood to be fairly represented would lead to a more stable balance between the religious and political spheres. (That seems to be the message of those who focus on religion as an aspect of civil society.)[43] But the lack of debate about the fundamental question of authority—the lack of freedom and security to talk freely about the origins and status of the sharia and to criticize the authoritarianism of the regime—make it unclear that democracy as a foundation of authority is acceptable to anyone. The religious and political spheres have not yet fully agreed upon an ideological foundation for the Egyptian state, but it does seem that there has been some narrowing of ideological differences. In defending itself against Islamic revolution, the Egyptian state has become significantly more religious in orientation.[44] The Islamist movement has succeeded in creating a more religious society and goading the state to greater religious sensibility. The movement has, however, also abandoned its revolutionary dream of a utopian Islamic state—never explicitly defined by Qutb or anyone else. Islamist ideology has penetrated the Egyptian state, and the state has produced a reshaping of Islamist ideology. The same sort of reciprocal influence has occurred in the domain of institutions.

Institutions

Modernization theory predicts greater and greater separation of church and state, but in Egypt the lines between religious and political institutions, never sharp, have become increasingly blurred. When D. E. Smith wrote his book on *Religion and Political Development* in 1970, the secular-minded state seemed to have overwhelmed religious institutions in Egypt, but the challenge of radical Islamist groups in the 1970s put the Egyptian state on the defensive, where it remains to this day. Institutions such as the office of the *mufti*, head of the fatwa office (Dar al-Ifta), and Azhar mosque-university, pronounced lifeless in the 1960s, have achieved resurrection.[45] And the Islamist movement, though deterred in its most radical inclinations, has made its influence felt in every aspect of Egyptian society.[46] The Muslim Brotherhood, now eighty years old, has become a semiofficial (though extralegal) part of the religious establishment.

One contemporary model of development proposes that religious organizations be seen as a part of civil society and that civil society be seen as separate from the state. By opening its doors and encouraging the growth of civil society, the Egyptian state would prepare the way for participatory democracy. All voices would find their expression through political parties vying for power. Democratic decision-making would fashion the balance between religion and politics; both religious and political power would be tamed. A liberated civil society would redefine the state.

However useful in thinking about the prerequisites of democracy, the model does not sufficiently reflect the complexities of the interlocking relationship between religious and political institutions. On the one hand, no religious organization can function without the security and regulatory framework the state provides; without the state there is no civil society. On the other hand, the state cannot function without the legitimacy provided by religious leaders and organizations, some of whom escape direct control. The state is the single most important actor in the religious sphere, and religious groups exercise critical influence in the political system. The religious establishment in Egypt, represented by Azhar and the Dar al-Ifta, constitute part of the state but also remain part of the country's religious structure. The Azhari establishment includes high officials closely beholden to the state and peripheral preachers who manage to critique the government and support militant Islamist positions from within what appears to be a state-controlled sphere.[47] And the Muslim Brotherhood, whose origins were antistate and anti-ulama, now finds itself an integral part of the political system it supports and opposes. There is no clear boundary between civil society and state, between religion and politics.

The state's assault on the autonomy of the religious sphere began with Muhammad Ali's confiscation of waqf land as a means of bringing the ulama, the native Egyptian elite, under his control. The assault continued throughout the nineteenth and twentieth centuries as the state elevated Azhar to a dominant position within Egyptian Islam and then seized direct control of it, established its own educational system to challenge the Azhari system, created the Dar al-Ifta as an official source of religious opinions, attacked and then eliminated sharia courts, replacing them with state courts fashioned on the European model, and regulated Sufi practices, abolishing some of the more extreme ceremonies. Gamal abd al-Nasir completed the long process of sub-jugating religious institutions to state control and making Islam a simple in-strument of the state.[48] State superiority over religious institutions appeared absolute but proved short-lived, even illusory.

In the 1940s and 1950s, the Muslim Brotherhood nearly reversed the power relationship, first with its challenge to the weak governments from 1942 to 1952, and then with its assault on the Nasirist regime in 1954. (Al-though the Brotherhood may not on either occasion have intended a full-scale assault on the regime, it certainly did nurture hopes of creating an Islamic state.) Then in the 1970s and 1980s, the radical groups that had spun off from the Brotherhood renewed the effort at violent overthrow of what they saw as a secular state. That effort also appears to have failed.

Azhar and Dar al-Ifta

Neither the state under Nasir nor the radicals who fought for power emerged entirely victorious. As a result, the waters are now muddied. The Egyptian state that is deeply involved in the regulation of religious organizations, albeit not in full control, battles semiautonomous religious organizations in the po-litical sphere. The religious and political spheres are engaged in an embrace that neither can break. Although the state retains the upper hand, the linger-ing threat of radical Islam and the mass appeal of Islamic symbols and pro-grams mean the state must accommodate religion. And the Muslim Brotherhood, breaking with its past and the militant offshoots, has decided to seek influence within the confines of the authoritarian state, tempering its message and compromising with state regulation in a variety of ways. Even now the Brothers must forgo direct control of a political party to remain within the body politic.

Two religious-political institutions reflect the tensions at the heart of the struggle between the religious and political: the Azhar mosque-university system and the Dar il-Ifta, office of the mufti. Both are, in different degrees, creations of the state designed to exercise state influence over Egyptian Is-lam. Both offices have dubious legitimacy in the minds of Islamist groups, but neither can be entirely ignored. Both are obliged in some measure to do the will of political elites, but Islamist pressures permit them to stiff the regime on some issues to maintain the legitimacy they need to do the job the state wants them to do. They demonstrate the way in which the state has re-shaped Egyptian Islam and at the same time made itself vulnerable to pressures from the religious sphere.[49]

At the moment of the French conquest in 1798, the Egyptian ulama constituted a small native elite headed by a council of nine or ten, of whom the shaykh of Azhar was one.[50] Muhammad Ali and his successors sought to subordinate the ulama by nationalizing the autonomous source of financial support, waqf, and by creating a chief among the ulama, someone who could take orders. By the beginning of the twentieth century, the state had raised the shaykh of Azhar to such a position.[51] Azhar successfully resisted reform of its teaching establishment on more than one occasion, declining a more effective role in the modern world in what was a losing effort to maintain autonomy. By the end of the Nasir regime, there was no longer any illusion of autonomy. Azhar, nationalized and reformed, constituted an arm of the state and seemed to have lost all legitimacy in the eyes of Islamist groups. Hasan al-Banna and the Muslim Brothers, although they recruited some members from among Azhari students, remained largely critical of the institution for tolerating foreign rule and political domination of Islam.

Azhar, together with the Ministry of *Awqaf* (Religious Foundations), became and remains the principal tool for state control of religious practice in Egypt. It administers a system of religious schools that expanded from a total of 90,000 students in 1970 to about 300,000 by 1980. The university itself came to enroll about 90,000 students; its faculty, employees of the state, constitute the elite of Egyptian ulama, all of them employees of the state. In addition, through the ministry of Awqaf the state employs several thousand preachers who staff official mosques around the country, most of them products of the Azhar system. Starting in the 1960s, Azhar's Institute for Islamic Research began to claim the right to censor Egyptian publications according to Islamic criteria. It has largely succeeded in exercising that right. The shaykh of Azhar, named by the government, is in theory the chief spokesman for Islam in Egypt, empowered to issue fatwas affecting every Muslim in Egypt.

The state created the Dar al-Ifta in 1895 as another tool in its effort to assert its control over the religious sphere. From the beginning the office annually issued thousands of fatwas, nonbinding judgments on the application of Islamic principles to problems and legislation. The office's prestige rose and fell according to the ability and qualifications of the mufti, who was always a political appointee selected from men educated in the religious tradition.

What is surprising in the case of the Dar al-Ifta, even more than in the case of Azhar, is that it has exercised increasing autonomy since the end of the Nasir regime as a result of the state's need for protection against the verbal assault of the Islamists. It has helped transform politics into a war of fatwas, reshaping Egyptian Islam as has the state's transformation and manipulation of an old institution, Azhar.

The history of these two institutions shows how the Egyptian state has transformed the institutional structure of Islam in Egypt. By its actions, it has politicized religion. Every religious institution must in some measure play politics to protect itself within the system. Virtually every religious act has acquired political significance. Every proclamation, every sermon, every study group, every nongovernmental organization (NGO) operated in the name of religion resonates within a structure defined by the government. The institutions differ in degree of government regulation and influence, but only the militant Islamist groups accused of murdering policemen and tourists are outside the system—in jail or invisible.

The Muslim Brotherhood

The Muslim Brotherhood grew outside the official religious establishment but within the legal framework of the Egyptian state. Its founder, Hasan al-Banna, was a layman, and the movement included few ulama in its early years. It eschewed politics but became a political force by virtue of its organizational strength. From a small society established in Ismailia it spread to Cairo and then to much of Egypt as a network of people drawn by Banna's charisma, by the group's schools and activities, and by its message of moral rejuvenation and nationalism.

> One friendly writer describes Banna as a man who knew the language of the Azhar and of the Sufis, who knew the dialects, the traditions, and the problems of the cities and towns, of the provinces, of the delta and the desert, and of Upper and Lower Egypt; he knew the psyche of the butcher and the little girl and the various types of people who inhabited the cities, including the thieves and murderers—he spoke to them all, says this observer, and "always his knowledge astounded his hearers." In this matter "he won individual after individual," binding them in an unbreakable bond to him as a representative of an idea and as a personal friend.[52]

Banna was, in short, an extraordinarily effective and talented politician with explicit, though deferred, political objectives: the liberation of Egypt and the creation of an Islamic state.[53] Although the Brotherhood did not advance candidates for office, it enjoyed a broader base of support than any of the existing parties, even the Wafd, which dominated Egyptian politics in the interwar period with a thin base of support in the landed elites. Membership in the Brotherhood may have totaled 1 million by World War II. It loomed as a threat to "liberal Egypt," the label commonly applied to Egypt from "independence" in 1923 until the revolution of 1952.

The Brotherhood's ability to survive first the loss of its founder and then two periods of official dissolution demonstrates the organization's strength. The government dissolved the organization in 1947. (The Brotherhood responded by assassinating Prime Minister Mahmud Fahmi al-Nuqrashi in 1948, and the government then apparently ordered the killing of Banna as retribution.) Reauthorized in 1952, the Brotherhood succeeded in putting thousands of demonstrators into the streets in a matter of hours. Banned again in 1954 and its leaders imprisoned after the assassination attempt on Nasir, the Brotherhood survived underground until its liberation by President Sadat in 1970. It soon made its presence felt with its publications, its affiliated organizations, and a strategy of capturing power in the universities and professional syndicates, such as that of engineers and lawyers. Although Presidents Sadat and Hosni Mubarek sought to harass and restrain the Brotherhood out of suspicion that it kept ties to radical factions engaged in violence, they stopped short of dissolving it a third time. The Brotherhood became a part of Egypt's religious, social, and political structures.

An Egyptian law that prohibits the formation of political parties based on religion has kept the Brotherhood from running candidates under its name in parliamentary elections, but it has succeeded in running candidates on other tickets or as independents. And its members of the People's Assembly have a tight, effective parliamentary group, boasting 80 members (of 454) after the 2005 elections.

The Brotherhood has often been critical of the official religious establishment (i.e., Azhar, Dar al-Ifta, and the Ministry of Awqaf) but some of the official ulama have expressed sympathy for the Brotherhood and its positions. Moreover, unofficial preachers working from private mosques have echoed Brotherhood positions and even sympathized with the radicals without being arrested. Their sermons circulate in an underground cassette trade that the government tries to suppress. Furthermore, many NGOs with Brotherhood sponsorship receive a portion of their resources from the government, and they could not function without government permission. These organizations provide a quality of service many Egyptians see as fulfilling important needs and as lacking from any other source. Hence, the government seeks to tolerate and even support them. In this sense the Brotherhood constitutes an unofficial, semiautonomous part of the religious establishment.[54]

Pluralism

The triangular relationship among government, the official religious establishment, and the unofficial establishment (the Brotherhood) remains unstable because the status quo depends upon the will of the state. The government continues to campaign against unauthorized preaching and unauthorized sermons on cassette, to regulate NGOs, to monitor elections to syndicates where Islamists have won power, and to censure publications that step beyond the line of "acceptable criticism." Religious groups push the state toward implementation of its proclaimed interest in democratization; by resisting, the state weakens its hand and exposes the instability of the situation it has created. Azhar once again exercises a certain autonomy, as does the Dar al-Ifta, because the regime needs the help of the official establishment in legitimating an unstable and fundamentally illegitimate system. The Muslim Brotherhood enjoys considerable liberty to organize, speak, and publish because its support helps the regime suppress radicals and helps affirm the state's loyalty to Islamic principles. The Brotherhood enhances its position if it wins the support of Azhar; Azhar magnifies its position within the state if it helps to satisfy the Brotherhood and to keep it within the domain of state control.

Despite government efforts over two centuries, the organizational structure of Islam in Egypt has become pluralistic. It is thoroughly politicized, except perhaps for the Sufi brotherhoods, which seem somewhat isolated from politics in Egypt, although Banna willingly acknowledged his own debt to Sufism.[55] (The organization of the Muslim Brotherhood under a Supreme Guide takes inspiration from the Sufi notion of disciples following a master.) Government efforts to control Islam and give it a single spokesman have failed. Even the official agencies do not speak with a single voice, and the Muslim Brotherhood, though it would aspire to follow a single line, has suffered a splintering that further complicates the picture. The New Islamists, for example, express their conviction that Islam must be the foundation of the Egyptian state but they welcome fresh thinking about the meaning of Islamic law from any and all quarters. They reject narrowness of interpretation from the Brotherhood, Azhar, and Dar al-Ifta. They criticize the government for its unwillingness to move toward genuine democracy.

The state has transformed the institutional structure of Islam in Egypt and incorporated it in various degrees into the structure of the state. The revolt of the Islamists intensified the state's need for regulation and control and contributed to an unintended Islamization of the state. Transforming Islam has transformed the state. Far from separated, religious and political institutions are more entangled than ever before, and neither sphere is happy: The religious groups chafe under the limitations placed upon them, and the state, still dominated by secular-minded elites, appears chagrined by the concessions it finds itself making. Both sides proclaim their commitment to democracy, and neither believes the other is sincere. The regime fears that democratization would empower Islamists to revise the configuration of the religious-political sphere currently guaranteed by the coercive powers of the state. It also fears that the Islamist commitment to democracy would end with access to power.

The case of Professor Nasr Abu Zayd, who was convicted of apostasy, illustrates the deep involvement of religion in state institutions and the partial ability of state institutions to regulate and enforce Islam. Islamists brought a civil case against Abu Zayd for teaching that, like any other document, the Quran must be subjected to close textual analysis and that understanding its implications is a human process open to continual revision. Islamists supported by some ulama brought the case to the state court system, which would enforce religious law only insofar as it is embedded in the Egyptian code. The court would normally have been concerned only with the effects of apostasy. One consequence in this case is that a Muslim who abandons Islam cannot be married to a Muslim woman. The court found Abu Zayd guilty not of abandoning Islam but of teaching and writing against it and, as a result, being illegally married to his wife. In finding guilt and dissolving his marriage, the court made it clear that Islam constitutes one of the foundations of the Egyptian state. The decision, a product of religious pressure on the state, nevertheless represented a state assertion of authority over religion.[56] In what can only be termed a humane response to an inhumane decision, the government subsequently permitted Abu Zayd and his wife to leave the country for the Netherlands, where he teaches at the University of Leiden.

The relationship between religious and political institutions remains unstable for at least two reasons: (1) Social and economic change in the form of urbanization, social mobility, improved communication, and increasing access to education continues to transform religious institutions. These changes have increased pluralism and produced conflict within the religious sphere. Some elements of the religious sphere have sought to profit from their strength to make religion a more prominent, or even a dominant, part of the state. (2) The state has responded by seeking to further subjugate religious institutions, undermining the power Islamic organizations have acquired in the past three decades. The state tries to further modify the structure of Islam in Egypt to protect the regime, and the Islamist groups seek to modify the state. The political and the religious, entangled though they are, have been somewhat successful in transforming each other.

Political Culture

The notion of political culture serves to help political scientists identify the attitudes of a society that are more enduring than opinions of the moment. Scholars have shown that there is a certain continuity in the way the French think about their political system and that French attitudes are distinct from those of Denmark, Great Britain, the United States—and Egypt, for that matter. Weber argued that the "Protestant ethic" affected the growth of capitalism in Europe. Inglehart claims that there are still traces of the distinction in European political culture between predominantly Catholic and predominantly Protestant countries. He argues that respondents from Muslim countries do not differ from other cultural groups in attitudes toward democracy but do distinguish themselves from other cultures on the equality of women and on homosexuality.[57] Differences in basic attitudes—the importance of religion in society, attitudes toward minorities, trust of other people—tend to endure within countries and, perhaps, within cultural areas.

Such attitudes are not, however, permanent. There is abundant evidence for long-term change in political cultures. Catholic Europe has become as dynamic economically as Protestant Europe. The authoritarian Germans have become democrats. Eastern Europeans are shedding communist values. And, as Lerner showed more than fifty years ago, Middle Eastern Muslim culture has evolved in significant ways.[58] A reading of the trilogy of novels by Naguib Mahfouz dramatizes the shifting mentalities of a single Egyptian family over thirty years.[59] It would be helpful to document the political attitudes of ordinary Egyptians in, say, 1810, 1860, 1910, and 1960, but the modern survey, dependent on computers, became available only in the 1950s. Since then the skepticism of the Egyptian government about any survey touching on politics has slowed research, but some survey data on Egypt are available to help test impressionistic accounts. While some Egyptian attitudes have clearly endured—witness the broad attachment to clitoridectomy (female circumcision), for example, even among city dwellers—others have evolved over time.

Change in social conditions would certainly be the primary explanation for long-term evolution of Egyptian political culture.

The most striking change in Egyptian political culture during the past fifty years is the apparent increase in commitment to Islam. The signs are everywhere—in dress, in behavior, in publications, in speech. The Islamist movement seems to have had an impact on the piety of ordinary Egyptians, even on many who are not formally a part of the movement. How does one explain this "awakening" in a country that seemed inclined to downplay religion in the 1950s? Many scholars have attributed the Islamist success to changing social conditions.

Islam has become a form of protest for regions and groups disadvantaged in the modernization process. The message of the militant Islamic Group, an offshoot of the Muslim Brotherhood powered by Qutbian ideology, found resonance in the underdeveloped south of Egypt.[60] By at least one analysis, the attacks on tourists and policemen represented an assault on northern dominance and southern weakness. Kepel has argued that the Islamist phenomenon has, in general, depended upon an appeal to two groups: a pious bourgeoisie and a lumpen proletariat, the wreckage of the modernization process. Where Islamists have succeeded, they have mobilized both groups, as in Iran.[61] Urbanization has overtaxed the state's ability to minister to the needs of its citizens. Migrants fleeing the poverty of the countryside end up in slums on the periphery of Cairo, which lack sanitation, decent housing, schools, and transportation. The radicals captured and held two such neighborhoods in the 1990s. NGOs, many of them supported by religious organizations, have often stepped into the breach by providing services unavailable from the state.[62] The rise in literacy and demand for public education has resulted in overcrowded schools, declining standards in education, and large numbers of educated young people unable to find jobs. To compensate, the wealthy hire tutors for their children or send them to private universities.

Training Citizens

Social dislocation does not, however, explain why individual Egyptians have been drawn toward Islam rather than into socialism, Arabism, or some other form of protest. It does not explain why so many Egyptians have ceased to think of their faith as a set of rituals and practices embedded in the social fabric and have begun to read about Islam and think about what it means to their lives. Changes in Egypt's educational system over the past century probably do more than social alienation to explain the growth of the Islamist movement. Of course, education may itself produce alienation in those who emerge with modern degrees but cannot find work. Lack of access to modern education also alienates those who have come to understand its magic properties but cannot acquire them. The two explanations are complementary.

The Islamist awakening comes in part from a transformation in the structure of Egyptian Islam that has followed from modernization. Starrett writes:

> In documenting the role of the contemporary school in teaching Islam, I hope to show how the expansion and transfer of religious socialization from private to newly created public sector institutions over the last century has led to a comprehensive revision of the way Egyptians treat Islam as a religious tradition, and consequently of Islam's role in Egyptian society.[63]

As education has reached ever larger percentages of the population, it has enabled more and more Egyptians to evaluate their faith and its implications. The Nasirist state forced reform upon the Azhari educational system after 1961, and one result has been ulama better prepared to lock horns in contemporary political battles, ulama whose background more closely resembles that of Islamist leaders, many of them products of state education. The Muslim Brotherhood and all its Islamist successors are products of modern education as well as propagators of their own versions of it. Already in the 1930s and 1940s the Brotherhood was publishing newspapers and journals to recruit and hold members. Since the 1970s, the number of religious publications has multiplied, and the government has been obliged to compete by mounting a publishing industry of its own.

Religious and political institutions find support in political culture. They respond to the culture as they find it, but they also seek to transform it. The Brotherhood exemplifies both sides of that assertion. It arose from its ability to respond to the sentiments of Egyptians caught in a process of change they could not fully comprehend. It sought to re-create a moral society inspired by the Quran and committed to a comportment consistent with Islamic law. The Muslim Brotherhood wanted to transform the existing political culture as a prelude to changing the state. Similarly, Gamal abd al-Nasir transformed a military coup into a popular "revolution" by virtue of his ability to reach ordinary Egyptians. His government launched land reform, formed agricultural cooperatives, and pushed medical clinics into villages. He appealed to the political culture as he found it, but he also set out to transform Egyptians into "good citizens," good Arabs, and eventually good socialists! The Brotherhood saw that education was the key to bringing Egyptians back to Islam. Nasir understood education as the key to secularizing society. Consensus on educational policy remains vital to stabilizing the relationship between religion and politics in Egypt.

Although Jamal al-Din al-Afghani revived the idea of using Islam as the rallying cry against European imperialism in the late nineteenth century, the British never came to see Islam as an obstacle to colonial rule. Instead, as Starrett shows, they sought to finish the job begun by Muhammad Ali and his successors, undermining the traditional elite by providing an alternative source of education in the society.[64] The elementary schools they established, though they reached a relatively small part of the population, included instruction about religion, which the British saw as a necessary component of citizenship.[65] In so doing they opened the way for a transformation of Islam in Egypt in ways that made possible the Muslim Brotherhood and the identification of Islam—a good Egyptian is a good Muslim—with the Egyptian state. But this was not any longer the Islam of the ulama in the early nineteenth century but the Islam of the Egyptian public schools.[66] The old Quranic schools based on memorization of the Quran began to lose sway.

Successive Egyptian governments, first under British tutelage and then independent of British rule, have followed the British line. Islamic identity reinforces Egyptian identity so long as the Islam in question is Egyptian Islam, a product of a curriculum designed and supervised by Egyptians. A survey of Egyptian university students found that 73 percent favored teaching religion in the national curriculum. A third wanted religious instruction extended to the university level. Most respondents said the current educational system in Egypt conflicts with Egyptian national character, presumably because it is insufficiently influenced by Islamic learning and culture.[67] According to Starrett, Egyptians see public education as the principal means of transmitting Islam to the younger generation. [68]

Nasir's regime sought to move that culture toward an Arab version of socialism, but those efforts did not succeed, nor did Islamist efforts to transform Egyptians into militant Muslims, willing to countenance violence in the name of an insurgent Islam. Both the state and the Brotherhood work at shaping the existing belief system through education, social services, and a barrage of mediated messages, but neither currently seems capable of transforming that culture. Instead, the competition has accentuated a bifurcation of the political culture between attitudes that one might term "religious" and "secular," and it seems unlikely that one tendency will vanquish the other.

To say that political culture resists change is not to say that it is immutable. Egyptian attitudes toward education, proper attire for women, international politics, and the responsibilities of the Egyptian government bear little resemblance to those same attitudes a century ago. The old saws about the incompatibility of democracy with Islam or Arab culture, built on notions that cultures are unchanging, seem utterly untenable. But, as Ahmed observes, change occurs not because a modern culture erases the traditional, but because participants in a culture find ways to preserve and innovate at the same time.[69] Are women who join Islamist groups and embrace "traditional" subordination of women to men acting in a modern or traditional way? They are both agents of change and agents of preservation.[70]

Education

Socialization is the key to maintaining and transforming culture. It is not surprising, then, that education has been a primary battleground between the religious and the political spheres in Egypt as elsewhere. From Muhammad Ali's initial effort to create European-style schools to the contemporary conflict over higher education in Egypt, the battle has raged. The state weakened and almost destroyed the hold of religious elites on the education of youth, but the resulting public school curricula reinforced the place of religion in Egyptian society. Now the Azhari system has bounced back in a new form combining secular and Islamic criteria. Secularizing liberals once constituted the forces for instability; now it is the Islamists who agitate for revision and change. The relative strength of religious and political institutions has determined the outcome of the struggle over education much more clearly and directly than it has the shape of Egyptian political culture as a whole. Education does not necessarily produce an intended result, as colonial powers and independent governments alike have discovered over time.

More than anything, education seems to have objectified religion. Educated Egyptians must now think about what sort of Muslim or what sort of Christian they want to be. If they choose to follow the old ways, it will be a matter of choice, not habit. They may choose to wear the hijab or the niqab or not. They may choose to vote for candidates of the Muslim Brotherhood or not. Islam is thus a variable and not a constant. To know whether an Egyptian is a Muslim may be less important politically than knowing how religious she is and whether she sees a relationship between faith and politics. Whether the average Egyptian actually has become more pious or whether piety itself strengthens or weakens identification with the state remains uncertain. Tessler and Nachtwey found that Egyptians who ranked high on piety did not necessarily support Islamist parties, and half of those who support Islamist parties did not report high levels of piety. They found no correlation between policy issues and religiosity measured by an index of piety.[71]

Formal education is one means of shaping and reshaping political culture. Political elites tend to imagine that law will reshape political attitudes. Religious elites rely on preaching, publications, and fatwas in an effort to heighten the public's moral perceptions and religious practices. Both groups necessarily acknowledge a set of habits and practices that resist change. To proclaim that clitoridectomy is illegal does not necessarily eliminate the practice. To declare certain Sufi rituals contrary to Islam or to intone against drunkenness does not necessarily produce the desired effects. From the perspective of both religious and political elites, political culture often appears static.

Both political and religious elites must respond to popular conceptions of ethics and rightful authority. For example, the Egyptian government has appealed to the public's general sense of right and wrong in its efforts to suppress radical attacks on tourists and policemen, and it seems to have been largely successful. The Muslim Brotherhood has had success in attacking the government for its hypocrisy and corruption; where possible the regime has responded by accusing the Brotherhood of corruption in its involvement with municipal administration.[72] There is no need for detailed Quranic exegesis to make these points, although both sides do invoke expert opinion to support arguments that most Egyptians, Christian or Muslim, accept without thinking. In these cases there is coincidence between the law and the common sense of morality.

Instability?

Divergence between morality and the law contributes to instability in the relationship between religion and politics. The importation of civil and criminal codes from Europe in the nineteenth century constituted an effort of the state to reshape moral sentiments, something more easily attempted in a thoroughly authoritarian state, willing to ride roughshod over religious objections. The reduction in authority of the sharia courts and their ultimate abolition constituted a wholesale assault on a political culture in which justice had been seen as a function of religion more than politics. The many tales of villagers ensnared by a law they did not comprehend testify to the conflict between law and morality.

The tables have now turned. Common perceptions of morality appear to be undermining the law and thereby threatening the state's authority. The Islamist movement has emphasized the responsibility of citizens to one another, and it has put renewed emphasis on the need for respectability in sexual relations. It is a matter not of creating a new morality, but of reemphasizing aspects of morality embraced by most Egyptians, Muslims, and Copts. The result is that court cases often become public causes, not because the law was or was not applied, but because the law seemed inadequate to express the morality of the case.[73] Public policy on matters such as clitoridectomy, AIDS, and prostitution reflect rather than challenge general conceptions of morality.[74] Individual citizens can drag other citizens into court on charges of immorality. That is what happened to Professor Abu Zayd, accused of apostasy.

While in the nineteenth century the Egyptian state thought it was changing the standards by which all citizens, including those in the religious sphere, would be judged, it increasingly appears that the state is to be judged by a set of criteria emerging from the religious sphere. Or rather, it is the religious sphere (of which state-supported actors are a part) that is reemphasizing old standards of respectability and responsible citizenship the government can scarcely deny or ignore. By acceding to these standards, leaders cede their power to the Islamist forces and thereby demonstrate weakness. In resisting these standards the government appears illegitimate and hypocritical; in fact, it must invoke them itself to ward off attack from radical elements.

This domain of encounter between religion and politics is thus quite different from those previously described. The strength of the political culture and its evolution does not depend on the state's Islamic identity or on ideological disputes about sovereignty. Both the religious and the political spheres depend upon the prevailing political culture in Egypt. Both spheres reflect ideas about morality, authority, and participation contained in that culture and have limited means to alter that culture in the short run.[75]

Social, economic, and political conditions appear to shape political culture more than does ideological discourse. The religious and political institutions do, however, reshape political culture in the long run by influencing social, economic, and especially educational policy. Outcomes necessarily reflect the relative strength of political and religious institutions. Institutions must function within an existing set of cultural conditions but must also think about their future welfare by attempting to mold culture in a way that favors their prosperity. Christians must socialize young Christians. Muslims must train new generations of Muslims.

Conclusion

The burgeoning literature on religion and politics in Egypt shows that modernization theory, with its predictions about the secularization of politics and society, does not accurately describe what has happened there. Religion and politics have become more and more thoroughly intertwined as social, economic, and political changes have affected all four domains in which politics and religion necessarily interact: identity, authority, morality, and organization. Destabilized by Muhammad Ali in the early nineteenth century, the religious and political spheres remain locked in an increasingly intense, uncomfortable, and unstable embrace. Neither sphere can be characterized as a force of tradition or modernity. Neither sphere can realistically contemplate victory. The question is whether further iterations of dialogue and conflict will magnify the oscillations in the relationship or whether there will be movement toward a more stable relationship.

This pattern bears the imprint of Islam. The relative lack of hierarchy in the Islamic establishment as Muhammad Ali encountered it in the early nineteenth century made it easier for him to seize waqf resources and reorganize the ulama. (Because of this lack of hierarchy, Smith calls Islam an "organic" religion as opposed to a "church" religion, such as Roman Catholicism.)[76] The egalitarianism of Islamic doctrine opened the way for lay challenge to the Islamic establishment; the plurality, even chaos, in the current configuration of Egyptian Islam stems in some measure from this fact. The character of the sharia has certainly conditioned the debate about legitimate authority.

Islam has shaped the nature of the interaction, but the dynamism and instability of the relationship come from forces of social and economic change that go beyond Egypt or even the Muslim world. They also result from developments peculiar to Egypt. Would indigenous rulers, beholden to the ulama, have been as aggressive as the Albanian Turkish dynasty of Muhammad Ali in seeking to subordinate the religious establishment to their agenda of modernization? Might not the relationship have evolved quite differently in the early twentieth century without British intervention, pushing modern education and galvanizing dissent? It is commonplace to see Egyptian politics as a product of British imperialism, the failure of liberalism, or the Nasirist fling with Arabism. But these are also the forces that have transformed the religious sphere in Egypt into the vibrant, cacophonous, polycentric force it is today.

The development of an Egyptian national state required the development of an Egyptian Islam. How does religious identity square with the claim that Egypt is a state distinct from others in the Muslim world? How do Copts fit into that identity? How does the authority of the nation-state square with God's authority? Does an Egyptian government represent truth and justice as it is commonly understood, or do religious leaders speak for general perceptions of morality? How do national political institutions relate to religious institutions? The development of the nation-state created these questions and requires answers.

The state was needy, and religion responded to this neediness. It evolved in response to changing political opportunities, gaining influence and authority along the way. The state fought back by limiting and altering those opportunities, trying itself to exploit the pluralistic structure of Egyptian Islam, and the result was ever greater intermixture of politics and religion. In moments of tranquility, the two spheres conducted a sharp but civilized dialogue; in moments of trauma, violence broke out on the margins. Much more than even thirty years ago, religion and politics today reshape each other daily by their interactions.

How might one envision a move toward stability in Egypt? How many more iterations of conflict will be required? It is difficult to imagine an Egypt that does not eventually become liberal and democratic, and it is equally difficult to imagine an Egyptian state willing to forgo the legitimacy that a link to Islam provides. What sort of state will the religious sphere be willing to tolerate? What sort of religious doctrines and organizations will political elites be willing to permit? In what sorts of encounters and forums is such a compromise likely to emerge? The lesson of the West would seem to be that the answer will be forthcoming from a long progression of interactions of the religious and the political.

For now the interactions of the state and religion seem to be producing a tight embrace that solidifies the regime's authoritarianism. The continued weakness of the state pushes it toward greater efforts to solidify its control over religious organization and ideology, and those efforts spur greater politicization of religious groups seeking to maintain their autonomy and influence. The resulting threat to state authority requires another twist of the authoritarian screw, which furthers the spiral of religious-political involvement in a pattern that might be called sacralized-bureaucratic-authoritarian. For now, conflict and plurality, which ought to be conducive to democratization, seem to be producing religious-political collaboration that serves to reinforce authoritarianism, despite the liberal, democratic rhetoric of both government and opposition.

Notes

1. D. E. Smith, *Religion and Political Development* (Boston: Little Brown, 1970), 2.

2. Ronald Inglehart, ever a partisan of the notion of secularization, nonetheless charts sharp variations in the degree of secularization within societies at all levels of income and all degrees of commitment to what he calls postmaterial values. See his *Modernization and*

Postmodernization: Cultural, Economic, and Political Change in 43 Societies (Princeton, NJ: Princeton University Press, 1997), 93.

3. "Secularization is inherently linked with Modernization. This holds true despite frequent assertions that a rapid growth of fundamentalist religion is taking place throughout the world. This interpretation reflects a misconception of what is happening, generalizing from two very different phenomena." He finds the European case very different from the Middle Eastern, where he says fundamentalism is linked with lack of modernization. Inglehart, *Modernization and Postmodernization*, 72.

4. Pippa Norris and Ronald Inglehart, *Sacred and Secular: Religion and Politics Worldwide* (Cambridge, UK: Cambridge University Press, 2004), 24.

5. Ibid., chapter 4.

6. Ronald Inglehart and Christian Welzel, *Modernization, Cultural Change, and Democracy: The Human Development Sequence* (Cambridge, UK: Cambridge University Press, 2005).

7. See the diagram in D. E. Smith, *Religion and Political Development*, 14.

8. See the extraordinary account provided by Abd al-Rahman al-Jabarti, *Napoleon in Egypt: AlJabarti's Chronicle of the First Seven Months of the French Occupation, 1798,* trans. Smuel Moreh (Princeton, NJ : M. Wiener, c1993).

9. Daniel Crecelius, "The Ulama and the State in Modern Egypt" (PhD dissertation, Princeton University, 1967), chapter 1.

10. Ibid., 362.

11. See Benedict Anderson, *Imagined Communities* (New York: Verso, 2006), for an account of how that nationalist idea seized Europe and then other parts of the world.

12. See George Antonius, *The Arab Awakening: The Story of the Arab National Movement* (New York: G. P. Putnam's Sons, 1946).

13. See Nikki Keddie, *An Islamic Response to Imperialism: Political and Religious Writings of Sayyid Jamal al-Din "al-Afghani"* (Berkeley: University of California Press, 1983).

14. See Sylvia Haim, ed., *Arab Nationalism: An Anthology* (Berkeley: University of California Press, 1964).

15. Richard P. Mitchell, *The Society of Muslim Brothers* (New York: Oxford University Press, 1993), originally published in 1969, remains the standard history of the organization. Sa'id Hawwa, *The Muslim Brotherhood*, trans. Abdul Karim Shaikh (Kuwait: Al Faisal Islamic Press, 1985), contains extensive material from the speeches of Hasan al-Banna. The book provides an uncritical account of Banna's approach and thinking. In many passages, it is difficult to know whether Hawwa or Banna is the author of the thoughts.

16. Israel Gershoni and James P. Jankowski, *Redefining the Egyptian Nation, 1930–1945* (Cambridge, UK: Cambridge University Press, 1995), 210.

17. See Robert R. Bowie, *Suez, 1956* (New York: Oxford University Press, 1974).

18. See Michael N. Barnett, *Dialogues in Arab Politics* (New York: Columbia University Press, 1998), and Malcolm Kerr, *The Arab Cold War* (London: Oxford University Press, 1967).

19. Gershoni and Jankowski, *Redefining the Egyptian Nation*, 163.

20. David Zeidan, "The Copts—Equal, Protected or Persecuted? The Impact of Islamization on Muslim-Christian Relations in Modern Egypt," *Islam and Christian-Muslim Relations* 10, no. 1 (1999): 56.

21. "Secularist" women interviewed by Nadje Al-Ali often defined a secular society as one in which Copts and Muslims were equally free to practice their religions, not as a soci-

ety (or a state) hostile toward religion. Nadje Al-Ali, *Secularism, Gender and the State in the Middle East* (Cambridge, UK: Cambridge University Press, 2000).

22. Zeidan, "The Copts," 64.

23. Paul Sedra, "Class Cleavages and Ethnic Conflict: Coptic Christian Communities in Modern Egypt," *Islam and Christian-Muslim Relations* 10, no. 2 (July 1999): 224.

24. Sedra, "Class Cleavages," 239.

25. World Values Survey 9062000, Question G015, "Which of the following best describes you?"

26. Gregory Starrett, *Putting Islam to Work: Education, Politics and Religious Transformation in Egypt* (Berkeley: University of California Press, 1998), 91. Also Asef Bayat, *Making Islam Democratic: Social Movements and the Post-Islamist Turn* (Stanford, CA: Stanford University Press, 2007), 147–154.

27. See Charles Hirshkind, "The Ethics of Listening: Cassette-Sermon Audition in Contemporary Egypt," *American Ethnologist* 28, no. 3 (August 2001): 623–649.

28. Al-Ali, *Secularism.*

29. Emad El-Din Shahin, "Political Islam in Egypt, CEPS Working Document #266" (May 2007), 3.

30. See note 201 in Bayat, *Making Islam Democratic,* 250.

31. Eldon J. Eisenach, *The Next Religious Establishment* (Lanham, MD: Rowman & Littlefield, 2000), 51.

32. On the salafiyya movement see Malcolm Kerr, *Islamic Reform: The Political and Legal Theories of Muhammad Abduh and Rashid Rida* (Berkeley: University of California Press, 1966); also Elie Kedourie, *Afghani and Abduh: An Essay on Religious Unbelief and Political Activism in Islam* (New York: Humanities Press, 1966).

33. Mitchell, *The Society of Muslim Brothers,* 326–327.

34. Meir Hatina, "On the Margins of Consensus: The Call to Separate Religion and State in Modern Egypt," *Middle Eastern Studies* 36, no. 1 (January 2000): 36.

35. Hatina, "On the Margins of Consensus," 50.

36. Sayyid Qutb, *A Child from the Village,* ed. and trans. John Calvert and William Shepard (Syracuse, NY: Syracuse University Press, 2004).

37. Sayyid Qutb, *Milestones* (Indianapolis: American Trust, 1990).

38. See Muhammad Abd al-Salam Faraj, *The Neglected Duty: The Creed of Sadat's Assassins and the Creed of the Islamic Resurgence in the Middle East,* ed. and trans. Johannes J. G. Jansen (New York: Macmillan, 1986).

39. Bayat, *Making Islam Democratic,* 141–142.

40. Malika Zeghal, *Gardiens de l'Islam: Les oulémas d'Azhar dans l'Egypte contemporaine* (Paris: Fondation nationale des sciences politiques, 1996), 156.

41. Hatina, "On the Margins of Consensus," 57.

42. William E. Shepard, "Muhammad Sai'd al'Ashmawi and the Application of the Sharia in Egypt," *International Journal of Middle East Studies* 28, no. 1 (February 1996): 43ff.

43. See Denis J. Sullivan and Sana Abed-Kotob, *Islam in Contemporary Egypt: Civil Society vs. the State* (Boulder, CO: Lynne Rienner, 1999).

44. For Bayat this follows from the success of the Islamist movement in Egypt, which has nonetheless failed to produce revolution. Iran achieved revolution without an Islamist movement, in his view.

45. See Jakob Skovgaard-Petersen, *Defining Islam for the Egyptian State: Muftis and Fatwas of the Dār al-Iftā* (Leiden, Netherlands: Brill, 1997). Also see Zeghal, *Gardiens de l'Islam,* and her chapter, "'The Re-centering' of Religious Knowledge and Discourse: The Case of al-Azhar in Twentieth-Century Egypt," in Robert W. Hefner and Mohammad Qasim Zaman, eds., *Schooling Islam: The Culture and Politics of Modern Muslim Education* (Princeton, NJ: Princeton University Press, 2007).

46. See Sullivan and Abed-Kotob, *Islam in Contemporary Egypt,* for a general survey.

47. Zeghal treats Azhar as a highly complicated institution that functions within and without the political sphere, one exercising some influence from within partly because it also exercises influence from without. See *Gardiens de l'Islam,* especially chapters 6 and 7.

48. Crecelius, "The Ulama and the State in Modern Egypt," 362.

49. See the magnificent studies by Jakob Skovgaard-Petersen and Malika Zeghal referred to above.

50. See Crecelius, "The Ulama and the State in Modern Egypt," chapter 1.

51. Ibid., chapter 3.

52. Mitchell, *The Society of Muslim Brothers,* 298.

53. Sayed Khatab, "Al-Hudaybi's Influence on the Development of Islamist Movements in Egypt," *The Muslim World* 91 (Fall 2001): 453.

54. Sullivan and Abed-Kotob, *Islam in Contemporary Egypt,* 59.

55. Ibid., 20.

56. Maurits S. Berger, "Apostasy and Public Policy in Contemporary Egypt: An Evaluation of Recent Cases from Egypt's Highest Courts," *Human Rights Quarterly* 25, no. 3 (August 2003): 740. See also Baber Johansen, "Apostasy as Objective and Depersonalized Fact: Two Recent Egyptian Court Judgments," *Social Research* 70, no. 3 (Fall 2003): 687–710.

57. Norris and Inglehart, *Sacred and Secular,* chapter 6.

58. Daniel Lerner, *The Passing of Traditional Society: Modernizing the Middle East* (New York: Free Press of Glencoe, 1958).

59. *Palace Walk,* trans. William Maynard Hutchins and Olive E. Kenny (New York: Doubleday, 1991); *Palace of Desire,* trans. Hutchins and Kenny (New York: Doubleday, 1991); and *Sugar Street,* trans. Hutchins and Botros Samaan (New York: Anchor, 1993).

60. Mamoun Fandy, "Egypt's Islamic Group: Regional Revenge?" *Middle East Journal* 48, no. 4 (Autumn 1994): 611–625.

61. Gilles Kepel, *Jihad: Expansion et déclin de l'islamisme* (Paris: Gallimard, 2000).

62. See Sullivan and Abed Kotob, *Islam in Contemporary Egypt,* 25–35.

63. Starrett, *Putting Islam to Work,* 6.

64. Ibid., chapter 2.

65. Starrett says 31 percent of elementary school time was devoted to the Quran in 1903, 11 percent to religion, and 29 percent to Arabic.

66. See Starrett, *Putting Islam to Work,* 129–135, for discussion of the teaching of Islam in elementary schools.

67. Bradley J. Cook, "Islam and Egyptian Higher Education: Student Attitudes," *Comparative Education Review* 45, no. 3 (August 2001): 379–409.

68. "It eclipses all other institutions, programs, and facilities, including the mosque, the home, radio and television broadcasting, and print in the importance attributed to it as a publicly directing Islamizing force." Starrett, *Putting Islam to Work,* 115.

69. Leila Ahmed, *Women and Gender in Islam* (New Haven, CT: Yale University Press, 1992), 244.

70. Saba Mahmood, "Feminist Theory, Embodiment, and the Docile Agent: Some Reflections on the Egyptian Islamic Revival," *Cultural Anthropology* 16, no. 2 (May 2001): 202–236.

71. Mark Tessler and Jodi Nachtwey, "Religion and International Conflict: An Individual-Level Analysis," in Tessler, ed., *Area Studies and Social Science: Strategies for Understanding Middle East Politics* (Bloomington: Indiana University Press, 1999), 106, 113.

72. Sarah Ben Néfissa, "Citoyenneté et participation en Egypte: l'Action vertueuse selon la Gami'yya Shari'iyya," *Monde Arabe Maghreb Machrek* 167 (January–March 2000): 4.

73. Baudouin Dupret, "Justice égyptienne, moralité publique et pouvoir politique," *Monde Arabe Maghreb Machrek* 167 (January–March 2000): 31.

74. Jean-Noël Ferrié and Saâida Radi, "Consensus national et identité morale: le sida comme analyzeur de la société égyptienne," *Monde Arabe Maghreb Machrek* (January–March 2000): 36.

75. This is the general perspective of the three articles from *Monde Arab Maghreb Machrek* (January–March 2000) cited above.

76. D. E. Smith, *Religion and Political Development*, 250.

4

The Transformation of Judaism in Israel

The state of Israel illustrates the inadequacy of dichotomies between secular and religious, modern and traditional. A product of Jewish nationalism, Israel is thoroughly modern in its economic, social, and political orientation, but it is not secular. Some dimensions of law bear the imprint of religious law (halakha), and religious institutions intertwine with those of the state. Yet the mixing of religion and politics in Israel reflects the decisions of an elected legislature always dominated by secular elites. Religious parties have influenced political outcomes but have failed to win control of the state. Secular elites of the Left and the Right have accepted the collaboration of the religious parties and concurred in funding religious institutions, in order to perpetuate secular dominance. Only small minorities at the two ends of the spectrum, secularist ideologues and some ultraorthodox groups, find the Israeli pastiche of secular and religious unacceptable. That is one reason why the political system has been stable.

The evolution of the Israeli system, from the early articulations of Zionism through independence to the transformation produced by the Six-Day War of 1967, illustrates the primacy of politics. Both Orthodoxy and Zionism emerged in nineteenth-century Europe in response to the emancipation of Jews from a ghettoized existence. The movement toward Orthodoxy, which eventually produced a political party called Agudat Israel, responded to the breakdown of the communitarian organization (the *kehilla*) of Jewish life.[1] Orthodoxy sought to fight assimilation by ensuring a separate life for Jews in Europe. Zionism responded to the apparent failure of assimilative processes and called for regeneration of the Jewish people, fragmented by geography and rejected in many societies. It was a modern, secular movement driven by a political objective.

Politics, not religion, drove the Jews toward independence, and politics dictated forgoing a constitution opposed by the forces of religion. David Ben-Gurion, a socialist who led the Jewish community in Palestine to independence, shunned the separation of religion and state because he wanted to control religion.[2] Twenty years later it was politics, not religion, that pushed Israel to victory in 1967 and to domination of the West Bank and Gaza Strip areas. The conquest triggered an outburst of religious enthusiasm, however, that fostered pressures for settlement and long-term retention of the conquered territories.

Ben-Gurion, the first prime minister of Israel (1948–1953 and 1956–1963), had no reason to feel threatened by the power of religion, nor did he probably imagine that state control would eliminate religious influence on the state. Were he alive today, he might nonetheless be astounded at the degree to which the controllers are controlled, and the extent to which the religious organizations and authorities controlled by the state have strengthened themselves to play a part in their own control. The state of Israel, though surely not in full control of even official Jewish Orthodoxy in Israel, has reshaped the Jewish religion within and without its boundaries. The religion that shapes Israeli politics bears the distinct mark of Israeli policy. Even anti-Zionist ultraorthodox groups have been seduced into playing the democratic game and into acknowledging the supremacy of positive law over Jewish religious law, the halakha.

Israel declares itself a state that is both Jewish and democratic. Whether it can be both remains open to question. Full democracy would imply equal rights for non-Jews, mainly Palestinian Arabs, who are predominantly Muslim and who might come to be the majority. It would mean equal treatment for Reformist and Conservative congregations in Israel, and under the Law of Return acceptance of immigrants who are not Jewish by halakhic standards, which define Jews as persons whose mothers are Jewish or persons converted by Orthodox procedures. For those on the secular end of the spectrum, a "Jewish" state suggests imposition of halakhic law on those who do not wish to live by it. It evokes rigorous enforcement of the Sabbath and of Jewish dietary rules (*kashrut*) and alienation of much of the American diaspora, dominated as it is by Reform, Conservative, and secular Jews. For Arabs who are citizens of Israel living within the borders established by the armistice of 1949, a Jewish state means formal citizenship but not full rights.

Judaism does not appear inherently more democratic than Islam or Christianity. (In fact, Jewish history provides only the sketchiest of suggestions about what a Jewish state might look like.[3] Israel is the first such state since classical times.) While some writers have found pluralistic tendencies in the Jewish tradition, it is God rather than human beings who dominates the Jewish version of history.[4] Many Jews who have resisted the Hellenistic and modern conception of the world as man-centered have joined the hurly-burly of

Israel's democracy despite theology. If Israel is largely democratic today, it is despite Judaism, not because of it.

Can the Israeli mix of secularism and religion, of Jewishness and democracy, of modernity and tradition, be maintained? Is the relationship between religion and politics conducive to political stability? Boat designers think in terms of primary and secondary stability. Primary stability is how a boat responds to small waves. A boat with good secondary stability can undergo considerable rocking but nonetheless show excellent resistance to capsizing. In the case of Israel, sharp debates about identity, the role of institutions, political culture, and ideology suggest primary instability fostered in part by religious issues. To listen to debates in the Israeli parliament, read the local press, or monitor the platforms of political parties is to see that the boat rocks continuously. Some critics have predicted the ship of state will capsize, but this has not happened.[5] Democratic procedures have so far garnered legitimacy and led to a continuous retouching of the balance, and secondary stability has been achieved. But, to the chagrin of political scientists, the result does not conform to any external model. In practice, the Israeli polity permits both the observant and the nonobservant to go on claiming it as their own, "Jewish and democratic," without being fully satisfied that it is either one.

Identity

Religion shapes Israeli identity. It is that identity that causes critics to charge that Israel is a racist state. The opening line of the 1948 Declaration of the Establishment of the State of Israel, which is also called the Declaration of Independence, proclaims: "Eretz Israel, The Land of Israel, was the birthplace of the Jewish People," and goes on to declare the establishment of "the Jewish State in Palestine, to be called Israel." Yet, the same document promises the non-Jewish inhabitants of the Israeli state "full and equal citizenship and due representation in its bodies and institutions—provisional or permanent." While the declaration promises that the state will be "open to the immigration of Jews from all countries of their dispersion," it guarantees the "full social and political equality of all" Israeli citizens, "without distinction of race, creed or sex." The perplexing paradoxes contained in this document frame the debates that still dominate Israeli political discourse over national identity.

Who composes this "Jewish People"? What is the relationship between the Jewish people and the Jewish religion? What constitutes the Jewish character of the state of Israel? Is it possible for the Israeli state to be Jewish in character while guaranteeing full citizenship to all of its inhabitants?

"Secular" Versions of Israeli Identity

For the first twenty years of Israeli statehood, Labor Zionism attempted to define Israeli identity by linking it to Jewish tradition without subordinating political decision-makers to traditional religious authorities and to the ritual practices and the theological worldview of Orthodox Jewry. Labor Zionism attempted to remove religious ritual and rabbinical law from the core of Jewish identity and replace it with a common nationalistic affiliation (*am Yisrael*) and with a historical connection to the Land of Israel (*Eretz Yisrael*) and the state of Israel (*Midinat Yisrael*). The construction of the state and the settlement of the land was, for the Labor Zionists, the reentry of the Jewish people into the history of nations. The attainment of a national homeland meant that the Jewish identity could be rebuilt through the worldly activities of settling the land and forging political independence.

The founders regarded the otherworldly orientation of the Orthodox (*dati*) community, with its emphasis on ritual observance and religious study, as a dysfunctional symptom of the Jewish nation's long exile from its homeland and inability to govern itself politically.[6] Rather than looking to religion, the founders sought to create a national identity based on cooperative effort to build a new Jewish civilization in the Land of Israel. "For this generation," Ben-Gurion wrote, "this land is more holy than for the tens of generations of Jews who believed in its historical and religious sanctity; for it has been sanctified by our sweat, our work, and our blood."[7] For Ben-Gurion, the labor of the settlers preempted the Torah as the basis of Jewish claims.

Far from abandoning tradition, however, the Labor Zionists tried to seize the "spirit" or basic values of the Jewish religion and present them as moral and cultural foundations of the Jewish nation. The Declaration of Independence, though it makes scant mention of religious ritual and law, credits the Jewish people with the creation of "cultural values of national and universal significance" and with giving "to the world the eternal Book of Books." This statement acknowledges the connection between Jewish nationhood and Jewish religious texts and ethics. Yet it describes the Bible not as a divine mandate but as a cultural accomplishment of the Jewish nation, and designates Jewish values not as a binding moral code but as an aspect of Jewish national character and ethos. Nahum Levin, a member of Ben-Gurion's team, went further:

> We have freed the biblical texts of their archaic quality and restored to them their concrete content: "Six days thou shalt labor—Thou shalt love

thy neighbor as thyself—that which is altogether just shalt thou pursue—
Proclaim liberty throughout all the land unto all her inhabitants" . . . These
have become foundations of the world view which we have sought to achieve
in the cooperative and communal settlements in particular, and in the Labor
movement in general.[8]

Labor sought to invoke Jewish values without reference to rabbinic Judaism
or belief in God. The "New Jew" would be the product of collective political
and social endeavor.

This effort to define the Jewish state by land and labor failed on two
counts. It did not incorporate many who were already living in the land, including Orthodox Jews, as well as those beyond its borders who were not part
of the effort.[9] The notion of identity constructed on the basis of collective effort to build the Land of Israel excluded Diaspora Jews. Were those who declined to help build the state really Jews? Moreover, the symbols Labor
Zionism used to forge a Jewish nation came from the theological, ritual, and
cultural tradition referred to as the Jewish religion. Ben-Gurion acknowledged this stubborn reality when he stated: "Even for a free-thinking Jew like
myself, our faith is still something that requires respect and any Jew who does
not revere Judaism in one way or another is alien to Jewish history."[10]

Even the Jews who immigrated in the first years of independence fit awk-
wardly into the dominant notion of the "New Jew." Between 1948 and 1951,
the number of Jews living in Israel more than doubled.[11] Most of the immigrants who arrived during the first twenty years of Israeli statehood came
from the Muslim countries of the Middle East and North Africa. They had
not experienced European discrimination or suffered from the Holocaust.
Religious practice defined them as Jews, whereas the concept of the "New
Jew" depended on a Labor Zionist conception of Jewish ethnicity.

In the 1960s and 1970s, as these Oriental immigrants (Mizrachim)[12] began to make their influence felt, and especially after Israel's conquest of the
Sinai, the West Bank, and the Golan Heights in 1967, the discourse of Israeli identity began to shift from what Shafir and Peled call "republican
virtue"—identified with collectivism, settlement, labor, and state-building—
toward a new form of reference they call "ethno-nationalism."[13] This new
discourse pulled the Jewish heritage from the periphery to the center of Jewish identity but still stopped short of embracing religious orthodoxy. Prime
Minister Golda Meir expressed the shift with her call for "the deepening of
Jewish education, an increased awareness and understanding of the Jewish
faith and heritage" that she argued were crucial to the "spiritual continuity of

our people and the reservoir of commitment and strength for the future of Israel."[14] Ethno-nationalism credited Jewish customs and culture with preserving Jewish life in a hostile gentile world.

In this emerging perspective, the Holocaust became central to Israeli identity. Whereas the concept of the "New Jew" treated the Holocaust as a product of Jewish passivity attributable to the "Old Jew," ethno-nationalism extolled instances of Jewish resistance to persecution, such as the Warsaw Ghetto Uprising. The subtitle of the Vad Vashem Holocaust memorial, begun in the late 1950s, reads: "Memorial Authority for the Holocaust and Bravery," and in the name of the official day of Holocaust remembrance: "Memorial Day for the Holocaust and Ghetto Uprisings." Israeli identity emerged from a tradition of suffering and bravery.

This emphasis on persecution and resistance fit conveniently with Israel's ongoing conflict with its Arab neighbors. The resistance of the Israeli Defense Forces (IDF) against Arab aggression echoed the rebellion of the Jewish communities of the Holocaust against gentile oppressors. The central myth of the Jewish nation, therefore, became the heroic resilience of the Jewish people and their vigilant determination to defend and maintain their culture (including religious traditions) rather than the Labor Zionist myth of a transcendent "New Jew" whose identity sprang from cultivation of a new Jewish civilization.

Labor Zionism and ethno-nationalism have both cloaked the state in traditional symbols of the Jewish religion for secular reasons. The Israeli flag bears the *magen* David (star or shield of David), a Jewish symbol said to date from the period of the First Temple (957–597 BCE). Israel adopted the seven-branch menorah, another ancient religious symbol, as its national symbol. Biblical verses adorn Israeli government buildings and stamps, and figure frequently in speeches by Israeli politicians.[15] Furthermore, as a result of compromise in Israel's constituent assembly, the Israeli parliament (Knesset) contains the same number of representatives as the Great Knesset, a governing body of the Second Temple period (516 bce–70 CE).[16] Saturday, the traditional Sabbath, is the official day of rest in Israel, and the state sponsors ceremonies on Jewish holidays.

Doubts about the Jewishness of Israel

These gestures give substance to the Declaration of Independence, which proclaims Israel a Jewish state, but they do not constitute divine sanction. From the Labor Zionist perspective, Israel is Jewish because Jews have built it. In the ethno-nationalist ethos, it is Jewish because Jews have suffered, and Israel is a refuge. For many religious Jews these standards do not suffice. Religious authorities do not rule the state; the halakha, "defined by religious authorities and encompassing all aspects of human activity," does not preempt or even guide positive law in most domains. Most Israelis reject the claim of some religious Zionists that Israel represents a step toward messianic redemption. The ultraorthodox and some secularists deny that the state has any religious significance whatsoever. Finally, in the eyes of some, the effort to define nationality independently of religion and to accord equal rights to all religious groups threatens Israel's identity as a Jewish state.

Since the first stirrings of modern Zionism, elements of the Orthodox Jewish community have regarded the "secular Zionist" movement with deep suspicion. For these rabbis and their followers, to admit that the modern state of Israel was Jewish in character or to acknowledge any relationship between Jewish identity and Israeli nationality was considered blasphemous. The memory of many false messiahs, including Jesus, Bar Kochba, and a seventeenth-century rabbi named Shabatei Tzvi, drove the prominent rabbinical authorities of the Diaspora into a deep conservatism regarding the migration of the Jewish people to the Holy Land. In the main, these rabbis taught that only miraculous, divine intervention could transport the people to the land.

To acknowledge Israel as a Jewish state carried troubling messianic implications. Benjamin Mintz, a prominent member of an Orthodox political party, triggered scandal when he admitted to saying that the formation of the Israeli state "might" have been the first step toward redemption.[17] The leaders of the Jewish state considered themselves secular, even atheist, and the laws they adopted diverged from the mandates of the Torah. Thus, for Mintz to acknowledge the state's Jewish character signified approval of what the Orthodox rabbinical establishment considered an illegitimate form of Judaism.[18]

A group known as Neturei Karta (Defenders of the City) and its leader, Amram Bloy, expressed an extreme version of this ideological conviction. The existence of a secular state in the Promised Land so appalled Bloy that he refused to recognize the legitimacy of the Israeli state, declared his unwillingness to defend the country, and announced that Neturei Karta would accept the rule of "any nation that the United Nations would choose, or the rule and protection of all of them together."[19] For this faction of the Orthodox community there could be absolutely no concrescence of Jewish and Israeli identities.

Elite intellectuals of the Israeli Left, including a group of scholars from Jerusalem's Hebrew University, formed a group known as Brit Shalom (Covenant of Peace) that distinguished Jewish national identity from the identity of the state. This group advocated the foundation of a binational (Arab-Jewish) state in the Land of Israel and curtailment of Jewish immigration to mandatory Palestine. Martin Buber, himself an Orthodox Jew and one of the leading Jewish scholars of the twentieth century, insisted that establishing peaceful coexistence with the Arabs was the primary religious challenge of the Jewish people in modern times.[20] Members of the peace movement including Hashomer Hatzair, a party based in utopian communities called kibbutzim, and later the Israeli New Left made similar arguments on behalf of binationalism.[21]

An even more extreme attempt to dissociate Jewish national identification from the Israeli state came from Uriel Halperin, publicly known as Yohanan Ratosh, a charismatic Israeli poet and the founder of the Hebrew Youth movement in the 1940s. The Hebrew Youth, commonly referred to as the Canaanites in the Israeli media, argued for the existence of a "Hebrew" nation that included people living in the Land of Israel and other parts of the Middle East. "Now it is possible," Ratosh declared before the Knesset, "for a new Hebrew nation to arise, young and strong and mighty, the liberator of its homeland . . . hand in hand with all its inhabitants . . . Jews, Christians, Moslems, Druze, and others."[22] The Hebrew Youth's formulation of a "Hebrew nation" that enveloped Jews and non-Jews in a Middle Eastern superstate constituted a radical secular effort to dissociate religion from national identity in Israel.

Who Is a Jew?

Both Labor Zionists and ethno-nationalists assume that Jews are an identifiable group. In 1950 the Knesset passed the Law of Return, which gave every Jew the right to join the nation "as an *oleh*"—one who immigrates by "rising up" to citizenship, but the Law of Return offers no conclusive specification of who qualifies as a Jew. Quite predictably this legislation generated long and intense debate. In 1958 the Knesset established a three-person committee to suggest a legal framework for determining who qualified for Jewish status. It proposed that "any person declaring in good faith that he is a Jew shall be registered as a Jew and no additional proof shall be required."[23] The Orthodox member of the committee resigned from the cabinet in protest. Leaving many issues unsettled, the Knesset went on to adopt a definition of Jewish identity that closely resembled the halakhic rule.

Some of the unsettled issues arose in a pair of court cases. In 1969 Binyamin Shalit, an Israeli citizen born of a Jewish mother, married a non-Jewish woman outside the country and settled in Israel. He then challenged the Israeli government to make the identity cards of his children say: "Nationality: Jew; Religion: None." Although Shalit admitted that his children did not qualify as members of the Jewish religion, he argued that they should be accepted as members of the Jewish nation. Despite much ambivalence, the Supreme Court found legal reasons to deny Shalit's request.[24]

The 1970 case of "Brother Daniel" exposed further contradictions in Israeli legislation. Brother Daniel was born in Yugoslavia to a Jewish mother. Named Oswald Rufeisen, he survived the Nazi occupation of Yugoslavia in a Catholic monastery. Later he became a Catholic monk, changing his name to Brother Daniel. He then requested that the Israeli government grant him permission to immigrate to Israel as a Jewish oleh, become an Israeli citizen, and live in a Catholic monastery in Jerusalem. Refused an oleh visa, he appealed to the high court, using the Talmudic argument that "a Jew, even if he has sinned, remains a Jew."[25] The Supreme Court ruled against Brother Daniel and denied him Israeli citizenship. In doing so the court acknowledged a distinction between Jewish religious identification and Jewish national identification.

In response to political pressures and the legal crisis caused by these cases, the Knesset amended the Law of Return in 1970. The amended law declared: "For the purposes of this Law, 'Jew' means a person who was born of a Jewish mother or has become converted to Judaism and who is not a member of another religion." This change confirmed that only persons who qualify as halakhic Jews may become members of the Jewish nation but also established that some halakhic Jews, who happen to have adopted another religion, may be denied legal Jewish status. The amended law also declared:

> The rights of a Jew under this Law and the rights of an *oleh* under the Nationality Law, 5712–1952, as well as the rights of an *oleh* under any other enactment, are also vested in a child and a grandchild of a Jew, the spouse of a Jew, the spouse of a child of a Jew and the spouse of a grandchild of a Jew, except for a person who has been a Jew and has voluntarily changed his religion.

This amendment diminished the importance of Jewish national identity by permitting close relatives of Jews to attain oleh status and Israeli citizenship.

This amendment has affected subsequent immigrant groups. As many as a fourth of those who have immigrated from the former USSR under this amended Law of Return are not halakhically Jewish.[26] Yet there is no sharp divergence in political and social behaviors between these people and the rest of the Jewish population. These immigrants have, in effect, joined the Jewish nation without joining the Jewish religion. To become Jewish in a religious sense, these non-Jewish immigrants would have to undergo conversion, and under the 1947 status quo agreement—a letter from David Ben-Gurion to the leadership of Agudat Israel—only institutionalized Orthodox rabbis can administer conversion in the state of Israel. Orthodox leaders and politicians fought fiercely against establishing a Joint Conversion Institute, which would have given Reform and Conservative (*masorti*) rabbis a role in the conversion process.

It matters who is a Jew in Israel. The approximately 23 percent of Israel's legal citizens, roughly 1.5 million people, who are not considered Jews under Israeli law, most of them Arabs, do not enjoy full citizenship rights in the state of Israel. While the Declaration of the Establishment of the State of Israel promises non-Jews "full citizenship," the religious symbols of these "minority" populations do not appear in Israel's institutions. Although minority religions receive funding from the state, the monies come from a fund separate from the one that subsidizes Jewish (Orthodox) institutions. Furthermore, the Israel Land Authority controls 93 percent of the land within the pre-1967 boundaries of Israel and decides who is entitled to lease property for which purposes.[27] Serving the needs of Jewish immigrants has been a primary purpose of public policy since the founding of the Jewish National Fund (KKL) in 1901.

Recent developments suggest some willingness to lessen the privileges of Jewish identity. The Supreme Court decision in the Qaadan case of 2000 challenged the right of the Jewish National Fund to discriminate between Jews and non-Jews in leasing land, and amendments to the Law of Return extended rights at least as far as relatives of Jews. These changes constitute an ideal of citizenship more in line with liberal-democratic ideology. The recent activism of the Supreme Court, coupled with the Knesset's adoption of two basic laws, Human Dignity and Liberty, and Freedom of Occupation, constitutes a gradual shift toward a value system that prizes equal application of the law over Jewish collective objectives. However, both the Law of Return and the Israel land laws grant Jews preferential status as citizens of the state of Israel.

Israel's Jewish identity has proved stable in its inconsistency. On the one hand, the state cannot renounce its Jewishness without undermining its reason for being. Hard as Zionists might try, they did not succeed in defining a Jewish people without some reference to religion. Beliefs, scholarship, rabbinic leadership, common rituals and ceremonies—all these held Jewish communities together in the Diaspora. An Israel without Jewishness cuts itself off from the Diaspora and from its links with Jewish history. On the other hand,

Israel cannot adopt unmitigated Orthodox definitions of Jewishness without cutting itself off from the nonorthodox Diaspora and from important elements of its own population, such as the Russian immigrants. Even a watereddown commitment to Jewishness makes it difficult if not impossible for Israel to achieve the democratic commitment contained in the Declaration of Independence. Non-Jews lack full status in the state. Arabs, who are Christians and Muslims, are third-class citizens behind the Jews of European origin (Ashkenazim), who enjoy primacy in the society, and the Mizrachim, who are still struggling for parity with the Europeans.

The conflict between Israelis and Palestinians may help stabilize the inconsistencies inherent in Israeli identity. The unexpected victory of 1967 opened the way for a new religious Zionism committed to do God's work in carrying settlement into the West Bank and Gaza—lands linked to Jewish history. These initiatives tipped Israeli identity toward the religious. The ratio of Israelis who put their Jewishness ahead of their identity as Israelis increased slightly and became a majority. The settlers and their supporters saw themselves as Jews doing the work of God. They attacked "mere" Israelis, who wanted to trade land for peace with the Arab states and the Palestinians. More generally this conflict reinforces Israelis' self-perceptions as a persecuted minority. Until this conflict ends, it seems unlikely Israeli society will embrace full democratic inclusion of its non-Jewish citizens.

Israel's identity remains distinctly Jewish. The Jewishness of the state results from a set of political decisions that reflect divergent and even contradictory notions of Judaism and Jewishness. The state remains too Jewish for some and insufficiently Jewish for others. The privileges accorded Jewish identity make the goal of full and equal citizenship for non-Jews unattainable. The elaborate use of religious symbols to legitimate the secular state strike some as a travesty. Yet many religious Zionists see the state as halfhearted and even hypocritical in its commitment to its sacred mission, the realization of God's promise to the Jews. Ultimately the Jewishness of Israel reflects a set of political decisions taken to realize the ambitions of Zionism. Nationalism requires an identity for a people, and no one has yet devised a definition of the Jewish people that does not refer to religion. The religious identity of the state is not a result of religious imperatives but of nationalist necessity.

Ideology

Israel's Declaration of Independence frames one of the central debates over Israeli political ideology. Ratified in 1948, it promises that the Israeli state will be "based on freedom, justice, and peace as envisaged by the prophets of Israel." While the document recognizes the visions of the Jewish prophets, it denies political authority to rabbis and makes no claim that the law of the state will reflect or abide by the traditional rabbinical laws of the Jewish religion. Instead the declaration explicitly promises that elected, regular authorities will govern the state of Israel in accordance with a constitution written by an elected constituent assembly. How much and in what ways should the law of the Jewish state reflect the religious law of the Jewish tradition? Should the Jewish state be governed exclusively by elected politicians and bureaucrats? Or should the traditional leaders of the Jewish faith who serve as interpreters of divine law hold positions of authority?

Pre-State Discourse

The most powerful politicians of the Zionist movement had no interest in turning over government power to rabbinical leaders. The religious conceptions of these men and women reflected the socialist and democratic ideals of the modern Zionist movement. The founders framed their call for the Jewish state in terms of political necessity, as had Theodor Herzl. They saw themselves as champions of a homeless people dispossessed from its native land, not of a movement to create a religious state. David Ben-Gurion, Israel's first prime minister, assured the devout that the government would show "understanding of your religious feelings and those of others," and would be "devoted to the values of Judaism" but would not make Israel into a theocratic state or impose religious law upon the people.[28] In the constitutional debate that followed the ratification of the declaration, a member of the Knesset loyal to Ben-Gurion proclaimed: "As a socialist and an atheist, I could never endorse a program that included a religious model."[29]

Few ultraorthodox Jews of the pre-state period regarded the Zionist project as divine. While Orthodox Jews did regard the Land of Israel (Eretz Yisrael) as sacred, most did not attribute holiness to the state of Israel (Midinat Israel), whose architects largely considered themselves secular Jews. Consequently, few Orthodox Jews believed in a divine mandate for the creation of a halakhic state and were thus willing to accept compromise on religious matters.

In the early nineteenth century, much of the Orthodox establishment evoked a rabbinical tradition that discouraged the formation of a Jewish political entity in the land of Palestine. Although Orthodox Jews everywhere believed that the "End of Days" and the coming of the Messiah would eventually bring the dispersed Jewish communities back to their homeland, most Orthodox rabbis taught that this migration would be of a miraculous nature. The Mizrachi movement among Orthodox Jews began a cautious shift in this long-held tradition. Created in Vilna in 1902 among Orthodox delegates to the Zionist Congress, Mizrachi sought to foster cooperation between two separate responses to modernism: Orthodoxy and Zionism.[30] In 1912, Agudat Israel split with Mizrachi to engage in Jewish settlement of Palestine outside the auspices of the World Zionist Organization. Although they supported the migration of Jews to Palestine and the foundation of a state in Israel, both groups regarded the secular Zionist movement with suspicion. But both came to cooperate with the World Zionist Organization on a practical level during the 1940s, when European persecution of Jews reached catastrophic proportions.

Suspicion of Labor Zionism led a large portion of deeply Orthodox Jews in Palestine in 1948 to reject the formation of a halakhic state and to deny that the modern Israeli state was holy or theologically significant. These groups feared that an Israeli state claiming a basis in modern Judaism would undermine the Orthodox cultural establishment in Israel. They attempted to persuade the Labor Zionists to refrain from engaging in Jewish cultural activities.

In the early twentieth century, however, there emerged an alternative Orthodox discourse that invested the Jewish state with religious meaning. Rav Abraham Isaac Kook argued that the establishment of a Jewish state in the Land of Israel was an "advent of redemption" and had not only religious but also messianic implications.[31] Yet he was willing to accept that Israel would at least temporarily be a secular, nontheocratic state. While he hoped and anticipated that Jews who had rejected rabbinic authority and traditional law would repent in the final stage of messianic redemption, he welcomed the work of the Labor Zionists in taking the land and creating a space for the physical salvation of the Jewish nation. These were necessary conditions for the spiritual salvation he believed would come later. Kook helped to create a discourse that permitted the formation of a sacred but nonhalakhic Israeli state. These Orthodox discourses eased the burden of the early Zionist leaders, who feared and rejected the idea of a halakhic state. Significant portions of the Orthodox population of Palestine and important Orthodox leaders discouraged involvement in the Jewish state, lest the integrity of traditional Judaism be compromised. Other Orthodox Jews and leaders accepted the sanctity of the state of Israel without demanding that it be governed immediately by religious law or religious leaders. Consequently, no significant movement for theocratic government surfaced as the Jewish community in Palestine (the Yishuv) prepared for statehood.

The Founding

Lack of demand for theocracy did not, however, prevent fierce debate over the role of halakhic law in Israel and the allocation of governmental power to Israel's religious leaders. Those questions dominated debate in the Constituent Assembly, which quickly declared itself the sovereign parliament, the Knesset, and eventually prevented adoption of a constitution. One member representing Agudat Israel argued that "only the Torah Law and tradition are sovereign in the life of Israel."[32] While the religious forces recognized that the creation of a halakhic state would be impossible, they fiercely opposed the drafting of a secular constitution they feared might sever the tie to the past.[33] "If the time is not yet ripe for our constitution to be based on the laws of our Torah," argued Agudat, "it is better that no constitution be passed and that we not be untrue."[34] The Knesset quit trying to draft a constitution, but the ideological battles over the role of religion in government were far from over.

Israeli leaders used two strategies of tempering ideological debates and creating a certain degree of ideological stability. Their first strategy was to frame policy and law so they conformed to the basic tenets of Jewish tradition even if they did not precisely reflect the halakha. David Ben-Gurion used this strategy frequently. In one speech he claimed, "Our activities and policy are guided not by economic considerations alone but by a political and social vision that we have inherited from our prophets and imbibed from the heritage of our greatest sages and the teachers of our own day."[35] Politicians such as Ben-Gurion embraced the political and social vision of Jewish religious leaders in an attempt to legitimate modern interpretations of ancient principles and traditions.

This rhetorical strategy required a clever ability to avoid discussing religious legitimacy with the Orthodox rabbinical establishment. Ben-Gurion insisted that the "Rock of Israel (*tsur* Israel)" was to be found in the "State of Israel and in the Book of Books."[36] And on at least one occasion, he referred to the modern Israeli state as the Third Kingdom, comparing it to the ancient Jewish communities of biblical times. By focusing on the Bible and on ancient Israeli civilization, Ben-Gurion attempted to steer ideological debate away from the Talmud and the halakha. This strategy permitted him to argue for the sanctity of state policies without deferring to the authority of contemporary religious authorities, who claimed to be the rightful interpreters of religious law.

Ben-Gurion's approach amounted to more than rhetoric. Attempts to embrace the basic principles of Judaism, and to couch legislation and institutions in the language of religious tradition, influenced the character of Israeli institutions and law. The status quo letter has long served as the foundation for political debate over religious issues in Israel. In this letter, Ben-Gurion promised that the religious character of the Jewish state would be respected and reflected in the policies and practices of the Israeli government. The first two points of the letter reflect the strategy of Israeli political leaders, described above. "Saturday shall be the national day of rest," the letter reads, and "the laws of *kashrut* will be observed in all government kitchens." These promises did not guarantee observance of halakha but committed the state to honor Jewish tradition in some domains.

To implement the promises of the status quo letter, the government passed the Law of Working Hours and Rest in 1951, limiting the workdays of Jewish employees and effectively barring most industrial activity on the Sabbath. Framed in modern legal language, the law did not, however, apply to self-employed Jews or to government utilities and services crucial to the proper functioning of the state. While the legislation honored a principle, it did not adhere to the letter of the halakha. Neither did it interfere with the practical necessities of the state.

A similar strategy led to compromise on kashrut. While the Israeli government was not willing to pressure its citizens to maintain these dietary laws in their own homes, the government did maintain kashrut in its kitchens and other facilities. Positive law prevented state-owned companies from importing pork and any other meat not slaughtered in accordance with religious law. The state hired Orthodox inspectors to ensure that military food was prepared according to religious standards. These and other compromises served to quell ideological conflict by covering state institutions with a veneer of religion. They went far enough to secure the continued participation of Orthodox Jews in government institutions, and especially in the military, without subordinating government authority to religious leadership.

The strategy of compromise proved insufficient. Traditional religious Jews, and the rabbinical establishment of Palestine, rejected Labor Zionism's efforts at modernizing Jewish tradition to fit a nationalist agenda. While many Orthodox Jews accepted compromise over the expression of religious ideals in the state's public activities, they would make no concessions in other domains. In response, Israeli leaders used a second strategy to soften ideological debates. The status quo letter promised that religious organizations would continue to receive funds from the state to maintain their autonomous school systems and that religious courts would have exclusive authority over matters of personal status, including marriage, divorce, conversion, and burial. The promises constituted small steps toward recognizing religious authority over particular, specified spheres.

Israeli citizens considered Jewish cannot engage in civil marriage within the state of Israel. Although the state recognizes civil marriages performed outside Israel, government employees appointed by religious courts of the fourteen religious denominations recognized by the Israeli government issue marriage certificates.[37] Judaism is but one of the fourteen, albeit the largest. These religious courts grant marriage licenses and perform ceremonies according to standards of religious law upheld by religious authorities in Israel. Governmentally recognized Jewish leaders supervise all conversions to Judaism and manage funerals and Jewish cemeteries.

In addition, the status quo agreement promises that "full autonomy of every education system will be guaranteed." At the state's inception, the Ministry of Education began to allocate funding among its many autonomous school systems according to the size of the populations they served. This includes explicitly Muslim, Christian, Druze, Bahai, and Jewish schools, which are free to teach religious curricula to their students as they see fit. By permitting autonomy, secular elites sought to dissuade religious groups from seeking influence over a broad spectrum of the state's laws and functions in return for domination of significant but specified and limited spheres of policy. While government officials handle a broad range of state functions according to codes of civil law, religious officials administer other domains according to their own interpretations of sacred texts and tradition.

The attempt to connect the law and institutions of the Israeli state apparatus to a modified version of Judaism, and the effort to grant specific spheres of influence to religious leaders and some autonomy to religious institutions constitute the two major strategies that early political leaders used to deal with the perplexing paradoxes of a Jewish republic. While protests over religious legislation did occasionally erupt, the early Israeli leadership managed to maintain a balance. Many religious leaders expressed discontent from time to time but also often articulated their gratitude to Ben-Gurion and his allies for their cooperation. Menahem Parosh of Agudat Israel said: "Ben-Gurion gave us more than anyone else, because he understood that if the state did not make concessions to us we would have to leave the country, and this he did not want."[38] So long as their own spheres of authority were not challenged or disturbed, Orthodox leaders could accept that the state of Israel did not abide by halakha or recognize their authority on other matters. And although some citizens rebelled fiercely when they thought religious leaders and authority figures had overstepped boundaries, few were willing to fight for their total disenfranchisement.

Ideological Shift

While there were occasional challenges to the status quo agreement, its basic lines prevailed through the first twenty turbulent years of Israeli history. Orthodox leaders had no practical ideas about how a halakhic state might be governed.[39] Because a modern nation-state must operate utilities, ensure security, and maintain other services, the Israeli government cannot observe the halakhic prescriptions of the Sabbath. Conversely, separation of religion and state did not seem possible or desirable. Most Israeli Jews, even those who consider themselves secular, wanted (and still want) the state to maintain its Jewish character for nationalistic reasons. Eliminating the symbolic manifestations of religious law would not resolve the contentious issues of education and military service. Most Israeli Jews have accepted the laws of the state of Israel as legitimate.[40]

The 1960s and 1970s, however, brought ideological shifts in the Israeli political landscape that eroded support for the fragile balance created by the status quo agreement. First, Israel absorbed more immigrants in comparison to its population than any other country.[41] Many of these immigrant groups belonged to religious communities. They did not share the ideals of the secular Zionists or support the idea of modernizing the Jewish faith to fit contemporary needs. Government mistreatment of the immigrants bred discontent, and attempts to indoctrinate them through education fomented hostility toward the ruling coalition. Second, two deeply traumatic events, the Six-Day War of 1967 and the Yom Kippur War of 1973, contributed to ideological reconfiguration. Although the stunning victory in 1967 left many with a feeling of elation and national pride, it ended with the Israeli occupation of vast territories and Arab populations that posed new and difficult questions. The more costly 1973 war had a deeply traumatic effect on the Israeli people and divided previously unified coalitions. It led to diplomatic negotiation and eventual peace with Egypt, but Israeli sentiment remained deeply divided about giving up more territory to create a Palestinian state.

The wars of 1967 and 1973 sparked shifts in Israel's most Orthodox communities. Rav Kook's son, Rabbi Zvi Yehuda Kook, interpreted the two battles and the acquisition of the historically and religiously significant areas of the West Bank as indicative of messianic times.[42] Through the institution of Merkaz Harav, a highly influential religious academy established by his father, the rabbi began to articulate religious arguments for expanding the Israeli state and settling the occupied territories. While Abraham Isaac Kook had argued that redemption of the land was a precursor to the spiritual redemption of the Jewish people and the world, Zvi Yehuda Kook portrayed the very conquest of the land as a holy endeavor.

A new generation of religious leaders began to utilize the vocabulary of Jewish tradition and to formulate a new ideology that justified and even commanded the forceful conquest of the Land of Israel. Rabbis such as Moshe Rom interpreted wars of conquest as "mandatory in Jewish tradition and argued against ceding any land to non-Jews as a religious sin."[43] Moshe Moskowitz, a leader of Agudat Israel, declared, "Do not doubt that the land and the people will find their mutual redemption."[44] These militant religious Zionists spread their ideas through a large network of yeshivas, academies of Jewish learning, where they found audiences of thousands of young, idealistic Jews.

The new ideology sparked settlement, and settlement solidified ideology. In 1968 Rabbi Moshe Levinger moved with a small group of pious followers to the city of Hebron. As one of four Jewish holy cities and the site of the cave of *machpelah*, thought to be the burial place of three of the Jewish patriarchs and their wives, Hebron held enormous religious significance to religious Jews. But the city was inhabited almost exclusively by Arabs, most of them Muslims who, like Jews, honor Abraham as the founder of their religion. Levinger began a settlement called Hameuchad, often considered the first religious settlement established in the occupied territories. A short time later religious settlers in Hebron organized the Gush Emunim (Bloc of the Faithful) around the militant religious ideology of Zvi Yehuda Kook. These settlers saw conquest of the entire biblical land of Israel as the divine right and obligation of the Israeli state; they claimed that this divine mandate transcended positive law. "We are commanded by the Torah according to the will of God," proclaimed one official Gush Emunim publication, "and therefore we cannot be subject to the standard laws of democracy."[45]

Rabbi Meir Kahane, who moved from the United States to Israel in 1971, took the new ideology of militant religious Zionism a step further by explicitly justifying the use of violence to secure the whole Land of Israel. Kahane not only hailed conquest as a noble and sacred activity but also claimed that militant conquest was the primary, divinely inspired purpose of the Israeli state. In an essay written in 1976, Kahane declared, "The State of Israel was established not because the Jew deserved it, for the Jew is as he has been before, rejecting God, deviating from his paths and ignoring his Torah." Kahane argued rather that the divine purpose of the state was "a Jewish fist in the face of an astonished Gentile world that had not seen it for two millennia."[46] Kahane proclaimed that "when the Jew is beaten, God is profaned!" He preached that the state of Israel was God's instrument of holy war.

Kahane expanded his ideological formulation into a full-fledged apocalyptic prophecy. In 1980, after being arrested by Israeli police for his involvement in a plot to blow up the Dome of the Rock, Kahane claimed on the basis of biblical texts that the formation of the Jewish state in 1948 was a sign of the impending messianic redemption. According to Kahane, the forty years following the establishment of the state were a grace period in which Jews could choose to repent their sins, obey God's law, and experience "a great and glorious redemption," or choose to remain in defiance of God and face a redemption brought about through "terrible sufferings and needless agonies; . . . holocaust more horrible than anything we have yet endured."[47] Predicting an impending catastrophe, Kahane advocated a "truly Jewish state, not a Hebrew-speaking gentilized one."[48] Kahane argued, among other things, that democracy should be suspended in Israel, that Arabs should be stripped of political rights and excluded from all spheres of work, that Jewish sovereignty should be proclaimed over all of the Land of Israel "by virtue of the promise of the Almighty," that Israeli public schools should teach a fully religious curriculum, and that dietary laws, censorship laws, and dress codes should be strictly enforced in public venues according to halakha.[49]

While Kahane's religious ideology and apocalyptic predictions galvanized his inner circle of followers, the rabbi also managed to appeal to a larger audience by couching his ideas in more secular and pragmatic language. He warned Israelis that the demographics of Israel were the real danger, playing on nationalist anxiety felt throughout Israeli Jewish society that a Jewish majority would no longer exist in Israel.[50] He appealed to poor Mizrachim by claiming that cheap Arab workers were undermining the Israeli labor market, and utilized racist biases to garner support. After several electoral bids to gain a seat in the Knesset, Kahane's party, Kach, gained 1.2 percent of the vote in 1984, enough to win a seat in parliament, but the Knesset barred Kach from taking its prize.[51]

The ideology of the settler movement developed on the fringe of the Israeli political spectrum, but the religious parties used the movement's precepts and spirit to mobilize political coalitions and push for favorable policies. In 1977, it was the defection of the National Religious Party after a series of disputes over Sabbath regulations that brought down a Labor government under the leadership of Yitzhak Rabin.[52] The Likud coalition that took power in 1977 shared many common interests with religious settlers, although it never adopted the ideological discourse of the militant settler movement. The religious parties exacted a high price for their support of the coalition in terms of increased state support of religious institutions and religious education.

The compromises and coping strategies derived from the status quo agreement did not work in the new political circumstances. While the Orthodox community had been primarily concerned with preserving its own privileges in the Israeli establishment, the ideology of militant religious Zionism demanded radical action. Because the radicals believed that the conquest of the land was a divine duty, they were unwilling to dismiss the actions of the Israeli state as theologically inconsequential as had non-Zionist Orthodoxy. And believing that they were living in times of impending messianic redemption, militant religious Zionists were unwilling to agree with the elder Kook that Israel could wait to fulfill its halakhic obligations.

Ideological debate sharpened after a government of the Left returned to power in 1993, interrupting a sixteen-year period in which the Likud party dominated coalitions. In an attempt to forge a peace process that would lead to a sovereign Palestinian state in the West Bank and Gaza, Yitzhak Rabin's government encountered resistance from a religious Zionist movement that regarded the surrender of the Holy Land to gentiles as a religious sin. Rabin pushed his peace plan in largely pragmatic terms, arguing that the social, economic, and moral cost of maintaining the occupation of the territories was unnecessary and damaging to the Israeli state.[53] As Rabin saw it, a government must pursue the best interest of its citizens, but the militant religious Zionist movement saw the state as God's designated instrument for the conquest of the Land of Israel.

A young Orthodox Jewish militant named Yigal Amir assassinated Prime Minister Yitzhak Rabin in 1995. When questioned, Amir offered the following explanation for his actions: "I acted alone on God's orders and I have no regrets. . . . I know Jewish law and *din rodef* means that if you have tried everything else and nothing works, then you have to kill him."[54] Amir took it upon himself to defy positive law to impose halakhic law on the state. The leader of the opposition, Benyamin Netanyahu, proclaimed Amir a "madman," implying that the logic he used lay beyond the legitimate spectrum of Israeli political discourse. Amir had, however, studied in a West Bank yeshiva with rabbis who propounded such ideas. Many secular Israelis accused right-wing politicians of tacitly cultivating a hostile political environment and of failing to denounce religious extremists when they called Rabin a murderer and a traitor. A fourth of Orthodox Israeli teenagers condoned the assassination.[55] Majority opinion sustained the government, however, in its use of positive law to punish the self-appointed enforcer of the halakha.

Already in the 1990s the ideological struggle had begun to transform itself into a struggle between two major institutions of the Israeli political system. Since 1977 the Right has usually dominated the Knesset and welcomed religious parties into coalition governments. These coalitions have encouraged and protected settlements, taken a hard line with the Palestinians, and cultivated Israeli particularism. Israelis of Middle Eastern and North African origins (Mizrachim), now the majority, have kept the Right in power and enabled the meteoric rise of Shas, a party with ultraorthodox leadership and a generally observant following. The Knesset became the champion of a "JEW-ISH democracy," while the defense of "Jewish DEMOCRACY" passed to the Israeli Supreme Court, which began to set itself up as the champion of religious freedom, equality, and human rights. The court has challenged the power of religious authorities and proclaimed a "constitutional revolution." Compromise and agreement (not to disagree) gave way to a test of wills between branches of government, each of them sustained by political forces.

Institutions

The history of Judaism contrasts with that of Islam in its relationship to political authority. A band of Muslims led by Muhammad founded a small community in Medina in 622, and that state grew into an empire. Muslims became rulers of the territories they conquered, and the majorities in those territories became Islamized over the centuries. In the first two centuries after Muhammad's death, the architects of Islamic law and doctrine worked in a context of political dominance. In contrast, Jews never enjoyed self-government after the destruction of the Second Temple (70 CE). Rabbinic Judaism produced the Talmud in exile. As long as the Abbasid caliphate survived, the exilarch of Baghdad enjoyed special authority within the Diaspora. Jews and Christians enjoyed some autonomy as peoples of the book under Muslim rule, but not since 1042 have there been Jewish institutions with any claim to centralized religious authority over world Jewry, dispersed across the globe under gentile rule.

Israel emerged from Zionism, and Zionism came from Eastern Europe, where Jewish communities survived by closing themselves off from the mainstream. In relatively small groups they sought to follow the halakha, which had been articulated for just such circumstances. In Poland and Russia the community (*kahal* or *kehilla*) shouldered responsibility for its own court system, for taxation, and for discipline of its members. While some Jewish bodies brought together communities to deal with central authorities, most decision-making lay within the individual communities. The halakha defined Jews as persons born of Jewish mothers, prohibited intermarriage, and prescribed a rather complicated set of rituals and ceremonials that preserved the community by setting it apart from society as a whole. The community took precedence over the individual, and the community functioned in the context of overarching political authority exercised by gentiles.[56]

The European Enlightenment of the seventeenth and eighteenth centuries brought nationalism and the destruction of the kahal. After the Peace of Westphalia in 1715, sovereign states with sharp boundaries sought increasing control over their own citizens. Napoleon made Jews full citizens in France, and the lure of assimilation affected German and English Jews, as well. In Russia the czar sought to centralize authority to push reform. He abolished the kahal in 1844 and transferred its functions to municipal councils, where Jews were in the minority. As Jews came to see themselves as citizens in the new "imagined community" of the nation-state, or as governments began to treat them that way, the internal solidarity of the kahal began to break down. Judaism, like Christianity, acquired a new shape as a result of Westphalian geography.[57]

Two political forces emerged within the Jewish community to challenge these threats to the old order. Orthodoxy was the first in order of appearance. It sought to resist the breakdown of the kahal by creating a set of ideas and organizations to protect the Jewish way of life from destruction. Rabbi Moses Sofer took a negative view of secular culture and responded by founding a yeshiva in Pressburg, Hungary, which became the largest in Europe. The Volozhin yeshiva founded in Lithuania in 1803 became even more important than Pressburg as a model. "The yeshiva became the locus of a Jewish counter-culture."[58] Whereas schools in the kahal had been local in character and conservative in message, these yeshivas reflected the new universalism of Europe even in rejecting it.

Then came Zionism. Moses Hess, Ahad Ha'am, and Theodor Herzl came to regard assimilation as a failure, but they sought a remedy not in resurrecting the kahal but in realizing Jewish peoplehood. Nationalist theory, with debts to Immanuel Kant and to romanticism, argued that peoples deserved to control their own political destiny. If the Jews are a people, then they deserve a state. Herzl argued that Jewish survival depended on it. Ha'am welcomed the possibility of cultural renewal. And these ideas reverberated with great success in Eastern Europe, where the herding of Jews into areas of settlement and official acts of discrimination violated the promises of the Enlightenment. Masses of Jews sought emigration.

The World Zionist Organization, formed at Basle, Switzerland, in 1897, sought to pull Jews together in an international organization. The impulse was secular and thoroughly modern. Some Orthodox rabbis rallied to the idea. Rabbi Abraham Isaac Kook, perhaps the most influential, insisted in somewhat mystical fashion that a coming together of Jews in Palestine might produce a spiritual revival. He declined, however, to identify settlement in Palestine with messianic redemption or with any immediate religious significance. Religious Zionists founded Mizrachi in 1903 to support the idea of settling Palestine, but other Orthodox rabbis "seceded" from the Zionist movement by founding Agudat Israel in 1911 in Eastern Europe. As a "transnational" organization, it sought to speak for a single Jewish tradition, thereby creating unprecedented hierarchy in Judaism.[59] One response to modernity, Orthodoxy, thus took its distance from another, Zionism, which it regarded as an unseemly effort to force the hand of God.

Jewish settlement of Palestine began under Ottoman rule and continued after World War I under the mandate for Palestine awarded to Great Britain. The Ottomans had treated Christian and Jewish communities as "millets," worthy of autonomy in administering some of their own affairs, especially matters of family and personal status—matters directly affected by religious law. The British carried this system into the mandate; the mandatory power treated Christians, Muslims, and Jews as separate communities, a practice Arabs regarded as unfair because it split them into two groups. Moreover, the mandate document entitled the Jews to "an appropriate agency" to serve as a liaison with the British government. Initially the World Zionist Organization (WZO) assumed that role, even though its leadership lived outside Palestine. Even in the first decade of the mandate, 1920–1930, the Labor settlement movement dominated the WZO and, hence, spoke for the Jewish community. A decidedly secular force thus represented the Jews, defined as a religious millet!

Labor Zionism dominated the Yishuv, and its leader, David Ben-Gurion, took the community to independence in 1948, but Israel's institutional structure came to reflect not so much the will of the majority as it did a power-sharing arrangement between secular and religious forces. Several authorities have called it consociationalism.[60] The majority could proceed only with the consent not just of religious Zionists but also of ultraorthodox elements whose attitude toward Zionism and the new state of Israel was anything but unambiguously positive. As Agudat Israel prepared to testify before the

United Nations Committee on Palestine in 1947, its leadership met with Ben-Gurion about conditions for supporting the state. Ben-Gurion, with the help of religious Zionists, supplied the status quo letter. Even then, Agudat avoided firm commitment to the state.

The Status Quo Letter

Ben-Gurion opposed separation of church and state, because he wanted the state to control religion. He avoided insistence upon a constitution, which the religious parties unanimously opposed. They said the Torah provided a sufficient backbone for the republic. Yet the religious Zionists welcomed state control of religion to assert their primacy over their ultraorthodox rivals. They favored the creation of a chief rabbinate, supported by a rabbinical council. The rabbinate would supervise both Jewish religious courts, which would retain exclusive control of marriage and divorce for the Jewish community, and local Jewish religious councils, which would supervise synagogues, ritual baths, and kashrut.[61] These institutions would depend on state funding.

The status quo letter promised that ultraorthodox schools would not come under state control. Before independence, the Jewish community in Palestine had supported four streams of education: Labor Zionist, General Zionist (liberal, nonsocialist), religious Zionist, and ultraorthodox. Labor now agreed to abandon its own schools and establish a single secular track, but religious Zionists insisted upon state-run religious schools, as well. Agudat maintained its schools, and the state established schools for Arabs. State monies flowed toward all these schools, even the Agudat yeshivas. The intensity and adequacy of state supervision constituted a greater point of dispute than the fact of funding.

The state controls religious institutions, and secular elites dominate the state. But the consociational nature of Israeli politics requires governments to win the cooperation and even support of the religious parties. The National Religious Party has normally supported the governing coalition and has normally dominated the Ministry of Religious Affairs, which is only one of many sources of funding for religious institutions. Sharkansky writes: "A variety of Israeli government offices provide aid to Orthodox and ultra-Orthodox bodies, but there is no central recording of how much goes to which institutions. The style of Israeli political competition may have something to do with this lack of record keeping."[62] He notes that the Ministry of Construction and Housing, the Ministry of Finance, the Ministry of Education, the Ministry of Welfare, and local municipalities all help fund religious institutions. The religious parties have focused their political efforts on winning cabinet-level appointments to at least some of these ministries. Because the religious parties have traditionally cared most about issues directly related to religion, they have been willing to accommodate the secular parties on other matters.

State control, mediated by Orthodox and ultraorthodox influence over state policy, has created an Israeli Judaism utterly at odds with much of the Diaspora. Reform and Conservative Jewish rabbis have no standing, get no state support, and cannot legally perform marriage ceremonies or convert anyone to Judaism. Yet these nonorthodox congregations dominate Judaism in the United States. Perhaps 5 percent of American Jews can be considered Orthodox, and the United States boasts more Jews than any other country in the world including Israel.[63] Muslims, Christians, Druze, and many other religious groups enjoy considerable autonomy in managing their institutions and ceremonies in Israel, but the state defines the institutional parameters of Judaism. By virtue of its controlling mission, the state has effectively fashioned an Israeli Judaism that is distinct from American Judaism or the Judaism imagined by Agudat Israel in the years before independence. Even some of the new generation of students in the ultraorthodox yeshivas now acknowledge the Israeli context in which they live.

Secular critics argue that Jews lack religious freedom in Israel, which accords rights to persons of other faiths, though it denies them first-class citizenship. Jews of Conservative or Reformist congregations would be freer if the state treated them as non-Jews! The harshest among Orthodox rabbis would do just that, while the more lenient see these congregations as defective and misguided, worthy of citizenship but unworthy of official religious rights and privileges. State control of religious institutions permits the logic of Orthodoxy to prevail.

From 1948 until 1967, the stability of the Israeli political system helped maintain the equilibrium of political and religious institutions sketched by the status quo letter. Mapai, the party of David Ben-Gurion, dominated the Labor settlement movement with its commitment to break with Jewish passivity, victimhood, and exclusivism through pioneering, cultural regeneration, and state-building. Labor depended upon the cooperation of religious Zionists in the National Religious Party, and only occasionally on the support of the ultraorthodox Agudat Israel. There were skirmishes about respect for the Sabbath, rules of kashrut, and the Law of Return, but neither Labor Zionism nor the religious parties sought revision of the understanding Ben-Gurion had championed in place of constitutional regulation.

Threats to the Status Quo

Even in that period, however, the immigration of Jews from the Middle East and North Africa, cultivated and welcomed by Labor Zionism, began to threaten the balance between religious and secular forces. The immigrants who arrived from Morocco, Yemen, Iraq, and other Muslim countries tended to be more observant of Jewish tradition than their European predecessors in the camps for new arrivals. Secular Israelis traveled to Iraq and Yemen, among other places, to encourage Jews to come to Israel. They trumpeted the virtues of Israel as the Holy Land to reinforce an identity distinct from Arabo-Muslim culture. In fact, the immigrants who arrived in Israel from Middle Eastern countries after independence in 1948 tended to prefer religious schools for their children. Fearing that these students would strengthen National Religious Party schools, Ben-Gurion and his colleagues moved quickly to establish a single state school system, albeit one divided into state general schools and state religious schools. To this day students from Mizrachi families constitute an overwhelming majority of students enrolled in state religious education.

Israel's unexpected conquest of the West Bank in 1967 proved to be a key event in further destabilizing the balance between religious and political forces. While mainstream Labor leaders such as Ben-Gurion talked about trading the conquered territories for a peace agreement with the Arab states, religious Zionists exulted not just in the freedom to pray at the Western Wall of the old temple but to go live in places of biblical significance, such as the city of Hebron. Labor-dominated governments authorized settlement for reasons that are unclear. Some settlements were supposed to protect Israel's eastern frontier along the Jordan River, but the pressures for settlement came increasingly from religious voices brought together in 1973 in the Gush Emunim (Bloc of the Faithful).

Powered by a fresh version of Zionism and by an outburst of organizational talent and energy, the Gush became the primary pressure group for the Land of Israel Movement. The Six-Day War, in which Israel had seized the West Bank from Jordan, the Sinai peninsula from Egypt, and the Golan Heights from Syria, constituted an act of God and the beginning of the promised redemption of the Jews, they said. It was providential that Jews could now live not just in Tel Aviv, a new city of no religious significance, but also in cities of ancient Judea and Samaria, the land most closely identified with the ancient Jewish kingdoms. This was land God had given the Jews, and the Jews needed to settle and defend this territory. The Gush organized settlements, the most daring of them in the center of Hebron, surrounded by a hostile

Arab population. With considerable support in the National Religious Party and in the right-wing nationalist party, Likud, the Gush pushed ahead and dared the government to stop it. "They grafted their own messianic religious discourse onto the old discourse of republican virtue [propounded by the Labor settlement movement], and claimed the mantle of the moral community attending to the common good by settling the Land of Israel."[64]

The institutional balance defined by the status quo agreement tipped further toward the religious forces in the so-called earthquake election of 1977. Menachem Begin, Ben-Gurion's great antagonist and critic, won power in a smashing victory of his Likud party over the Labor Alignment. The primary reason was clear: Mizrachim now dominated the body politic, and Likud won a majority of their votes. It was a victory of "ethnic nationalism" over "republican virtue."[65] The ideology of Likud, an offshoot of Vladimir Jabotinsky's Revisionist movement, did not emphasize religious claims to the Land of Israel. Revisionism had always emphasized military power as the key to building and preserving a state. Likud opposed Labor's ostensible policy of trading land for peace for reasons of security: distrust of the Arabs, distrust of the United Nations, distrust of great power guarantees. Israel under Likud would not be content to trust God for protection, but Begin himself was personally observant as well as charismatic. Religion became a more important foundation of the so-called Second Republic than it had been of the first, the era of Labor dominance.

Designated as the new prime minister, Begin pleased Mizrachi supporters by inviting the National Religious Party and ultraorthodox forces to join his coalition. They accepted. State subsidies began to flow more generously toward religious institutions, and the government began officially encouraging settlement. The Land of Israel Movement, powered by the Gush Emunim, seemed preeminent, though it suffered temporary disillusionment when Prime Minister Begin agreed to pull back from Sinai in return for peace with Egypt. The Gush took the 1981 withdrawal of settlers from Yamit, required by the treaty with Egypt, as a sign of betrayal.

The birth of two new political parties in 1984 epitomized the shifting institutional balance between religious and secular forces. Kach, founded by Rabbi Meir Kahane, openly proposed expelling Arabs from the West Bank. In America, where he created the Jewish Defense League, Kahane had not hesitated to violate the law in God's name. He saw all gentiles as enemies of the Jews. God would hence approve even acts of violence against those who had systematically repressed his "chosen people." The Israeli Knesset ultimately banned Kach. The second party born in 1984 called itself Shas. Its founder was Rabbi Ovadia Yosef, former chief Sephardic rabbi of Israel. He split with Agudat Israel to establish an ultraorthodox party of Middle Eastern and North African Jews. Of Iraqi origin, Rabbi Yosef chafed at the lack of adequate Sephardic schools for rabbinic training. He dreamed of restoring Oriental Judaism to "its past splendor," identified in his mind with Muslim Spain. At first Shas split the ultraorthodox vote with Agudat Israel, but it soon achieved much wider appeal among Mizrachim, thanks in large measure to Arie Deri, of Moroccan origin, who felt he had suffered discrimination at the hands of the establishment. Deri demonstrated remarkable political talents and found himself director-general in the Ministry of the Interior after Shas joined the governing coalition. Soon he was acting minister and diverting large sums of money to religious institutions. The party, which won 3.1 percent of the vote in 1984, advanced to 4.7 percent in 1988 and 5 percent in 1992. In 1996 it leaped to 8.5 percent after a change in the electoral system created two ballots, one for parliament and one for prime minister. When Shas joined a new coalition headed by Benyamin Netanyahu, it received two ministerial posts and two slots for deputy ministers; three years later, even after charges of corruption forced Deri to stand aside, the party reached 14.1 percent of the vote and claimed four ministries.

Shas reached well beyond the ultraorthodox in its appeal by targeting Mizrachi resentment against Ashkenazi dominance in the society, the economy, and politics. It began to see itself as the representative of underprivileged Israelis. It established a special program to help marginal youths in the Oriental community by bringing them into Orthodoxy. At the same time it reached out to a mystic, Rabbi Yitzhak Kaduri, who helped legitimize religious practices common among North African Jews, including belief in charms and the power of saints. "Six to seven millions persons annually are reported to make pilgrimages to tombs of saints in Israel," writes Weissbrod.[66] Despite their commitment to Orthodoxy, Shas leaders have avoided criticizing such practices.

In the 2003 election Shas suffered the loss of one-third of its seats in the Knesset. It dropped from 14.1 percent to 8.9 percent of the vote but remained the fourth largest party in Israel. For the first time in nineteen years it was excluded from the governing coalition. The shift back to a single ballot probably is the single most important explanation. Voters needed to calculate how their votes for party lists would affect selection of the prime minister, as they had before 1996. Some voters apparently thought Shas had failed to fulfill its promises to help the underprivileged, but Rabbi Ovadia Yosef campaigned by saying, "Those who are for God follow me."[67] A secular political force of the center-right, Shinui, identified Shas as its principal enemy. In return, Yosef called on the electorate to vote against the evil Shinui. The viciousness of the attacks and rebuttals showed that both sides feared the balance of religious and secular forces was at stake.

The electoral success of Shas and its resulting influence in the ministries has permitted the construction of an educational system that guarantees lasting influence. Weissbrod reports that Shas established 270 centers in poor Mizrachi communities and neighborhoods to provide adult religious education, supplementary religious education for school-age children, hot meals for the needy, nursery schools, and more.[68] It moved toward providing modern education as well as religious instruction for girls as well as boys, and seemed prepared to move toward professional training in fields as diverse as social work and finance—all in the name of advancing the social well-being of the Mizrachi community. Whether these programs succeed in moving Mizrachim toward Orthodoxy remains to be seen, but they strengthened Shas as a political force.

Immigration and war explain much of the threat to institutional balance in Israel since 1967. The influx of Jews from the Middle East and North Africa after independence created an underclass of Israeli Jews susceptible to political mobilization. Menachem Begin and the Likud party succeeded in reaching some of this group, and then after 1984, Shas rode Mizrachi votes to power and influence. Meanwhile, the war of 1967 triggered new cries for "settlement of the Land of Israel." Religious Zionists flocked to the Occupied Territories, bolstered by convictions that they were carrying out the will of God, supported by the Gush Emunim and rabbinical proclamations. A few extremists such as Kahane jumped into the mix. The threat represented by Shas and by the Gush Emunim, on the other hand, came through the electoral system and the Knesset. Nothing could prevent the Knesset from changing things, other than a constitution that impinged on the Knesset's authority.

"Constitutional Revolution"

The Knesset usurped its authority at the birth of the state of Israel. Elected as a Constituent Assembly charged with preparing a constitution, it transformed itself at its very first meeting into a legislature and postponed the constitutional task. In 1950, after intense discussion of constitutional issues including the place of religion in the state, the Knesset adopted a resolution proposed by Haim Harari that said, in essence, that the constitution of the state would take shape one chapter at a time in the form of a set of basic laws. "The Harari

Compromise . . . enabled circumvention of the ideologically controversial issues which divided the religious and the secular publics by avoiding any explicit formulation of the relationship between religion and state in Israel."[69]

The Knesset proceeded to adopt a set of basic laws that defined the way Israeli government functions. These laws mostly confirmed established practices. They elicited little controversy until 1989, when the minister of justice, Dan Meridor, proposed the Basic Law on Human and Civil Rights. The religious parties objected that such a law would undermine the status quo. That proposal failed, but pieces of it re-emerged three years later in two parts: the Basic Law on Human Dignity and Liberty and the Basic Law on Freedom of Occupation. These bills won passage but only after an amendment provided that existing law would not be affected. The religious parties wanted to protect prevailing practice.[70]

Justice Aaron Barak of the Israeli Supreme Court proclaimed that passage of these two basic laws represented a "constitutional revolution." "Israel has transformed itself from a parliamentary democracy to a constitutional democracy," he said, because the Supreme Court had acquired the right to review legislation. In making these claims, he sharpened the lines of conflict: court against Knesset, secular against religious forces. By one account, Ashkenazi Jews, having lost control of the Knesset, were using the court to reassert their control over the state of Israel.[71] The "constitutional revolution" threatened to neutralize, if not reverse, the advances made by the religious parties since 1967. Secular forces on the left and the right cheered these changes. Shinui on the right found votes in attacking Shas for its support of special favors to the religious community (military deferment, allowances for large families). Rising electoral fortunes made Shas the principal opponent of the "revolution."

The bitterness of this confrontation suggested the possibility of instability, if Justice Barak pursued his constitutional aims. In fact, much of the ensuing controversy emerged from cases that produced modest change in the interpretation of Israeli law, nothing worthy of the term "revolutionary." The "pork case," involving the importation of nonkosher meat, showed the potential explosiveness of the issues, but the resolution also illustrated the secondary stability available in the Israeli system. The Knesset, upon recommendation of the government, undercut the apparent victory of the court system and defused the "constitutional revolution." The case (*Mitral v. Prime Minister*, 1993) arose after the Knesset privatized the frozen meat industry in 1992. Mitral, a meat importer, appealed a government decision that even private importers could not bring in nonkosher meat. Mitral said the decision violated the Basic Law on Freedom of Occupation, which guarantees any resident of Israel the right to practice any occupation, profession, or trade. The Supreme Court, sitting as the High Court of Justice, accepted the appeal and ruled that any further legislation of the Knesset that sought to ban nonkosher meat would contradict the clause of the basic law exempting previous legislation from its effects. But the government then won Knesset approval for an amendment to the Basic Law on Freedom of Occupation specifying that future legislation could constitutionally contradict the basic law, if that legislation included a clause exempting it from the provisions of the basic law![72]

Despite the clarity of that victory of Knesset over court and religious over secular forces, the antagonism did not end. On one side, the court chipped away at the authority of religious courts in matters such as the division of matrimonial property in divorce (Bavli case) and the right of women to pray at the Western Wall. The Supreme Court has "established the right to equality as a fundamental right," but "the Knesset has put personal status law . . . beyond the reach of the principle of equality and the courts have not challenged this."[73] Feminists and others concerned with civil liberties find the "constitutional revolution" rather tame, but religious forces have nonetheless attacked the Supreme Court and the chief justice repeatedly and viciously. Rabbi Meir Porush, a leader of Agudat Israel, proclaimed he was ready to die in the struggle against Justice Barak. In 1999 ultraorthodox (*haredi*) religious leadership forbade its leadership, members of the Knesset, and civil servants to obey rulings of the High Court of Justice on exemption from military service, conversions to Judaism, and the inclusion of Reform and Conservative Jews in local municipal councils. More than a quarter of a million Orthodox Jews demonstrated against the Supreme Court in February 1999.[74] Proposals to create a constitutional council to replace the Supreme Court in that role reached the Knesset. Those efforts met defeat in 2002 but ultraorthodox hostility to the court and to Barak continued.

The smoldering institutional rivalry that marks the relationship between politics and religion in Israel probably stems from an underlying clash of ideologies. Shafir and Peled write of the encounter between ethno-nationalist discourse and liberal democracy. Barak is explicit about wanting to put Israel more squarely in line with the Universal Declaration of Human Rights and with democratic principles. He has declared that "the meaning of the Jewish nature of the state is not in the religious-Halacha sense, and hence the values of the State of Israel as a Jewish state should not be identified with Jewish Law."[75] Lerner portrays the conflict as one between consociationalism and majoritarianism. The religious parties seek to maintain the consociational structure that has given them an effective veto power over Israeli political life. Those who champion equality want greater majority control in all matters and a reduction of what they perceive as religious privilege. The change of the electoral law to permit direct election of the prime minister seemed to be a step toward majoritarianism. Yet the unintended result was growth of the smaller parties, including Shas, a modern defender of the enduring consociational arrangements. Repeal of the provision for direct election of the prime minister signaled the resurgence of consociationalism.

Political Culture

Independent Israel grew out of a nationalist movement of European origin. European Jews, products of czarist rule in Poland and Russia, some of them survivors of Nazi Germany, brought with them a set of aptitudes and attitudes that continue to mark Israeli politics. When Israel took its independence, its political culture already accepted labor unions, political parties, and proportional representation. It also knew something of dictatorship and repression. As Ben-Gurion and his colleagues began to shape a new political culture, they were not working with virgin clay or starting from that hypothetical "state of nature" so important to liberals from Thomas Hobbes to John Rawls.

At independence, Israel distanced itself from the World Zionist Movement and from its longtime leader, Chaim Weizmann. Ben-Gurion seized the controls as prime minister, but Weizmann's presence on the stage as the first president and Israel's obvious debt to the WZO evoked an issue of enormous importance. Did the Israeli state respond to the Jewish people as a whole or was it responsible only to its citizens? What was Israel's relationship to the Diaspora? More Jews lived (and still live) outside Israel than live within. For some Jews, both within and without, Israel suddenly replaced God as the center of Judaism. In the first euphoria of independence, leaders seemed to have expected that most Jews would return "home." Constitution-making could be postponed until the great flood of immigrants had arrived. Any Jew who did not go there was not "fully" Jewish. To this day 83 percent of Israelis believe they have an obligation to the Diaspora, and a high proportion of American Jews support Israel even if they do not intend to move there.[76] For some, to oppose Israeli policies is tantamount to anti-Semitism, so much is Israel identified with the Jewish people as a whole.

Zionism asserted the existence of a single Jewish people, but the emergence of an independent Jewish state including only a minority of world

Jewry created a political culture quite distinct from that of the Diaspora. In Israel, Jewishness can become trivialized. As a twenty-year-old Israeli woman put it, "My Jewish identity is as much a part of me as my name—but really of no greater consequence."[77] Israelis divide evenly on whether they see themselves first as Jews or first as Israelis. An American Jew is more likely "to seek personal and spiritual meaning in religion than is his Israeli counterpart."[78] For many American Jews, political activism, not religion, cements identity. American Jews help define American political culture.

For some Jews, Israel has no religious significance. Leibowitz argues that the deep involvement of the state in religious affairs damages religion. "Religion as an adjunct of a secular authority is the antithesis of true religion," he writes.[79] Israel uses religion to bolster its identity and its standing with the Diaspora, but "nationalism and patriotism as such are not religious values."[80]

In a similar vein, Lockard writes: "It is not religion that makes me be ashamed of being Israeli today, but nationalism."[81] For Leibowitz and Lockard, nationalism separates Israel from the "Jewish people" and, of course, from the "Arab people" as well. The ultraorthodox accept Israel as a reality of their existence but stop short of sanctifying the state and seeing it as the center of Judaism.

The attitudes of the Diaspora constitute one element of Israeli political culture, but Israeli nationalism—propagated by Labor Zionists intent upon settling the land and building a state, and more recently by ethno-nationalists preoccupied with security issues—has emphasized the uniqueness of the setting, the problems, the people, and relevant solutions. The land itself, including the Occupied Territories, has become central to Israeli identity. The political system reflects and responds most directly to the attitudes of its Jewish citizens. The nation-state outweighs the Diaspora as the popular context of Israeli politics.

Secular or Religious?

Highly devout segments of the Israeli body politic fear majoritarian rule from their sense that the Israeli political culture is highly secular. The conventional wisdom, propagated by academics and the media, was that a third of Israeli Jews observed most religious traditions, and of that third, roughly half voted for the religious parties. (The ultraorthodox Agudat Israel and Poalei Agudat Israel garnered less than 3 percent of the vote.) The Guttman Institute Report, based on surveys taken in 1991 and 1993, provided a much more complete and complicated picture. It confirmed that a minority of Israelis are highly observant of religious traditions, but it also showed that an ample majority of Israelis observe some religious traditions. Israelis rated their own degree of religiosity this way:

Strictly observant	14 percent
Observant to a great extent	24 percent
Somewhat observant	41 percent
Totally nonobservant	21 percent[82]

Four-fifths of the population appears to be observant, and even this number may understate religious practice. The study reported that 77 percent of the respondents regard the Sabbath as important to their lives, "including 39 percent of those who consider themselves 'totally nonobservant.'"[83] Liebman writes: "The report found that the Jewish religion retains an influence that many had heretofore refused to acknowledge."[84]

The Guttman Report undermined the conventional wisdom about Israel's "secular" majority, but it did not convince everyone that Israelis are deeply religious. "Why do 50% think good deeds will be rewarded but 27% think bad deeds will be punished? Why do 50% see Torah as divine while only 14% observe commandments?"[85] Many Israelis may follow religious traditions for family or nationalistic and patriotic reasons.[86] One in six think public life in Israel should be more religious, and one in three think it should be less religious, but the rest of the Jewish population would keep the balance of religion and politics where it is.[87] "Israeli society has a strong traditional bent and, as far as religious practice is concerned, . . . there is a continuum from the strictly observant to the nonobservant rather than a great divide between a religious minority and a secular majority."[88]

These numbers help explain why neither secular nor religious forces have been successful in their efforts to tip the balance of Israeli politics. Secular opposition to restrictive Sabbath policies has not produced legal change, but the state does not enforce all the rules dear to religious Jews. "Could anyone in the 1960s have predicted that movie theaters, restaurants, and pubs would operate undisturbed in downtown Jerusalem on Friday nights?"[89] Orthodox rabbis continue to perform all marriages, but fewer and fewer Israelis choose to get married in Israel. Cyprus is a popular venue. Survey results do not directly confirm a great divide on religious matters but neither do they affirm a consensus.

Political culture in Israel appears to be evolving toward postmaterialism in the manner Inglehart predicted.[90] The spirit of the early Yishuv was decidedly collectivist. The kibbutz represented the collective, socialist spirit better than any other institution. Building the economy, the society, and the state required the subordination of the individual to group aims. Bourgeois Zionism stayed in the background until the 1960s, when economic prosperity began to produce a new emphasis on liberalism, individualism, self-realization, and secularism, at least among people of European origin. Israelis as a group may be relatively observant, but the elites are overwhelmingly secular, postmaterialist, and Western in orientation.[91]

Political attitudes slipped in the opposite direction, however, as a result of the immigration of Middle Eastern and North African Jews. These immigrants found themselves at the lower rungs of Israeli society, fighting for material gain and political influence rather than postmaterial values. They swelled the ranks of the observant and mostly observant, categories that came to be described as masorti (traditional). The Mizrachim appeared remarkably religious to secular Jews from Europe, and remarkably eclectic in their patterns of religious observance to the Orthodox community of European origin. The label "traditional" carried all the baggage associated with it in the "traditional-modern" distinction made by Inglehart and other modernization theorists, who argue that tradition must give way to modernity. Immigration thus produced an increase of religiosity that tended to counterbalance the decreasing religiosity of long-established Ashkenazim. The relative stability of survey numbers disguised offsetting changes.[92]

Change threatens both sides. S. N. Eisenstadt asserts that the religious feared the rising tide of secularism in the 1950s, whereas it is heightened religiosity and the strength of the religious parties that cause fright among secularists now.[93] The proportion of citizens who see themselves as Jews rather than Israelis has edged upward. The commitment to land as a sacred object has increased. The haredim seem to have advanced in strength relative to the Orthodox. Shinui has played on these fears to advance its political standing.

The attitudes that constitute a political culture show greater stability than popular perceptions of policy, but political culture nonetheless changes over time. Inglehart has tried to demonstrate that in Europe.[94] The case of Germany, decidedly authoritarian when the Civic Culture study was done in the 1950s, appeared remarkably democratic two decades later. Political practice is surely one of the primary influences. Democracy trains democrats. But socialization also occurs in families, the workplace, and, most important, schools. The organization of schools and content of education necessarily become critical to the revision or stability of political culture.

Remaking Political Culture

From the beginning, Zionism aspired to transform Jewish political culture. It sought to break with Jewish passivity and to create a new image of the Jew as adventurer, pioneer, worker, activist, and good citizen of the state. Israel was to be a "visionary democratic state" rather than a "service state." The dominant Labor party, Mapai, operated its own school system before independence, which invoked the Jewish heritage "mainly in historical terms, as a humanistic tradition, whose expression lay in the commandment 'Thou shall not kill.'"[95] The Labor schools saw the Sabbath as a day of rest, Passover as a festival of liberty. While perhaps not antireligious, the schools were nonetheless anticlerical. The schools run by the secular, liberal parties taught more Jewish subjects than did those run by Labor but tended to emphasize the Bible rather than the Talmud, the principles of Judaism as opposed to the rabbinic tradition. After independence, in 1953, these two streams of education merged into the state general schools. Resnick concludes that the national image conveyed in these schools in the 1950s was one of a "nation with a right to a state," a right seen as coming from Jewish history and international recognition.[96] The socialism of the Labor schools gave way to a message of nationalism in the merged general schools, which accommodated about 70 percent of Jewish pupils at the moment of merger.[97] Mainstream schools sought to transform Jews into citizens of the new state, distinct from Jews in the Diaspora.

The haredi, whether supportive or not of Zionism, found this transformative vision unacceptable, because it threatened the ability of the religious minorities to sustain themselves. Even before independence, about one-fourth of all Jewish pupils attended religious schools. Religious Zionists resisted a single, secular school system, and the Labor movement resisted complete autonomy for the religious schools. The resulting compromise produced two streams of state education: general and religious. In addition, groups such as Agudat Israel could and did establish independent schools. Thus, the religious forces sought to protect their distinctive cultural niches from the corrosive power of the secular schools.

Already in the 1950s the transformers began to be transformed. As immigrants poured into Israel from North Africa and the Middle East, Labor Zionists established camps and set up schools, but these immigrants preferred religious schools. Fearful they would all emerge as eventual supporters of the National Religious Party, dominant elites began to nudge the general schools toward greater consideration of religion. The governing coalition settled on new "basic principles" for education in 1955:

In primary, secondary and higher education the government will take care to deepen Jewish consciousness among Israeli young people, to root it in the Jewish people's past and historical heritage, and to strengthen its moral tie to world Jewry based on the awareness of a common destiny and the historical continuity which links all Jews from all countries.[98]

Resnick calls this image a "nation by right of religion" and says it came to be broadly implemented in the 1960s.

The objective of Jewish consciousness was to incorporate the Diaspora and to overcome the ever more visible split between religious and nonreligious Jews, between Sephardim and Ashkenazim. The evocation of religion as a treasure chest of memories and symbols available for political purposes did not, of course, satisfy even religious Zionists, much less the non-Zionist Orthodox groups. This deflection of Labor Zionism toward religion reflected a sense that arriving waves of immigrants and a growing religious school system might threaten secular domination. The threat warranted a tempering of the message to acknowledge more explicitly the role of religion in uniting the Jewish people. The state general schools still do not teach religion as much as they teach *about* religion.

Far from disappearing, state religious education gained in numbers but suffered in quality from the influx of immigrants. In the early 1990s, Mizrachim constituted 80 percent of the enrollment in state religious schools, compared with 57 percent in the general schools. Then, after the 1967 conquest of Sinai and the West Bank, those schools acquired fresh significance in justifying retention and settlement of the whole Land of Israel. The schools teach that Israel constitutes a step toward the redemption of the Jews. They are also supposed to prepare their students for modern life and teach that it is possible to "live as a Jew" in a democratic country.[99] The claim is that about 70 percent of the students in this track emerge as observant Jews. Since roughly 20 percent of Israeli pupils attend such schools, some 14 percent of the population would maintain or acquire Orthodox habits in these schools. Another 10 percent of pupils attend non-Zionist Orthodox schools, which emphasize religion but do have some state supervision. Roughly 4 percent of all pupils attend ultraorthodox schools, which follow religious curricula. If the independent religious schools succeed in keeping all pupils within the realm of Orthodoxy, then about 30 percent of Israeli youth would be drawn along in Orthodox patterns. This suggests relative stability in patterns of belief.

Religious education acquired new resources after the Right won election in 1977. It also suffered at home and abroad from the actions of settlers who took the law into their own hands. In the state general schools, there emerged a new emphasis on Israel as a democracy and a champion of universal human rights, pluralism, and the rule of law in response to the abuses of Israeli rule in the West Bank and Gaza. Religious forces saw Labor's return to power in the early 1990s as a fresh assault of Hellenism and universalism on Jewish particularism. The Oslo Accords opened the way to possible peace with the Palestinians and to ceding much of the West Bank. When Yigal Amir assassinated Prime Minister Rabin, religious education took some of the backlash. Overall, though, religious education does not appear to be gaining or losing strength.

Education has not fashioned a homogeneous political culture in Israel. A case study of ceremonies commemorating Rabin's death suggests that the two school systems differ in the way they socialize students into politics. On the one hand, the religious schools portrayed the assassination as "abrogation of a religious commandment rather than a political act." They used readings from the Torah to stress the need for tolerance, the sanctity of life, and the need to prevent civil war. The general schools, on the other hand, devoted much more time to the ceremonies, which included music, dance, and speeches. They emphasized the need for peace with the Palestinians and Arabs, and the need to work for goals by democratic means. From interviewing students, the author of this case study found those from religious schools referring to "us" as religious Jews, and those from the general schools using "us" as the equivalent of peace-loving democrats. She noted that these ceremonies, like the better established ceremonies commemorating the Holocaust, did not pertain to Arab schools—or even to yeshivas, for that matter.[100]

The autonomous yeshivas of the ultraorthodox contrast even more sharply with the state general schools in their approach to political socialization. In such schools boys don traditional garb and devote themselves to the study of the Torah to the exclusion of almost everything else. They enjoy deferment from the military service imposed on all other qualified Israeli males. Some students remain in the yeshivas until age forty-two, when deferments become exemptions, remaining all the while a burden on the state and delaying any contribution to the economy. Deferments for yeshiva students, which numbered about 500 in the 1950s, now total some 30,000 a year.[101] Criticism has mounted with the numbers, but the ultraorthodox, some of whom still disdain the state, fend off critics by saying that learning is the greatest asset of the Jews and because of this, yeshiva students contribute to the defense of the nation. The lure of military deferment has increased the power of the yeshivas as a socializing force and increased the state's financial burdens. It is estimated that two-thirds of the haredim live on welfare.[102]

Despite the intent of Labor Zionists to create a single civil religion, the Israeli school system has solidified pluralism. State general schools are too secular for religious tastes. The state religious schools are insufficiently orthodox for some and insufficiently secular for others. The autonomous yeshivas run by ultraorthodox forces constitute an unwarranted refuge from military service, in the eyes of some, as well as an inadequate preparation for modern life. The Hesder yeshivas run by the National Religious Party produce poor scholars and poor soldiers, in the eyes of critics. Schools for Arabs remain separate but include heavy doses of Jewish history and inadequate treatment of Islam. No single set of schools can satisfy the fragmented political culture of Israel. Only a segmented school system can sustain the plurality of attitudes that has shaped the polity from the early days of Zionism.

Politics has "created" and maintained the religious diversity that divides the body politic. Secular Zionism generated religious Zionism. Religious Zionism sharpened the reactions of Orthodoxy, which was, like Zionism itself, a reaction to modernity. Independent Israel separated itself from the Diaspora at the same time that it welcomed Jews from the Diaspora, and especially from the Middle East and North Africa. Immigration produced a split in Orthodoxy and the creation of Shas. The dominance of Orthodoxy ensured by the state fostered secular reactions of both the Left and the Right in the form of Meretz and then Shinui. All these groups, including most of the ultraorthodox, avail themselves of politics to protect their organizations and their constituents. Does this mean that the political culture is religious or that religious culture is thoroughly politicized? Both seem to be true.

Stability of Israeli political culture is a byproduct of the interdependence of religious and political attitudes. The effort to instill a single understanding of democracy may not have succeeded, and many proponents of the halakha may still remain theoretically opposed, but not even they can afford to put themselves outside the democratic maelstrom. How they behave politically may be a more important lesson for their students than what they teach. They may teach that politics depends on religion, but behavior of all groups suggests that religion depends on politics.

Conclusion

Israel calls itself a Jewish state and thinks of itself as democratic, but it is not democratic because it is Jewish. Some of the most religious elements of the society have rejected participation, and others have used their influence in democratic politics to block measures to liberalize and democratize the society. The early Israeli settlers, most of them secular in orientation, brought democratic ideas with them from Europe. Consociational political arrangements emerged not from the Talmud but from the practical need for cooperation within the Jewish community in Palestine under British mandate. The democratic procedures initiated in those years carried over directly into the independence period.

Israel is Jewish because, by a process of negotiation and democratic decision-making among its Jewish citizens, it has decided to be Jewish. Zionism began as a secular movement but found itself obliged to invoke religion, if only as a source of cultural commonality, to explain the common identity of the Jews. Labor Zionism flaunted its irreverence as it launched its program of settlement and state-building, but it could not in the end ignore the political strength of Orthodox groups. The status quo letter acknowledged the power and prestige of the Orthodox. The National Religious Party demonstrated its effectiveness at the polls and earned a lock on cabinet positions, guaranteeing the enforcement of status quo policies. The heavy immigration of Middle Eastern and North African Jews after independence pushed both Left and Right to sustain and even enhance their secular commitments to uphold religion. In these new demographic circumstances, the Right recruited voters more successfully than the Left and came to power in the earthquake election of 1977. In the aftermath, coalition governments based in the Right catered to the needs and desires of the religious parties, further solidifying the state's religious character. Israel has become progressively more religious by virtue of its democratic politics. The Arabs who live within the Green Line borders established in 1949 and enjoy full voting rights have been unable to exert significant influence over this process.

By becoming a Jewish state, Israel has transformed Judaism. For many Jews, Judaism acquired a center, a focus, and therefore a structure it had not had since the destruction of the Second Temple. Many Israelis saw themselves as occupying holy ground and playing a central role; the word "aliya" used to describe immigration evoked religion. Those who did not immigrate suddenly found themselves less Jewish than those who did. Reform and Conservative congregations, dominant in America, found themselves at odds with the Orthodox establishment, which had for political reasons achieved preeminence in Israel. A whole new line of religious thinking, initiated by Rav Kook, argued that the formation of the state might open the door to messianic times. Political bargaining led to the creation of parallel Orthodox rabbinates, one for the Jews of Europe, the other for those of the Middle East and Africa. Judaism, previously fractured into communities all over the Diaspora, acquired elements of order and hierarchy that brought parts of the world Jewry together but divided Israelis from the Diaspora, Zionists from anti-Zionists, Orthodox from Reform and Conservative congregations, West from East. If Judaism is the sum of what Jews believe, think, and do, then it is substantially different from what it was a century ago.

While religious doctrine and practice has indubitably affected the state of Israel in at least superficial ways, political opportunities and necessities have shaped religious thinking in more profound ways. The state agreed to honor the Sabbath, to practice kashrut in its establishments, and to protect the autonomy of religious institutions, but never agreed to wholesale implementation of the halakha. It does permit Jews to live their lives according to the halakha, as long as they don't violate the positive law of the state. The disciplining of Kahane and Amir demonstrates the supremacy of state law over halakha. Moreover, it was state action, the conquest of the West Bank in 1967, that triggered change in religious ideology. Suddenly, for an activist minority of Orthodox Jews, the Zionist project of settlement became a sacred enterprise of helping God fulfill his promise to the Jews. Retention and settlement of conquered lands became a religious imperative as a result of political conditions.

Conflict over institutions similarly arose not from religious doctrine but from the outcome of particularistic political bargaining. As the religious parties gained political clout and the control of key ministries, they reinforced their educational facilities and programs through the allocation of government funds. Representative government became the tool by which religious forces protected the Sabbath, encouraged settlement, ensured the future of religious education, and secured ongoing settlement in the West Bank and Gaza. These forces exploited their electoral strength and encountered resistance only in an unelected institution, the Supreme Court under Chief Justice Barak. The court challenged the sovereignty of the Knesset in the name of an Israeli "constitution" invoked against the legislative will. The strength and autonomy of religious institutions in Israel reflect the politics of the country more than the politics reflect religious institutions.

Religion has prevented Israel from achieving a single, unified political culture. Only a unified educational system common to people of all faiths and to the secular as well as the religious could build a unified political culture. Particularistic religious groups would not, however, be able to perpetuate themselves if they were not permitted to run their own schools. (The same thing might be said of Christian sects in the United States.) It is not Judaism that prevents unification. Rather, the diversity of the political culture and the consociational spirit that emerges from that diversity provides the political guarantees of religious diversity. Democracy of the Israeli sort helps create and sustain religious fragmentation.

In these three domains—ideology, institutions, and political culture—the intermixture of religion and politics seems not to thwart democracy but to be a result of it. Israeli politics has reshaped Judaism, and, as conditions change, it may do so again. Religion is a variable in this perspective and largely one that depends upon political circumstances and political interaction. Religious forces have become formidable players in Israeli politics because they have shaped and reshaped themselves to win elections, control ministries, approve budgets, and administer programs. They have seized their political opportunities and transformed themselves in the process. What they become in the future depends less on religious doctrine than on future political opportunities.

With the question of national identity, the prospects seem somewhat different. Early Zionism sought a national identity that was distinct from religious identity, but it could not define a Jewish people without reference to Judaism. Jewish leaders decided Israeli identity depended upon the invocation of religious symbols. This decision precludes full democracy in the state by denying non-Jews full citizenship. While it is theoretically possible to untangle national and religious identity, it is much more difficult to imagine separation than it is to imagine political decisions to give back the West Bank or to limit deferments to yeshiva students. Unlike many of the decisions about ideology, institutions, and political culture, this one does not seem to have been a product of democratic politics as much as a product of world history. The identification came out of medieval anti-Semitism, Russian pogroms, Hitlerian atrocities, British imperialism, American guilt, and much more. The identification of Israel with Judaism necessarily comes from politics, not religion itself, but it is not clear that a mere majority in Israel could undo what history has done.

Notes

1. Jonathan Sacks, *One People? Tradition, Modernity, and Jewish Unity* (London: Littman Library of Jewish Civilisation, 1993), 27–31.

2. Tom Segev, *1949: The First Israelis,* trans. Arlen Neal Weinstein (New York: Free Press, 1986), 261.

3. See Aviezer Ravitzky, "Is a Halachic State Possible? The Paradox of Jewish Theocracy," *Israel Affairs* 11, no. 1 (January 2005): 137–164.

4. For example, Ira Sharkansky, *Rituals of Conflict: Religion, Politics, and Public Policy in Israel* (Boulder, CO: Lynne Rienner, 1996), 152.

5. See Norman L. Zucker, *The Coming Crisis in Israel: Private Faith and Public Policy* (Cambridge, MA: MIT Press, 1973).

6. Charles S. Liebman and Eliezer Don-Yehiya, *Religion and Politics in Israel* (Bloomington: Indiana University Press, 1984), 51.

7. Liebman and Don-Yehiya, *Religion and Politics in Israel*, 50.

8. Segev, *1949*, 208.

9. Ibid., 222.

10. Ibid., 222.

11. Asher Arian, *The Second Republic: Politics in Israel* (Chatham, NJ: Chatham House, 1998), 27.

12. The Jews of Middle Eastern and North African origin are often called Sephardic as well as Oriental. Mizrachim has become the common term.

13. Gershon Shafir and Yoav Peled, *Being Israeli: The Dynamics of Multiple Citizenship* (Cambridge, UK: Cambridge University Press, 2002).

14. Virginia Dominguez, *People as Subject, People as Object: Selfhood and Peoplehood in Contemporary Israel* (Madison: University of Wisconsin Press, 1989), 57.

15. Liebman and Don-Yehiya, *Religion and Politics*, 15.

16. Segev, *1949*, x.

17. Ibid., 238.

18. Rael Jean Isaac, *Israel Divided: Ideological Politics in the Jewish State* (Baltimore: Johns Hopkins University Press, 1976), 27.

19. Segev, *1949*, 239.

20. Isaac, *Israel Divided*, 78.

21. Ibid., 78.

22. Segev, *1949*, 291.

23. Shafir and Peled, *Being Israeli*, 145, quoting Zucker, *The Coming Crisis*, 173.

24. Dominguez, *People as Subject*, 172.

25. Ibid., 172.

26. Shafir and Peled, *Being Israeli*, 318.

27. Elia Werczberger and Eliyahu Borukhov, "The Israel Land Authority: Relic or Necessity?" *Land Use Policy* 16, no. 2 (April 1999): 129–138.

28. Segev, *1949*, 258.

29. Ibid., 262.

30. Mizrachi is an abbreviation of "Mercaz Ruchani" or "spiritual center." See Bernard Avishai, *The Tragedy of Zionism: Revolution and Democracy in the Land of Israel* (New York: Farrar Straus Giroux, 1985), 95, for an account of its formation.

31. Shafir and Peled, *Being Israeli*, 138.

32. Segev, *1949*, 262.

33. Hanna Lerner, "Democracy, Constitutionalism, and Identity: The Anomaly of the Israeli case," *Constellations* 11, no. 2 (June 2004): 239.

34. Lerner, "Democracy, Constitutionalism, and Identity," 239, citing Ralph Benyamin Neuberger, *The Constitution Debate in Israel* (Tel Aviv: Open University in Israel, 1997), 40.

35. Segev, *1949*, x.

36. Isaac, *Israel Divided,* 43.

37. Martin Edelman, "A Portion of Animosity: The Politics of the Disestablishment of Religion in Israel," *Israel Studies* 5, no. 1: 206. A 2007 law permits civil marriage for persons not considered Jews by Orthodox standards.

38. Quoted in Segev, *1949*, 261.

39. See Aviezer Ravitzky, "Is a Halachic State Possible? The Paradox of Jewish Theocracy," *Israel Affairs* 11, no. 1 (January 2005): 137–164.

40. Arian, *The Second Republic,* chapter 10.

41. Ibid., 3.

42. Yehudah Mirsky, "Inner Life of Religious Zionism," *New Leader* 78, no. 9 (December 4, 1995): 10–14.

43. Isaac, *Israel Divided,* 61.

44. Ibid., 62.

45. [Ralph] Benyamin Neuberger, *Religion and Democracy in Israel,* trans. Deborah Lemmer (Jerusalem: Floersheimer Institute for Policy Studies, 1997), 30.

46. Ehud Sprinzak, "Violence and Catastrophe in the Theology of Rabi Meir Kahane: the Ideologization of Mimetic Desire," in *Terrorism and Political Violence* 3, no. 3 (Autumn 1991): 50.

47. Ibid., 54.

48. Raphael Cohen-Almagor, "Vigilant Jewish Fundamentalism: From the JDL to Kach (or 'Shalom Jews, Shalom Dogs')," *Terrorism and Political Violence* 4, no. 1 (Spring 1992): 54.

49. Ibid., 59.

50. Sprinzak, "Violence and Catastrophe," 58.

51. Cohen-Almagor, "Vigilant Jewish Fundamentalism," 51–52.

52. Efraim Ben Zadok, "State-Religion Relations in Israel: The Subtle Issue Underlying the Rabin Assassination," in Efraim Karsh, ed., *Israeli Politics and Society Since 1948: Problems of Collective Identity* (London: Frank Cass, 2002), 139.

53. See Mirsky, "Inner Life of Religious Zionism."

54. Ben Zadok, "State-Religion Relations in Israel," 141.

55. Lisa Beyer, "The Religious Wars," *Time,* May 11, 1998, 32.

56. Alan Dowty, *The Jewish State: A Century Later* (Berkeley: University of California Press, 1998), chapter 2.

57. See Lari Nyroos, "Religeopolitics: Dissident Geopolitics and the 'Fundamentalism' of Hamas and Kach," *Geopolitics* 6, no. 3 (Winter 2001): 135–157.

58. Sacks, *One People?* 61.

59. Ilan Greilsammer, *Israel: les hommes en noir* (Paris: Presses de la fondation nationale des sciences, 1991), 191.

60. See, for example, Hanna Lerner, "Democracy, Constitutionalism, and Identity."

61. Edelman, "A Portion of Animosity," 207.

62. Ira Sharkansky, "Assessing Israel," *Shofar: An Interdisciplinary Journal of Jewish Studies* 18, no. 2 (Winter 2000): 5.

63. Liebman and Don-Yehiya, *Religion and Politics,* 9.

64. Shafir and Peled, *Being Israeli,* 168.

65. The terms are those of Shafir and Peled.

66. Lilly Weissbrod, "Shas: An Ethnic Religious Party," *Israel Affairs* 9, no. 4 (Summer 2003): 96.

67. Etta Bick, "A Party in Decline: Shas in Israel's 2003 Elections," *Israel Affairs* 10, no. 4 (Summer 2004): 118.

68. Weissbrod, "Shas," 85.

69. Lerner, "Democracy, Constitutionalism, and Identity," 239.

70. Ibid., 244.

71. Ran Hirschl, "Constitutional Courts vs. Religious Fundamentalism: Three Middle Eastern Tales," *Texas Law Review* 82, no. 7 (June 2004): 1819–1870.

72. Lerner, "Democracy, Constitutionalism, and Identity," 247.

73. Frances Raday, "Women's Rights: Dichotomy between Religion and Secularism in Israel," *Israel Affairs* 11, no. 1 (January 2005): 94.

74. Lerner, "Democracy, Constitutionalism, and Identity," 249.

75. Ibid., 249.

76. Liebman and Don-Yehiya, Religion and Politics, 4.

77. Ibid., 7.

78. Ibid., 10.

79. Yeshayahu Leibowitz, *Judaism, Human Values, and the Jewish State*, ed. Eliezer Goldman (Cambridge, MA: Harvard University Press, 1992), 176.

80. Ibid., 227.

81. Joe Lockard, "Israeli Utopianism Today: Interview with Adi Ophir," *Tikkun*, November–December 2004, 21.

82. Shlomit Levy, Hanna Levinsohn, and Elihu Katz, "Believers, Observances and Social Interaction Among Israeli Jews," in Charles S. Liebman and Elihu Katz, eds., *The Jewishness of Israelis: Responses to the Guttman Report* (Albany: State University of New York Press, 1997), 3.

83. Levy, Levinsohn, and Katz, "Believers, Observances and Social Interaction," 7.

84. Charles S. Liebman, "Academics and Other Intellectuals," in Liebman and Katz, eds., *The Jewishness of Israelis*, 69.

85. Bernard (Baruch) Susser, "Comments on the Guttman Report," in Liebman and Katz, eds., *The Jewishness of Israelis*, 170.

86. Gerald J. Blidstein, "The Guttman Report—The End of Commitment?" in Liebman and Katz, eds., *The Jewishness of Israelis*, 128; and Susser, "Comments on the Guttman Report," 169.

87. Levy, Levinsohn, and Katz, "Believers, Observances and Social Interaction," 21.

88. Ibid., 31.

89. Menachem Friedman, "Comments on the Guttman Report," in Liebman and Katz, eds., *The Jewishness of Israelis*, 142.

90. See Ronald Inglehart, *Modernization and Postmodernization: Cultural, Economic, and Political Change in 43 Societies* (Princeton, NJ: Princeton University Press, 1997).

91. Charles S. Liebman, "Cultural Conflict in Israeli Society," in Liebman and Katz, eds., *The Jewishness of Israelis*, 111.

92. Elihu Katz, "Behavioral and Phenomenological Jewishness," in Liebman and Katz, eds., *The Jewishness of Israelis*, 74.

93. Quoted in Liebman, "Academics and Other Intellectuals," Liebman and Katz, eds., *The Jewishness of Israelis*, 67.

94. Inglehart, Modernization and Postmodernization.

95. Segev, 1949, 202.

96. Julia Resnick, "Particularistic vs. Universalistic Content in the Israeli Educational System," *Curriculum Inquiry* 29, no. 4 (Winter 1999): 491.

97. Mordechai Bar-Lev, "Politicization and Depoliticization of Jewish Religious Education in Israel," *Religious Education* 86, no. 4 (Fall 1991): 609.

98. Resnick, "Particularistic vs. Universalistic Content," 492.

99. Zehavit Gross, "State-Religious Education in Israel: Between Religion and Modernity," *Prospects* 33, no. 2 (June 2003): 158.

100. See Jo-Ann Harrison, "School Ceremonies for Yitzhak Rabin: Social Construction of Civil Religion in Israeli Schools," *Israel Studies* 6, no. 3 (Fall 2001): 113–134.

101. Edelman put the number at 28,277, 8 percent of all eligible draftees, in 1997. Martin Edelman, "A Portion of Animosity: The Politics of the Disestablishment of Religion in Israel," *Israel Studies* 5, no. 1 (Spring 2000): 215.

102. The National Religious Party has founded some Hesder Yeshivot, where students alternate between their studies and military service.

5

The Politics of Religion
in "Secularist" Turkey

The first nation-state to emerge from the defeat and breakup of the Ottoman Empire in World War I, the Republic of Turkey decided to separate religion from public life. It accepted the idea that modernization requires secularization of society and politics. From a Western perspective and from that of many Turks, Turkey became proof that a Muslim country could become modern, liberal, and democratic. From another perspective, advanced ever more insistently in the past forty years, Turkey had betrayed its heritage, its neighbors, and itself. Both perspectives are misleading, because they confuse intent with result.

Mustafa Kemal Atatürk, the first president of republican Turkey, pursued policies he regarded as secularist, *laik*. Many writers took the regime's self-proclaimed secularism as a description of fact, even though Turkish "secularism" never meant separation of church and state. Quite the contrary, secularism in Turkey "refers to state control of all aspects of religious life."[1] Secularist elites proclaimed the liberation of the country from the strictures of Islamic doctrine, customs, and what they called superstitions inconsistent with modernity, but they never convinced most Turks to abandon their religious beliefs and practices.

The Kemalists, followers of Mustafa Kemal Atatürk, who seem to have interpreted their dreams as reality, fueled the efforts of Western social scientists to propose Turkey as a model for modernizing societies. The Turkish case confirmed theory: Secularization leads to modernization. But recent scholarship suggests a definition of *laiklik*, the Turkish term for secularism, that conflicts with the one propagated by Kemalists and Western scholars of an earlier epoch. The new scholarship portrays a continuum of development in which a series of political changes has altered the balance between religion and politics in Turkey.

Mustafa Kemal created an official Islam and outlawed nonofficial versions. As a product of the democratization process undertaken since World War II, however, the outlawed strands of Islam have been progressively reintegrated. The search for a new equilibrium of religion and politics reflects changing political opportunities and the responses of religious groups to these opportunities. Modern Islamic movements, reshaped by the politics of the past century, are now reshaping politics. They have helped bring neglected segments of the Turkish population into the political process. The rediscovery of Islam in Turkey has resulted from and promoted modernization and democratization.

Atatürk sought to create a Turkish nation whose identity depended on Turkishness rather than on Islam. Under the Ottoman Empire, a true citizen was both a Turk and a Muslim, although many Ottoman subjects were neither Turkish nor Muslim. In winning the war against the Greeks that set the Turks free of European ambitions, the Young Turks, including Mustafa Kemal, invoked Islam to rally the country and especially the Kurds against the foreigners. Yet, once the war was won, the new Turkish republic made the Turkish language and Turkish history the foci of national identity, making it difficult for Kurds, speaking a non-Turkish mother tongue, to feel a part of the state. In fact, the Kemalist elites cut themselves off from much of rural Turkey by virtue of their apparent hostility to religion. The emphasis on Turkishness and official Islam "helped to politicize nascent identities such as Kurdish ethnicity and Sunni/Alevi Islam."[2]

The gradual reconciliation of Islam with Turkish identity began in the 1950s but progressed more quickly with the emergence of Islamist parties in the 1970s.[3] The election of an Islamist mayor of Istanbul in 1994, and the accession of Necmettin Erbakan to the premiership two years later, pulled the country toward reintegration of Islamic symbols with those of the republic. The old Ottoman capital, Istanbul, began to reassert itself against republican Ankara, the country's modern capital. Even the military, a bastion of Kemalist secularism, fostered the growth of religious schools, and the graduates of these schools slipped into the bureaucracy. Since 2002 the government headed by Recep Tayyip Erdoğan, himself a product of the Islamist movement, has reopened Turkey's connections to its Ottoman and Muslim past without negating the nationalist tradition constructed by Atatürk. Erdoğan evokes the past as he moves Turkey toward a future in Europe.

While Islam served as a foundation for Ottoman law and morality, it can scarcely be regarded as an Ottoman ideology. Ottoman rule depended both upon dynastic legitimacy and upon the linkage of the dynasty to Islam. Ideology is a modern concept. Most modern political ideologies have emerged from revolution, and the Turkish revolution against Ottoman rule led by Mustafa Kemal and his band of Young Turks in the military produced an ideology of secularism that has marked Turkey ever since. The idea of divorcing politics and religion drove changes in language, dress, social habits, and even the choice of the capital city. Atatürk sought to remake Islam into a state-supporting ideology, propagated by official preachers and public schools—an ideology dedicated to eradicating Islam from public life. Not surprisingly, this ideology created alienation and resistance.

To implement his secularizing ideology, Atatürk created a set of central institutions to define and direct religion. He disbanded the religious hierarchy and outlawed public meetings of unofficial religious organizations such as the Sufi brotherhoods, which were forced underground. The Republican People's Party, guardian of the revolution, won support from an educated, urban, secular elite that regarded religious practices as badges of backwardness. The institutional monopoly seemed unassailable, and yet, forgoing politics, religious leaders such as Said Nursi nurtured a modernist, nonconfrontational set of Muslim study groups and organizations. Some of these groups eventually moved toward political action through the National Outlook movement, which spawned a series of political parties. The regime banned one and then another of the parties, but always there was a successor to replace it. It became apparent that the Turkish state, despite its best efforts, had not succeeded in maintaining control of all religious institutions, although it had made religion invisible in public life.

The Kemalist state partially succeeded in remaking Turkey's political culture in an image of European enlightenment and secularism. Elites adopted European dress, manners, entertainments, and the attitude that religion is a private matter. Yet Turkish society as a whole remains religious to roughly the same degree as those of Egypt and Iran. Roughly 80 percent of all three populations report that God is "very important" in their lives.[4] The regime found itself teaching religion in the public schools to advance the "correct" Islam, and in the 1950s it opened special schools for preachers. Immensely popular, these religious schools were soon pumping graduates not just into the mosques and teaching positions but also into business and the bureaucracy. Muslim organizations did their part with study groups and scholarships. "Islamic businesses" began to flourish, and prosperous businesses funded Islamist organizations. The political culture, never as broadly secular as the Kemalists would have wished, began to appear more and more religious in attitude even as it advanced toward liberal democracy. Any Kemalist hope of generating a monolithic, secular political culture in Turkey had disappeared by the twenty-first century.

Religion has once again become an important element in Turkish identity.[5] "Although Turkey has been strictly secular since 1928, Islam is becoming the semi-official religion of Turkey."[6] One writer calls contemporary Turkey a "semi-secular state."[7] The secularist ideology demanding complete separation of religion from political life has broken down, and state monopoly of religious life has failed. The political culture has come to be marked by high religiosity, strong commitment to democracy and liberalism, and marked plurality of religious and political commitments. Turkey seems to be reintegrating the religious and the political as it charges toward more democratic political arrangements.

Identity

To speak of equilibrium under the Ottoman Empire would be to suggest that religion played the same role in 1300 as it did six hundred years later. While Islam constituted an element of Ottoman identity from beginning to end, the role and significance of religion evolved. The founder of the eponymous state, Ösman (Turkish version of Uthman, the name of the third caliph), won fame as a warrior for the faith on the southern frontier of the Byzantine Empire. Yavuz writes: "Frontier societies tend to be fluid, institutionally fragmented, and multiple in their loyalties and shared understandings—laws, norms, customs, and overlapping roles."[8] Islam was not the sole basis of the Ottoman state. Kushner writes:

> In time the dynasty acquired the sanctity which kept it in power for centuries. An Ottoman gentleman, until well into the nineteenth century, would therefore identify himself as a Muslim and an Ottoman, never as a Turk, a term which was used either to differentiate between Turks and non-Turks, or as a derogatory reference to the ignorant peasant or nomad of Anatolia.[9]

The Ottoman state built its legal system on the sharia (*şeriat* in Turkish), but the periphery "maintained its segmentary Sufi and eclectic character."[10]

The identification of the Ottoman state with Islam came under pressure in the nineteenth century both from within and from without. Ottoman losses to the Russians in the north and then to the French in Egypt led sultans starting with Selim III to begin a process of modernization, first of military forces and then of political institutions. The suppression in 1826 of the janissary corps, which had once been the fearsome heart of the Ottoman infantry, and the issuance of the Rose Chamber Rescript in 1839 demonstrated an Ottoman effort at defensive modernization. The principles of the *tanzimat* (reorganization) first articulated in the Rose Chamber Rescript, such as equal rights for and protection of minorities, derived from European thought and practice. The nationalist idea was driving European development in the wake of the French Revolution. Now the Ottomans began to cultivate the idea of a national monarchy. With a new emphasis on Ottomanism, they sought to bring together "all peoples living in Ottoman domains, Muslim and non-Muslim, Turkish and Greek, Armenian and Jewish, Kurd and Arab."[11]

By the second half of the century a group of intellectuals calling themselves the New Ottomans began to criticize these policies. Namık Kemal, perhaps the most prominent thinker of the group, faulted the Ottomans for inattention to the sharia. "The Ottoman state is based on religious principles and if these principles are violated, the political existence of the state will be in danger."[12] Namık Kemal saw Islam as the key to legitimacy and believed the sharia to be consistent with constitutional politics and educational reform. Any such appeal to Islamic identity tended, of course, to divide the empire's Muslim and non-Muslim subjects.

At the end of the nineteenth century a powerful, reform-minded, autocratic sultan, Abdülhamid II, took some of Namık Kemal's advice. Although he ignored Kemal's plea for constitutionalism—in fact, he set aside the constitution accepted by his predecessor in 1876—he invoked Islam as a rallying point for the empire. He called himself caliph, a title initially adopted by the immediate successors to the Prophet Muhammad as leaders of the entire Muslim community. In doing so he reached out to Muslims beyond the Ottoman domains as well as to Sufi orders within, even as he promoted reform. He opened new schools at the elementary and secondary levels to offer both European education and Islamic instruction under the same roof. These schools began to produce graduates who entered the bureaucracy and began to influence policy. "In other words, in the process of transforming society, the state itself was transformed by societal forces."[13] Abdülhamid used Islamism to further reform.

In 1906 the Young Turk movement staged a revolt and won control of the empire. The insurgents appealed to Turkism rather than either Ottomanism or Islamism as the rallying point of the endangered empire. That decision exposed Armenians, Kurds, and other minorities to discrimination and even subsequent massacre. Suspected of sympathizing with Russia, the Armenians of eastern Anatolia died in what they regard as genocide during World War I. (Turkey has systematically denied wrongdoing.) The Young Turks opted to join Germany and the Austro-Hungarian Empire in that war, a choice that brought defeat and partition at the hands of the victorious allies. Russia, Britain, France, Greece, Italy—all were to have their piece of the Ottoman pie at the end of World War I.

The Europeans imposed the Treaty of Sèvres on the defeated Ottomans in 1920, but a group of Young Turk officers refused to accept foreign occupation. They challenged Greek forces for control of Anatolia and did not hesitate to use Islam in their efforts to rally non–Turkish speakers, especially the Kurds who dominated southeastern Anatolia, to the armed struggle. Mustafa Kemal, an officer in the Ottoman military and a Young Turk who had distinguished himself at the battle of Gallipoli in 1915 against British, French, and Australian forces, emerged to lead the struggle for Turkish independence.

Breaking with Islamic Identity

After the war waged for Turkish independence, religion temporarily preempted language in defining nationalism for those who had fled the new Turkey for Greece and who had left Greece for the new Turkey.[14] Only after victory was secure and an independent Turkey had emerged from the 1923 Treaty of Lausanne did Mustafa Kemal take radical measures against both the political and religious establishments of the truncated empire. Breaking with the Ottoman dynasty proved much less difficult than distancing the new Turkey from Islam. The proclamation of the Turkish republic in 1923 ended the Ottoman experiment with a "national monarchy."[15] However, the attachment to Islam depended not just on Abdülhamid's proclamation of the "caliphate"—which the new republic now abolished—but upon the power and prestige of the ulama, upon a legal system they helped administer and schools they ran, upon Sufi orders such as the Bektaşis and the Nakşibendis, and upon a set of symbols that tied Turkey to Islam and to the old regime. Mustafa Kemal and his supporters (subsequently referred to as the Kemalists) acted against all these dimensions of the Ottoman heritage.

The Kemalists sought to revive Turkishness as an identity for the new nation-state and to portray Ottoman Islam as a symbol of backwardness. Istanbul had been the capital of the Ottoman Empire ever since its conquest from the Byzantines in 1453, a trophy city that as Constantinople had been the most important city in Christendom before it became the most important city of Islam. Its mosques and palaces are among the most famous in the Muslim world. Yet the Kemalists abandoned Istanbul as their capital in favor of Ankara, a small town in Anatolia of no particular religious or political distinction, dramatizing their intent to reshape Turkish identity. The decision to abandon the Arabic script used to write Ottoman Turkish and to adopt the Western alphabet for modern Turkish further emphasized the shift. Arabic is the language of the ulama and the Quran everywhere in the Muslim world. Its alphabet also serves the Persian language, which was the literary language of Ottoman elites. By adopting the European alphabet, Mustafa Kemal tipped Turkish identity toward Europe and favored an elite already familiar with European languages.

The Kemalists exalted in "pure" Turkishness as the badge of authenticity, evoking pre-Islamic Turkish history and customs to justify social changes such as the uncovering of women in public places.[16] Women in ball gowns and bathing suits became symbols of the new Turkey.[17] A Turkish woman introduced as the granddaughter of the last shaykh al-Islam, chief religious official of the Ottoman Empire, won the Miss World beauty pageant in 1932.[18] "The appearance of women who broke with the Islamic tradition was to be a major sign of a new form of social life."[19]

Mustafa Kemal Atatürk convinced much of the world that he had effectively cut Turkey free of its identity with Islam. The West applauded. Scholarship of the 1960s portrayed him as a secularizing, modernizing hero, a model for the Middle East.[20] Some Muslims described Atatürk as one of the great enemies of Islam. Both views now appear extreme. Rather than suppressing Islamic identity in Turkey, Atatürk actually cultivated it, politicizing religion and making religious reaction almost inevitable. By abolishing sharia courts and closing the meeting places of the Sufi brotherhoods, he struck blows against versions of Islam he deemed inimical to the new Turkey, even as he created the Directorate of Religious Affairs to control and propagate an Islam he thought benign. Ümit Cizre has written: "Atatürk set in motion the republican tradition of employing Islam to promote the ideas and policies of the secular state."[21] The Turkish masses outside the capital and even in the middle-and lower-class neighborhoods of Istanbul remained attached to the substance and symbols of Islam.

The failure of the Kemalists to establish a viable equilibrium of religion and politics became evident after 1950. When Atatürk's successors opened the system to competitive elections after World War II, the Republican People's Party lost its control of the country. The victors of 1950, the Democrats, made clear their sympathies with the rural areas and their sensitivity to religious belief. In their decade of domination, the Democrats began a long process of bringing Islam back into public life. The process continued in the 1960s under the Justice Party and further accelerated in the 1970s with the emergence of the National Outlook movement, which spawned a series of Islamist parties including the National Order Party, the National Salvation Party, the Welfare Party, the Virtue Party and, finally, the Felicity Party.

Bringing Back Islam

Transition from the Kemalist effort to separate Turkey from centuries of identity with Islam toward the reintegration of Islam into Turkish identity has already spanned more than half a century. Three moments stand out as turning points in the progressive modification of the Turkish identity. After the army intervened in 1980 in response to a decade of conflict and violence, it recognized the need to cultivate the religious needs of ordinary Turks by making religious instruction mandatory in primary and secondary schools. The military wrote this requirement into the 1982 constitution.[22] President Kenan Evren, dressed in military uniform, delivered sermons "as if he were the Grand Mufti."[23] As representatives of Atatürk's memory and policies, the military legitimated the reintroduction of Islam into politics.

Once the military had returned politics to the politicians, a remarkable leader, Turgut Özal, assumed power at the head of the Motherland Party. By breaking with protectionist policies and opening the country to international competition, he triggered economic expansion and political liberalization. He also spoke publicly about his religious devotion. "As comfortable with Western leaders as in a mosque,"[24] he was the first prime minister of the Turkish republic to identify openly with Islam, and, even more particularly, with Sufism, a variety of Islam disdained by early Kemalism. He was a member of the Nakşibendi Sufi order, and "to him, rather than being a burden, [Islam] was an asset that could be utilized for the stability and prosperity of the country."[25] By recalling Ottomanism and its acceptance of plural identities, he sought to bring the Kurds, alienated by Turkish unwillingness to recognize their culture, back into the political fold. Özal said: "Our state is secular. But what holds our nation together, what serves in a most powerful way in our national cohesiveness and what plays the essential role, is Islam."[26] Özal's actions constitute a second important moment.

The sweeping victory of the Justice and Development Party in 2002 under the leadership of Recep Tayyip Erdoğan constitutes a third moment. Erdoğan came out of the National Outlook movement, a movement that sought to identify Islam with Turkish nationalism and the future of Turkey. Elected as mayor of Istanbul in the 1990s, he scandalized Kemalists by proposing a mosque in the city's Taksim Square with a minaret among the tallest in the Middle East. Taksim is the neighborhood the Kemalists had chosen for their administrative hub to escape the Islamic architecture and influence of the old city center south of the Golden Horn. Istanbul became the capital of "an alternative, Islamist, nationalist project."[27] Erdoğan welcomed a United Nations conference on habitat in 1996 in an effort to advance a new vision of national identity. The accession of Erdoğan to the prime minister's post with an overwhelming parliamentary majority in 2002 demonstrated that the Turkish political system, far from purging itself of Islamic influence, had been Islamized even as it sought to democratize and liberalize as preparation for entry into a predominantly Christian Europe.

This account neglects the contribution of Necmettin Erbakan and the National Outlook movement (Milli Görüş). His party, Welfare (Refah), assumed the leadership of the Turkish government in 1995 as part of a coalition. The soft coup that brought Erbakan's resignation in 1997 reflected his inability, despite his rather mild but awkward attempts to enact the Welfare Party's agenda, to bring Kemalists and the military into his project. Yet his effort was one of enhancing and enlarging the Turkish national identity, not undercutting it in the name of an internationalist Islam. He saw himself and his movement as saving the Turkish state by restoring its Islamic identity. His party advocated a Just Order (Adil Duzen) to effect a "division of labor and equality among the Muslim brothers comprising all ethnic groups of Turkey."[28] Banned from politics after the dissolution of the Welfare Party, Erbakan must have watched with some amazement when only five years later his protégé, Erdoğan, managed an electoral victory without triggering further military intervention. Erdoğan had tweaked the Islamist message and wooed support in quarters where Erbakan could not have hoped to be successful.

Contemporary Islamism

The renewed identification of the Turkish state with Islam may complicate the Turkish case for entry into the European Union (EU), although Europeans have never ceased to identify Turkey with Islam and Muslims. Kemalist secularism did not change the political complexion of the country any more than laïcité has stripped France of its underlying Catholicism. Ninety-nine percent of all Turks carry identity cards indicating they are Muslims. The Turks were supporters of Bosnian Muslims after the breakup of Yugoslavia, as they are naturally advocates of Turkish emigrants who reside in Germany and elsewhere in Europe. The rediscovery of Islamic identity reinforces the logic of such foreign policies, as it facilitates integration of Turkey's Kurdish minority—distinct in language from the Turkish majority but united with most Turks by religion. The National Outlook movement has enjoyed strong support in the Kurdish areas. In fact, military hostility to the Islamist revival in Turkey probably reflected, in part, the Kurdish issue, until the armed resistance in Kurdistan collapsed after the arrest of its leader, Abdullah Öcalan. Treatment of the Kurds has been one of the sticking points as the Turks negotiate with Europe for entry into the EU. (The Europeans have effectively blocked Öcalan's execution.) For that reason, a sharper Islamic identity that brings Kurds closer to national purposes may augment Turkey's chances to join the EU.

The downside of heightened emphasis on Islam lies in the alienation of hard-line Kemalists, some of them Alevis. The Ottomans identified formally with Sunni Islam. The Islamist movement in Turkey has been Sunni in general orientation, while Alevis, who believe that Ali, the nephew and son-in-law of the Prophet, should be seen as his rightful successor, have much in common with Shii Islam but their syncretistic beliefs and practices make them suspect in the eyes of many Muslims, both Sunni and Shii. Faruk Bilici argues that Alevis have, in fact, played an important role in Turkish Islam by raising questions: "Which Islam? Which Quran? Which Sunna?"[29] Asking those questions and implying that there is more than one possible answer does not win them friends among devout Sunnis and many in the Islamist movement. Alevis constitute between 10 percent and 25 percent of the Turkish population. Some are Kurds.

A majority of Alevis have been sympathetic to the secularism of Kemalism, and some have gone beyond Kemalism to support parties of the extreme Left.[30] Some highly religious Alevis feel close to Iranian Shiism and share its belief in twelve legitimate imams starting with Ali. They want a return to the sharia. Another strain of Alevism centers on Bektaşi Sufism, its associations, and its lodges. It tends to be mystical and apolitical. Ultranationalist Alevis tend to see themselves as authentic inheritors of ancient Turkish tradition. Alevis have thus been anything but united in their political views, but the rise of the Islamist parties triggered an Alevi revival both in Germany and in Turkey. An Alevi Manifesto issued in 1990 called for acceptance of the Alevi faith and culture and equal opportunities in education and politics. Many Alevis fear that Islamist efforts to reassert the centrality of Islam will lead to a single acceptable interpretation of Islam.

The greatest benefit of the gradual reintegration of Islam into Turkey's political identity lies, however, in the solidification of Turkish democracy that appears to have occurred with the victory of Erdoğan and his Justice and Development Party. The party captured not just support of National Outlook voters, who had brought Erbakan to office in the 1990s, but a broad swath of center-right voters who had swelled the ranks of the Democratic Party in the 1950s, the Justice Party in the 1960s, and Özal's Motherland Party in the 1980s. Erdoğan's victory was as much about class as religion, as shown by Turkish reactions when he sent his daughters to the United States for education. "He is no longer a Muslim."[31] It was said he had betrayed his class and his religion, but his actions also demonstrated that he was not a religious ideologue. Erdoğan avoided sensitive religious issues but proceeded with the confidence born of broad-based political support to advance the Turkish application to Europe.

The reemergence of Islam in Turkish identity opens the way toward reconciliation with the Ottoman past, which in turn links Turkey to Europe. The Ottomans constituted a formidable European power from the moment they bypassed the Byzantines in Constantinople to establish a beachhead in Europe until their defeat in World War I. The core of Istanbul stands on the European side of the Bosporus, together with a smidgen of hinterland that permits a continued geographic claim to be a part of both Europe and Asia, the bridge between the two. Ottoman elites hailed from the Balkans, and Balkan refugees swelled the population of Anatolia in the last years of the empire, as it progressively lost European provinces.[32] If the EU were to admit Turkey to full membership, one would expect even greater dependence on Ottomanism and its tolerance for ethnic and religious minorities in the further construction of Turkish political identity.

Political identity is always a work in progress.[33] Islamism, Ottomanism, Turkism, Westernism—all became tools for the construction of a national identity, even though each of the concepts lends itself to transnational interpretation. While Turkey has reached out to the Turkish-speaking republics of Central Asia, those states have not warmed to the formation of a trans-Turkish union. Turkey has shown little enthusiasm to unite with all Muslims in a revival of the umma, and none for the revival of Ottomanism. The drive to enter Europe reflects a desire to further strengthen the nation in economic and political terms rather than a wish to escape the nation-state formula and the bundle of identities it represents. Fortunately for the Turks, the EU remains a group of states with multiple identities, not a superstate with a monolithic perception of itself. If Europe were to become such a superstate, the accession of Turkey would become even more complicated, requiring, perhaps, further exploration of the cultural riches attached to the Ottoman past.

Ideology

States may incorporate religious values into law without elevating them into ideology. The Ottomans based their legal system on Islamic law but theirs was a dynastic state, not an ideological state. The French Revolution produced the world's first ideological state, which came to threaten all of Europe with its zeal for universal republican ideals. German writers took this French "universalism" for what it was, French nationalism, and responded with theories of German nationalism, grounded deep in the collective memory of the *volk*, the German people. Nationalism, socialism, liberalism, anarchism, syndicalism—all spilled forth in the nineteenth century. Even empires such as the Austro-Hungarian and the Ottoman, which were the objects of ideological attack, began to see advantage in appealing to one or more of these ideas.[34]

Kemalist ideology emerged in the context of late-nineteenth-century European ideologies, spurred by a philosophical movement called logical positivism, whose proponents argued that truth must be empirically verifiable. Natural science produced hypotheses. When those hypotheses could be verified empirically, positivists took them as truth. Observations such as "God exists" cannot be verified and do not satisfy the positivist criterion for truth. Marx claimed to be a scientist whose theories explained the dynamics of history and the workings of the capitalist system. While rejecting Marx, Weber and other sociologists offered theories of modernization and change that pushed religion to the margins of society. Durkheim posited that societies create religions to satisfy social needs. The more modern the society, the less it needed religion. In positivist perspective, secularization of European society had come to be fact, not mere theory, at the end of the nineteenth and beginning of the twentieth century.

The Ottomans had looked to France to help them modernize education. The military schools in which Mustafa Kemal and other Young Turks received their educations reflected the influence of the French curriculum. At a moment when France was regarded as the quintessential modern country, the Third French Republic (1871–1940) found itself deeply at odds with the Catholic Church. Not until 1896 did the Catholic Church rally to support the republic, but the Radical Party, largely defined by its hostility to the Church, joined socialists to press for the secularization of education and the body politic. The French vision of secularism comported overt suspicion of the Church and a political arena in which any reference to personal religious belief came to be seen as improper.

Positivists came to see religion as superstition. In Turkey those educated in science who imbibed this notion felt estrangement from those who followed a course of religious study. Mardin has argued that secularism relied on a book culture and pulled elites apart from the "non-book world of the more humble subjects of the sultan."[35] Positivist science made language the secure basis of nationhood, and nationhood an inevitable outgrowth of modernity.

Kemalism

Mustafa Kemal established an ideological state in Turkey. "All new ideologies are in essence oppositional," writes Moaddel.[36] The republicanism and nationalism of the French Revolution responded to the monarchy. Marxism emerged in opposition to capitalism. Secular nationalism in Turkey, fueled by positivism, used the Ottoman Empire as its foil. Mustafa Kemal set out to reshape the lives and even the consciousness of his fellow citizens by indoctrinating them with the new ideology, which was unabashedly Western.

> This state not only claimed the monopoly of the legitimate use of the physical means of violence, to use Weber's terminology, but also a monopoly of the means and content of legitimate discourse. . . . Cultural expression was at the same time political expression. Cultural opposition was also political opposition.[37]

Questions of dress were fundamental. The fez, adopted by the Ottomans in the early nineteenth century as modern headgear, was proclaimed passé. Only the European hat was suitable for a modern man. In 1926 a decree prohibited the wearing of the veil in public places. Images of Atatürk in a tuxedo, the elegant host of ballroom dancing, suggested a new standard for the elite. Not even clergy could wear traditional Muslim garb, except when they were exercising their functions.

By putting costume at the forefront of cultural concerns and by focusing on the role of women in society, Kemalists responded to the Western image of the Muslim world. The Orientalist fixation on the veiled eroticism of the East stirred Kemalist response. The adoption of a secular civil code in 1926 replaced the sharia and opened the way for the advancement of women. It continued to treat men as heads of households and required women to obtain permission to work outside the home, but it outlawed polygamy and marriage by proxy and accorded equal rights to women in divorce, custody, and inheritance. Women received the right to vote in 1934–35.[38] While rural women remained largely beyond the scope of this "state feminism," the results were nonetheless impressive. White calls Turkey "one of the most important success stories of women's empowerment in the early twentieth century."[39]

The military came to epitomize and defend secular values. Atatürk took power on the shoulders of the Turkish military, victorious over the Greeks in the fighting that followed World War I. His army saw itself as the vanguard of the modernization movement. The military still occupies a privileged position in the constitution. It enjoys "an autonomy that no other democratic state would accept," powerful in its control of the National Security Council and solid in its relationship to big business.[40] The officer corps enjoys superior schools and acquires a sharp sense of duty to protect the state against external threats and against "dangerous" people and ideas. "An officer who prays, shuns alcohol or is married to a woman who wears a head scarf not only is an unlikely candidate for advancement but runs the risk of being cashiered."[41] The military has been the guarantor of secularist ideology.

"Secularist ideology" must be distinguished from mere secularism. The Kemalists did not merely abolish the sultanate/caliphate and undermine the political authority of the ulama. They established an official version of Islam and sought to outlaw or discredit every other version. Propelled by positivist thinking, Kemalist ideology drew a line between modern and traditional, urban and rural, "white Turks" and "black Turks," the cultured and the uncultured, enlightenment and superstition, elites and masses.[42] "Members of Turkey's elite and foreign dignitaries marched to Chopin music, while the masses marched to Qur'anic chants."[43] Or, as Pamuk, born into a wealthy Istanbul family, recalls:

> As westernized, positivist property owners, we had the right to govern over these semiliterates, and we had an interest in preventing their getting too attached to their superstitions—not just because it suited us privately but because our country's future depended on it. If my grandmother discovered that an electrician had gone off to pray, even I could tell that her sharp comment had less to do with the small repair job he had left unfinished than with the "traditions and practices" that were impeding "our national progress." [44]

Turkey's enemy, "medieval" Islam, lurked within the country.[45]

Kemalist ideology posited a dichotomy between science and religion, modernity and tradition, but that dichotomy began to erode even as ideological Kemalism continued to dominate the political scene. One important factor was an extraordinary individual, Said Nursi, who suffered through government harassment, trials, and imprisonments to attain the status of sainthood among his followers. Bediüzzaman ("without equal in our times") Said Nursi combined popular religion with an appeal to literacy and reason that challenged the dichotomy Kemalists were making between tradition and modernity. A nationalist from start to finish, Nursi denied he was undermining the state by using religion for political purposes, but the Kemalists felt threatened by the following he generated no matter where they forced him to live.

The Nur Movement

Said Nursi crossed intellectual boundaries. Born into a Kurdish family in Bitlis near Van in eastern Anatolia, Nursi struggled to bring modern, university-level education to the Kurdish region. The son of an *'alim*, a man of religion, he distinguished himself as a boy by his prodigious memory and capacity for learning, but he never permitted his erudition to separate him from the Nakşibendi (Sufi) environment that nurtured his spiritual instincts or from popular religion that deviated from the practices of the formal Sufi orders. Endowed with personal magnetism and the qualities of a Sufi shaykh—sometimes he acknowledged divine inspiration and sometimes he denied it[46]—he gathered disciples and followers in the traditional Sufi pattern but then insisted on burial in an unknown tomb, to prevent his worship after death. Unlike a traditional Sufi shaykh, he created a body of writing called the *Risale-e Nur* (*Epistle of Light*), which he regarded as his legacy. He pushed his followers toward the study of text and away from the adoration of a holy man in the Sufi tradition.

Nursi fought Kemalist secularism without trying to create a counterideology. He had sought to shore up the failing Ottoman state in its final decade. He joined the army to fight against the Russians on the eastern front in World War I without jumping on the anti-Armenian bandwagon. He supported the republic from its beginnings in 1923 and redoubled his efforts to get a university established in Kurdistan. As Mustafa Kemal steered the country toward a radical separation of religion and state, the proposal for a university languished in the Grand National Assembly, and Nursi, "the New Said," gave up on politics and launched a spiritual renaissance. Nursi quoted himself as having told Atatürk, who had offered him a job in the public service as a preacher: "The New Said wants to work for the next world and cannot work for you, but he will not interfere with you either."[47] Bringing Islam in line with science and modernity was part of his project. Merging the lessons of formal Islam with those of popular religion was another. Nursi's idiom was Sufi even though he did not try to found a new Sufi order.

Although Nursi did not support the Kurdish Revolt of 1925, the government used that uprising as an excuse to move Nursi out of the East and into forced residence in the province of Isparta in western Anatolia. The government claimed Nursi represented the superstition and mysticism that Mustafa Kemal identified with the Ottomans. Nursi irritated the authorities by wearing his turban in defiance of dress laws. ("The turban comes off with the head," he said in 1943.) He wrote his great work, the *Risale-e Nur*, in the forbidden Arabic script. Nursi had learned Turkish as a third language after Kurdish and Arabic. His somewhat stilted prose, heavy in words of Arabic derivation, evokes the spirit of the Quran. He believed the Ottomans had fallen on hard times not from devotion to religion but because they had neglected Islam. Modernism with its emphasis on materialism was diverting Turkish Muslims from their ethical responsibilities. Nursi nurtured a spiritual revival.

It was probably Nursi's modernism even more than his traditionalism that irritated the Kemalist authorities. Nursi had supported the Constitutionalist movement and the deposition of Sultan Abdülhamid. He favored progress and opposed despotism.[48] He argued for the integration of a modern curriculum into the advanced schools of religious learning, the *madrasas (medrese)*. Nursi must have seemed dangerous to the government, because he pushed his followers to read texts and analyze them, to think about religious issues in a modern way, to go beyond oral transmission of scripture and clerical intermediaries to confront spiritual questions on their own. Secular culture was book culture.[49] Nursi pushed his followers toward book culture to oppose secularism, weakening the government effort to link Islam with superstition and backwardness.

Even without a printing press at his disposal, Nursi managed to reach a broad public. The government prevented publication of the *Risale-e Nur*, but his disciples copied it by hand and distributed it in channels beyond government control. It is estimated that various versions of this work had been copied 600,000 times before it reached print in the new alphabet in 1956.[50] At his trials (and there were many, because the government would not give up on prosecuting him) Nursi argued that genuine secular government would make all citizens free to practice any religion they wished.[51] He professed utter loyalty to the Turkish republic and Turkish law. This modern savvy saved his neck and irritated the Kemalists.

Nursi threatened the regime by exposing the ideological, positivistic, religious character of the Kemalist commitment to secularism. His fearlessness, willingness to endure deprivation, ability to inspire devotion in his followers, and eloquence in articulating his message made him a formidable opponent for the Kemalists. His work opened the way for challenges to Kemalist practice in the 1950s, after the Democratic Party took power. Nursi even modified his apolitical stance to endorse the Democrat program, which put religion back in public schools and led to the creation of Imam-Hatip schools to prepare preachers and teachers. But the Nur movements inspired by Nursi's book that continue to animate modern Turkey have, for the most part, retained the founder's distaste for ideology and honored his fondness for education and spirituality. Fethullah Gülen, the most prominent of Nursi's disciples (known as Nurcus), continues to combine pragmatism, modernism, and a commitment to education with a core belief that Turkey must be true to its Islamic heritage.[52]

The Kemalist elite cut themselves off from the masses with their ideology of secularism and authoritarian approach to enforcement. Yavuz writes: "By suppressing Islam, the state ruptured the formative ties between politics and culture, and this estranged the majority of the population from the state."[53] Nursi addressed that estrangement. Mardin suggests Nursi responded to aspirations arising from the mobilization of a "new class," "the middling level of the rural and small-town population of Turkey."[54] He was pulling this class toward a modern, text-based world once reserved for the elites but doing it in a familiar, recognizable idiom. New economic opportunities and modern schools had begun to produce fresh ambitions together with frustrations at the erosion of established customs. The communications revolution had begun to bring the countryside in touch with the shocking, Westernized habits of the Turkish elites and a government bent on steamrolling particularistic customs into a smooth, monolithic culture.

The Nurcus were not alone in reaching the relatively disempowered segments of Turkish society before 1950. The Kemalists had banned the Sufi orders (*tariqat*) and bolted the doors of their meeting places, the *tekkes*, but the orders merely went underground. "The Naqshbandiya, with its sobriety and emphasis upon the sharia, could well dispense with the tekkes, and it was thus particularly well-equipped to defy the attempted abolition of the tariqats."[55] Nursi had himself come from a Nakşibendi environment. The

Nakşibendi, who take their name from Baha al-Din Naqshbad from Bukhara (d. 1389), look to Maulana Khalid (b. 1776) of Kurdistan as their founder. In the modern era they have split into many sections following different shaykhs, some oriented toward Kurdistan and others involved in opposing Mustafa Kemal's secular state. One spin-off group, the Süleymancis, engaged themselves in creating underground Quranic schools with the explicit aim of colonizing the government's Directorate of Religious Affairs, which controlled official Islam.[56]

When Atatürk's successors opened the door to multiparty competition, the opposition parties sought votes among the "black Turks" of the hinterland, where the Nur movements and the Sufi orders had been carefully working the terrain. The ideology of the Republican People's Party did not change, and even the opposition parties—first the Democrats and then their successors in the Justice Party—did not challenge the notion of the secular state. Instead, they reached out toward popular Islam with small reforms that produced important long-term consequences. They co-opted the Nurcus and the Nakşibendi, or at least important segments of their groups, to support Imam-Hatip schools for the training of preachers and prayer leaders, to create a faculty of divinity at Ankara University, to permit the use of Arabic in the call to prayer and to authorize religious radio broadcasts, and to make religious instruction available in primary schools on a voluntary basis. The Democratic Party enacted these measures to win votes.[57]

The military coup of 1960 threatened to interrupt this movement toward the accommodation of popular Islam, but in fact the military junta, which produced a new constitution and then put government back in the care of civilians, did not reverse the trend. General Cemal Gürsel, interim president, in fact proclaimed: "The cause of our backwardness is not our religion but those who have misrepresented our religion to us. Islam is the most sacred, most constructive, most dynamic and powerful religion in the world." For him there were, however, two Islams: "one secular and dispassionate, the other reactionary."[58] It was both a restatement and a softening of Kemalist secularism.

The military had abolished the Democratic Party and executed its leader, Adnan Menderes, but the Justice Party, which emerged to dominate the 1960s, endorsed many of the Democratic Party's policies toward Islam. Fear of communism and the Soviet Union dominated Turkish politics in both the 1950s and 1960s. The Justice Party saw Islam as a counterforce and a link to its allies on the Right. The government brought a few Muslim technocrats into the government and cultivated the support of the tariqat and the Nurcus, but it did not launch a direct assault on the longstanding ideology of secularism.[59]

Islamist Ideology

Ideological opposition emerged first in the 1970s with the National Outlook (Milli Görüş) movement, which spawned a series of political parties over the next thirty years. The founder was a prominent Nakşibendi, Mehmet Zahid Kotku, who believed much of Turkish society would support a politics based on identity and justice.[60] The name "Milli" (millet, a term used by the Ottomans to designate religious groups) already evokes religion as the national focus and suggests opposition to cosmopolitanism and Westernism. "National View" might be another translation.[61] With Just Order (Adil Duzen) as its only genuine platform, the movement suggested a return to the sharia without actually committing itself to that objective. The National Outlook movement appealed directly to the "other" Turkey, with a "reconstruction of Ottoman-Turkish norms and associations to challenge the alienating aspects of the Kemalist project of radical positivism."[62]

The National Outlook movement created a succession of political parties, every one of which was eventually suppressed by the state. The National Order Party, banned in 1971, became the National Salvation Front, which eventually gave way to the Welfare Party. When Welfare was outlawed, the Virtue Party surfaced, only to disappear quickly in favor of Felicity. Every name bore religious connotations. And the leadership fell primarily to one man, Necmettin Erbakan, first elected in 1969 to the Grand National Assembly. In 1974 he became a deputy prime minister when his National Salvation Party joined a coalition government. But the great success of the National Outlook movement came twenty years later, when the Welfare Party took control of twenty-nine large municipalities. In the parliamentary elections of the following year, it won 21.4 percent of the vote and 158 of 550 seats. Erbakan stepped to the fore as prime minister of a coalition government.

The National Outlook movement did not initiate the politicization of religion in Turkey. The Ottomans had taken steps in that direction, and Mustafa Kemal had moved several steps further by attempting to force a single official version of Islam on the country. The opposition parties of the 1950s and 1960s had used Islam to enhance their appeal in the rural areas and small towns of Anatolia. But it was the National Outlook movement that imparted an ideological fervor to Islamism. It offered an alternative version of Turkish nationalism to the secular ideology (and official religion) of the Kemalist state.

The emergence of Islamist ideology in Turkey provoked sympathetic response among the Kurds and negativity among the Alevis. The Kurds saw the sharia as providing space in which ethnicity would be irrelevant. But at the same time that Kurdish Islamists cloaked themselves in universalist Islam against the Turkish particularism of the state, they also defended Kurdish particularity against Islamic universalism.[63] The Alevis were themselves divided and pluralistic and worried about what they saw among the Sunni Islamists in the National Outlook movement. They feared an effort to reduce Islam to a single interpretation, albeit a different interpretation than that of the Kemalist regime. They also worried about regime efforts to cast them as "true Turks" as opposed to the Kurds, some of whom are Alevis. The Alevis began looking to the past and trying to reinvent a culture, perhaps because so many Alevis were moving or already had moved away from it.[64] The Alevis resisted Islamist ideology without being able to offer one of their own. One Alevi group, the Democratic Peace Movement, demanded in 1995 that the Directorate of Religious Affairs be shut down, but the group was shut down instead.[65]

The appeal of Islamist ideology suffered from the policies of Turgut Özal, the soft coup of 1997, and the acts of an extremist group, the Turkish Hizbullah.[66] First as prime minister and then as president, Özal opened Turkey to the world with his policies of economic liberalization. He resisted secularism, state control of the economy, and nationalism as homogenizing influences in favor of tolerance for minorities whether ideological, religious, or ethnic. A devout Muslim, he worked to bridge the differences between the religious and secular communities. Yet, despite his efforts to blunt the Islamist appeal, an economic downturn in the 1990s combined with international tensions brought the Welfare Party to power in 1995.

The Turkish armed forces, with their eighteen directives to Prime Minister Erbakan on February 28, 1997, seemed to have struck Islamism a fatal blow. "The goal of the military was to roll back the Muslim sectors of civil society by closing off their opportunity spaces."[67] When the Constitutional Court closed down the Welfare Party in January 1998, it said the party had violated "the principles of the secular Republic." It enforced Kemalist ideology.

Finally, a shootout at a villa on the Bosporus in January 2000 led to the discovery of a reign of terror by a Turkish organization known as Hizbullah, whose victims were thought to number at least sixty. Hundreds of arrests followed. It may be that the state looked aside as Hizbullah built strength in the Kurdish areas, looking on it as a means to counter the radical Kurdistan Workers' Party, or PKK.[68] Hizbullah spread from the Kurdish zone into the squalid urban milieus of western Turkey. "While not organically linked to the Islamists of the Virtue Party, Hizbullah certainly grew out of an atmosphere of tension between the secular state and the desires of political Islam." It was the first time that Turks had seen violence from Islamism, and the image of the Virtue Party and the National Outlook movement in general suffered as a result.[69]

The parliamentary elections of 2002, in which Recep Tayyip Erdoğan, the former Islamist mayor of Istanbul, led his Justice and Development Party (AKP) to overwhelming victory, may come to be regarded as the end of two ideologies: Kemalism and Islamism. The AKP gathered into its camp many of the conservative voices and categories that had supported the Democratic Party in the 1950s, the Justice Party in the 1960s, and Özal's Motherland Party in the 1980s. Erdoğan also appealed to the Islamists of the New Outlook Movement, from which he came. But, unlike Erbakan, who was prime minister in 1996 and 1997, Erdoğan did not announce an Islamist agenda or even take immediate action on what Kemalists had long regarded as the headline issue, the head scarf. Pulling Islamists toward the system, he pushed them toward full support for global initiatives and entry into Europe. His policies seemed both post-Islamist and post-Kemalist. He attempted to depoliticize religion.

Erdoğan takes his place among a set of Turkish leaders who have sought to bring Turkey back toward its Ottoman, Muslim heritage. Even the military, especially after the 1980 coup, has edged in this direction, even if the directives of 1997 represented a throwback to an earlier era.[70] By gradually separating themselves from the ideological secularism of Kemalism, they have extended the reach of Turkish democracy to minorities and the rural areas, to those who have left the rural areas for the slums of the urban areas, to those who are just now feeling the effects of education and higher standards of living, to the nonelites whom Kemalists hoped to convert to "modern ways," and to all those for whom the Islamic idiom rings true and familiar.

Kemalists brought Turkey toward a liberal, democratic system, but their ferocious secularism eventually impeded further democratization. Islamism as an ideology helped undermine Kemalist ideology and brought conflict and crisis rather than reconciliation, but the return of Islam as a bridge to a plural, heterodox cultural heritage appears to be moving Turkey forward toward liberalism and inclusiveness. Said Nursi and the Nakşibendis initiated this change. Nurcus such as Fethullah Gülen have carried it forward. Islam as an identity draws together Kurds and Turks, Alevis and Sunnis, Sufi orders, various other practitioners of popular Islam, and so-called secular Muslims. In

Turkey, the diminished intensity of ideological conflict has reinforced democracy and the state's legitimacy.

Institutions

Turkish secularism has never meant separation of church and state. Rather, the Turkish state sought to take complete control of every aspect of religion—prayer, language, preaching, teaching, meetings, doctrine, places of worship, personnel, calendar, finances, everything. A government agency called the Directorate of Religious Affairs (Diyanet İşleri Başkanlığli or DBI) was its primary tool. The Kemalists abolished, at least in theory, unofficial religious organizations and outlawed analysis or propaganda from any source suggesting that religion should count in public affairs. In taking these measures, they thought they were promoting modernity and condemning Ottomanism.

Democratization and liberalization opened the way for political parties. To combat the Kemalists and their Republican People's Party, the new parties needed to mobilize the minorities, the rural areas, the "other Turkey." The only organizations with strong roots in the "other" Turkey depended on religion as a bond. As industrialization and urbanization pulled people away from their familiar settings, they turned to religious associations for support, comfort, and advice. These parties and organizations found financial backing in a newly prosperous, small-town and rural bourgeoisie, created in part by the economic liberalization programs undertaken in the 1980s and held together, in part, by association with the Islamist movement. Their money financed newspapers, magazines, and television stations, where Islamist intellectuals talked and wrote about the relationship of religion to public life. More and more graduates of religious schools, funded by the state in deference to the pressures of these parties and movements, invaded the sanctuaries of the secular state, including the Directorate of Religious Affairs. In short, liberalization led to a relationship between organized religion and the state utterly different from that imagined by the early Kemalists.

The Ottomans looked to the mainstream Sunni tradition for legitimacy. They accorded a place of honor and responsibility to the ulama, scholars and prayer leaders who were the defenders of the sharia. Ottoman judges, the cadis, applied the sharia as well as the positive law (*qanun*) adopted by the Ottoman sultans. Many of the qanun reflected dispositions of the sharia. Not a part of the military-bureaucratic elite recruited by the *devshirme* (forced conscription) in the European provinces and converted to Islam, the ulama achieved a measure of autonomy from state control. As in other parts of the

Islamic world, gifts in perpetuity for the support of religious institutions (*vaqf* in Turkish, or *waqf* in Arabic) ensured financial well-being. The ulama enjoyed close family connections with the Muslim bourgeoisie. The sultan appointed the shaykh al-Islam, chief of the religious establishment, from the corps of ulama, which tended to reproduce itself in a bourgeois milieu. Most important, the ulama derived power and influence by virtue of their specialized knowledge of Arabic and Islam.

As the Ottoman dynasty undertook modernization in the nineteenth century, it began to regard the ulama, some of whom objected to the guarantees of rights to minorities and to the moves to secularize schooling, as obstructionist. Bureaucrats began to echo the positivistic tendencies of European thought. Meanwhile, the Nakşibendi order expanded its networks all across Anatolia, perhaps as a response to the pressures for change. Islam itself appeared to be in flux. The last powerful Ottoman sultan, Abdülhamid II, renewed the dynasty's appeal to Islam, while other voices called for an Islamic constitutionalism that Abdülhamid had renounced. In short, the Ottoman state never enjoyed full control of religious organizations even at the height of its glory. Even Hamidian efforts to restore sultanic authority failed to counter the subversive effects of liberalization, which opened the way toward still greater pluralism and "multiple modernities."[71]

State Control

The Kemalist revolution sought to reverse these trends by eliminating not just the official religious institutions of the Ottoman state but the unofficial networks that challenged or supplemented the Sunni establishment. The sultan was deposed, the caliphate abolished, the office of shaykh al-Islam and the corps of ulama disbanded, the madrasas shut down, the sharia courts abolished, the tekkes closed, and the brotherhoods themselves disbanded. A new court system and the Swiss Civil Code replaced the cadis (judges) and the sharia courts. The new Directorate of Religious Affairs took over the management of mosques and ceremonies. The regime thus sought to deny religious organizations and groups the opportunity to intervene in public policy and obstruct progress toward "modernity" as the Kemalists defined it.

Achieving effective state control of legalistic, Sunni Islam proved easier than bringing personalistic forms of Islam to heel. The state could and did replace formal structures with new courts, legal codes, and supervisory personnel, thus supplanting some of the legitimating apparatus of Ottoman rule. But closing the Sufi lodges (of which there were some three hundred in Istanbul in 1920) and replacing them with People's Houses did not suffice to eliminate the power of the Sufi brotherhoods. The Sufi orders (tariqat), prevalent in both Sunni and Shii Islam, all look to eponymous founders, shaykhs, who pass their secrets to successors and train disciples to "remember God" in the fashion particular to their order. Some of these Sufi masters gain honor as saints in their own right. Their followers may come to see themselves as new groups within the larger tradition. While the closure of meeting places reduced the capacity of the orders to perform their ceremonies of remembrance (*dhikr*), the government could not destroy the networks of personal relationships between masters and disciples that underpin Sufism. For example, the Nakşibendi order, which accounted for about a fourth of all the lodges in Istanbul in 1920, sprang back into public view and influence once the ban on Sufism was lifted. The Nur movement survived and prospered because it, too, depended on the personal ties characteristic of Sufism.

The state has become much more realistic in assessing its influence on religion than it was in the early days of the republic. Ali Bardakoğlu, president of the Directorate of Religious Affairs, acknowledges three sorts of influences over the public perception of Islam in contemporary Turkey: official agents, unofficial agents and institutions, and the mass media.[72] The directorate employs the official agents, who number 80,000. It controls 69,000 mosques and employs some 63,000 chaplains and preachers.[73] "Unofficial agents and institutions" run the gamut from local holy men through Nurcu and Sufi groups to political parties. The mass media have opened space for a new set of religiously oriented intellectuals.

Bardakoğlu insists that the directorate does not impose a single understanding of Islam. "The Diyanet does not support an essentialist idea of Islam," he writes. Yet he says his organization generates "authentic knowledge" and encourages "sound knowledge and scholarship." He implies that some religious knowledge is inauthentic and unsound. The directorate does not regard religion merely as a "theoretical belief system," he says, but as a "sociological phenomenon."[74] With that statement he acknowledges the diversity of Islam, ranging as it does from "mystical and folk Islam to a conservative and more moderate understanding of Islam." The directorate aims to foster "social peace and trust" by promoting tolerance, education, "independent" research, and "moderate" understandings of Islam. Bardakoğlu says that the Kemalist state created the directorate in an effort to create "moral religiosity."[75] The opposite would probably be "political religiosity" or perhaps "religious activism" rather than "immoral religiosity"!

Beyond State Control

The unofficial agents of Islam in Turkey fall into three categories: nonactivist and nonpolitical, activist and indirectly involved in politics, and explicitly political. The first category would include local holy men practicing varieties of folk religion loosely derived from a multiplicity of religious traditions and some of the Sufi orders. The mystical Alevism associated with Hacı Bektaş Veli would be an example.[76] The second would include many of the offshoots of Nakşibendi including the Nurcus, the Süleymancis, and the most prominent of the neo-Nurcu groups, the Fethullahci (followers of Gülen), which have promoted education, economic development, and social mobilization. The third category consists of political parties, principally those associated with the National Outlook movement since 1969, together with their supporting groups.

The second category paved the way for the third. The Nakşibendi and the Nurcus supported the loosening of Kemalist secularism championed by the Democratic Party in the 1950s and the Justice Party in the 1960s, but their activities were aimed at promoting modern ideas and economic progress in the name of religious identity. Their success cannot be separated from the emergence of a new Islamist bourgeoisie capable of financing the movements and from the development of mass media—newspapers, radio, television, book publishing—by which their message was spread. One prominent Nakşibendi shaykh, Mehmet Zahid Kotku, based in Istanbul, "transformed the structure of the mosque-based community into a semi-political movement."[77] He became a spiritual adviser to Turgut Özal, the first prime minister to acknowledge his Sufi ties. Another major Nakşibendi leader, Süleyman Hilmi Tunahan (1888–1959), who took on consumer culture and secularism but also Wahhabism and Shii Islam, generated a following of some 4 million members. The Süleymancis dominated the Directorate of Religious Affairs until 1965, controlled a large number of mosques in Germany, and ran a network of dormitories for university students in Turkey.[78]

Said Nursi died in 1960 but his followers continued to meet and read aloud his *Epistle of Light*. The emphasis on text freed them from control of the official ulama and distinguished them from Sufi groups. Their meetings generated socioeconomic and even political networks. "The Nurcus are mostly university graduates who either work for small companies or own small businesses." Their networks served as the means of distribution for a number of household products.[79] As time went on, they split into more than ten groups, the most prominent of them headed by Fethullah Gülen, who started his career as a state preacher in Edirne. He read Nursi and other Islamist thinkers and by the late 1960s had begun to build an organization. His basic thesis: In Seljuq and then Ottoman times the Turks achieved an Islamic synthesis that draws not just on the Quran and the sunna but on Sufism. "Sufism has spread among Turks more than others."[80] Modern intellectuals must work from this synthesis, he argued. "He drew much of his support from engineers, the new Anatolian bourgeoisie, academics, and other professionals."[81] By the 1980s and until the soft coup of 1997, the Fethullahci exercised increasing influence in public life with great emphasis on rationality, education, moderation, tolerance, and pursuit of the good life based in a religious understanding. More than Said Nursi, Gülen emphasized action. The movement bought a newspaper and made it into a leading daily, the fifth largest newspaper in Turkey by 2002 and one distributed in thirteen countries with large Turkic, Muslim populations. The movement also owns a television station and radio stations.

The media explosion included many groups besides the Fethullahci. By 1994, Islamic groups owned nineteen television stations and forty-five radio stations.[82] The outpouring of books, journals, magazines, and newspapers reflected the advances in literacy achieved in Turkey and furthered the "creation of a new genre of Muslim intellectuals."[83] It represented a quantum leap in a trend initiated by Said Nursi that pulled Turks toward new forms of imagined community based in text and interpretation rather than personal, oral communication. While government agents and publications could compete in this new marketplace of ideas, they could not control the production of religious "knowledge."

The liberalization of economic policy under Turgut Özal in the 1980s favored this pluralization of Islam. As prime minister, Özal opened the Turkish economy to international competition and thus unleashed a more competitive business environment in Turkey itself. Soon these changes produced a new prosperity and a new Anatolian, Islamist middle class. Small and medium-sized businesses emerged to challenge the state-favored monopolies. Some of these new businesses made specific appeals to a religious clientele. Barber shops, bakeries, restaurants, resort hotels—even some in the luxury category, such as the Caprice on the Adriatic Coast—hung out signs that proclaimed friendliness to devout Muslims. "The hotel suggests that Islamists are not immune to the seductive powers of consumption, pleasure, commodity, and property acquisition—the patterns dictated by global and local trends in the market economy. It underscores the transformative power of the market system in which leisure is 'Islamicized.'"[84]

Islamist businessmen formed an association called MÜSIAD, which built a membership of some 3,000 companies, in parallel to the older, Kemalist-dominated industrial organization called TÜSIAD, which claimed only some 400 members, most of them larger enterprises with bases in Istanbul.[85] The economic strength of the Islamist business community and the creation of a new modern, attentive middle class supported the expansion of mass media aimed at an Islamist public. Islamist businesses also became the material foundation of the openly Islamist political parties, which emerged in Turkey after 1969.

These developments diminished the capacity of official agents to keep Islamic ideas and sentiments out of political life. The collective activities of the Nakşibendis, the Nurcus, the new media, the new Islamist bourgeoisie, and the new Islamist intellectuals transformed the conditions of Turkish politics, even if many of the individuals continued to sidestep direct political involvement. The military leaders who took power in 1980 furthered the change in atmosphere by their appeals to Islam as a source of national unity. Turgut Özal's economic and social policies furthered the growth of the Islamist movement without government acceptance of Islamist ideology.

Islamist Success

Only some of these individuals and groups came to support direct political action to move Turkey toward a more explicit identification with Islam. The prime mover of the National Outlook movement, Necmettin Erbakan, did come out of the Nakşibendis movement but did not take all Nakşibendis with him into the string of political parties he led. The parties of the National Outlook movement challenged the Kemalist idea of separating religious organizations from public life. Kemalist theory depended upon notions that the state could keep religion out of public life by controlling it and by outlawing autonomous religious organizations. The theory did not correspond with reality even when the Kemalists retained authoritarian control of the country, and it broke down completely after they lost parliamentary dominance in multiparty elections. Only force could prevent the use of Islam for political purposes, but the use of force to maintain it jeopardized Turkey's emerging democracy and the country's chances of entering the European Union.

The organizational success of the Islamist parties in Turkey reflected international context, the Turkish past, the Kurdish problem, internal migration, economic growth, the mass media, the veil as a symbol, and the tireless efforts of activists, many of them women. The wave of Islamist activity ignited by the Arab defeat by Israel in 1967 seems to have affected Turkey, a non-Arab state. The Iranian Revolution of 1979 accelerated the growth of Islamism all across the region, even though Turkish Islamists, most of them Sunni, did not rally to the Iranian plea for Muslim unity under Shii leadership. In the case of Turkey, the National Outlook movement sought to reconnect the country with its Ottoman past without negating the Turkish nationalism on which Mustafa Kemal had sought to construct an independent state. Kemal had used Islam to cement Kurdish support during the war of independence. Now the Islamists cultivated Kurdish support, and they took heavy criticism from the Kemalists for doing so, at least until the capture of Abdullah Öcalan and his subsequent denunciation of violence diminished the power of the PKK. The Nakşibendis and the Nurcus had deep roots in Kurdistan. As Kurds and other rural Turks moved to the suburbs of the big cities in the 1970s and 1980s, they found themselves drawn into the Islamist networks providing social integration, education, economic support, and more. Ownership of media gave the Islamists access to a large public even without access to the mosques. The head scarf, or the "turban," as it came to be called to distinguish it from the more traditional head scarf, became the symbol of the movement.

The Islamist movement brought new categories of women into political activity at the same time that it reasserted a set of traditional family values. Powered in good measure by men and women educated in religious schools, the movement drew more women into education, study groups, voluntary associations, and even local government. On the one hand, the conservative Islam they imbibed from the male leadership of the movement discouraged them from employment outside the home.[86] On the other hand, work with other women for the benefit of the party constituted acceptable activity. Many highly educated women who were forgoing professional opportunities to rear their children in traditional ways worked long hours to advance the cause.[87] The Welfare Party mounted grassroots campaigns without precedent in Turkey and won political control of twenty-nine large cities including Istanbul in 1994. Then in the 1995 parliamentary elections they won 21.4 percent of the vote and 158 of 550 seats in the legislature. The victory, coupled with the disarray of the secular parties—none of them able to capture even a fifth of the electorate—enabled the party to enter a coalition government as senior partner.

Neither the success of Welfare in the 1990s, nor the soft coup that appeared to jeopardize the achievements of Islamism in 1997, transformed the relationship between religion and politics. Necmettin Erbakan's government undertook ill-considered initiatives that alarmed Kemalists. He reoriented Turkish foreign policy away from Europe and toward the rest of the Muslim world.[88] The directives handed down by the military on February 28, 1997, did seek to weaken Islamism by pulling back on state-supported religious schools, but not even powerful non-Islamists such as the center-right Mother-land Party supported the changes. The courts banished the Welfare Party and banned Erbakan from politics but could not prevent successor organizations from emerging. At that point, however, the National Outlook movement split, and Recep Tayyip Erdoğan, former Islamist mayor of Istanbul, engi-neered a new party with a post-Islamist outlook, Justice and Development (AKP), which stormed to victory in 2002 with overwhelming support from Islamists and a wide swath of non-Islamist voters who had normally sup-ported parties of the center-right.[89] The Turkish word *ak* (as in the AK Party) means "white" and "clean," suggesting freedom from corruption. The party logo was a shining lightbulb, and the slogan was "continual light."[90] In its emphasis on enlightenment the imagery is strikingly Kemalist. It also evokes Nursi's *Epistle of Light.*

That victory, followed by assurances that the AKP planned no major over-haul of the system in the name of Islam, did not provoke further military in-tervention. Female AKP candidates did not wear head scarves.[91] The AKP lacked incentive to attack the Directorate of Religious Affairs or even official policies on the wearing of the "turban," because many Islamists had already penetrated the directorate as well as other parts of the Turkish bureaucracy, most of them products of the religious schools. The state had already stopped strict enforcement of the rules against beards and turbans in public places, such as universities. The new government portrayed itself as the protector of all religions and all types of Islam. "Official Islam" had become more circum-spect, unwilling to endorse one version of Islam, quite willing to acknowledge that official preachers were not the sole voices of Islam. Kemalist fears ap-peared to diminish. [92]

The election of 2002 showed that Islamists could win in the democratic marketplace of Turkey. It may have demonstrated, as well, that Turkish Is-lamists can win only in a democratic setting. (Only in Iran has revolutionary Islamism carried the day.) Islamists transformed Turkish democracy by ex-panding political participation and became democrats by virtue of political expediency. They pulled the "black Turks"—rural elements, the poor, the up-rooted, the alienated—toward the political system to gain political power for themselves, not by virtue of following instructions in the Quran or the ha-dith. To veer subsequently from the democratic path toward theocracy would be to court rejection from the EU and further military coups from within. Religion has helped secure democracy, and democracy has restored religion as an element of Turkish identity.

Political Culture

As Turkey has edged its way toward liberalism and democracy, it has also moved toward an understanding of politics that incorporates elements of both secularist and Islamist ideologies. State institutions play a leading role in shaping religion, and nonofficial religious organizations help shape the political debate. The lines between public life and religion are much less sharp than the Kemalists thought (or think) they should be. One explanation of these developments lies in Turkish political culture, which combines religiosity, modernism, nationalism, liberalism, and democracy.

Modernization theory hypothesizes that the secularization of societies depends primarily on their degree of economic and social development. Norris and Inglehart argue that "postmodern" societies are more secular than "industrial societies," which are more secular than "traditional societies." They classify Turkey as an "industrial society" and the United States as "postmodern." Yet these two societies score equally high in religiosity. The United States ranks higher than Turkey in the degree to which respondents report religious participation ("How often do you attend services?") and somewhat lower than Turkey in people who say religion is "important" to them. The Turks are slightly more inclined toward "traditional" values than Americans, but these countries both fall outside the norms of their respective groups (postmodern for the United States and industrial for Turkey) by virtue of the religiosity and "traditionalism" of their views.[93] Even more than the Turks, the Americans are outliers, far removed in attitudes from the secular norms of Northern and Eastern Europe. Turkey and the United States resemble agrarian societies more than industrial or postindustrial groups in their relative attachment to religion.[94]

The United States appears exceptional in the context of liberal, democratic states of the postindustrial sort. Turkey appears exceptional among Muslim states struggling with Westernization and modernity. Mardin traces that exceptionalism to the Ottomans, who, of their own accord, decided to embrace change—in education, the military, even in politics—without abandoning the old. They sought to strengthen religious commitments and dynastic authority as a means of achieving modernization. They resisted seeing modernity as the negation of tradition, as the Kemalists later did.[95]

The Ottomans cultivated and maintained a second source of Turkish exceptionalism: religious heterodoxy. Although Ösman built his reputation as a warrior for the faith (*gazi*), his successors never sought to convert all their subjects to Islam. While the Ottomans came to rely on Sunni Orthodoxy for dynastic legitimacy, they seem to have done so only rather late, after Safavid Persia had decided to adopt Shii Islam as the national faith. Never did they seek to suppress the rich traditions of popular Islam that marked the Muslim portions of the empire. Several authors assert that the Turkish proclivity for Sufism exceeds that of other Muslims. Some link the proclivity to ancient Turkish shamanism. The Ottomans never sought to create a monolithic religious culture.

A third strand of exceptionalism in Turkish political culture stems from its lack of colonial experience. In most of the Middle East, modernization arrived as a set of policies propounded by the agents of foreign domination. Napoleon arrived in Egypt in 1798 and imposed change. In North Africa, from Morocco to Libya, and in the Fertile Crescent—Iraq, Syria, Lebanon, Palestine—Christian powers brought "civilizing" agendas, and often they saw Islam as an obstacle. They favored Christians and other minorities, took control of mosques, created European-style schools, and wrote constitutions that reflected European experience. In the minds of many Egyptians, "liberalism" served the purposes of the British. For some Egyptians and many other Muslims, modernity meant replacing traditional morality with materialism, wantonness, and corruption. Turkey, spared direct colonial intervention, avoided this identification of modernism with imperialism. Quite the contrary, it was the hero of the independence movement, Mustafa Kemal, who unabashedly and wholeheartedly adopted Westernization as his program.

The Kemalists wanted to create a monolithic culture based on the Western model, and they failed. They launched a cultural revolution, which unquestionably changed attitudes in the urban areas, especially among the bourgeoisie. To be a true Turk was to do everything the European way! Pamuk remembers a member of the upper class with nothing better to do than have tea at the Hilton Hotel "because it's the only place in the city that feels like Europe."[96] Mardin argues that Mustafa Kemal did not push too hard for change in the rural areas. The Kemalists created a bifurcated political culture, in which only the secularized, Westernized elite of the cities represented the real Turkey, the new Turkey, the pure Turkey.

The Kemalists imagined that the new alphabet would cut the country loose from its Islamic and Ottoman past, but the change immediately affected only the literate, perhaps 3 percent to 5 percent of the population.

Many of those persons would have acquired literacy in Quranic schools without any modern elements in the curriculum. Some of the most prominent would have been ulama, such as Said Nursi, whom the Kemalists would have been happy to exclude from public discourse. The Kemalists needed schools to propagate the new culture. Education, reeducation, and consciousness-raising would be vital training for citizens. The genius of Said Nursi, who combined his Islamic learning with European philosophy and history, lay in his understanding that education would be the key to combating Kemalist secularism.

Education

Even the most liberal and democratic governments normally seek to shape their public school curricula to support political legitimacy. The Kemalist version of civic education promoted Turkish nationalism, the heroism of Atatürk, and the values of modernity. The government took control of all schools in 1923 and adopted the Law on the Unification of Instruction the following year, which imposed a single curriculum, thus abandoning the dual-track (religious-modern) system of the Ottoman period. "It meant the abolition of public religious education as well as religious education provided by various religious orders."[97] These schools offered no instruction in Islam. There was initially no provision for training mosque personnel. Only in the 1940s did the Republican People's Party, then the only legal party of the state, permit the creation of optional courses of religious instruction in elementary schools, and a few courses in secondary schools to train preachers and prayer leaders. The state also created a faculty of theology at Ankara University. The Kemalist intent was "to ensure that religious instruction remained within the secular principles of the state," but the state could not sustain official Islam without teaching Islam.[98] The alternative was to let the Nakşibendis, Süley-mancis, Nurcus, and others supply religious education.

After 1950, with the Democratic Party in power, the state increased the place of religious instruction in public schools. In elementary and secondary schools, children took optional courses in religion unless their parents requested in writing that they be exempted. The courses for preachers and prayer leaders became separate Imam-Hatep schools, which were initially established in seven cities and then extended to sixteen. By 1997 Imam-Hatip schools numbered 600 and were turning out 50,000 graduates a year.[99] By then almost a third of the graduates were female, even though women could not become imams. By the 1990s only 15 percent of the graduates of the I-H schools were entering the religious sector; many graduates went on to universities, where their options expanded.[100] Some ended up in business, the professions, education, and the state bureaucracy, adulterating the secular climate in the state apparatus and penetrating the ranks of the Turkish elite. After the soft coup of 1997, the military insisted upon closing down the middle-school sections of these Imam-Hatip schools, greatly restricting the overall enrollment, but the state continued to maintain the I-H high schools to limit radicalism, appease the public, and train functionaries. The state also manages about 5,000 Quranic schools with some 200,000 students.[101] The forces of Islamism continued to support these schools, despite suspicion of state control, as the best way to nurture their bases of support.

The constitution adopted under military rule in the wake of the 1980 coup provided for the mandatory teaching of "religious culture and moral education" in primary and secondary schools. Section VI, Article 24 of the Constitution of 1982 (amended in 2001) specifies that the state is to supervise the control of "education and instruction in religion ethics." But it also refers to "other religious education and instruction." Presumably that phrase refers to higher education.[102] A manual of instruction to teachers produced by the Ministry of Education says schools must offer "correct" information about religion so that "others" do not "brainwash" students on religious matters. The ministry urges teachers to explain the utility of religion: "For example, in this context ablution helps keep one sufficiently clean; daily prayers discipline one into being organized; and fasting is good for one's health."[103] Teachers must uphold the secularist gospel of the Kemalists, which requires utter separation of religious and political affairs.

The courses themselves may violate that precept, however, by virtue of efforts to sanctify nonreligious values. Texts on religion used in the schools vaunt patriotism, the homeland, religious duty, the military, and social harmony. "Because 'protecting the homeland from all kinds of attacks is a sacred responsibility,' 'it is improper for a Turkish man to evade conscription or avoid joining the army using various excuses.'"[104] "The state, from the religious point of view, is an institution that Allah created for mankind's benefit."[105] Islam serves the cause of social stability. It holds diverse groups together in the interests of the nation, imparting happiness even when differentials of wealth or status may give reason for jealousy. "Thus justice does not mean the eradication of wealth differentials but 'equal' treatment of people without reference to their level of material well-being."[106] The rush of students toward the Imam-Hatip schools, and the protests occasioned by the decision after 1997 to eliminate Imam-Hatip middle schools, show that some

TABLE 5.1

Turkish Student Attitudes Toward Religion—Percentage Agreeing
with Statements in Two Surveys

STATEMENT	1978	1991
"God really exists"	54	81
"Day of Resurrection exists"	64	77
"There is a Heaven and a Hell"	36	75
"Quran is God's commandments"	47	77
"Day of Judgment exists"	59	70
One should "make decisions by Quranic principles"	39	26
"Religion is search for truth and beauty"	64	66

Source: Kayhan Mutlu, "Examining Religious Beliefs among University Students in Ankara," British Journal of Sociology 47, no. 2 (June 1996): 355.

Turkish parents found official treatment of religion in the ordinary public schools inadequate.

As in Egypt, the efforts of the Turkish state to promote and control Islamic education may have helped elevate religiosity in the society. Results from a pair of surveys done among university students, the first done in 1978 on the eve of the Iranian Revolution, the second in 1991, when Turgut Özal had become president of the republic, suggest sharp changes in attitude toward religion. Table 5.1 gives the percentage of students responding positively to a series of statements. The average increase for the first five items was 24 points. The statement "religion is a search for truth and beauty" won roughly equal support from both cohorts, but "making decisions by Quranic principles" actually diminished in support, suggesting that heightened religiosity did not translate into support for an Islamic state that would enforce the sharia. A 1999 survey indicated that 21.2 percent of Turks wanted such a state but only 10 percent thought Islamic law should regulate marriage, divorce, and inheritance, and a mere 1.4 percent favored Quranic punishments, such as stoning, for adultery.[107] "When the implications of Islamic law for marriage, inheritance, or criminal penalties are made clear, support for sharia falls away to nothing."[108] There is presumably heavy overlap between the 21.2 percent of the population favoring the establishment of an Islamic state and the 21.4 percent of the electorate who voted for the Welfare Party in 1995.

The same 1999 survey suggested a high level of tolerance in Turkey. Nine of ten respondents "found tolerance of differences of faith and belief to be important for social peace." Four-fifths said one could be a good Muslim without fasting at Ramadan or, in the case of a woman, without covering one's head, although three-fifths said women who are Muslims ought to wear head scarves.[109] Responses to the 1991 survey of university students also revealed considerable tolerance. Four respondents in five agreed that minorities should be able to worship freely, but more than a third were intolerant of deviation from religious norms. The minority said: (1) head scarves are necessary for women; (2) only Muslims will go to heaven; (3) only a Muslim can be a "truly good person." A fourth of the respondents said that the "secularist" policies of the Turkish state should change, even though two-thirds favored secularism and efforts to gain entry into the European Union.[110]

Turkish Exceptionalism

While religiosity in Turkey remains high—97 percent of the 1999 sample said they were Muslims, and only 2.6 percent reported they were atheists—Turks also show relatively high commitment to democratic ideals. Tessler and Altınoğlu, analyzing data from the World Values survey of 1997, found support for democracy higher (86.5 percent "high" or "somewhat high") than support for freedom (52.5 percent "high" or "somewhat high"). While religiosity did not help explain support for democracy among these respondents, religiosity and "traditionalism" did correlate negatively with the support for political liberty. Tessler and Altınoğlu found that social tolerance, trust in ordinary citizens, attentiveness to public affairs, and positive attitudes toward government performance helped explain why about one-third (the so-called high-high group) of the sample showed "high" support for both democracy and freedom. Traditionalist attitudes correlated negatively with "high" support.[111] Female respondents with less education, low trust in other people, and low attentiveness to government affairs tended to show low support for both democracy and freedom (25 percent of the sample fell in this "low-low" group). Religiosity did not emerge as a significant independent variable in either the high-high or low-low groups.[112]

Turkish exceptionalism appears secure. The influence of heterodoxy within Islam so apparent in the Ottoman era is more visible today than in the early years of the republic, when the state sought to repress unofficial Islam. The Kemalists sought to build on the modernist initiatives of the late Ottoman period to fashion a new, monolithic political culture, and they succeeded in that endeavor among a relatively prosperous urban elite. The broad support for democracy in Turkey and, to a lesser extent, for basic freedoms bear witness to that success.

Resistance to Kemalism came not in the name of superstition and traditionalism but from an alternative vision of modernity. A number of Kemalist values have won overwhelming approval—the sanctity of the nation, respect for the military, orientation toward Europe—but the majority of Turks also appear to accept Islam as a foundation of the state. Surveys suggest that most Turks do not see a conflict between Islam and national independence, Islam and democracy, or Islam and human rights. Kemalist fears of religion and Islamist fears of secularism seem to be diminishing. The victory of the AKP in 2002 shows that a large share of the voting public will rally to an Islamist who proclaims his loyalty to most of the Kemalist program. The Kemalist search for a monolithic political culture has not given way to a monolithic Islamism but rather to an acceptance of plurality and heterodoxy. Only groups dedicated to violence, the PKK and Hizbullah, have enjoyed broad censure.

That does not mean that liberal democracy and a healthy respect for human rights have been fully integrated into Turkish political culture. Under increasing pressure from Europe, the Turkish government has often blamed "exceptional circumstances" for human rights abuses. It continues to deny Turkish responsibility for the Armenian massacres of the WWI era and even to deny the right of Turks to talk about that problem. Pressures from Europe make human rights a question of national pride. Foreign governments and nongovernmental organizations have their interests and agendas. Pressures from the Islamists on the head-scarf issue awaken Kemalist fears of Islamist imposition of the sharia, but the Kemalist agenda to unify and democratize Turkey has itself all too often led to the employment of force against those groups, such as the Kurds, believed to stand in the way of unification. Human rights issues cannot be divorced from contemporary politics in Turkey or from history. Ümit Cizre writes: "Most of all, integration of human rights into a liberal democratic order requires coming to terms with the past."[113] Turks are still in the process of doing that.

Turkish exceptionalism began with the Ottomans, who began to pull the country toward Europe to defend themselves against Europe. Modernization came from within. That exceptionalism continued into the republican era in a different form: a commitment to modernization and its concomitant, secularization, at all costs. No other Middle Eastern state was prepared to follow the Turkish lead, and no other Middle Eastern state can contemplate such policies in the postcolonial era. Even with policies muted by the times, the

Turks appear exceptional in their embrace of liberalism and democracy, despite and even because of an Islamist movement. Turkey combines a high quotient of religiosity with tolerance for diversity that is exceptional. Bülent Aras has talked about "the construction of a Turkish style of Islam and the Islamization of the Turkish nationalist ideology."[114] In the minds of many contemporary Turkish intellectuals, Turkey can go forward in its exceptionalism by looking back toward the Ottoman period for its pluralism, tolerance, and cultural achievement.[115]

Conclusion

To judge by the constitution, religion is much less central to the Turkish state than it is to Egypt, Israel, or Iran. The preamble says that "as required by the principle of secularism, there shall be no interference whatsoever by sacred religious feelings in state affairs and politics." It does not mention Islam. Article 2, which is qualified as an "irrevocable provision," defines Turkey as a "democratic, secular, and social state governed by the rule of law." Article 2 refers to the "fundamental tenets set forth in the Preamble," thus making "the principle of secularism" an irrevocable part of the constitution. Yet the overwhelming majority of Turks are Muslims. In a population now put at 72 million, there are about 400,000 Greek Orthodox Christians, 65,000 Armenian Christians, and 20,000 Jews. Religious minorities thus constitute about 0.7 percent of the population. Ali Bulaç, a leading Islamist intellectual, claims no other country in the world is so overwhelmingly Muslim.[116] He complains that the Turkish state inadequately protects both Muslim and non-Muslim rights.

The Kemalist fear of identifying state and religion came out of a particular period and a particular notion of modernity. The elites who hailed from that period and shared positivist views of modernity imposed a secular Turkish identity on the state, which survives in a formal sense but suffers steady erosion. Nothing symbolizes the erosion better than dress. The head scarf and the beard, traditional symbols of religiosity, never disappeared from rural Turkey, but the return of the head scarf and the beard to the universities and to fashionable, educated, modernist milieus suggests that the identity issue is anything but resolved.[117] The Kemalists made dress a central element in their effort to define modern Turkey; Said Nursi was attached to his turban; and young Islamists now flaunt various types of Islamic fashion to express their identities, drawing praise in some circles and derision or even prejudicial action in others.[118]

External factors also push Turkey toward a sharper identification with Islam. Europeans identify Turks as Muslims and Turkey as a Muslim state. The Bosnian crisis caused Turks to identify with fellow Muslims. As prime minister, Necmettin Erbakan overplayed his hand when he traveled to Iran and Libya to reopen dialogue with Muslim pariah states, but he will surely be remembered, too, for trying to spring Turkey from its self-imposed isolation from its region. Other Muslims identify Turkey with the Ottoman Empire and with long-term struggles against Christian Europe. Turkey is itself a member of the Organization of the Islamic Conference, an organization principally dedicated to planning the annual hajj (pilgrimage). These forces pull Turkey inexorably toward an identity that Mustafa Kemal sought to shed.[119]

The progressive inclusion of Islam as a part of Turkish national identity has not yet resulted in any significant shift toward implementing Islam as an ideology. In Egypt the constitution specifies the sharia as the principal source of legislation, and secular courts have increasingly bowed to religious pressures and applied religious law—convicting Abu Zayd of apostasy, for example—even where the legal foundation of the judgment was unclear. The pressures of the Muslim Brotherhood and elements of the official religious establishment harp incessantly on the need for more thorough enforcement of the sharia. In Turkey, quite to the contrary, Islamists have achieved electoral success by promising to work within a "secular" state. The Justice and Development Party under Recep Tayyip Erdoğan has not sought legislative remedy for the head-scarf issue, much less modification of the constitution. It promises protection of all religious practices and beliefs, as guaranteed by the constitution. Secularism as ideology appears to be giving way to a more pragmatic secularism as practice, and Islamism seems to have relinquished some of its ideological fervor in the process. As long as only a fifth of the Turkish electorate favors implementation of the sharia, and even fewer favor the application of religious rules in particular domains, it is unlikely that the Turkish majority will endorse Islam as ideology.

Turkey and Egypt both propagate an official version of Islam. The organizational structure resulted in both countries from the need to consolidate national power. Muhammad Ali began to undermine the autonomous power of the ulama in early-nineteenth-century Egypt. The Ottomans sought to harness the ulama to the needs of the "national monarchy." But it was the independent nation-states created in Turkey and Egypt after World War I that thoroughly subjugated religion to national purposes. These nation-states nationalized Islam as quickly and efficiently as some states later nationalized oil. The Islamization of these nation-states occurred more slowly.

The governments determined the structure and even the content of religion in their countries to a significant degree, but they worked, of course, with different material and without a common set of guidelines. On the one hand, the Turks worked with a highly heterodox Muslim culture. On the other hand, the Egyptians dealt with a Christian minority far larger than any non-Muslim minority in Turkey. Egyptian geography favors centralized government control. The mountains of Turkey help protect localism and diversity of all sorts. It is thus not surprising that the Kemalist effort to impose a uniform Islam on that country did not succeed and that the Egyptian government needed only to confirm the relative uniformity of Islam in that country as it sought greater control over religious affairs.

Islam shapes political culture in both Egypt and Turkey. High religiosity marks both peoples, yet neither country makes the list of the "most religious states" in the world.[120] No Muslim state figures in the list of the least religious countries. It is not possible to argue that Islam itself explains the high level of religiosity in Muslim countries, any more than one can say that Protestantism makes the United States highly religious or that Catholicism explains Ireland's high religiosity. Other factors are at work.

Governmental educational policies constitute one such factor. Egypt has long taught Islam in its schools. After the first twenty-five years of independence, Turkey reversed course and introduced religious studies at every level of education. The Imam-Hatip schools, begun as a means of training prayer leaders and preachers, have become a general avenue of secondary education that feeds the university system, the corporate world, and the state bureaucracy. The Islamist movement in Turkey has supported this system of schools and benefited from the support of many graduates. The state involved itself in religious education in both countries for similar reasons: to train loyal citizens. Official religious education tied moral behavior to religion and to citizenship in both countries long before a resurgence of Islam became apparent across the Middle East and North Africa. The two governments tied religion to politics, albeit in quite different ways, and both reaped some of the fruits of their labor. Opposition movements sought to make politics answerable to religion. These reciprocal actions have produced high religiosity.

The Turkish republic under Mustafa Kemal did not succeed in its efforts to reduce Islam to a personal religion, eliminate the identification of religion with the state, subordinate all religious institutions to state control, and reduce the religiosity of the society via public education. But the actions of the state under Atatürk and his successors provoked creative reactions among individuals and groups, who generated a new dynamic in Islam. That dynamic contributed to the democratization process and to a gradual modification of state policies that fed a re-Islamization of the society. The new Islam in Turkey is, however, quite different from that of the Ottoman Empire or from that of Egypt. As Turkey has transformed itself in economic, social, and political terms, it has transformed Islam as well. Modernization has brought Turkey closer to Europe by virtue of capitalist development, social mobilization, and political liberalization, but modernization has not eliminated the unique qualities of the Turkish attachment to Islam.

Despite the impact of globalization, the Turks have accentuated the distinctiveness of their approach to religious politics. Mustafa Kemal Atatürk surely deserves less of the credit than is usually attributed to him. (The Turkish constitution, prominent monuments, government Web sites—all give him full credit for everything that is good about Turkey!) He did, however, initiate a process of revamping Islam to suit the needs of the nation-state. European states had already done it with Christianity. Other Muslim states of the Middle East are still following his example, even though the times no longer permit the "secularism" he espoused.

Notes

1. Whit Mason, "The Future of Political Islam in Turkey," *World Policy Journal* 17, no. 2 (Summer 2000): 58.

2. M. Hakan Yavuz, *Islamic Political Identity in Turkey* (New York: Oxford University Press, 2003), 52.

3. Christopher Houston writes that "Islamist best denotes those movements, groups and individuals who reject republican law and desire to substitute Islamic Law (seriat) for it, or live under its aegis." He also notes: "The meaning of Islamist then is self-referentially constructed against the state's official Islamic position, and is not a description of a person's religiosity." Houston, "Civilizing Islam, Islamist Civilizing? Turkey's Islamist Movement and the Problem of Ethnic Difference," *Thesis Eleven* 58 (August 1999): 87.

4. World Values Survey, 2000–2001, Question F063, "How important is God in your life?" from 1=not important to 10 =very important. Analysis online.

5. There is an outpouring of literature on the topic. The Yavuz book, *Islamic Political Identity in Turkey*, is the most substantial. Here is a sample of other recent works that focus on identity: David Kushner, "Self-Perception and Identity in Contemporary Turkey," *Journal of Contemporary History* 32, no. 2: 219–233; Dov Waxman, "Islam and Turkish National Identity: A Reappraisal," *Turkish Yearbook of International Relations* 30 (2000): 1–22; Hasan Kosebalaban, "The Impact of Globalization on Islamic Political Identity: The Case of Turkey," *World Affairs* 168, no. 1 (Summer 2005): 27–37; Ihsan D. Daği, "Transformation of Islamic Political Identity in Turkey: Rethinking the West and Westernization," *Turkish Studies* 6, no. 1 (March 2005): 21–37; Feroz Ahmad, *Turkey: The Quest for Identity* (Oxford, UK: Oneworld Publications, 2003).

6. Arif Payaslyoğlu and Ahmet Içduygu, "Awareness of and Support for Human Rights Among Turkish University Studies," *Human Rights Quarterly* 21, no. 2 (May 1999): 524.

7. Pinar Tank, "Political Islam in Turkey: A State of Controlled Secularity," *Turkish Studies* 6, no. 1 (March 2005): 5.

8. Yavuz, *Islamic Political Identity*, 39.

9. Kushner, "Self-Perception and Identity," 219.

10. Yavuz, *Islamic Political Identity*, 39.

11. Selim Deringil, "The Invention of Tradition as Public Image in the late Ottoman Empire, 1808 to 1908," *Comparative Studies in Society and History* 35, no. 1 (January 1993): 5. Deringil calls the empire a good example of what Benedict Anderson, *Imagined Communities*, calls "official nationalism."

12. Joseph G. Rahme, "Namik Kemal's Constitutional Ottomanism and Non-Muslims," *Islam and Christian-Muslim Relations* 10, no. 1 (March 1999): 32.

13. Yavuz, *Islamic Political Identity*, 45.

14. Brian Silverstein, "Islam and Modernity in Turkey: Power, Tradition and Historicity in the European Provinces of the Muslim World," *Anthropological Quarterly* 76, no. 3 (Summer 2003): 510.

15. For a fascinating discussion of Ottoman efforts to create a more coherent political entity, see Deringil, "The Invention of Tradition," 5ff.

16. Nilüfer Göle, *The Forbidden Modern: Civilization and Veiling* (Ann Arbor: University of Michigan Press, 1996), 45, which quotes Ziya Gökalp (1876–1924) as saying, "The most significant characteristic of the early Turks is feminism."

17. See Alev Çinar, *Modernity, Islam, and Secularism in Turkey: Bodies, Places, and Time* (Minneapolis: University of Minnesota Press, 2005), 64, for an illustration.

18. Çinar, *Modernity*, 73. Islamists later saw this as a moment of humiliation.

19. Ibrahim Kaya, "Modernity and Veiled Women," *European Journal of Social Theory* 3, no. 2 (May 2000): 201.

20. See, for example, Bernard Lewis, *The Emergence of Modern Turkey* (London: Oxford University Press, 1961), and Robert E. Ward and Dankwart Rustow, eds., *Political Modernization in Japan and Turkey* (Princeton, NJ: Princeton University Press, 1964).

21. Ümit Cizre Sakallioğlu, "Parameters and Strategies of Islam-State Interaction in Republican Turkey," *International Journal of Middle East Studies* 28, no. 2 (May 1996): 236.

22. Section VI, Article 24.

23. Ersin Kalaycioğlu, "The Mystery of the Türban: Participation or Revolt," *Turkish Studies* 6, no. 2 (June 2005): 234.

24. Henry J. Barkey, "The Struggles of a 'Strong' State," *Journal of International Affairs* 54, no. 1 (Fall 2000): 99.

25. Berdal Aral, "Dispensing with Tradition? Turkish Politics and International Society during the Özal Decade, 1983–93," *Middle Eastern Studies* 37, no. 1 (January 2001): 84.

26. Quoted in Waxman, "Islam and Turkish National Identity," 17.

27. Çinar, *Modernity, Islam and Secularism*, 127.

28. Burhanettin Duran, "Approaching the Kurdish Question via *Adil duzen*: An Islamist Formula of the Welfare Party for Ethnic Coexistence," *Journal of Muslim Minority Affairs* 18, no. 1 (April 1998): 115.

29. Faruk Bilici, "The Function of Alevi Bektashi Theology in Modern Turkey," in Tord Olsson, Elizabeth Ozdalga, and Catharina Randvere, eds., *Alevi Identity* (Istanbul: Swedish Research Institute in Istanbul, 1998), 62.

30. The classification is that of Tahire Erman and Emrah Göker, "Alevi Politics in Contemporary Turkey," *Middle Eastern Studies* 36, no. 4 (October 2000): 105–110. Bilici, "The Function of Alevi Bektashi Theology," uses the same categories.

31. Haldun Gülalp, "Whatever Happened to Secularization? The Multiple Islams of Turkey," *South Atlantic Quarterly* 102, no. 2/3 (Spring/Summer 2003): 394.

32. Silverstein, "Islam and Modernity," 503.

33. See, for example, Christopher Houston, "Profane Intuitions: Kurdish Diaspora in the Turkish City," *Australian Journal of Anthropology* 12, no. 1 (April 2001): 15–31.

34. Benedict Anderson, *Imagined Communities: Reflections on the Origin and Spread of Nationalism* (London: Verso, 1991).

35. Şerif Mardin, "The Just and the Unjust," *Daedalus* 120, no. 3 (Summer 1991): 125.

36. Mansoor Moaddel, *Islamic Modernism, Nationalism, and Fundamentalism: Episode and Discourse* (Chicago: University of Chicago Press, 2005), 15.

37. Ibid., 342. In that context he was writing about the "rise of the ideological state" in Algeria, Egypt, Iran, and Syria, but the observation applies equally to Turkey.

38. This discussion owes much to Ayşe Kadioğlu, "Women's Subordination in Turkey: Is Islam Really the Villain?" *Middle East Journal* 48, no. 4 (Autumn 1994).

39. Jenny White, "State Feminism, Modernization and the Turkish Republican Woman," *NWSA Journal* 15, no. 3 (Fall 2003): 158.

40. Eric Rouleau, "Ce pouvoir si pesant des militaires turcs," *Le monde diplomatique*, September 2000, 8.

41. Stephen Kinzer, *Crescent and Star: Turkey Between Two Worlds* (New York: Farrar, Straus and Giroux, 2001), 168–169.

42. M. Hakan Yavuz, "Cleansing Islam from the Public Sphere," *Journal of International Affairs* 54, no. 1 (Fall 2000): 21–42.

43. Yavuz, "Cleansing," 27.

44. Orhan Pamuk, *Istanbul: Memories and the City,* trans. Maureen Freely (New York: Random House, 2006), 182.

45. Haldun Gülalp, "Enlightenment by Fiat: Secularization and Democracy in Turkey," *Middle Eastern Studies* 41, no. 3 (May 2005): 362. He says Kemalism replaced religion as absolute truth. It became a "quasi-religion," 357.

46. Şerif Mardin, *Religion and Social Change in Modern Turkey: The Case of Bediüzzaman Said Nursi* (Albany: State University of New York Press, 1989), chapter 5.

47. Sükran Vahide, *Islam in Modern Turkey: An Intellectual Biography of Bediuzzaman Said Nursi* (Albany: State University of New York Press, 2005): 172.

48. Mardin, *Religion and Social Change*, 86.

49. Mardin, "The Just and the Unjust," 125.

50. Vahide, *Islam in Modern Turkey*, 204.

51. Ibid., 220.

52. See Bekim Agai, "Islam and Education in Secular Turkey: State Policies and the Emergence of the Fethullah Gülen Group," in Robert W. Hefner and Mohammad Qasim Zaman, eds., *Schooling Islam: The Culture and Politics of Modern Muslim Education*

(Princeton, NJ: Princeton University Press, 2007), 149–171. For a sample of Gülen's thought, see Fethullah Gülen, *Advocate of Dialogue* (Fairfax, VA: The Fountain, 2000).

53. Yavuz, *Islamic Political Identity*, 267.

54. Mardin, *Religion and Social Change*, 222.

55. Hamid Algar, "A Brief History of the Naqshbandi Order," in Marco Gaborieau, Alexandre Popovic, and Thierry Zarcone, eds., *Naqshbandis: cheminements et situation actuelle d'un ordre mystique musulman . . . : actes de la table ronde de Sèvres . . . 24 mai . . . 1985* (Istanbul: Isis Yayımcılık Ltd, 1990), 34.

56. Altan Gökalp, "Les fruits de l'arbre plutôt que ses racines: Le suleymanisme," in *Naqshbandis*, 429.

57. Cizre Sakallioğlu, "Parameters and Strategies," 237.

58. Ibid., 239.

59. Ibid., 240.

60. Yavuz, *Islamic Political Identity*, 207.

61. Daği, "Transformation," 21.

62. Yavuz, *Islamic Political Identity*, 212.

63. Houston, "Civilizing Islam," 93

64. Karin Vorhoff, "Academic and Journalistic Publications on the Alevi and Bektashi of Turkey," in Olsson, Ozdalga, and Randvere, eds., *Alevi Identity*, 23–50.

65. Sefa Şimşek, "New Social Movements in Turkey since 1980," *Turkish Studies* 5, no. 2 (Summer 2004): 130.

66. Rainer Herman, "Political Islam in Secular Turkey," *Islam and Christian-Muslim Relations* 14, no. 3 (July 2003): 274.

67. Yavuz, *Islamic Political Identity*, 244.

68. Asli Aydintaşbaş, "Murder on the Bosporous," *Middle East Quarterly* 7, no. 2 (June 2000): 18.

69. Ibid., 21.

70. For a list of those directives, see Yavuz, *Islamic Political Identity*, 275–276.

71. Şerif Mardin, "Turkish Islamic Exceptionalism Yesterday and Today: Continuity, Rupture and Reconstruction in Operational Codes," *Turkish Studies* 6, no. 2 (June 2005): 147.

72. Ali Bardakoğlu, "Moderate Perception of Islam and the Turkish Model of the Diyanet: The President's Statement," *Journal of Muslim Minority Affairs* 24, no. 2 (October 2004): 367–374.

73. Yavuz, *Islamic Political Identity*, 48.

74. Bardakoğlu, "Moderate Perception," 370.

75. This paragraph reflects the views expressed by Bardakoğlu in his article "Moderate Perception."

76. Erman and Göker, "Alevi Politics," 106.

77. Yavuz, *Islamic Political Identity*, 141.

78. Ibid., 146–47.

79. Ibid., 167.

80. Fethullah Gülen, *Advocate of Dialogue* (Fairfax, VA: The Fountain, 2000), 56.

81. Yavuz, *Islamic Political Identity*, 184.

82. Ibid., 104.

83. Ibid., 103.

84. Nilüfer Göle, "Snapshots of Islamic Modernities," *Daedalus* 129, no. 1 (Winter 2000): 111.

85. Ziya Önis, "The Political Economy of Islamic Resurgence," *Third World Quarterly* 18, no. 4 (December 1997): 743–766, 14 in EBSCO online version.

86. See Yesim Arat, *Rethinking Islam and Liberal Democracy: Islamist Women in Turkish Politics* (Albany: State University of New York Press, 2005), on the work of "ladies' commissions."

87. Jenny B. White tells this story in *Islamist Mobilization in Turkey: A Study in Vernacular Politics* (Seattle: University of Washington Press, 2002).

88. Ziya Önis, "Political Islam at the Crossroad: from Hegemony to Co-existence," *Contemporary Politics* 7, no. 4 (2001): 285

89. The term is from Daği, "Transformation," 31.

90. R. Quinn Mecham, "From the Ashes of Virtue, A Promise of Light: The Transformation of Political Islam in Turkey," *Third World Quarterly* 25, no. 2 (March 2004): 348, 351.

91. Ibid., 353.

92. For excellent analysis of the results of the 2002 election, see Ömer Çaha, "Turkish Election of November 2002 and the Role of 'Moderate' Political Islam," *Alternatives* 2, no. 1 (Fall 2003): 95–116, and Ümit Cizre and Menderes Çinar, "Turkey 2002: Kemalism, Islamism and Politics in the Light of the February 28 Process," *South Atlantic Quarterly* 102, no. 2/3 (Summer 2003): 309–332.

93. Pippa Norris and Ronald Inglehart, *Sacred and Secular: Religion and Politics Worldwide* (Cambridge, UK: Cambridge University Press, 2004), 239.

94. Ibid., 226.

95. Şerif Mardin, "Turkish Islamic Exceptionalism."

96. Pamuk, *Istanbul*, 192.

97. Soon-Yong Pak, "Cultural Politics and Vocational Religious Education: The Case of Turkey," *Comparative Education* 40, no. 3 (August 2004): 326.

98. Jeremy Salt, "Nationalism and the Rise of Muslim Sentiment in Turkey," *Middle Eastern Studies* 31, no. 1 (January 1995): 14.

99. Pak, "Cultural Politics," 334.

100. Payaslyoğlu and Içduygu, "Awareness," report that 23 percent of students writing university entrance exams in 1997 were from the religious schools.

101. Sencer Ayata, "Patronage, Party and State: The Politicization of Islam in Turkey," *Middle East Journal* 50, no. 1 (Winter 1996): 47.

102. Section VI, Article 24 of the constitution as amended in 2001: "Education and instruction in religion and ethics shall be conducted under state supervision and control. Instruction in religious culture and moral education shall be compulsory in the curricula of primary and secondary schools. Other religious education and instruction shall be subject to the individual's own desire, and in the case of minors, to the request of their legal representatives."

103. Özlem Altan, "Sanctifying the Nation: Teaching Religion in Secular Turkey," *ISIM Newsletter*, June 12, 2003, 52. He analyzes religious studies texts for the fourth through eighth grades.

104. Ibid., 53, quoting from religious texts by Ömer Yilmaz, Hasan Sarisoy, and Vehbi Vakkasoğlu.

105. Ibid., quoting from Samuel Kaplan, "Education and the Politics of National Culture in a Turkish Community" (PhD dissertation, University of Chicago, 1996).

106. Altan, "Sanctifying the Nation," 53.

107. Binnaz Toprak, "Islam and Democracy in Turkey," *Turkish Studies* 6, no. 2 (June 2005): 170.

108. Mason, "The Future," 60. He bases that conclusion on a study of religion done by the Turkish Foundation for Economic and Social Studies (TESEV) in Istanbul.

109. Toprak, "Islam and Democracy," 176.

110. Kayhan Mutlu, "Examining Religious Beliefs Among University Students in Ankara," *British Journal of Sociology* 47, no. 2 (June 1996): 356.

111. Note that the "traditional" versus "secular" scale constructed from questions posed in the World Values Survey taps attitudes closely related to religion.

112. Mark Tessler and Ebrin Altınoğlu, "Political Culture in Turkey: Connections among Attitudes Toward Democracy, the Military and Islam," *Democratization* 11, no. 1 (February 2004): 21–50.

113. Ümit Cizre, "The Truth and Fiction about (Turkey's) Human Rights Politics," *Human Rights Review*, October–December 2001, 75. This whole paragraph owes much to Cizre's analysis.

114. Waxman, "Islam and Turkish National Identity," 5.

115. Jenny White talks about the Islamist commitment in that direction in *Islamist Mobilization*.

116. Ali Bulaç, "The Logical Basis for Religious Violence," *Zaman*, October 4, 2006.

117. Haldun Gülalp, "Whatever Happened," 385.

118. Ali Bulaç reports that landlords sometimes refuse to rent to tenants dressed in Islamic garb.

119. Jean-Paul Sartre, *Anti-Semite and Jew* (New York: Schocken Books, 1948), argues that identity stems from how one is viewed by others.

120. Norris and Inglehart, *Sacred and Secular*, 60. The "most religious" countries on that scale are Uganda, Zimbabwe, Philippines, Bangladesh, Ireland, Poland, South Africa, Mexico, and the United States. The rating depends on two indices, how often one participates in religious services, and how often one prays outside of religious services.

6

State Shiism in Iran

A casual observer might easily conclude that religion has dictated the course of political development in Iran, but careful analysis suggests, to the contrary, that politics has refashioned religion in that country. Political decisions and opportunities have recast a version of Islam (Twelver Shiism) from a passivist, minority stance into a badge of national identity, a religious establishment like no other in the Muslim world, a set of competing political ideologies, and an authoritarian effort to promote religion. Neither Islam, nor Shii Islam, nor even the Iranian variant of Shiism as a set of doctrines and beliefs constitutes a sufficient explanation for the major events of modern Iranian history, including the revolution of 1978–1979, but those events go far to explain the place of Islam in that country today. Politics and religion have become intricately entangled for political reasons.

Few are the states where national identity depends as heavily on religion as Iran. Israel seems similar, because its religious identity is its raison d'être, but Iran differs from Israel in that it is only one of many Muslim states, whereas Israel is the only country to identify itself as Jewish. Iran identifies with the Muslim community as a whole but nonetheless uses that identity to distinguish itself from all other states and to reinforce Iranian nationalism. In Iran, political and social revolution brought to power a clerical class that turned Islam from one of many cultural characteristics of the country into the defining element of its identity. Iran became the country of bearded men and veiled women, an "Islamic" form of government, and a rhetoric of Muslim rectitude reinforcing a version of Iranian identity.

The Iranians do not get full credit for turning Islam into political ideology. Jamal al-Din al-Afghani, Abdülhamid II, Hasan al-Banna, Abul ala Mawdudi, Sayyid Qutb, Mustafa Kemal Atatürk, and others played roles in that transformation. Within Iran Ruhollah Khomeini and Ali Shariati probably did the most to convert Shiism from a set of beliefs, customs, rites, and ethical principles into a political program. Khomeini, Shariati, and a few others

213

discovered in Shiism the resources they needed to construct ideologies of combat and governance. Like others before them, they claimed knowledge of the revolutionary intent of Muhammad, the spiritualism of Ali, the tradition of the designated imams, and the truth of the Quran. But if theirs were the only possible readings of the tradition, then the ulama of Twelver Shiism ought to have come to the same conclusions centuries sooner. As a matter of fact, the doctrines of Khomeini, Shariati, Morteza Mutahhari, Muhammad Kazem Shariat-Madari, and Abdolkarim Soroush are unimaginable except in the modern circumstances of the late twentieth century. These writers responded to the cultural cacophony of modernity, the onslaught of imperialism, and the authoritarianism of Iran's Pahlavi dynasty. The peculiarities of the Iranian situation closed the door on other ideologies and opened the way for Islamist thinking.

The clerical establishment in Iran proved to be the great secret of revolutionary success. There is no comparable case where the scholars of Islam, the ulama, have themselves taken political action. It is commonplace to assert that there is no separation of church and state in Islam, but the power of the clergy in Iran resulted precisely from the relative autonomy the clerical establishment achieved and maintained under the Qajar dynasty (1796–1925) and especially under Pahlavi rule (1925–1979). The advent of the Islamic Republic brought government to the clergy and the clergy closer to government, but not even twenty-five years of republican rule wiped out the distinction between government and the religious establishment, some of whom declined to endorse constitutional arrangements, refused to endorse Khomeini's successor, Ali Khamenei, and deplored the authoritarianism of the regime. By making religion a civic duty, the Islamic Republic renders suspect all professions of belief, undercuts religious rites and rituals by making them political, and undermines respect for the independence of the ulama. Clerical rule appears to have divided and weakened the religious establishment that gave birth to the revolution.

It is by no means certain that the Islamic Republic has transformed the political culture of Iran. One form of authoritarianism has followed another. Iranians bowed to the shah with an obsequiousness tinged with contempt. Scholars reported high levels of personal distrust in prerevolutionary Iran.[1] Iranians lived in fear of the secret police (Savak), berated the bureaucracy, and mocked efforts to proclaim and teach about the glories of monarchy in Iran. The regime has certainly sought to transform these and other aspects of political culture through policies, propaganda, and changes in school curricula. To judge by the way women dress, the content of the media, and the propaganda of the regime, Iran has become more moral, more honest, and more Islamic than it was under the shah, but it is no less focused on individualism and competition. Local elections still seem to turn on garbage collection, parks, recreational facilities, and taxation. The society is more bureaucratic rather than less, and perhaps no less a victim of corruption, mutual suspicion, fear, and authoritarianism than it was before the revolution.[2] Authority by emanation, once anchored in the myths of monarchy and nobility, and now reflected in the mystical superiority of the clergy, seems secure.[3] The Islamic Republic has sacralized familiar patterns of behavior more than it has transformed them.

What is it about Iran that is obstructing the constitutional promise of liberalism and democracy? The success and failure of the reform movement suggests that neither religious doctrine nor the religious class is the primary obstacle. The reformist former president Muhammad Khatami was himself trained as a cleric. His supporters invoked the legacy of the Ayatollah Khomeini, founder of the Islamic Republic, whose religious standing far outshone his successor's, in support of their advocacy of greater openness and flexibility. Khomeini himself repeatedly invoked the "public interest" over narrow interpretations of Islamic law. Clerics of great authority, such as Ayatollah Husayn Ali Montazeri, have accepted both the principle of Islamic government and the need for democracy. The obstruction comes from the use of a complicated and contradictory constitution to support the agenda of Supreme Guide Ali Khamenei and his traditionalist friends, who invoke religion to legitimate their position.

Identity

The revolutionary government of Iran reinvented that country's identity by creating not just a republic (as opposed to a monarchy) but an Islamic republic. The preamble to the constitution says the Islamic Republic reflects the wishes of Iran's "Muslim people." The new government claimed that the previous regime had ignored or neglected the Muslim character of the country and propagated instead a vision of Iran as a product of the Persian language, Aryan race, ancient dynasties, and devotion to monarchy. The revolutionary government attempted a major overhaul of Iranian self-perception and of the country's image in foreign affairs.

A sharp shift in identity has often accompanied the great revolutions of modern history. The French discovered that they were not just part of a state ruled by a king but were a nation capable of determining the future of that state. The Russians discovered that they were a multiethnic empire of workers held together by a commitment to communism. Enlightenment thinking proclaimed universal rights, and Marxist ideology denigrated national identities in favor of communist internationalism. The Iranian revolutionaries called upon all Muslims to join them without distinction of race, ethnicity, or nationality. Yet all three revolutions, however much they began with a commitment to universalist principles, ended up creating or solidifying a conception of national identity.

Although Muslims constitute a majority in about forty countries and several countries proclaim Islam as the state religion, very few have equated national identity with Islam.[4] Pakistan, created as a refuge for Indian Muslims, would be an example. One constraint on most Muslim states is the existence of significant non-Muslim minorities. Another is the apparent conflict generated by invoking a universal, transnational religion as the principal defining element of a nation. Just as defining one's country as an Arab state points toward the need to dissolve the fatherland into a broader Arab nation, proclamation of an Islamic state implies that it is coterminous with the umma, the community of believers. To identify with the umma suggests utopian expectations of unifying all Muslims in a single nation-state or, alternatively, the dissolution of the nation-state and the incorporation of its people into some larger agglomeration.

How, then, can one explain that Iran, a country with substantial non-Muslim minorities—a country quite unlikely to submit itself to union with Pakistan, Saudi Arabia, Morocco, or any other Muslim state—would undertake the bold and improbable action of identifying the nation with Islam?[5] One hypothesis relies upon the prevalence of Twelver Shiism in Iran; Shiism has perhaps predisposed Iranians to thinking of themselves first and foremost as Muslims. Iran is not just another Muslim state; it is a unique Muslim state, where religion and state are inseparable concepts.[6] A second hypothesis attributes the recourse to Islamic identity to the "prism of colonialism" and the "mirror of modernity."[7] Because these external forces affected many Muslim countries besides Iran, it was the particular Iranian encounter with colonialism and modernity that pushed Iran to think of itself in religious terms. Finally, one might explain Iranian identity with Islam in terms of the political context of Iran under the Pahlavi dynasty. "We are Muslims" served to unite revolutionaries against a nationalist monarchy dependent on Western support. It solidified the nation by opposing the secular nationalism of the shah and the international system of nation-states. By that hypothesis, Islam has become an identity of political convenience.

The first hypothesis surfaced almost immediately after the revolution in the minds of many Sunni Muslims. As Egyptians, Saudis, and others awoke to the change of regime in Iran and heard Ayatollah Khomeini invite others to follow him into a supranational Islamic umma, their leaders were quick to observe that Iran is predominantly Shii. Muslims and non-Muslims alike made Shiism a primary explanation of the Iranian phenomenon: Shiis are more devout than Sunnis; Shiism is more violent than Sunnism; Shiism cultivates revolt and dissent while Sunnism promotes obedience and submission. Shiism requires religiously inspired leadership; Sunnism accepts a separation between religion and politics. So went the explanations of why Islamic revolution had swept Iran but not other Muslim countries. Sunni elites dismissed Iranian claims to lead the Muslim community as a whole, because the Shia remain a distinct minority in the Muslim world as a whole.

There can be little doubt that Shii Islam has contributed to Iranian identity, but it is difficult to disentangle cause and effect. Neither the history nor the doctrines of Shiism as a whole constitute a sufficient explanation of its importance or development in Iran. Shiism was not born in Iran and it has never been limited to Iran. Moreover, Iran includes important Sunni minorities. Even the Iranian variant of Shiism, called Imami or Twelver Shiism, includes adherents beyond the frontiers of Iran. For those reasons, the decision of the Safavid family in 1501 to make Twelver Shiism the state religion in what was then called Persia outweighs all other factors in explaining the linkage between national identity and Shiism. The Qajar and Pahlavi dynasties nurtured this connection.

Early Shiism

The Shia trace their history to the struggle for leadership of the Islamic community between Ali ibn abi Talib, cousin and son-in-law of the Prophet Muhammad, and Muawiya, governor of Syria. Muawiya belonged to a distinguished Meccan family that opposed the Prophet early in his career. Muawiya won appointment from the second caliph, Umar, to govern the new province of Syria, and, after Umar's death, Muawiya's kinsman, Uthman ibn Affan, acceded to the leadership of the Muslim community. The assassination of Uthman some eight years later by a band of Muslims disaffected from the caliphate triggered the first civil war in Islam.

The Shia later argued that Muhammad had wanted Ali as his successor. The companions of the Prophet wrongly overlooked him when they selected Abu Bakr as the first caliph. The Shia believe the injustice continued with the selection of the next two caliphs, Umar and Uthman. Ali finally won the position of leadership after the assassination of Uthman, but he refused to denounce those guilty of taking Uthman's life. Incensed by the treatment of his kinsman, Muawiya declared war on Ali. An army recruited in Syria marched into Iraq to oppose Ali and the force he had recruited in Arabia. A series of fateful events led ultimately to Ali's defeat and the transfer of authority to Muawiya and his family, the Umayyads, who came to rule the Islamic community from Damascus.

The followers of Ali, or at least some of them (whom scholars call Alids in the early centuries), remained permanently alienated from the mainstream. The Alids found symbolic support for their alienation when the second son of the heroic Ali, Husayn, marched into a battle he knew he would lose against the Umayyad caliph Yazid in the year 684. The massacre of Husayn and his little band constitutes an annual occasion of mourning and self-flagellation in the Shii community to this day. During the revolutionary days of 1978–1979, the annual passion plays commemorating the martyrdom of Husayn ibn Ali cast Shah Muhammad Reza Pahlavi in the role of the evil Yazid. The Ashura celebrations honoring Husayn fueled the fervor of the protest against the ancien régime.

While Alids played some role in bringing down the Umayyads in what is known as the Abbasid Revolution (750), they found themselves disappointed with their treatment by the new dynasty in Baghdad. But another century or more passed before there emerged a set of doctrines one might call Shii. Watt argues that Shiism emerged as a response to the development of a mainstream Muslim body of jurisprudence and theology.[8] Berkey suggests it was the other way around. The development of Shii doctrines pushed the mainstream to generate the ideas that came to be identified with Sunnism.[9] Shiism needed a doctrine to hold it together. Sunnism needed a doctrine only once challenged by the Shii minority.

The common thread of Shii doctrines is charismatic leadership. While the Shia avoid putting Ali on the same plane as the Prophet Muhammad—whom the Quran describes as the seal of the prophets, the last in a long line of human beings called upon to carry God's message—they believe Ali embodied inspired religious leadership and inherited the primary responsibility for the spiritual welfare of the Muslim community. Only from him and "designated" descendants can the Muslim community look for legitimate leadership. The historic leaders are imams. For all Shia, Ali is the first designated imam, his first son, Hasan, is the second, his son Husayn is the third, and the line continues from there. Some Shia look back to five such historic figures, some cling to seven (Ismailis), but the largest group came to believe in eleven such imams and a twelfth who disappeared as a child but will reappear some day. These are the Twelvers, or the Imamis, who dominate in Iran.

Sunni doctrine downplays any notion of divine leadership after the death of the Prophet and emphasizes the development of a moral code, gradually built into five schools of law, that governed rulers and ruled alike. A class of scholars who codified the law and articulated theological doctrines became the primary spokesmen for Islam. The caliphs, few of them noted for their piety, found themselves ever more dependent on the ulama for the fragile legitimacy they enjoyed. Their power was bureaucratic and military, and even that power diminished as non-Arabs seized effective control of the empire, leaving the caliphs in place as figureheads.

With the disappearance of the twelfth imam, and the beginning of a period called the Greater Occultation, the Twelver Shia lacked divinely inspired leadership. Many interpreters see the Occultation as a rationale for passivism, which perhaps reflected the condition of the Shia as a minority in most Muslim settings. Even the tenth century, often called the Shii century because Shii families ruled in Persia, Egypt, and parts of Arabia, did not promote the Shia from minority to majority status in the Muslim world. As minorities in most areas, the Shia kept a low profile, waited for the return of the Twelfth Imam, and lied about their beliefs if challenged by the Sunni authorities. Their doctrine permitted this sort of dissimulation.

While Iran looks with pride upon this history of the early Alids and of Shiism more generally, there is no unique link between Iran and Shiism as a whole or Twelver Shiism in particular before the Safavid dynasty took control of the country in 1501. As Keddie puts it:

> Before then, although there were many Iranian Shiis, the great majority of Shiis were non-Iranian and the majority of Iranians were Sunni. The Zaidi, Ismaili, and Carmathian Shiis are still found mostly outside Iran; the great majority of Shii dynasties were outside Iran, with only the Buyids as a major partial pre-1501 exception; and the great majority of Iranian dynasties have been Sunni. . . . The legendary marriage of Imam Hosain [Husayn] with a Sasanian princess, which has no historical basis, was useful in cementing the identification of Iran with Shiism, but such legends are usually available when needed.[10]

Although conversion to Islam began after the Arab overthrow of the Sasanian Empire in the seventh century, Iran became Shii as a result of the Safavid conquest. By the time the Safavids lost control of the country to Sunni Afghans in 1722, most Iranians had apparently come to identify with Shiism.[11]

Monarchy and Modernization

The Safavids (1501–1722), like the Qajars and the Pahlavis who followed them to the throne, invoked both Iranian (monarchical) and Islamic legitimacy, but the Safavids emphasized their religious legitimacy and permitted creation of a religious establishment largely subservient to their monarchical ambitions. The Safavids were Sunnis from Ardebil in Azerbaijan with strong affinity for Sufism. They found themselves drawn toward Twelver Shii teachings, apparently from contact with nomadic tribes in Anatolia. With the energy of converts convinced of their divine empowerment, the Safavids mustered tribal followers and swept to power in Tehran. Only then did they begin to concern themselves with Shii orthodoxy, creating a set of theologians recruited inside and outside of Persia to articulate a legal and religious order supportive of their rule. "More than most Islamic dynasties the Safavids worked for conversion to their branch of Islam and for ideological conformity."[12] The identity with Shiism helped the Safavids differentiate their empire from that of their principal enemies, the Ottomans in the West and the Uzbeks in the north, who were Sunni.

The Safavid conquest of Iran and the continuing need for Islam as a prop for political legitimacy under the Qajars and the Pahlavis contribute more to the explanation of Iran's religious identity than the history of Shiism per se. The search for modernity and Iran's encounter with imperialism served in the nineteenth and twentieth centuries to reinforce the identity with Islam. Imperialism and modernity arrived later in Iran than in the Ottoman Empire to the west, but their impact was perhaps more devastating. The decision of the Russians and the British to partition Iran into zones of influence in 1908, only two years after the country had adopted a new, liberal constitution, represented a cynical response to Iranian weakness that has lingered in the collective memory. Reza Khan seized power in 1921 as an Iranian nationalist, even though some suspected he held power only with British indulgence. About twenty years later, when Reza resisted Allied efforts to take effective control of his country in order to resupply the Soviet Union during World War II, he found himself pushed into exile. His son, who replaced him, could not resist Allied efforts. That son, Muhammad Reza Shah, retained his throne in 1953 only because British and American secret services incited an uprising against the popular prime minister, Muhammad Mussadiq (Mossadegh). From that point on, the shah depended heavily on American support for his security services, his military machine, his educational establishment, and the technology for his economy.

This record of imperialism spurred secular nationalism. Mussadiq, who had opposed the Pahlavis with consistency since the 1920s, galvanized nationalist support with his nationalization of oil in 1952, the act that provoked British and American intervention. A few maverick *mujtahids* (ulama specializing in the law) supported the Mussadiq government in the beginning but backed away from him as they perceived increasing leftist influence of the Tudeh Party, supported by Moscow, in his coalition. Tudeh support for Mussadiq disturbed American and British policy-makers caught up in the cold war. Imperialism in Iran could never be entirely separated from modernism, and modernism came to be seen by some as a threat to Islam and to Iranian identity, by others as a promise of change. Secular nationalists such as Mussadiq thus provoked both applause and alarm among the clergy.

A great admirer of Atatürk, Reza Shah plunged ahead with a program of modernization and secularization in the 1920s and 1930s. With a series of measures, he continued policies initiated in the nineteenth century to secularize education. In addition, he implemented a civil code in 1928 and diminished the clerical role in administering justice. As had Atatürk, Reza Shah tried to modernize dress. The clergy and the masses came to see Reza Shah as hostile to religious celebrations and religious institutions. Ruhollah Khomeini wrote a book in 1941, *The Revealing of Secrets* (Kashf al-Asrar), that expressed some of these frustrations.

As increasing oil revenues enabled ever more rapid change in Iran after World War II, the secularization and Westernization of Iranian lifestyles proceeded rapidly in the big cities and especially in Tehran. Muhammad Reza Shah epitomized the opulent style of the old nobility and the nouveaux riches. In 1972, evoking the memory of Cyrus the Great, he celebrated 2,500 years of monarchy in Iran by feasting on its symbol, the peacock, with a crowd of international dignitaries in the ancient Persian capital, Persepolis. Maxim's, the Paris restaurant, catered the affair. On the one hand, the king appeared to diminish and even assault the Islamic identity of his country by glorifying an authoritarian, pre-Islamic tradition. On the other hand, he cemented the linkage of progress and modernity with foreigners. It is little wonder that the Iranian writer Jalal Al-e Ahmad struck a sympathetic chord when he evoked the "Westoxication" of Iran.[13]

Vahdat argues that Iran has vacillated between two complementary but competing notions of modernity, subjectivism and universalism, both of them originating in the thought of Immanuel Kant.[14] Kant maintained that the mind has no direct access to external realities. Truth must, therefore, come from within. It is necessarily subjective, but human rationality is nonetheless capable of discovering truths that are universal in validity. Insofar as students of politics and society map patterns of modernization and development—the spread of markets, the growth of urban areas, improved communication and transportation, the secularization of society, the burgeoning of bureaucracies, and the democratization of society—they reflect Kant's confidence in the universal qualities of modernity. But those champions of individualism and liberty, who see modernity as innovation, creativity, self-determination, and self-fulfillment, reflect the subjective dimension of modernization. The Pahlavis pushed relentlessly on the universalist understandings of modernity. Their critics reevoked subjectivism to argue that Iranians were losing touch with themselves, their "authentic" beings, in a hell-bent rush to become modern. Al-e Ahmad, Ali Shariati, and other intellectuals began to argue that Iran could recover its subjectivity and rediscover its authentic self through a return to Islam.

Before 1960 Islam seemed a remnant of the Iranian past, nurtured mainly in the superstition and backwardness of villages. From 1960 it started to become the Iranian future, thanks in part to Ayatollah Ruhollah Khomeini and other ulama and in part to a set of circumstances more specific than colonialism and modernity. The writings of Al-e Ahmad and Shariati played a role, but so did the inability of secular nationalists to pull the shah toward genuinely liberal reform; the failure of the shah's land reform policies to produce rural prosperity; the forced pace of modernization, which began to alienate traditional sectors of the bourgeoisie; the shah's ability to ward off revolution by manipulating the "new middle class," which was dependent on his policies and largesse; and his inability to control the clergy, which maintained its standing with the general public by keeping its distance from the monarchy. From a stance of separation the clergy moved toward opposition. The defiance of Khomeini from exile in Iraq and then Paris excited the country and energized many of his fellow clerics.

The Islamization of Identity

In these circumstances the architects of revolution managed to transform Shiism into a national, revolutionary doctrine. They exploited some characteristics—"historical victimization, divine mission to restore justice, and the culture of sacrifice (martyrdom)," all illustrated in the early history of the Alids.[15]And they ignored other characteristics, such as the long subsequent period of quietism among Twelvers awaiting the return of the Hidden Imam. They also ignored the transnational character of Islam and even Imami Shiism to focus on the national struggle against monarchy. They altered the prevailing conception of Iranian identity from that of a Muslim country to that of an Islamic nation.

By renaming Iran "the Islamic Republic" and by adopting a constitution that trumpets the state's allegiance to Islam, the founders of the new Iran asserted the new identity. In doing so, they confirmed Iran's place in the world of modern nation-states and confirmed its allegiance to constitutionalism, a thoroughly modern, secular idea. If identity depends upon constitutional confirmation, then it is conventional, not primordial. It may be true "that Iranians cannot even think of, or 'imagine,' themselves as a political community in purely secular terms."[16] The word for nation, *mellat*, is the same as that for people, and it connotes people of the faith. (The Ottoman millet system treated each major religious group as a community.) Yet the revolution, with its vigorous assertions about Iran's identity, sought to go beyond the natural bonds of faith that held Iranians, or various groups of them, together and to make Iran "truly Islamic." Iran became authentically Islamic only when it became constitutionally Islamic.

By making Islam a matter of convention rather than faith, the regime reached out to minority groups. Some linguistic minorities in Iran, such as Kurds, Arabs, Turkmen, and Baluch, are predominantly Sunni in religion. As inhabitants of outlying mountainous or desert regions they have often been peripheral to the state, but the Islamic state, though Shii in its origins and instincts, pulls these groups into the majority. In the Islamic state, Azeri (Turkish-speaking) Shia, who constitute 20 percent of the population, are not officially seen as a minority. Half-nomadic groups such as the Qashqay, Lur, and Bakhtiari, all Shii but unorthodox in their practices and beliefs, do not attract attention as minorities, either. The only genuine minorities are non-Muslim groups, and even Christians and Jews enjoy some status as "peoples of the book." However, the Bahais, who number perhaps 200,000 to 300,000, do not command even this sort of respect. They put themselves beyond the Muslim community as defined by the regime, by their belief in prophets beyond Muhammad. They do not qualify as Iranians.

Language takes second place to religion as a determinant of nationality in this scheme of things. Paul puts Shii Persians and Azeri (Shii) Turks at the top of the pyramid of Iranianness. The Sunni groups fall in the middle, and the non-Muslim official minorities occupy the bottom. The tribes are marginal, and the Bahais are outcasts. But anyone can be an Iranian by behaving like a true Muslim and joining the fight against imperialism and Zionism.[17] A Shii is an activist, a "true Muslim," one who is not content to believe but acts on the basis of his or her beliefs. While Arabic is the language of Islam and serves as a link between Iran and the Arab world, Khamenei called Persian "the language of true . . . and revolutionary Islam."[18] It would seem to follow that the only country with a Persian-speaking majority would be the locus of the "true Islam." Paul concludes: "The commitment to the Islamic Revolution can now be understood as generating the very commitment that it was originally meant to replace: that to the nation and the home-country."[19]

"Who is a Muslim" becomes as important in an Islamic state as is "who is a Jew" in a Jewish state. In time of revolution it is relatively easy to say that those who join the struggle are "true Muslims," whether or not they are believers. The Iran–Iraq War provided ample opportunity for activism and martyrdom. Once peace was restored on that front, activists could still vent their anger against the United States and Israel. The constitution calls upon citizens to vote, which could also be interpreted as activism of the sort demanded of "true Muslims." Candidates for public office, however, by the standards enforced by the Guardian Council, must be not just citizen believers but "true Muslims."[20] They must have already distinguished themselves by their commitment to the Islamic Republic. To be an activist dissident, which was in revolutionary days the quintessential way to prove one's true colors as a "true Muslim," has now become dangerous in the extreme. Many of those who criticize the repressiveness of the regime risk prison or execution, even though all profess loyalty to the Islamic state. A "true Muslim" is thus one who behaves in approved, conventional ways, whatever he or she believes.

Iranian identity depends not on the fact that most Iranians are Muslims, or Shii Muslims, and not entirely on the fact that their constitution says Iran is an Islamic state. Rather, identity depends on its being an authentically Islamic state, which means that its citizens behave as "true Muslims." In the case of women, that means they cover their heads and wear modest dress. If actions outweigh belief, then dress becomes a critical bit of testimony. To show too much hair or wear colors that are too bright suggests a woman is not a "true Muslim." By this logic any woman inappropriately dressed constitutes proof that Iran is not an authentic Islamic state. Perhaps that helps explain why women's behavior and dress remain a matter of inordinate concern for the regime.

The question of veiling also illustrates a fundamental dilemma of a Shii polity nominally committed to egalitarianism. The Quran proclaims the equality of all believers, but the Shia came to believe that Ali and his descendants were spiritually inspired. While the learned men (ulama) of the Sunni tradition worked out a legal system consistent with the Quran and the sunna of the Prophet that obviated the need for any further human interpretation, Twelver Shiism progressively empowered a class of mujtahids to be privileged interpreters of the law. Every believer was expected to subject himself or herself to the guidance of an exemplary, living mujtahid, a *marja*. A clerical class emerged that enjoyed a status unimaginable in Sunni countries. The clerics are a bit more equal than other Muslims in Iranian society and thus feel empowered to define who is a "true Muslim." The constitution refers to the "continuous ijtihad of the fuqaha' possessing necessary qualifications, exercised on the basis of the Qur'an and the Sunnah of the Ma'sumun, upon all of whom be peace."[21] By this logic, Iran is Islamic not only because the constitution declares it so but because the constitution allocates power to those who are "true Muslims" and because Iranians behave as "true Muslims" by dressing appropriately and acquiescing in the judgments of those in power. The identity of the state with religion may thus depend on inequality of status.

Shii Islam does not account for Iranian identity but it does help explain how that identity came to be asserted. It also helps explain why Islamic identity depends more on the rule of the clerical class than on an ideological unity or purity. Without the conversion of Shii Islam into ideology, the revolution might never have occurred in Iran, but the success of the revolution in creating institutions, and the success of the clergy in dominating those institutions, freed the Islamic Republic from all but the most elementary ideological standards. It could afford to be a "dissonant" state, where competing ideological notions often paralyze action and force the elites to privilege expediency over consistency.[22] What it cannot tolerate, or will not tolerate, is a revival of revolutionary ideology that would undermine the institutions established by the revolution.

Ideology

The transformation of Islam from a set of religious beliefs into a program of political action occurred in Iran at about the same moment as it occurred elsewhere in the Muslim world. Iran trailed Egypt in the development of an Islamist movement by forty years. In the early 1970s, observers such as James A. Bill who predicted revolution in that country focused on the secular nationalist movement as the likely source of revolt.[23] Influenced by the failure of Mussadiq, the nationalists contrasted the authoritarianism of the shah with liberal-democratic theory. The Marxism of the Tudeh Party also enjoyed some support. Yet it was what Dabbashi calls the "theology of discontent" that powered the revolution, a theology that emerged from the writings of persons such as Jalal al-e Ahmad, Ali Shariati, Morteza Mutahhari, Sayyid Mahmud

Taleqani, Allamah Sayyid Muhammad Husayn Tabatabai, Mehdi Bazargan, Abolhasan Bani-Sadr, and Ayatollah Khomeini.[24] These thinkers deserve much of the credit (or blame) for making Islam into a political ideology in Iran.

Ideologies transform values and philosophies into actionable ideas. Iran was the first country to experience modern political, economic, and social revolution under the banner of Islamic ideology. Once triumphant, the revolutionaries sought to implement one version of Islamist ideology and to stamp out competing ideologies.

> The dominant religious discourse, based on an ideological understanding of Islam, is by its very nature militant, exclusivist and populist; it demands unquestioning obedience and conformity to its ideological elite—the clergy. The politicization of religion has made postrevolutionary political discourse in Iran equally stifling.[25]

While the revolution represented a triumph of Islamist ideology, the statement ignores the diversity of ideologies lurking within the revolutionary discourse. Ashraf and Banuazizi put Shariati and Khomeini at opposite ends of the ideological spectrum.[26] Dabbashi portrays Khomeini as a "traditionalist" and thus quite separate from the development of "the Islamist ideology" of Shariati.[27] The politics of the Islamic Republic came to be marked not only by repression of those who challenged the fundamental concepts but also by ferocious, open debate among partisans of competing Islamist views. Where everyone claims to be an Islamist and every proposal is made in the name of Islam, some other criterion for choice must be invoked. Who is empowered to make choices is more important than the relationship of choices to the Quran or the sunna of the Prophet.

The Iranian constitution specifies a single ideology based in the sharia. While Article 3 sketches a general set of orientations, Article 4 is precise:

> All civil, penal, financial, economic, administrative, cultural, military, political, and other laws and regulations must be based on Islamic criteria. This principle applies absolutely and generally to all articles of the Constitution as well as to all other laws and regulations, and the fuqaha of the Guardian Council are judges in this matter.[28]

Following as it does a list of "beliefs" in Article 2 and a set of "goals" in Article 3, Article 4 makes it sound as if the Islamic Republic of Iran would function within a very narrow set of limits imposed by the sharia. References to the sharia are everywhere in the document.[29] But in fact, the tradition of law in the Shii world had long ago turned away from a single, definitive, codified understanding of the sharia. In contrast with the Sunni practice, the Shii tradition came to emphasize the ongoing work of Islamic lawyers to reinterpret the Quran and the sunna of the Prophet—the primary sources of the law in both Sunnism and Shiism—in the light of contemporary circumstances. Since the victory of the Usulis over the Akhbaris in the eighteenth century (see below), Twelver Shiism has typically revered several living interpreters of the law, mujtahids seen as worthy of emulation (*maraji*), and even at times when Shii recognized a single marja (sing. of maraji), his interpretation was not taken as valid into the next generation. Shiism came to emphasize the deciders as conveying legitimacy to what is decided, and this has enabled the current regime to avoid commitment to a single ideological perspective. The government has frequently invoked "necessity" to justify policies that do not conform to "Islamic criteria" in the eyes of the Guardian Council.

Islamist movements in Sunni countries, such as Egypt and Turkey, have sought to transform Islam into a revolutionary ideology by calling for the enforcement of Islamic law, the sharia. Mawdudi and Qutb, the two great Sunni theoreticians of radical Islam, insist upon the absolute sovereignty of God. Human beings have no right to final authority over other human beings. God has, however, left the administration of worldly affairs to ordinary human beings with only revelation to guide them. God's law, based in the Quran and the sunna of the Prophet, is the only legitimate foundation for a human community. No human being is closer to God than any other; no human being can set himself above others as anything but the enforcer of the rules God has laid down.[30]

Although Sunni radicals criticize the Umayyad family and all subsequent dynasties for veering away from these principles and establishing monarchy in the Islamic community, they tend to regard the law developed in the Umayyad and especially the Abbasid periods as complete and faultless. The great Islamic jurists dissected the Quran for what little guidance it provides in the domain of law and then mined the sunna of the Prophet for additional help. In the first generations after the Prophet's death, the sunna was simply the living tradition, what good Muslims and companions of the Prophet continued to regard as behavior consistent with his views and practices. As time went on, jurists became increasingly reliant on written accounts of what the Prophet had said and done, the *ahadith* (sing. is hadith). The lawyers constructed a legal system on the fragmentary Quranic material, on the voluminous hadith material (winnowed to eliminate obvious fraud), and to a much lesser extent on the living tradition, suspected of being corrupted. The ideal was to construct a law so complete that subsequent generations of jurists would have nothing to do but apply it. The notion of a timeless and universal law (even though it had been assembled by ordinary mortals over the space of a century or more) became a foundation of Sunnism and a foundation of radical Sunnism in the twentieth century.

Ruhollah Khomeini

Ruhollah Khomeini argued as early as 1941 that Pahlavi authoritarianism violated precepts of Islamic law. "Reason can never accept that a man who is no different from others in outward or inward accomplishments, unless maybe he is inferior to them, should have his dictates considered proper and just and his government legitimate, merely because he has succeed in gathering around himself a gang to plunder the country and murder its people."[31] The government of God is the government of reason. "The duty of our government . . . is to conform to his legitimate government by making the laws passed by the Majlis a kind of commentary on the divine law." Implementation of Islamic law "will lead to the establishment of the Virtuous City."[32] At that point Khomeini, perhaps already influenced by the writings of Mawdudi, sounded much like a Sunni in his legalism. "If just one article of the Constitution were to be implemented, that specifying that all laws contrary to the sharia are invalid, everyone in the country would join together in harmony, and the country would move forward with the speed of lightning."[33]

Thirty years later Khomeini, who had become a leader among religious scholars and the primary clerical opponent of the shah, argued a different theory, one more consonant with the history of Imami Shiism. In a series of lectures he argued that God would never have left the Shii community without leadership during the period of Occultation. As the community waited for the return of the Hidden Imam, it would necessarily follow God's law and would therefore be dependent for leadership on the legal experts, the *fuqaha* (plural of faqih). With great care to cite precedents and relevant hadith, he constructed a case for the governance of the leading jurist of each generation, the velayat-e faqih, placeholder for the Hidden Imam.

In the earlier work, Khomeini had written: "We do not say that government must be in the hands of the *faqih*; rather we say that government must be run in accordance with God's law."[34] In his later lectures he emphasized the need for government and the need for scholars to provide leadership. The decline of the Muslims vis-à-vis the West could be explained by "our lack of a leader, a guardian, and our lack of institutions of leadership."[35] If justice is to prevail, it depends upon the law. Any legitimate ruler must turn to the faqih (jurist) for advice about the law. "This being the case, the true rulers are the *fuqaha* themselves, and rulership ought officially to be theirs." He then argues that when a jurist with a sound knowledge of law and justice "arises and establishes a government, he will possess the same authority as the Most Noble Messenger . . . in the administration of society, and it will be the duty of all people to obey him."[36] One cannot establish justice without law and one cannot have a society of law without government, or government without leadership. Khomeini thus pulled his Islamist campaign toward a focus on leadership, which is the essential orientation of Shiism. The twelve designated imams provided such leadership. When the twelfth went into hiding, the community was not helpless, according to Khomeini, because there were always fuqaha available to lead.

For Sunni Islamists such as Hasan al-Banna and Sayyid Qutb, both of them laymen, the scholars of Islam constituted a part of the problem, not the solution. They argued that the ulama of Egypt had been loyal servants of the monarchy and of the military regime that followed. The government of Egypt had in the space of two centuries deprived the ulama of their bases of financial support and their control of mosques and vital educational institutions. Ali Shariati made roughly the same case against the ulama of Iran. He portrayed them as defenders of tradition and authoritarianism, at roughly the same moment Khomeini was calling upon his fellow clergy to rise up against the monarchy and establish the velayat-e faqih. Khomeini's success in carrying a few of his fellow scholars and much of the country with him may have more to do with his own charisma and political skill than the persuasiveness of his argument. The case for scholarly leadership did, however, enjoy a plausibility in Iran that it could not have had in Egypt.

Ali Shariati

The thinking of a lay preacher and pamphleteer, Ali Shariati, probably did more to inspire revolt than the lectures of the Ayatollah Khomeini. Son of a cleric from Mashad, Shariati pursued modern studies in Paris but then combined his knowledge of European thought with his own study of Islam. His lectures at the Irshad Hosseini in the late 1960s played to ever greater crowds until the shah felt the need to close down the institute. "Shariati made Islam into an ideology," but it was scarcely a simple plea to implement the sharia and it was certainly not a call for clerical rule. Shariati feared a theocracy would turn into a despotism of the clergy, which he termed "the worst and most oppressive form of despotism possible in human society."[37] He portrayed the clergy as a reason Islam had become sclerotic. He contrasted what he called the radical, "red Shiism" of Ali and his followers with the "black Shiism" of the Safavids and their successors—conventional, conservative, passive, and antimodern. Shariati preferred red to black.

Shariati regarded the determinism of Western thought, and Marxist thought in particular, as corrosive of human will. Evoking the early egalitarianism of Islam as an antidote for Western materialism, he found a model for Islamic feminism in the example of Fatima (wife of Ali and daughter of the Prophet) and a model for universalism in the mystical coming together of those making the pilgrimage to Mecca. Shariati's thought combined modernism with nativism, mysticism with social analysis, a denunciation of the old Islam with an appeal to the "true," "red," revolutionary instincts of the religion.[38] High-ranking clerics rejected Shariati for his lack of traditional Islamic education and, doubtless, for his harsh words about the mullahs (clerics). The shah hounded him for his hostility to the regime and his ability to attract followers. In fact, the partisans of Shariati believe he died at the hands of the shah's agents in London, more than a year before the revolution gained momentum.

For one analyst, "Islamic ideology" came to an end with Shariati's death.[39] While Shariati's ideas did not die with him, his revolutionary Shiism has not had a decisive influence on the policies of the Islamic Republic of Iran. His greatest champions, the Mujahideen-e Khalq (Leftist Fighters for the Faith), encountered repression and then obliteration. By seizing power and then claiming legitimacy by virtue of his institutional theory, Khomeini pushed aside programmatic ideology as a foundation of the regime. After the revolution, Khomeini's ideas and not Shariati's became visible in the earliest version of the constitution, but the constitution went well beyond anything sketched in Khomeini's lectures on Islamic government. It reflected both ideas of popular sovereignty and velayat-e faqih. Its complex system of checks and balances owed something to the constitution of 1906, something to the Fifth French Republic, and a great deal to the political creativity of those who wrote it. While it intoned the need to establish Islamic principles of governance, it established processes of decision rather than a set of irrevocable, ideological standards to be followed.

Velayat-e Faqih

Legitimacy flows from those authorized by the constitution to make decisions rather than from the coincidence or lack of it between those decisions and some preestablished template of Islamic ideology. As long as Khomeini was alive, his office, his position in the religious hierarchy, and his charisma provided such authority. When an elected president got in his way, that president, Bani Sadr, was forced to flee. When the Guardian Council blocked proposals of the Majlis (parliament) in the name of Islam as the constitution permits, Khomeini moved to create the Expediency Council (Council for Assessing the Interests of the System) that could move the country forward in the name of "necessity."[40]

Debates about the constitution and about policy in the Islamic Republic have always depended on arguments about Islam. Islam has become the language of politics. Every candidate, every group, every office rationalizes positions and actions in the name of Islam. The government first opposed birth control in the name of Islam. Then it changed its mind and endorsed birth control as permitted by Islam. Some legislators have championed public enterprise and expansion of the welfare state in the name of an egalitarian Islam. Others have championed privatization in the name of Islamic commitment to private property. Khomeini found it necessary to make peace with Iraq, although the war was a jihad against an enemy of Islam, Saddam Hussein. Necessity dominated ideology. "Ultimately, the imperative of governance has forced the rulers of Islamic Iran to resort to the same foundation for laws as used by secular states: the interests of the regime. They have rationalized that this transformation is justified by a juristic principle, *maslahat* (public interest), long rejected by Shiism."[41] Policy followed from politics, not ideology.

The great debate in Iran turns on who holds the authority and by what right. By the time he took power, Khomeini had become a marja, a model for emulation, one of a handful of clerics at the top of the pyramid. He permitted others to refer to him as the Imam, which suggested a mystical relationship to the Hidden Imam, although Khomeini never explicitly claimed any such relationship. The popularity he achieved in Paris before his triumphal return to Tehran in January 1979 made him a hero from the start, a father of the revolution. Thus, he enjoyed both a spiritual and popular legitimacy even before the constitution was adopted. Popular ratification of the constitution further affirmed his legitimacy.[42]

Three competing principles of legitimacy—*marja-e taqlid,* velayat-e faqih, and popularism—coincided in support of Khomeini as Supreme Leader.[43] They do not coincide to legitimize the rule of his successor, Ali Khamenei, who was not a marja or even a distinguished cleric. Certainly not the most distinguished jurist (faqih) of his generation, he was simply a revolutionary leader who won selection to office by the Assembly of Experts, a body made up exclusively of clerics.[44] His legitimacy is thus procedural rather than religious. Khamenei sought to become designated as a marja but then withdrew in the face of clerical opposition. Because the constitution draws its legitimacy from popular ratification and the voters choose the Assembly of Experts, albeit from a list of qualified candidates, one could argue that the faqih is the servant of public opinion, but there is little sign that Khamenei enjoys a popular mandate. Overwhelming opposition to Khamenei and his candidate for the presidency, Ali Akbar Nateq-Nuri, brought Muhammad Khatami to the presidency of the republic in 1997. Yet the Supreme Leader, Khamenei, fought off the challenge.

Reform

Khatami took office with promises of reform: greater political liberty, greater freedom of expression, and expanded rights for women. He argued for the rule of law, and more specifically, for the enforcement of the 1979 constitution. He endorsed the independence of the judiciary, warned the secret services directed by the Supreme Leader against the transgression of individual rights, and even introduced a bill to increase the power of the presidency. Khatami alerted Iranians to the potential of the law, if rigorously enforced, but his failure to achieve greater compliance within the executive branch only contributed to the "public's cynicism and mistrust."[45] He spent two four-year terms in the presidency without being able to convert two overwhelming victories at the polls into significant reform of the system. By staying in office rather than resigning on principle, he reinforced the concept of velayat-e faqih and the authority of the Supreme Leader.[46] He tacitly acknowledged the weakness of the presidency.

The election of Mahmoud Ahmadinejad as president to succeed Khatami in 2005, while a rebuke to the reformists for their failure to produce concrete results, did not resolve the underlying ideological ambiguity of the Iranian regime. Himself a populist with strong appeal in the rural areas, Ahmadinejad launched a one-man crusade to develop nuclear power in Iran, or at least he called attention to a program already in development. (Even the shah had been interested in developing nuclear power.) As Ahmadinejad's campaign put Iran increasingly at odds with Europe and the United States, not to mention Arab neighbors, many in the West seemed to assume he represented the Iranian government as a whole, even though these same analysts had come to understand that Khatami, as president, did not control Iranian policy, internal or external. As Khamenei began to distance himself from Ahmadinejad's aggressiveness and regime spokesmen downplayed a conference Ahmadinejad organized to discredit the Holocaust, it became increasingly clear that the infirmities of the presidency affected Ahmadinejad just as much as his predecessor. Electoral outcomes and the rule of law remain subordinate to the political interests of the ruling clerics.

President Ahmadinejad sought to tighten the enforcement of dress codes for women. His efforts illustrate the impact of not just "the Islamic ideology" but also rival notions of ideology, and even the irrelevance of ideology. The imposition of a dress code said to originate in Islamic law constitutes the most visible effect of ideology on women. A 1983 law enacting "Islamic punishments" made it an offense to appear in public without the hijab. The regime enforced the law with vigor.[47] That code came as a shock to educated, urbanized, middle-and upper-middle-class women, many of whom were accustomed to dressing in Western style in public as well as in the privacy of their homes.[48] By banning the veil in 1938, Reza Shah had made Iran look more Western, as Atatürk had similarly made women the symbol of Turkish modernity. In the Islamic Republic, women again came to symbolize the transformation of Iran.

Other actions to implement the sharia were more fundamental but also more ambivalent and impermanent. The new regime banned women from certain jobs such as judgeships. Shirin Ebadi, eventual winner of the Nobel Peace Prize, lost her post as a judge after the revolution of 1979 and was denied authorization to practice law until 1992. Subsequently, she took on the defense of prominent dissidents. Women were at first barred from studying certain subjects, but those restrictions were removed in 1986. Divorce laws established as consistent with the sharia were amended in 1992. Contraception, banned in the early days of the revolution, became available in 1988. Sixty percent of university students are now women. "Educated women's demands have led to calls for a strategic change in the governance of the Islamic state."[49]

The Islamic Republic promoted women to participate in the economy and the body politic at the same time it emphasized their "duties" under Islamic law and their subordination to men. The Ayatollah Khomeini, not generally a champion of women's rights, "called for . . . millions of Iranians including women to join the Islamic *Jihad* . . . against poverty and social deprivation."[50] Women joined revolutionary demonstrations in the last days of the shah's regime. They received the right to vote and have exercised it in great number. Several women have been elected to the Majlis.[51] The rate of women's employment in Iran rose more sharply in the 1990s than it had under the shah in the 1960s and 1970s. Women constituted slightly more than 25 percent of the workforce in Iran by the year 2000, compared with about 20 percent at the moment of the revolution. Female employment in Muslim countries ranges from a low of 13 percent in the United Arab Emirates and Oman to about 35 percent in Morocco, compared with 40 percent to 46 percent in industrialized countries.[52] Bahramitash concludes: "The rise of political Islam broke the barriers to participation in public life that had previously existed for women, especially those of lower socioeconomic background."[53] In contrast, many upper-class women have felt the pinch of restriction in the Islamic Republic.

Several men who have championed women's rights have been punished by the regime. Abdollah Nuri, a cleric who first lost his position in the presidential cabinet by action of the Majlis, was brought to trial before the Special Court for the Clergy in 1999 for a newspaper article that criticized official imposition of the hijab. He said the hijab as a form of dress should be seen as an aspect of lifestyle and accused the regime of trying to impose a lifestyle. But the government argued that the notion that people should live as they wished contradicts the Islamic duty to promote virtue and prohibit vice. Nuri received a five-year sentence but managed to publish a book called *The Hemlock of Reform*, reiterating his views on personal freedom, before he was incarcerated. It achieved best-seller status before the 2000 elections.[54]

Another dissident voice, that of Hasan Yousefi Eshkevari, a champion of democracy and human rights, argued that the hijab is a matter of belief, not obligation. To not wear modest dress might be a sin but it should not be a crime. In April 2000 Eshkevari attended a conference in Berlin called "Iran after the Elections, and the Dynamics of Reform in the Islamic Republic." The conference suffered interruption from groups protesting the policies of the Islamic Republic. One protester was a "woman wearing nothing but a bikini and a head scarf as a gesture of protest against 'the oppression of women in Iran.'"[55] Eshkevari agreed to sit on a panel about women's rights, although he had not been scheduled to do so, and there he ended up making a statement. He distinguished belief or dogma from basic values of Islam, which he called ideology. He put religious rulings in a third category and then distinguished rulings about worship, which are unchanging, from rulings that must be adapted to social circumstances. He put matters of women's rights in that category, since they emerged from a different set of social circumstances, those of pre-Islamic Arabia. On his return from Germany, Eshkevari was arrested and brought before the Special Court for the Clergy on charges of apostasy, conspiracy to overthrow the Islamic Republic by spreading lies, and insulting the regime by his presence at the conference. Originally sentenced to death, he won a reduced sentence of four years for "insulting the sanctities" and one year for going to Berlin and propagandizing against the regime.[56]

Law and Ideology

The case of women's rights in Iran illustrates the strengths and weaknesses of ideology as a determinant of politics. Khomeini's position, which emphasized governance of the clergy, prevailed over other ideological positions, including that of Shariati. The new governing institutions were supposed to defend an ideology that could not be defined with precision. One solution would have been to further open debate and give the proponents of democracy an opportunity to make their case, but that solution endangered the sovereignty of the faqih and the clergy.[57] It endangered the interests of the regime, which then preferred to impose its version of Islamic ideology, however partial and incoherent, and to repress other versions. It was not the persuasiveness of the faqih that prevailed but the power of the office, not the strength of the official ideology but the political strength of those it protected from democratic challenge. The sharia, prominently mentioned in the constitution as the foundation of the Islamic ideology, affects Iranian life only where and if the political institutions decide it should. "The controlling factor in the Iranian legal system, in fact, has been the interests of the ruling conservative clergy."[58] It is the political power of the clergy in political life that makes the Islamic Republic of Iran Islamic.

Islamic ideology has affected dimensions of the law in Iran. Legislation has been drafted to reflect "Islamic criteria," and the Guardian Council has rejected some legislation in the name of the same criteria, but much of Iranian law remains unchanged. Mayer writes that the legal system "remains essentially French in orientation." It is based in law codes developed originally in Europe and applied in a judicial system based on the French model. "Islamic law should not be treated as the central determinant of Iran's post-revolutionary legal system," she writes.[59] The reasons are several: the adoption of European law codes in the early twentieth century that continue to govern property, business, commercial transactions, and many other dimensions of Iranian life; the long Shii tradition of judges who offer differing interpretations of Islamic law; the resulting clash of authorities about which "Islamic criteria" are relevant in any given situation; and, most important, the unwillingness of the regime itself to put law above the interests of the governors.

Mayer characterizes law in Iran as "political law" rather than either "traditional" or "professional" law. Professional law as exercised in Western democracies depends upon a separation of political and judicial functions. Independent judges, though elected or named through a political process, interpret the law in a largely autonomous fashion and apply it even to those exercising political authority. In postrevolutionary Iran as in prerevolutionary Iran, the judicial system remains subject to the whim of the ruling power. "The official reason for subordinating sharia to the State law is to achieve the higher interest of the Islamic State and hence of Islam. But here again it is the political instance which decides what is essentially Islamic, in opposition to the prescribed rules of the sharia."[60] While the law guarantees freedom of expression and the right to political participation, the Supreme Guide and the ruling establishment have used the law and courts to pursue both political opponents and dissident intellectuals. They created the Special Court for the Clergy to try dissident clerics.

Islamic ideology does not explain the Iranian regime. Banuazizi argues that the Iranian experience shows that Islam can be utilized to mobilize resistance, "but, as the hegemonic ideology of a modern bureaucratic state, it is no less susceptible to corrupting influences of power and privilege than other, secular ideologies."[61] The ideology is hegemonic in the sense that supporters, critics, and outright opponents who do not openly seek the overthrow of the regime must formulate their arguments in the language of Islam. The greatest challenge comes not from those who would reject velayat-e faqih, as do many members of the clerical establishment, but from those who accept it and interpret it differently. Grand Ayatollah Montazeri, himself a participant in the revolution, has advanced a theory that Islam requires the faqih to bow before democratic politics.[62] Intellectuals who have supported reform (and gone to jail, in some cases) have done so within the Islamic context.

The most notable critic, one who has escaped punishment, is Abdolkarim Soroush, a philosopher who has sought to differentiate religion from the religious knowledge of human beings, which is inevitably fallible and changing. He has argued that genuine faith is possible only if a believer is free to choose to believe or not to believe. Faith and freedom are inseparable. "Soroush identified protection of the freedom of faith and creation of social conditions conducive to such freedom as the main tasks of a democratic religious state."[63] An Islamic state cannot, therefore, seek guidance in Islamic ideology understood as an unchanging set of principles or even understood as a principle of leadership, such as velayat-e faqih. According to Soroush, the faqih, not to mention the author of the idea (Khomeini) himself, is a mere mortal interpreting the immortal and unchanging will of God from a particular vantage point amidst the vicissitudes of history.

Another dissident, Mohsen Kadivar, insists on the necessity of protecting freedom in the private sphere. "The private sphere is the sole prerogative of the individual," he writes.[64] He says the sharia starts from the assumption that no issue is public and that individuals, even non-Muslims, are protected in their options and in their private activities. "The rights of the individual in his or her private sphere are guaranteed to a higher degree in an Islamic society than in a secular one," he says.[65] The boundary between public and private is the question. Giving absolute power to an Islamic state, and putting the Islamic state above the principle of free choice, may reflect good intent, but the state cannot succeed in imposing belief. "Deceit, duplicity, and maintaining appearances are only some of the pitfalls of imposed religiosity. . . . Islamic thought finds absolute and despotic rule alien and does not sanction interests not already delineated in Islamic terms."[66]

Iran is a place where ideas have mattered. From its rich intellectual history there reverberate echoes of Ferdowsi's Shahnameh from the pre-Islamic period, the great Sufi poets, the Islamic philosophers, distinguished ulama, liberal reformers, Marxists, and Islamists. The ideas of Jalal Al-e Ahmad, Ali Shariati, and Ruhollah Khomeini affected the revolutionary outcome. The regime has chosen principles of the sharia and written them into positive law, but, as Naim observes, the sharia "cease[s] to be the normative system of Islam by the very act of enacting it as the law to be enforced by the state."[67] The Islamic Republic is a product of all these ideas together with many from non-Iranian and non-Islamic sources. The state is not a result of an unambiguous Islamic ideology, because no such thing exists. The "Islamic ideology," which many would see as a force in modern Iranian politics, is best understood as an outcome of state decisions. The state is not Islamic by virtue of the ideology. The ideology is Islamic by decision of the state. It is secondary to institutions.[68] Because one segment of the clerical class dominates the state, that segment fashions the laws, decrees, sermons, and proclamations that have come to be seen as the "Islamic ideology."

Institutions

Neither an Islamic identity nor an Islamic ideology suffices to explain political and religious institutions in Iran. No concept of Islamic identity adequately

accounts for the emergence of a strong, relatively hierarchical religious institution in Iran, which is quite unlike the religious structure of other Muslim
states, such as Egypt or Turkey. Nor does any concept of Islamic ideology suffice to explain the elaboration of a constitution that owes so much to Western
conceptions of political engineering. In the wake of the Iranian Revolution,
many Westerners argued that the Islamic Republic of Iran reflected an Islamic
requirement for the complete merger of religion and politics. Scholars soon
pointed out, however, that the revolution occurred because the clergy in Iran
had developed an autonomy from political domination over a period of five
centuries. This autonomy permitted the clerical class to act against a monarchy that had long strived to control religious personnel and observance.
When a portion of the clerical class took power, it broke with another substantial group of clerics who believed in separation. A number of distinguished clerics never accepted the legitimacy of the velayat-e faqih, and while
the Ayatollah Khomeini enjoyed remarkably broad support as both the supreme political leader and the supreme object of religious emulation (marja-e
taqlid), his successor, the Ayatollah Ali Khamenei, has not dared assert the
same sort of religious preeminence. The political hierarchy does not coincide
with the religious hierarchy. Tehran, the political capital, is only one hundred
miles from Qom, the center of religion, but the psychological distance between these cities remains significant.

The dominance of clerics creates an impression that the religious establishment dictates political outcomes in Iran. The situation may be analogous to
the Egyptian revolution led by military officers. In the wake of that revolution in 1952, military officers occupied many of the highest positions in the
state and accepted assignments in almost every aspect of the Egyptian bureaucracy, but Colonel Gamal abd al-Nasir largely abandoned his uniform, as did
many of his fellow officers who entered politics. The military remained a separate organization from the nonmilitary bureaucracy. Nasir's Egypt could be
considered a military state, but it also became nationalist, reformist, socialist,
and pan-Arab in ways that could not be predicted by simply calling it a military regime.

Some analysts predicted that military dominance in Egypt or elsewhere
would produce more rapid modernization, since the military was necessarily
made up of "modern men." Others predicted that military regimes would necessarily back off and permit democratic rule, as had the Turkish regime. Still
others predicted that regimes dominated by the military would necessarily im-
poverish their societies for the benefit of the military and engage in bellicose
behavior. None of these predictions proved entirely correct. The presence of

military officers in governmental positions does not guarantee a military regime of any specified type. It does not guarantee that the army as an organization makes political decisions. Similarly, clerical domination does not mean identity with a set of political outcomes necessarily predictable from the identity of the decision-makers. Clerics in Iran have fallen into conflict with one another over issues such as the role of government in the economy, the nature and function of institutions, and the place of women in society.

What distinguishes Iran from other Muslim countries is the degree to which the religious establishment enjoys (1) internal coherence and hierarchical structure and (2) relative independence from political interference. The Qajar and Pahlavi dynasties tried in the nineteenth and twentieth centuries to subjugate the ulama by undercutting their bases of financial support, eliminating the religious courts, and reducing the role of ulama in education. But governments never got full control. Instead, a portion of the clergy began as early as the nineteenth century to utilize its ties to the commercial middle class in particular and to the people more generally as bases for political influence. Ruhollah Khomeini built upon this long tradition of political engagement and capitalized upon the construction of a religious hierarchy that had begun under the Safavids and matured under the Qajars. Reza Khan (Pahlavi) benefited from the support of that hierarchy when he had himself crowned shah in 1925, but his son Muhammad Reza Shah found himself increasingly at odds with the hierarchy after 1963. His crude, ill-considered efforts to throttle the rising voice of the clerics merely magnified their prestige and authority. It was the separateness of the ulama from the political system that made them popular and credible. It was their distinctiveness (in dress and language) and organizational coherence that made them a powerful force for revolution.

The emergence of an autonomous, distinctive corps of ulama—a religious establishment separate from the political establishment—owed something to Safavid rule and even more, perhaps, to the eventual disappearance of the Safavids. The early Safavids were "extremists," tribal Sufis from Azerbaijan who seized power according to the pattern outlined a century earlier by Ibn Khaldun. They were religious extremists sweeping in from the marches to seize power and establish a dynasty in the name of moral purity. Their link with theological Shiism was tenuous or nonexistent, and they took control of an Iran marked by multiple religious tendencies. The Safavids cultivated a group of ulama to bolster their legitimacy in the name of Twelver orthodoxy.

The Safavids appointed the imams of the primary mosques in the cities, but there also developed a category of unofficial ulama. The most distinguished became known as mujtahids, who claimed the right to engage in the process of ijtihad, offering opinions on theology and law. Toward the end of the Safavid rule (early eighteenth century) some mujtahids seem to have been claiming the right to give the ruler advice.[69] By the end of the Safavid period the word "Sufi" had already become synonymous with extremist and heretical, even though the Safavids had originally been Sufis. The Safavid rulers themselves, so eager to assert their virtue in the early years, had become the civilized, corrupted conservatives that Ibn Khaldun predicted would ultimately make every dynasty subject to overthrow.[70]

The Qajars and the Ulama

The weakening of the monarchy made it more dependent on the ulama. The eruption of Afghan forces into Iran in the eighteenth century ended Safavid rule and drove many of the ulama into the Shii shrine cities of Iraq, where they were largely invulnerable to the blandishments of political authority in Iran. When the Qajar dynasty established its hold on Iran after an interregnum of relative anarchy, they did so without religious pretension or claim. They were from the beginning suitors of a religious establishment led by mujtahids, most of them living beyond the political control of the Qajars. A struggle among the mujtahids in the late eighteenth century pitted a group known as *akhbaris*, who claimed that the role of the mujtahids was limited to the application of inherited wisdom, and another group known as the *usulis*, who insisted that wisdom must be reinterpreted in every generation. They said the concept of "perfect man" in Islamic thought must necessarily reflect time and place, and they portrayed themselves as the keeper of that tradition, as the models for the emulation of ordinary believers. Their success led to increased prestige and influence for the mujtahids in particular and the clerical class in general. In the absence of the Twelfth Imam, they asserted their claim to religious leadership of the society about two centuries before Ruhollah Khomeini proposed velayat-e faqih.

The Qajar dynasty never enjoyed the power of the founding Safavids. The Qajars courted the religious establishment without advancing any religious claim. Enforcement is what governments could traditionally offer in support of religious law. The mujtahids had enforcers of their own, thugs called *lutis*, who carried out sentences pronounced in religious courts, but they welcomed the help of the state, particularly in dealing with heretical minorities and practices. The monarch curried favor with the mujtahids by prosecuting Sufis and a movement inspired by Sufism called Shaykhism in the early nineteenth century. The ulama saw even greater threat in a man named Sayyid Ali Muhammad, who claimed in 1843 to be the Bab, the "door" or "gateway" to the Hidden Imam. His was an explicitly anticlerical message, although some of his leading supporters came from the lower ranks of the ulama. Only one seems to have been a mujtahid. "Had the Bab been acknowledged as the Hidden Imam, the function of the ulama would have ceased to exist."[71]

The ulama responded by seeking to discredit the Bab and repress the movement. They demanded his execution, and with some hesitation and delay, the state obliged in 1850 after outbursts of unrest attributed to the Bab and his partisans. But, as is so often the case with religious figures, death did not settle the matter. Babism became Bahaism under the leadership of Abd ul-Baha, who reaffirmed the Bab's hostile attitude toward the clergy and the state.[72] Repression of the Bahais continues to this day.

The state appointed a few official religious figures but failed to bring the religious establishment to heel. It appointed an official called the *sadr al-ulama* and named imams to head mosques in key cities. It thus caused a division in the clergy between those seeking promotion within the state system and the larger number identifying themselves with the autonomous ulama. The emergence of Shaykh al-Ansari Murtada as the sole model for emulation (*marja-e taqlid matlaq*) in the mid-nineteenth century provided an unprecedented unity for the Twelver Shii world as a whole. That unity did not survive beyond the life of his successor and has rarely been re-created, but Murtada's dominance further strengthened the corporate identity of the autonomous clergy. His position as a teacher in Najaf, Iraq, put him beyond the control of the Iranian monarchy. Algar claims the predominant attitude of the ulama in this period was one of disdain for the Qajars and opposition to their policies.[73]

Foreign influence became the principal bone of contention. The Qajars started to modernize their country almost a half century later than the Ottomans, and they did it by appealing for foreign assistance, first for the military, then for the reorganization of the state and the economy. The ulama resisted growing foreign influence, positioning themselves as defenders of the Iranian people and their traditional way of life. They opposed the 1872 concession to the Baron Julius de Reuter, an Englishman, of rights to exploit mineral resources, build railways, and found a national bank, among other things.[74] But the shah went ahead, saying he respected the mullahs but "refused to permit their intervention in matters of state."[75]

The activist elements of the ulama achieved greater success in their fight against the tobacco concession in the 1890s and in the struggle for a constitution in the following decade. In both cases alliance with the merchant class, the bazaaris, was the secret of success. The families of bazaaris and ulama intertwined. As prosperous members of Iranian society, the bazaaris helped choose by their financial support the mujtahids who rose to become models of emulation.[76] Bazaaris needed the educational and judicial services of the clergy, and the clergy needed the financial support of bazaaris. Both groups found themselves threatened in their livelihood by the monarchy's reliance on foreign advice and money. In opposing royal absolutism they joined a group of modernizing intellectuals determined to promote political as well as economic and social change.

The shah's grant of a monopoly on the production, sale, and export of tobacco in Iran in 1890 served as a warm-up for the constitutional struggle that would follow more than a decade later. A cleric who preached against the agreement in Shiraz, where there was resistance, earned expulsion to Iraq. The resistance spread to Tabriz and other cities, with ulama leadership of mass protest. In December 1891, the clerical establishment produced a fatwa declaring that the use of tobacco constituted an attack on the Hidden Imam. The effect was dramatic. Mass demonstrations in Tehran led to violence and a number of deaths, and the government, after attempting to negotiate a partial renunciation, finally backed away from the entire concession in early 1892. The alliance of ulama with bazaaris and modernizing liberals had prevailed, and the ulama emerged as "a central force, which could be allied with, manipulated, combated, but never ignored."[77]

The same alliance proved critical in the success of the constitutional revolution in Iran. The assassination of Nasir al-Din Shah in 1896 weakened the Qajar monarchy. While scarcely an exemplary ruler—Keddie notes his lifelong preoccupation with women, young boys, and material gain—he held power for forty-eight years. His successor, Mozaffar al-Din Shah, switched from one minister to another in the search for resources to satisfy creditors of the throne and the "needs" of his courtiers and himself. Clerical contempt for the monarchy's moral weaknesses and indifference to national sentiment only increased. In December 1905, the governor of Tehran ordered the beating of sugar merchants who refused to lower their prices. Some mullahs and bazaaris assembled to protest, but the government broke up the meeting and provoked the ulama into withdrawing from the city. Algar calls it "a symbolic demonstration of the illegitimacy of the government."[78]

The ulama came back to Tehran once the government promised to implement a House of Justice. After further pushing and shoving between government and opposition that lasted ten months, the first representative assembly, the first Majlis, met in October 1906 to draft a constitution, which was signed by the dying Mozaffar al-Din Shah in December. Article 1 made Imami Shiism the religion of state, and Article 2 created a five-member board composed of top religious leadership to review legislation. These would seem to be important trophies for the ulama, who were presumably less committed to the freedoms of citizenship, assembly, and press the new document guaranteed. Unfortunately, the machinations of a new shah and foreign powers, especially the 1907 agreement between Britain and Russia to divide Iran into zones of influence, eventually brought the constitutional experiment to a standstill. The alliance of ulama, bazaaris, and constitutionalists brought change but not stability to the country.

The Pahlavis

The chance for stability emerged twenty years later, after Reza Khan, who had risen within the Russian-trained Cossack Brigade, overturned the Qajar dynasty. The religious establishment, or most of it, apparently preferred a new monarchy over a republic and the possibility of further chaos.[79] Reza Khan, who took power in 1921 and the crown in 1925, understood his dependence on the goodwill of the ulama, and perhaps that, together with his admiration for Mustafa Kemal Atatürk, helps explain why he systematically sought to undermine the power of the religious establishment over the next two decades. Already the creation of modern schools, begun after 1850, had eroded the power of the ulama in education. The adoption of a civil code in 1928 diminished the power of sharia courts, and a 1932 law deprived them of the revenue generated by the registering of documents. After 1936 the ulama could not serve as judges. Akhavi sums up the impact of Reza Shah's tenure on the religious establishment:

> On the whole, the Shah's legacy in the matter of clergy-state religions was that of a ruler who sought to prohibit the public enactment of passion plays, narratives or even mourning for the death of contemporary *maraji-yi taqlid*, rather than a ruler who received petitions of redress from the clergy, solicited their support in establishing order and stability, and sought their spiritual guidance, as mandated by the Constitution.[80]

The military strength of Reza Shah, who managed to subdue tribal areas and to initiate the creation of a modern infrastructure in Iran, permitted him to disregard the views of the ulama but did not enable him to domesticate the religious establishment. His reforms marginalized the ulama and deepened the divide between church and state. The adoption of a dress code in 1928 set clergy apart by permitting them to dress in a traditional manner. Everyone else was to appear in public in Western dress.[81]

Clerical influence rebounded after the allies—Britain, Russia, and the United States—pushed Reza Shah from the throne in 1941 and permitted his young son, Muhammad Reza Pahlavi, to take power. The veil came back and, in fact, mujtahids issued fatwas in 1948 forbidding women into public markets without the veil. One faction of the clergy led by the Ayatollah Kashani favored active intervention in politics and supported the rise of Muhammad Mussadiq to the prime minister's position. Mussadiq's nationalization of Iranian oil touched off an international crisis. His popularity threatened the position of the shah, who was forced to flee the country in 1953. He returned after a coup d'état engineered by Washington and London. But most of the clergy, including the young Ruhollah Khomeini, remained loyal to the leading ayatollahs, Muhammad Husayn Borujerdi and Muhammad Musavi Bihbihani, who resisted direct political involvement. While unwilling to cooperate openly with the shah, they gave him tacit support. The monarch, relatively weak until 1953, courted the support of Qom, which had replaced Najaf, Iraq, as the primary locus of the Iranian religious establishment.

Ayatollah Borujerdi solidified the organizational integrity of the religious establishment. Respected in his later years as the sole marja-e taqlid, he held together a set of factions and dampened conflict with the regime in the name of spirituality, the seminaries in Qom, a united front, and sufficient economic resources. Khomeini, who had studied with him, kept his radicalism under control while Borujerdi was alive. When Borujerdi died in 1961, he left behind a religious establishment that was more autonomous, coherent, and prosperous than the one he had inherited—an establishment better suited to supporting any political action, even revolution.

It was by no means obvious, however, that this establishment could prevail in a contest with the monarchy. By 1961 Muhammad Reza had been in power for twenty years, thanks in part to foreign assistance with police, education, and industry. He was launching the ambitious White Revolution in an effort to win the hearts of the peasantry with land reform, which some of the clergy opposed. The religious establishment appeared weak and ineffective. Akhavi puts the total number of clergy at 10,000, of whom 100 ranked as mujtahids. They staffed 20,000 mosques.[82] There were some 138 madrasas in 1968 and some 7,500 students, and the state was progressively taking control of those institutions to modernize the curriculum. The state had taken ownership of religious endowments in 1937 under Reza Shah.[83] (The autonomous clergy still enjoyed the benefits of direct contributions from believers in the form of the religious taxes.)[84] By the 1970s the state's Endowment Organization was using funds to support students in madrasas and to create the Department for Religious Propaganda to work in the rural areas. "Together with their associates in the Literacy Corps, they were meant to be the 'mullas of modernization.'"[85] The state sought to undermine the autonomy and power of the religious establishment.

At least two factors explain the establishment's transformation in a period of twenty years (1960–1980) from a position of relative obscurity and acquiescence into a force capable of taking political power. The first is the remarkable leadership of Ruhollah Khomeini, who turned the regime's awkward efforts at repression into incitement of revolution, and the second was the preaching of lay radicals such as Jalal Al-e Ahmad and especially Ali Shariati, whose revolutionary but anticlerical message aroused the masses in Tehran and prepared them to follow revolutionary religious leadership.

When Khomeini began systematic verbal attacks on the shah in the spring of 1963, he was already a prominent religious leader, one of three or four leading ayatollahs and objects of emulation, maraji. Some clerics objected to the shah's land reforms. Others protested the plan to give women the right to vote, although voting itself was largely meaningless in Iran at that point. Khomeini attacked the shah for the tyrannical nature of his rule and for his dependence on the United States. A proposed law to exempt American military personnel in Iran from prosecution under Iranian law exemplified his complaints. The regime triggered protests in major cities by arresting Khomeini in March 1963. Subsequently released, rearrested, released again, and then expelled in 1964 to Turkey, Khomeini ended up installing himself in the old stronghold of Shiism, the city of Najaf in Iraq, where he could teach and rail upon the Iranian regime with impunity. It was there he gave a series of lectures expounding his theory of velayat-e faqih.

From Quietism to Activism

By his long patience with the quietism of the Ayatollah Husayn Borujerdi, and by his denunciation of the shah from the prestigious Faiziyeh madrasa in Qom, Khomeini acted with full consciousness of the need to pull the clerical class with him toward political activism. He articulated a theory of Islamic government that depended on the rule of a mujtahid. Quite to the contrary, Ali Shariati helped found an institute in Tehran, Irshad Hosseini, outside the traditional religious structure, from which he and others intoned against the regime for its favoritism, its elitism, and its tyranny. Shariati preached a revolutionary version of Islam that categorized the clerical class as defenders of the status quo. Shariati called for a return to spiritualism and a reshaping of Iranian culture. Soon he attracted the attention of the regime, which put him in prison, but in the long run he helped Khomeini by portraying the shah as opposed to the authentic, democratic, egalitarian nature of Islam. After Shariati's death in 1977, Khomeini and his clerical entourage carried the message forward and transformed it into an Islamic government.

The religious establishment prevailed in Iran by virtue of its success in maintaining distance from the regime. Alone among Iranian institutions, it was relatively untainted by the crassness of authoritarianism. It prevailed because of the hierarchical structure, developed over centuries, that permitted top ayatollahs to exercise financial and political control. It prevailed thanks to a structure that reached into nearly every village. Mosques seem to have escaped the surveillance of Savak, the shah's secret police and intelligence agency. Sermons on cassette shipped from Europe carried Khomeini's message to the far reaches of the country. It prevailed by virtue of astute leadership that caught foreigners, and perhaps the shah himself (then suffering from cancer), by surprise. The United States struggled at the last minute to make contact with the leadership and failed. Ignored and disdained by academics and intelligence agencies, Khomeini and his revolutionary cohorts could not be restrained.

The arrival in Tehran of Grand Ayatollah Ruhollah Khomeini in February 1979 united religious and political power in a manner reminiscent of Safavid Iran. Khomeini had advanced himself to the pinnacle of the Shii hierarchy in Iran. The new constitution, with its consecration of the velayat-e faqih, opened the way for him to rule as "the most distinguished jurist" of his generation. The Guardian Council necessarily included members of the clerical class, and the Council of Experts entrusted with choosing the faqih included only members of the clergy. In addition, clerics repopulated the judiciary, dominated the new foundations designed to promote the purposes of the new regime, and ran for election to national and local offices. While laymen were eligible to fill offices and run for election, the regime vetted officeholders and candidates for religious credentials. It was not enough to be a Muslim. To get past the gatekeepers, one needed to have helped further the revolution. Under Khomeini, the religious establishment became the political establishment.

Such a statement is, however, misleading. First, a number of leading clerics stood aside and refused to acknowledge the legitimacy of velayat-e faqih. The clerical class was not united behind the regime. Some believed the clerical involvement in politics would sully Islam. Second, the constitution did not specify the relationship between the faqih and the religious establishment. Khomeini was a marja, but his successor, hastily promoted to ayatollah from a more modest status, did not persist in trying to attain marja status. He is the primary political leader but a secondary religious leader. Third, there is no constitutional necessity for clerics to dominate the Majlis or the presidency of the republic. Khomeini said the faqih inherited all the power of the Prophet, but the constitution balances that power with institutions based in popular sovereignty. Fourth, the clerical class has been split into factions vying for influence within the system. Are members of the Majlis and functionaries who are products of religious training to be regarded as clerics even when they have become professional politicians and bureaucrats? The Association of Teachers in the seminaries at Qom continue to control education and function with relative autonomy from the government. There remains a distinction between the government and the religious establishment, appearances notwithstanding.

Separation of Institutions

The selection of Ali Khamenei to succeed Imam Khomeini reaffirmed the separation between religious and political institutions.[86] At that moment, all the remaining grand ayatollahs with the exception of Husayn Ali Montazeri stood opposed to the idea of velayat-e faqih, and Khomeini had already broken with Montazeri, who ended up under house arrest for advocating Islamic democracy. Buchta puts the number of grand ayatollahs at 14 in 2000. Khamenei did not even rank as an ayatollah when he took office as the Supreme Leader. Of 5,000 clerics at this rank in the year 2000, Buchta estimates that 80 (including Khamenei after promotion) worked for the government. When Khamenei took office, he held the rank of hojjatoleslam, a title accorded to graduates of theological seminaries. Buchta puts the number of such people at 28,000 in 2000, of whom about 2,000—including former President Ali Akbar Hashemi Rafsanjani and the speaker of the parliament Ali Akbar Nateq-Nuri—serve in the government. He also estimates that some 4,000 clerics (out of a total of 180,000) with little or no seminary training hold government positions.[87]

If these numbers are roughly correct, then the size of the formally trained clerical class has increased about threefold from the early 1960s, from 10,000 to 33,000. Mosques, seminaries, and religious associations multiplied in the

1960s and 1970s in a period of relative prosperity. "By the mid-1970s, perhaps for the first time in Iranian history, the religious establishment was large enough to be able to send preachers to the most distant of Iranian villages."[88] Keddie puts the number of people in Iran holding religious posts or having some religious training at 180,000 in the early 1980s.[89] The total might be more than 210,000 today (about .35 percent of the population), as indicated by the Buchta figures. The clerical class constitutes a small part of the population (1 person in 350), and few of the clerical class (roughly 6,000 of 210,000, or 3 percent) hold government positions.

While clerical rule has transformed some government departments, such as the judiciary and education, others have retained much of their prerevolutionary character, largely unscathed by clerical influence. Clerics have gained power through the great foundations created after the revolution in the name of good works and charity. The bonyads, as these foundations are called, now control about 40 percent of the Iranian economy.[90] Examples would be the Foundation for the Disabled and Oppressed, the Martyrs' Foundation, the Imam Reza Foundation, the Fifteenth of Khordad Foundation, and the Farabi Foundation. Enjoying nonprofit status and reporting to the Supreme Leader, these foundations engage in moneymaking activity but also draw heavily on the state budget. Perhaps because they depend on the Supreme Leader, or perhaps because of their ostensibly charitable purposes, clerics play key roles in most if not all of the foundations.

It is impossible to assert that there is a clear separation of religion and politics in Iran, but it is likewise impossible to assert that the two realms are one. Some religious institutions, such as the seminaries, continue to function with relative autonomy. The religious hierarchy centered in Qom is distinct from the political hierarchy, topped by the Supreme Leader in Tehran, who is not and never was a primary religious leader. The fear he evokes inside and outside the government depends not upon his ability to allocate religious rewards but upon his control of the armed forces, police, and intelligence agencies (the modern lutis) in addition to the powers of appointment and dismissal that reside with his office. The presidency, the Expediency Council, and the Majlis, not to mention most of the government ministries, are not religious institutions. If political institutions were identical with the religious institution, there would be no need for a constitution and the complicated system of elections it creates.

In Iran, the Qajars and then the Pahlavis sought to subjugate the Shii establishment but with much less success than rulers in Egypt or Turkey. The hierarchy and autonomy of the religious institution contributed to the revolution and seemed to disappear into it, but fusion was never achieved, and the trend now appears to be toward greater separation. The reform movement headed by former President Khatami talked about creating a civil society, an intermediate zone between the spiritual life of the individual and the realm of government. Government would then acknowledge limits imposed by the rules of civil society, which are already articulated in the Iranian constitution. It would acknowledge the supremacy of constitutional and positive law, which conflicts with the supremacy of religious inspiration, the justification of the faqih's role. The constitution, the religious establishment, and Iranian tradition prevent complete fusion of religion and politics. The current constitution, as interpreted by the Supreme Leader, Ali Khamenei, prevents separation. Such is one definition of "dissonant politics"[91]

Political Culture

The hope of any revolutionary regime is to transform the political culture in its image. Lenin and Stalin hoped to create a society of communists. Mustafa Kemal Atatürk hoped to make Turkey a nation of secular Muslims. The Iranian revolutionaries succeeded by appealing to the Muslim loyalties of men and women who flocked to the revolutionary standard. But the leadership also hoped to transform their countrymen into "true Muslims," those who would abandon the miniskirt, give up wine and beer, rededicate themselves to their families, and, when necessary, stand ready to sacrifice their lives for the country. The revolutionaries hoped to displace memories of pre-Islamic Iran dear to the deposed shah with a fresh commitment to Islam, and to Iran as the leader of the Muslim world. As with every revolutionary regime, education became the key to achieving such objectives. Propaganda may sway some of the older generation, but the new, purified generation will come from the schools. Unless a revolutionary regime can transform the political culture to fit its ideals, it will eventually be forced to continue with postrevolutionary repression or relinquish its vision of utopia.

The struggle over political culture in Iran has focused on religion for a century. Reza Shah and his son Muhammad Reza Shah drew from Atatürk's vision of modernity, which called for secularization of the political culture. They worked at the level of symbols (dress codes), law (civil and criminal codes), and especially education. By creating modern elementary and secondary schools run by the state, they undercut the role of the clergy and helped propagate a message of nationalism and modernization. The schools taught religion as a tool for achieving these objectives.[92] The creation of a law school in 1936 and then modern universities after World War II offered an alternative to the madrasas run by the ulama, and even the madrasas became subject to government regulation. The Pahlavis sought to reduce the impact of the religious establishment on the law, the enforcement of the law, education, and the mores of the country.

To some extent they succeeded. They succeeded among the upper classes in the great cities of Iran, especially Tehran, where Western fashion, automobiles, industry, commerce, and education wrought enormous changes. As Iran became richer from its oil production, the shah spent freely on military hardware, oil technology, and big business. New wealth and opportunities abounded for elites, but there also emerged resentment against the incursion of foreign ways. Western cinema, Western experts, Iranian students returning from abroad, American television shows broadcast in Iran—all affected the culture in Tehran. The modernizing, secularizing vision of the Pahlavis rallied an urban elite against the ulama and religion. In a survey of some 167 members of the Iranian elite in the late 1960s, Marvin Zonis found that two-thirds of his respondents

> felt that the ulema were performing a negative service for Iran—a rather conclusive demonstration of the fundamental bifurcation between the religious and political elite and a rationalization for the political campaign being waged against them. Inasmuch as the regime has been unsuccessful in mobilizing the religious elite for regime policies, the regime's response has been overwhelmingly negative, both against the ulema themselves and against religion per se (although this latter point is not one that would be conceded by the regime).[93]

But Zonis found the elites highly mistrustful of one another, cynical about human nature, and disdainful of some other groups in society not closely related to the purposes of the regime. One exception was the peasantry, which fared well in the estimation of elites. The shah's White Revolution to redistribute land to the peasantry probably explains the elite responses, not the peasantry's traditional attitudes toward religion. One cannot help wondering how much elites knew about the peasantry they were rating more positively than, say, members of the Majlis or professionals of the media. Elites who evinced the most respect for other groups in society also expressed the most favorable attitudes toward foreigners. Those more disdainful of Iranian groups were also more disdainful of foreigners.[94]

The Advent of Islamism

Beyond the elites, the tide was beginning to shift about the time Zonis conducted his survey. With the leadership of the Ayatollah Khomeini, the ulama began to reciprocate the elite's disdain. Al-e Ahmad was writing about Westoxication. Shariati began to preach about revolutionary Islam as the proper recourse for Iran. An Islamic revival began about the same time in other Muslim states. The Israeli victory over the Arabs in 1967 triggered new interest in Islam. Why had God abandoned the Arabs? Sadat released members of the Muslim Brotherhood from prison to help combat the Leftists he feared. An Islamist movement began to emerge in Syria, Turkey, and elsewhere. While the changing tide in Iran does suggest that the shah failed in his broadest efforts to combat religion, it would be difficult to establish that Iran was naturally more disposed toward Islamism than other countries or that the religious revival in the Muslim world began in Iran. As frustration with the promises of modernizing ideologies such as socialism and liberalism mounted, religion became the language of political dissent in Iran as elsewhere in the region.

In an effort to legitimize the illegitimate, the shah sought to link his throne to Persian monarchs of the pre-Islamic era. When he celebrated the 2,500th anniversary of the Peacock throne at Persepolis in 1971, he linked himself to tales of the past reported in the great epic poem by Ferdowsi, the *Shahnameh*. Writing in the Islamic era, Ferdowsi recounts bloody tales of ancient warfare in which kings and heroes act first and reflect later. When they reflect, they often invoke concepts of right and wrong and invoke the support of God (in the singular), but they also confront jinns (devils) and demons, monsters, and magic. Women figures are mostly bearers of children but at least one dons armor and takes the battlefield to avenge a family wrong. Wine flows freely at banquets that go on for days. Regarded as one of the first and most important examples of Persian literature, the *Shahnameh* neither exalts religion in the pre-Islamic period nor banishes it from consideration. Belief in a single God seems to characterize this ancient society.

The simple existence of Persian literature calls attention to the fact that the coming of Islam did not mean in Iran, as it did elsewhere in the Middle East and North Africa, the victory of Arabic. Names changed, as Bulliet observes in charting the slow conversion of Iranians from Zorastrianism to Islam, but the predominant language of everyday discourse did not.[95] Moreover, the Persian penchant for mystical poets such as Rumi and Hafiz further distinguishes

Iranian Islam from that of places such as Saudi Arabia, where Sufism has long been suspect. The passion plays honoring the death of the Imam Husayn draw upon a love of theater, poetry, and mysticism. The late shah sought to neglect elements of the Iranian heritage he considered inimical to modernization and his legitimacy. The ulama sought to filter the heritage of its non-Islamic and "heretical" elements (such as the Bab) in order to ensure its own dominance in religious affairs.

The Pahlavis, father and son, tried and failed to significantly reduce the role of religion in Iranian society. The Islamic Republic has sought to enhance the place of religion by (1) establishing norms of dress and behavior; (2) establishing religious criteria for holding political office; (3) revising school curricula and devising new educational programs; (4) restricting the flow of information in the name of protecting morality; and (5) encouraging religious groups, religious celebrations, religious language. The long-term result of these measures is still uncertain.

The regime has been successful in changing the way women dress in public, or at least the way bourgeois women dress. Nonurban and lower-class women have been less affected, because many continued to cover their heads. Women have necessarily complied, but they have complied in different ways and to different degrees. Some show a bit of hair, wear some makeup, or don scarves of bright colors. Any small distinction in a sea of gray and black calls attention to the bearer and the body. Covering the body is a way of calling attention to it. In short, women still show personality and make themselves attractive. The question is whether changing dress has affected the woman's role in the family and society. While the employment of women outside the home dropped after the revolution, it now appears to be rising again. And while girls suffered discouragement in the educational process and were prohibited from studying abroad without escort, these restrictions now appear to have been lifted. A society long steeped in misogyny is still misogynistic but nonetheless changing in directions predicted by modernization theory.

By demanding that candidates for public office hold religious credentials, the regime has sought to reduce the possibility that municipal councilors, members of the Majlis, and the president of the republic would act in ways injurious to religious rules. In fact, the criterion is loyalty to the regime. A similar requirement prevailed under the shah. Only authorized political parties were permitted to contest elections, and only authorized candidates were permitted to run. The old Majlis had little authority and the new Majlis has rather limited authority as well. Imposing religious criteria diminishes the democratic legitimacy of the assembly, as did the vetting process of the ancien régime. Because all legislation of the Majlis is subject to review by the Guardian Council, which looks for incompatibilities with Islamic law, there is no need to have members of the Majlis who meet religious criteria. What seems to be a process to promote religion turns out to be an inherited suspicion of democratic procedure.

Educational Reform

Education is the major tool of any government for reshaping or maintaining political culture. The Islamic Republic has taken a number of measures designed to reorient the schools toward moral purpose, to energize the teaching corps as models for behavior, to reinforce the teaching of religion, and to mobilize support for the Muslim world and against the West and Israel. Iran continues to permit non-Muslim religious groups to provide their own religious instruction and examinations. Non-Muslim students are exempt from examination on the Quran.[96] The texts call upon non-Muslim believers to join Muslims in opposing infidels (including Bahais). While students learn in high school that the leadership of the Muslim community passed to a line of twelve imams, as the Imami Shia believe, the high school texts refrain from criticizing Sunnis, who do not believe the imams were inspired leaders designated by God and Muhammad.[97]

The purpose of religious education in the schools is to train pious Muslims and encourage them to become champions of revolutionary Islam in the world at large. The classroom is a place for the teaching of moral values, proper dress, modesty, and chastity. One of the first actions of the new regime was to separate the sexes in all schools.[98] Instructions for teachers remind them that they are models for their pupils and must therefore conduct themselves in righteous fashion. Texts appropriate to each level come from the Religion Team of the Office of Planning and Compilation of School Textbooks, part of the Ministry of Education. In 1980 the government created a separate division of the ministry, the Bureau of Fostering Affairs, which aims specifically to propagate the regime's ideology and to create followers of the faqih. In 1999 the ministry began creating centers for teaching boys and girls the Quran and Arabic in segregated settings from age five. Some six hundred such centers enrolled 800,000 students by 2000–2001.[99]

The textbooks reflect an aggressive tone on behalf of Islam. In the Pahlavi era the schools emphasized modernization and Iranian nationalism as the primary objectives. Now the textbooks advocate jihad in defense of the homeland, defined not as Iran but the Dar al-Islam, the house of Islam. They mention not just the martyrdom of the Imam Husayn, but also the deaths of others on behalf of Islam, which the texts portray as threatened. Mehran says the texts show that the regime feels insecure. "Framing the threat in terms of Islam and Shiite Muslims as oppressed victims versus ambiguous others directs feelings of patriotism toward the Islamic state and its clerical rulers."[100] The school texts treat Iran as a homogenous country with a single, unambiguous pattern of historical development. They ignore Iranian history before Islam. They treat the great personalities of Iranian history only in their relationship with Islam, and they neglect, even if they largely refrain from attacking, the existence of linguistic and religious minorities. Iran is and always has been Shii and Persian by these textbook accounts. Its fate is identical with that of the Muslim world as a whole. This notion conflicts, of course, with the reality of international relations, where Iran has often been at odds with other Muslim countries.

Efforts to politicize the teaching of Islam in the primary and secondary schools carry forward into the university, where entrance now requires not just the requisite diplomas but a religious-political screening process. "This means that admission to university is contingent upon evidence of praying and fasting, proper veiling for female students, and loyalty to the Islamic Republic, in particular the religious jurisprudent [faqih]."[101] The authorities closed the universities for four years in the 1980s in an effort to cleanse them of classes, faculty, and students potentially critical of the regime. Reconstructed, the universities have nonetheless generated expressions of dissent and support for reform that have rocked the regime.

The Islamic Republic has made great strides in carrying education to remote villages. Illiterate parents want education for their children, and literacy rates have risen impressively, especially for girls and women. The demand for university education exceeds capacity, and the needs of the economy and society—the oil industry, the nuclear industry, modern communications—require an emphasis on education. One result is the increase in self-reflexivity that Adelkhah observes in Iranian culture. She notes the outpouring of manuals on food, marital relations, physical education, and raising children. Both sexes flock to the gym for exercise and self-improvement. The birthrate has fallen. Consumers make complicated decisions befitting a modern economy. There is a passion for competitions of all sorts, including Quran contests, and the country is mad about sports.[102] A film portrays women skydiving from the mountains north of Tehran—their Islamic garb intact from launch to landing.[103] Iran's qualification for the World Cup finals in soccer galvanized the nation. Women demanded and achieved access to soccer games.

Studies have long regarded heightened individualism and self-consciousness as a characteristic of "modernity" as defined in the West. Individualism and self-reflexivity rise with levels of education as they do with exposure to the media. While the regime in Iran has often censored newspapers or intimidated their owners and sought to control the spread of satellite dishes, it fights a losing battle over access to sources of information. Adelkhah refers to great public debates about soap operas. The regime takes advantage of Ramadan to broadcast programs designed to heighten religiosity and loyalty to the regime, but adherence to Ramadan fasting appears to have diminished, and those who follow it often offer as a reason its benefits to mind, body, and social interaction—not religious tradition. Even official programming on television turns a religious celebration into a variety show. Ramadan has become a time for great consumption, gifts, travel, and sporting competition.[104]

Deeply suspicious of cinema in general, the regime has nonetheless permitted a revival of the Iranian film industry. The government understood the propaganda potential as well as the risks. The makers of the documentary *Divorce Iranian Style* struggled for months to get the requisite permissions to film a family court.[105] Told they should find a more positive subject, they replied that what would be more positive in the eyes of the government would be seen more negatively abroad. On the one hand, the film shows the obstacles women face in making a case for divorce. On the other hand, it shows women of great will and determination who outmaneuver their husbands in the courtroom and a judge more open to their arguments than one might expect.

Increasing Religiosity

The Islamic Republic has poured religious propaganda into the schools and tried to use the media to promote political Islam. It has also made religion more convenient than it was forty years ago. The Quran is available in every size and shape. Every family can own not just one, as was once the case, one that needs to be protected from harm, but many of them. Cemeteries have been computerized and rationalized. A family in need of a funeral service can choose from among options online with specified prices. The Web site of the Iranian embassy in Canada offers believers a choice of maraji (those ayatollahs worthy of emulation) for advice on a wide range of issues. The Internet offers access to the sermons of great preachers and to religious information. The regime has institutionalized, bureaucratized, and rationalized religion, and it has enormously enhanced incentives for conforming to religious norms and supporting political Islam.[106]

TABLE 6.1

"How Important Is God in Your Life?"

	IRAN (2000)	ISRAEL (2001)	TURKEY (2001)	EGYPT (2000)
Less important 1–8	9.5%	39.1%	13.0%	9.0%
More important 9–10	89.6%	58.5%	86.7%	91.0%
Don't know, no answer	0.9%	2.4%	0.3%	0.0%
N=	2,532 (100%)	1,170 (100%)	3,401(100%)	3,000 (100%)

Source: World Values Surveys, 1981–2004, online analysis. Question FO63.

To what extent have Iranians become more devoted to the spiritual life? Survey data collected in 2001 suggest that Iranians are about as religious as Muslims in Turkey and Egypt. For example, when respondents in these countries were asked about the importance of God in their lives, on a scale of one to ten, 89.6 percent of Iranians responded with a nine or a ten ("very important," see Table 6.1). The figure for Egypt was 91.0 percent and 86.7 percent for Turkey. Israel appears much less religious by this measure. Only 58.5 percent of the respondents chose similar responses. In Iran, Turkey, and Egypt, the percentage of respondents saying they believe in God ranged from 97.4 percent in Turkey to a high of 100 percent in Egypt. In Iran, 2,504 of 2,532 respondents, or 98.9 percent, said they believed in God. Eighty-two percent of the Iranian sample defined themselves as "religious persons" as distinguished from "not a religious person" or a "convinced atheist." The percentage was 98 percent in Egypt and 79 percent in Turkey (see Table 6.2). Iranians appear about as religious as Egyptians and perhaps more religious than Turks by another measure. Asked how often they attend religious services, 45 percent replied that they do so once a month or more. Thirty-nine percent of Turks and 45 percent of Egyptians chose those responses. Iranians were more likely than Turks or Egyptians to say they attend services only on special holy days. Few Iranians (4 percent) responded that they "practically never" attend services, while 35 percent of Turks and 25 percent of Egyptians chose that response.

Because this was the first World Values Survey done in Iran, it is impossible to know whether these data represent change toward greater religiosity, as the regime might hope, or decline in spiritual belief and religious practice, as critics predict will be the result of forcing religion on citizens. What can be

TABLE 6.2

Three Questions About Religion

	IRAN (2000)	TURKEY (2001)	EGYPT (2001)
"Do you believe in God?"	98.9%	97.4%	100%
"Are you a religious person?"	82.3%	78.8%	98.4%
Attend religious services once a month or more*	44.8%	38.9%	44.7%
Attend religious services only on special holy days	40.1%	15.7%	24.9%

Source: World Values Surveys, 1981–2004, online analysis. Questions F050, F034, and F028.
Combines responses of "more than once a week," and "once a week" and "once a month" to the question "How often do you attend religious services?"

said is that efforts of the Islamic Republic to propagate religion do not, after the first twenty years, catapult Iran into a special category of religiosity. On a graph plotting religious participation against the propensity for religious beliefs, Norris and Inglehart locate Iran close to Egypt, Turkey, and Jordan— and not far from the United States, Chile, and Canada![107] On the Norris-Inglehart scale of traditional to secular-rational values (a scale heavily influenced by religious values and behavior), Iran appears slightly more secular than Egypt, Pakistan, Uganda, and Zimbabwe, and at about the same level as the Philippines, Indonesia, and Brazil.[108]

The Iranian government has pushed its citizens to see themselves first as Muslims and only later as Iranians. In contrast, the old regime pushed national over ethnic or religious identity. On a World Values Survey question about how a respondent would best describe himself or herself, 61 percent of Iranians chose "above everything else, I am a Muslim," almost twice as many (34 percent) as chose "above everything else, I am an Iranian" (see Table 6.3). But in Turkey, reputed to be a more secular country where Kemalism has been preaching Turkism for almost a century, the percentages were 64 percent for "I am a Muslim" and 29 percent for "I am a Turk." In Egypt, they were 79 percent and 10 percent. Israelis were more balanced: 44 percent chose "Jew" and 31 percent said "Israeli." Once again the Iranian results appear unexceptional for a Muslim country.

Two studies of the Islamic Republic done fifteen years apart reach roughly the same conclusion. Religion has always been an important element of the

TABLE 6.3

"Which of the Following Best Describes You? . . . "

	IRAN (2000)	ISRAEL (2001)	TURKEY (2001)	EGYPT (2001)
"I am Iranian" or Israeli, Turk, etc.	34.1%	43.9%	29.0%	9.8%
"I am a Muslim" (or a Jew in Israel)	61.0%	31.2%	64.0%	79.4%

Source: World Values Surveys, 1981–2004, online analysis. Question G015. Wording may have varied slightly with country.

political culture in Iran, but it is scarcely the only factor shaping that culture or even the most important one. In a book published in 1986, Behnam emphasizes Iran's long-standing love-hate relationship with outsiders. As early as the nineteenth century Iran began to resent the outside influence that it also courted and cultivated. Behnam notes the high degree of distrust of others to be found among Iranians (a distrust Zonis found among the elites).[109] Family is a refuge from such distrust and from the class distinctions that further undermine social solidarity. One can, in the end, depend only upon family ties. This message, already conveyed in the *Shahnameh*, is not likely to disappear.

In a study done in the 1990s, Adelkhah looks at the continual adaptation of an old idea, the Iranian "man of integrity," the *javanmard*, who demonstrates four characteristics: (1) a generous, giving nature; (2) a set of contacts that show he has "back [influence]"; (3) practical skills and abilities that bring success; and (4) unifying acts that come to constitute the self. But she says that the javanmard is also a person who manages to overcome the self. In many respects Khomeini embodied the ideal, but that ideal then runs up against the need for solidarity and institutions.[110] Bill observes that leadership in Iran has long depended on "emanation" for its success.[111] Khomeini's legitimacy emanated from the Hidden Imam and incarnated, perhaps, the Iranian ideal of the javanmard. But both these ideals conflict with the primary trends of the Islamic Republic: institutionalization and bureaucratization. Can Khomeini be reinvented without challenge to the institutions he helped create?

Adelkhah concludes that the social and economic forces propelling modernity, which include technological innovation, urbanization, global communications, and increasing literacy, continue to reshape mentalities in the Islamic Republic. Change compounds choice and causes the individual to develop capacities and rationales for choice. The regime claims religion governs social policy, and it does to some extent. Islam is "part of Iran," she observes,

> certainly a central part, but not necessarily more important from the social point of view than, say, the reality of cities, the search for knowledge, the economic crisis, the upward thrust of youth, the regional environment and family obligations.[112]

Adelkhah shows that political culture changed considerably in the first twenty years of the Islamic Republic, but only some of that change reflects intended consequences of government policies. For example, birthrates apparently started to decline even before the government reversed itself and began to promote birth control. It had previously argued that birth control contravened Islamic law. Government policies responded to social realities, and individuals responded to both microlevel realities and government policy. Iran has resumed a trend toward lower fertility rates and smaller families established under the ancien régime but now this trend enjoys religious sanction.

Iran's political culture, long marked by contradictions such as obedience to political authority and contempt for it, continues to evolve in ways that seem to reflect the forces commonly identified with modernity. While religious rhetoric and practice have become more prominent, the changes may be more superficial than profound. The wants and desires of Iranians do not seem to differ significantly from their neighbors. Asked to choose among four priorities, 69 percent list a stable economy as their first or second choice, a slightly higher percentage than in Turkey, Egypt, and Israel. In Inglehart's terms they are overwhelmingly "materialist" rather than "post-materialist," as one would expect from Iran's GNP per capita. They were much more likely than Egyptians and Turks to duck a question about democracy. About a third responded "don't know" to three questions about democracy that they may have seen as heavy in political implications. There is, in other words, little evidence that the aspirations of the average Iranian differ significantly from those of people anywhere else on the globe. Modernization does not require secularization. It requires only that people find means of accommodating modernization within religious ideas and of adapting religious practice to fit its exigencies. Iran appears to be engaged in accommodation and adaptation.

Conclusion

Religion varies with political circumstances, sometimes influencing those circumstances and sometimes changing as a result of them. The downfall of the

Sasanian empire at the hands of the Arabs brought Islam to Iran and resulted in the eventual demise of Zoroastrianism. The Safavid dynasty converted the country to Shiism and created a religious establishment that began to assert its political influence under the Qajars in the nineteenth century. The Pahlavis sought to push the establishment aside and to reinvent a national identity tied to the pre-Islamic past, but the overthrow of the Pahlavis brought Islamic revolution, which reworked the nation's identity, its political ideology, its religious institutions, and, to some extent, its political culture. It was the political success of the religious establishment that made possible a dream of religious transformation. Politics have been more cause than effect of religious change.

From a long-term perspective, every aspect of the relationship between religion and politics has fluctuated. No single analytical scheme can account for any one of them. Iran's identity with Islam, which the regime regards as total, has varied in intensity over the centuries and millennia. Persian literature ties the country to a geographical and cultural entity that predates Islam. The whims of fortune carried it toward Shiism, then toward secular nationalism, and finally back to identification with universal Islam. Religion has sometimes been dominant in the ideological predisposition of a regime, as with the Safavids, and receded into the background at moments such as the early twentieth century, when European law codes and political ideas carried the day. While political institutions have generally prevailed over religious institutions, the religious institution has exercised greater influence in moments of political weakness—in the Qajar period, during the Constitutional Revolution, in the 1970s as the Pahlavi dynasty began to come unraveled. Greater organization and greater hierarchy within the religious establishment enabled the clergy to create a revolution, which then altered the balance of power between politics and religion. The victory of the clergy led to a fresh assertion of political domination over religion. Yet the government has not been successful in translating that domination into a general transformation of the way people think about political authority and political actors.[113] The election of President Khatami in 1997 caught the regime by surprise, as did the election of President Ahmadinejad in 2005.

The key question about Iran is not how religion will transform the country. It is, rather, what the political system will do to religion. Will it continue to insist that Islam requires rule by a Supreme Leader, the faqih, who is above the law, or will those clerics who hold power ultimately decide, with Grand Ayatollah Ali Montazeri, that even the Supreme Leader must be subject to the law and the constitution? President Khatami took that position but failed in his efforts to uphold it. A reversal of that verdict would transform the Iranian system without eliminating religion from the public sphere. It would confirm the loss of sacredness in the political system, which began with the adoption of a constitution and accelerated with the death of Khomeini. It would perhaps save religion from the secularization it currently undergoes as a tool of government. Will the clerical elite who are now governing have the wisdom to liberate religion from its servitude to politics? To free it of the responsibility it bears for everything from the price of gasoline to foreign policy?

The government has transformed the relationship between religion and politics in Iran by claiming a monopoly on truth. Those who oppose this regime from within the Islamic tradition find this claim of a monopoly on truth to be the root of the problem. Such a monopoly contradicts the tradition of plural maraji, a choice among mujtahids as objects of emulation. Even though the current faqih does not claim to be a marja, much less the only marja, he cannot effectively be challenged from either inside or outside the political structure. While Imami Shiism has known periods in which there was a single marja-e taqlid, those have been exceptional periods. The regime need not be secular, but if it is to evolve toward democracy, it must become tolerant of diverse opinions, lifestyles, and religions. Such tolerance could certainly be achieved within an Islamic republic and even under a slightly modified version of the current constitution, but current elites may not permit change of that sort. Persistent rigidity would create a precondition for further revolution.

Notes

1. See Marvin Zonis, *The Political Elite of Iran* (Princeton, NJ: Princeton University Press, 1971).

2. Fariba Adelkhah, *Being Modern in Iran*, trans. Jonathan Derrick (New York: Columbia University Press, 2000).

3. James A. Bill, "The Cultural Underpinnings of Politics: Iran and the United States," *Mediterranean Quarterly* 17, no. 1 (Winter 2006): 22–33.

4. An additional half dozen countries are approximately 50 percent Muslim in population.

5. Bahais constitute the largest non-Muslim minority in Iran at 200,000 to 300,000. Ludwig Paul, "'Iranian Nation' and Iranian-Islamic Revolutionary Ideology," *Die Welt des Islams* 39, no. 2 (1999): 200.

6. Ibid., 205ff.

7. The terms are those of Hamid Dabbashi, "The End of Islamic Ideology," *Social Research* 67, no. 2 (Summer 2000): 502.

8. W. Montgomery Watt, "The Significance of the Early States of Imami Shiism," in Nikki R. Keddie, ed., *Religion and Politics in Iran: Shiism from Quietism to Revolution* (New Haven, CT: Yale, 1983), 21–46.

9. See Jonathan Berkey, *The Formation of Islam: Religion and Society in the Near East from 600–1800* (Cambridge, UK: Cambridge University Press, 2004).

10. Nikki R. Keddie, *Modern Iran: Roots and Results of Revolution* (New Haven, CT: Yale, 2003), 8–9.

11. Ibid., 11.

12. Ibid., 11.

13. Jalal Al-i Ahmad, *Occidentosis: A Plague from the West*, trans. R. Campbell, ed. Hamid Algar (Berkeley, CA: Mizan Press, 1984).

14. Farzin Vahdat, *God and Juggernaut: Iran's Intellectual Encounter with Modernity* (Syracuse, NY: Syracuse University Press, 2002).

15. Mahmoud Alinejad, "Coming to Terms with Modernity: Iranian Intellectuals and the Emerging Public Sphere," *Islam and Christian-Muslim Relations* 13, no. 1 (2002): 32.

16. Paul, "Iranian Nation," 195.

17. Ibid., 205.

18. Ibid., 211.

19. Ibid., 217.

20. A. William Samii, "Iran's Guardians Council as an Obstacle to Democracy," *Middle East Journal* 55, no. 4 (Autumn 2001): 650.

21. Constitution of the Islamic Republic of Iran, Article 2, 6, a, www.salamiran.org.

22. See Daniel Brumberg, "Dissonant Politics in Iran and Indonesia," *Political Science Quarterly* 116, no. 1 (2001): 381–411.

23. James A. Bill, *The Politics of Iran: Groups, Classes and Modernization* (Columbus, OH: Merrill, 1972).

24. Hamid Dabbashi, *The Theology of Discontent: The Ideological Foundations of the Islamic Revolution in Iran* (New York: New York University Press, 1993).

25. Forough Jahanbaksh, "Religious and Political Discourse in Iran: Moving Toward Post-Fundamentalism," *Brown Journal of World Affairs* 9, no. 2 (Winter/Spring 2003): 245.

26. Ahmad Ashraf and Ali Banuazizi, "Iran's Tortuous Path Toward 'Islamic Liberalism,'" *International Journal of Politics, Culture and Society* 15, no. 2 (Winter 2001): 238.

27. See Dabbashi, "The End of Islamic Ideology," 475–518.

28. See the translation available on the Web site of the Iranian Embassy in Ottawa, Canada, www.salamiran.org.

29. Asghar Schirazi, *The Constitution of Iran: Politics and the State in the Islamic Republic*, trans. John O'Kane (London: I. B. Tauris, 1997), chapter 1.

30. See Sayyid Qutb, *Milestones* (Indianapolis: American Trust, c1990).

31. Ruhollah Khomeini, *Islam and Revolution: Writings and Declarations of Imam Khomeini*, trans. Hamid Algar (Berkeley, CA: Mizan Press, 1981), 169.

32. Ibid., 170.

33. Ibid., 171.

34. Ibid., 170.

35. Ibid., 54.

36. Ibid., 62.

37. Hama Omid, "Theocracy or Democracy? The Critics of 'Westoxification' and the Politics of Fundamentalism, in Iran," *Third World Quarterly* 13, no. 4 (December 1992): 681, footnote 32.

38. See, for example, his *Marxism and Other Western Fallacies: An Islamic Critique* (Berkeley, CA: Mizan Press, 1980); *On the Sociology of Islam: Lectures* (Berkeley, CA: Mizan Press, 1979); and *Red Shiism* (Houston: Free Islamic Literatures, 1980).

39. Dabbashi, "The End of Islamic Ideology," 481.

40. Keyvan Tabari, "The Rule of Law and the Politics of Reform in Post-Revolutionary Iran," *International Sociology* 18, no. 1 (March 2003): 101.

41. Tabari, "The Rule of Law," 106. See also Schirazi, *Constitution*, 233.

42. The best account is that of Daniel Brumberg, *Reinventing Khomeini: The Struggle for Reform in Iran* (Chicago: University of Chicago Press, 2001).

43. Saïd Amir Arjomand, "The Rise and Fall of President Khatami and the Reform Movement in Iran," *Constellations* 12, no. 4 (December 2005): 505. See Ervand Abrahamian, *Khomeinism: Essays on the Islamic Republic* (Berkeley: University of California Press, 1993), chapter 1, for a treatment of Khomeini as a populist.

44. Ashraf and Banuazizi, "Iran's Tortuous Path," 246.

45. Tabari, "The Rule of Law," 106.

46. Arjomand, "Rise and Fall," 503, reproaches Khatami for not taking a firm stand and provoking a constitutional crisis.

47. Ziba Mir-Hosseini, "The Conservative-Reformist Conflict Over Women's Rights in Iran," *International Journal of Politics, Culture and Society* 16, no. 1 (Fall 2002): 42.

48. Azar Nafisi's *Reading Lolita in Tehran: A Memoir in Books* (New York: Random House, 2003) conveys that point of view.

49. Jaleh Shaditalab, "Islamization and Gender in Iran: Is the Glass Half Full or Half Empty?" in *Signs* 32, no. 1 (Autumn 2006): 19.

50. Roksana Bahramitash, "Islamic Fundamentalism and Women's Economic Role: The Case of Iran," *International Journal of Politics, Culture and Society* 16, no. 4 (Summer 2003): 560.

51. See Azadeh Kian, "Women and Politics in Post-Islamist Iran: The Gender Conscious Drive to Change," *British Journal of Middle Eastern Studies* 24, no. 1 (May 1997). Also Haleh Afshar, "Women and Politics in Iran," *European Journal of Development Research* 12, no. 1 (June 2000): 188–205.

52. Bahramitash, "Islamic Fundamentalism," 552. What women do in the villages of Iran (or other Muslim countries) probably does not get included in such figures. Neither do the number of women who do volunteer work, as in the campaign to eradicate illiteracy.

53. Bahramitash, "Islamic Fundamentalism," 565.

54. Mir-Hosseini, "The Conservative-Reformist Conflict," 45–46.

55. Hasan Yusefi Eshkevari, *Islam and Democracy in Iran: Eshkevari and the Quest for Reform*, Ziba Mir-Hosseini and Richard Tapper, eds. (London: I. B. Taurus, 2006), 149.

56. Ibid., 173.

57. By one account, the election of President Khatami in 1997 constituted a direct threat to the "ideological foundations of the Islamic Republic." Ali Gheissari and Vali Nasr, "The Conservative Consolidation in Iran," *Survival* 47, no. 2 (Summer 2005): 177.

58. Tabari, "The Rule of Law," 106.

59. Ann Elizabeth Mayer, "The Islamic Law as a Cure for Political Law: The Withering of an Islamist Illusion," *Mediterranean Politics* 7, no. 3 (Autumn 2002): 139.

60. Olivier Roy, "The Crisis of Religious Legitimacy in Iran," *Middle East Journal* 53, no. 2 (Spring 1999): 207.

61. Ali Banuazizi, "Faltering Legitimacy: The Ruling Clerics and Civil Society in Contemporary Iran," *International Journal of Politics, Culture and Society* 8, no. 4 (Summer 1995): 570.

62. Geneive Abdo, "Re-Thinking the Islamic Republic: A 'Conversation' with Ayatollah Hossein 'Ali Montazeri," *Middle East Journal* 55, no. 1 (Winter 2001): 9–24.

63. Vahdat, *God and Juggernaut*, 208.

64. Mohsen Kadivar, "An Introduction to the Public and Private Debate in Islam," *Social Research* 70, no. 3 (Fall 2003): 663.

65. Ibid., 669.

66. Ibid., 678.

67. Abdullahi A. Al-Naim, "Re-affirming Secularism for Islamic Societies," *New Perspectives Quarterly* 20, no. 3 (July 2003): 39.

68. This conclusion sustains the main argument of Anthony Gill and Aran Keshavarzian, "State Building and Religious Resources: An Institutional Theory of Church-State Relations in Iran and Mexico," *Politics and Society* 27, no. 3 (September 1999): 431–465.

69. Keddie, *Modern Iran*, chapter 1.

70. Ibn Khaldun, *The Muqaddima: An Introduction to History*, trans. Franz Rosenthal (Princeton, NJ: Princeton University Press, 1967).

71. Hamid Algar, *Religion and State in Iran, 1785–1906: The Role of the Ulama in the Qajar Period* (Berkeley: University of California Press, 1969), 148.

72. See Algar, *Religion and State*, chapter 8.

73. This is Algar's general assessment in *Religion and State*.

74. Keddie, *Modern Iran*, 54.

75. Algar, *Religion and State*, 171.

76. Ahmad Ashraf, "Bazaar-Mosque Alliance: The Social Basis of Revolts and Revolutions," *Politics, Culture and Society* 1, no. 4 (Summer 1988): 538–567. "The politics of the bazaar was intermingled with the politics of informal campaign for candidates of the highest office in the Shii hierocracy," 542.

77. Azar Tabari, "Shii Clergy in Iranian Politics," in Nikki Keddie, ed., *Religion and Politics in Iran* (New Haven, CT: Yale, 1983), 55.

78. Algar, *Religion and State*, 246.

79. Shahrough Akhavi, *Religion and Politics in Contemporary Iran: Clergy-State Relations in the Pahlavi Period* (Albany: State University of New York Press, 1980), 29.

80. Ibid., 59.

81. Roy Mottahedeh, *The Mantle of the Prophet: Religion and Politics in Iran* (New York: Pantheon, 1985), 234.

82. Akhavi, *Religion and Politics*, 129.

83. Homa Omid, *Islam and the Post-Revolutionary State in Iran* (New York: St. Martin's Press, 1994), 21.

84. "The *Shias* are expected to part willingly with one-fourth of their surplus worldly goods, *zakat*, and one-fifth of their surplus liquid cash, *khoms*, each year, to meet the needs of the poor and the needy; not those of the state and government. So the religious dues are paid to a religious leader of one's choice and never find their ways to the coffers of the state." Omid, *Islam*, 141.

85. Akhavi, *Religion and Politics*, 141.

86. "It is obvious that from the beginning the prevalence of politics over religion was in Khomeini's mind." Roy, "The Crisis," 205.

87. Wilfried Buchta, *Who Rules Iran? The Structure of Power in the Islamic Republic* (Washington, DC: Washington Institute for Near East Policy, 2000), 54. See his note on p. 55, too.

88. Omid, *Islam*, 33, citing Ervand Abrahamian, *Iran Between Two Revolutions* (Princeton, NJ: Princeton University Press, 1982), 433.

89. Nikki Keddie, Introduction, *Religion and Politics*, 17.

90. One writer, Katajun Amirpur, declares, without specifying a source, that "unofficial estimates" put 80 percent of the Iranian economy in the hands of the "clerical conservative establishment." "The Future of Iran's Reform Movement," in *Iranian Challenges*, Chaillot Paper #89, Amirpur and Walter Posch, eds. (Paris: European Union Institute for Security Studies, 2006), 29–40.

91. Brumberg, "Dissonant Politics."

92. Omid, *Islam*, 20.

93. Zonis, *Political Elite*, 315.

94. Ibid., 316.

95. Richard Bulliet, *Conversion to Islam in the Middle Period: An Essay in Quantitative History* (Cambridge, MA: Harvard University Press, 1979).

96. Golnar Mehran, "Iran: A Shi'te Curriculum to Serve the Islamic State," in Eleanor Abdella Doumato and Gregory Starrett, eds., *Teaching Islam: Textbooks and Religion in the Middle East* (Boulder, CO: Lynne Rienner, 2007), 56.

97. Ibid., 64.

98. Omid, *Islam*, 157. Chapter 8 treats the efforts of the regime to reshape the political culture.

99. Mehran, "Iran," 58.

100. Ibid., 62.

101. Ibid., 59.

102. Fariba Adelkhah, *Being Modern in Iran*, trans. Jonathan Derrick (New York: Columbia University Press, 2000), chapter 6.

103. "Iran: Veiled Appearances" (First Run/Icarus Films, 2002).

104. See Fariba Adelkhah, "Le ramadan comme négotiation entre le public et le privé: le cas de la République d'Iran," in Adelkhah and François Georgeon, eds., *Ramadan and politique* (Paris: CNRS, 2000).

105. Ziba Mir-Hosseini, "*Divorce Iranian Style*," in Richard Tapper, ed., *The New Iranian Cinema: Politics, Representation and Identity* (London: I. B. Taurus, 2004). The movie is by Women Make Movies, New York, 1998.

106. Adelkhah, *Being Modern*, 133

107. Pippa Norris and Ronald Inglehart, *Sacred and Secular: Religion and Politics Worldwide* (Cambridge, UK: Cambridge University Press, 2004), 226.

108. Ibid., *Sacred and Secular*, 239.

109. Zonis, *The Political Elite*.

110. Adelkhah, *Being Modern*, chapter 2.

111. Bill, "Cultural Underpinnings," 27.

112. Adelkhah, *Being Modern*, 178.

113. Delphine Minoui asserts that the regime "has not succeeded in infusing its population, the majority of which is young, with its political-religious ideology." "L'Iran des réformes: la société face au pouvoir," *Politique étrangère* 67, no. 1 (January–March 2002): 114.

7

Reconciling Religion and Politics

The debate about religion and politics degenerates all too frequently into exaggeration. On the one hand, living in Colorado Springs one can easily imagine that religious organizations such as the New Life Church and Focus on the Family are exerting inordinate influence on local schools, state government, and even national politics. Zealots push for the teaching of creationism in public schools. Many support the Bush administration's call for religious organizations to perform social services in the name of the government and its appointment of judges with strong religious convictions. On the other hand, living in Southern California one can easily imagine that secular humanism sweeps all before it, including school observance of religious holidays. The campaign for recognition of gay marriage evokes fear and objection among many of the devout. The American Civil Liberties Union plays the role of the devil in that context, as the religious right does in the other. The culture wars rage on in America without victor or vanquished.

Exaggeration also marks the discussion of religion and politics at the level of comparative politics. Some Europeans look at America with astonishment. How can a prosperous nation with a high level of literacy and education continue to have such high rates of church attendance and such large percentages of the population who believe in God? Americans view Europeans with some worry about a loss of not just religion but moral purpose. Europeans join Americans in deep concern about the growing strength of Islam in the West and of political Islam in many parts of the world. They link Islam with traditionalism, oppression of women, authoritarianism, and even terror. Some see the West locked in a clash of civilizations. Meanwhile, some of the exponents of political Islam see the secular humanism embedded in Western social, economic, and political theories as inimical to their ways of life. They see threats to the survival of Islam and welcome a clash of civilizations.

What these observations share is a common exaggeration about the importance of religion (or absence of religion) in political life. Social scientific studies of the 1950s and 1960s argued that religion diminishes in importance as countries become wealthier and better educated. Those studies downplayed the importance of religious leaders and political leaders with claims to religious legitimacy. Religion loomed as an obstacle to development. Then came religious revival in the Muslim world, and social scientists responded with a veritable deluge of studies of Islam and Islamism. The Iranian revolution was the key event. The question had to be reopened: Is Islam compatible with social and economic development? Professor Edward Said triggered a debate about Orientalism that pitted skeptics about the capacity of Islam to evolve with the times, such as Bernard Lewis, against optimists such as Said, who blamed Western scholars for having created distortions about Islam that Muslims themselves had come to accept. Both sides have focused on the importance of religion in the Muslim world and of scholarly efforts to understand it. The debate about Orientalism has helped temper the deterministic modernism of social science in the 1950s and 1960s, which downplayed the importance of religion, and the reactive overemphasis on Islam characteristic of the 1980s and beyond.[1]

While this study joins the stampede to study religion, it seeks to establish a plane of comparison that goes beyond any single religion or region of the world and beyond an assumption that religion determines politics. A survey of events in Europe and America shows that religion has played a part in shaping political life on both continents, especially at certain moments in time. In the great span of history, however, politics is a more important determinant of the religious configuration of a country than religion is a determinant of politics. Political necessities have driven religion to accommodate identity with the nation-state, the supremacy of positive law, the political regulation of religious institutions in the West. Politics has required recognition of religious pluralism and mutual toleration. Christianity, however influential, cannot account for the overall shape and course of political development in the West. Modern Christian thought and organization reflect political realities.

The investigation of four case studies in the Middle East confirms a similar pattern. Islam alone cannot explain three diverse patterns of political development in three Muslim nation-states: Egypt, Turkey, and Iran. It is impossible to describe the phenomenon we call Islam without descending to the nation-state or even the substate level. If Islam is merely the Quran and a set of core ideas divorced from those who propound and believe them, then one can speak of it as an abstraction. If Islam means not just a book and ideas but people, what they think, how they are organized, and what they do, then one must study them in a physical space, and that space is now divided into nation-states. Just describing Islam requires working within one or more nation-states. If religion is not merely an abstraction, then it cannot be treated as a single, undifferentiated phenomenon. If it were, and if it were determinant, it would create the same result everywhere. Judaism would have produced the same result in America as it has in Palestine, but it has not. In every case examined here, politics comes to explain more about religion than religion can explain about the condition of politics in a particular nation-state.

Politics is the determining factor. If religious forces gain control of a state, as in Iran, they do so by political means. It is the state that determines how religion—its representatives, its organizations, its believers, and its doctrines—will be treated. The state may find itself desperately in need of the legitimacy religious support can provide. It may discover that propagating a certain version of religion serves its purposes. It may need to suppress dissident religious groups, either to please the religious majority or to prevent religious dissent from becoming political dissent. It may have an ideological interest, as did the Soviets, in suppressing religion. Perhaps more than anything, the state has an interest in a stable relationship with the dominant religious group and its representatives. That interest in stability and legitimacy gives religious groups leverage. They may be able to bargain over national identity, over the nature of the law, over regulation of organizations, and over civic and religious education. Their political influence, or lack of it, will affect the outcome.

There exists a "balance" between religion and politics not when the two domains are equal in weight—what would that mean?—but rather when neither the state nor religious groups want radical change in the relationship. Of course, neither side may ever be happy with the balance that is struck. The culture wars in America attest to that fact. Many Americans apparently vote in solidarity with a religious denomination or from personal religious conviction.[2] Groups resort to referenda, legislatures, Congress, the presidency, and the courts to seek modification of the ground rules governing religion and politics. Secular-minded groups push back in all those venues. The American system permits continual adjustment of policy without risk of a major shift in structure. One may speak of an approximate "balance" or a "settlement" that is achieved in a particular context in a specific moment of history.[3]

Egypt in the nineteenth century serves as a case of imbalance where the state was the revisionist party. Starting with the reign of Muhammad Ali, the Egyptian state sought consistently to reduce the power and authority of the ulama by diminishing their financial resources and bringing them under state supervision. Egypt since World War II serves as an example of the opposite sort of imbalance. The Muslim Brotherhood assembled a political force with a capacity for armed action that challenged the monarchy and contributed to its demise in 1952. The new strongman, Gamal abd al-Nasir, felt threatened by the Brotherhood, and he outlawed the organization. Free again after 1970 but never legal, the Brotherhood has spun off groups dedicated to the forcible overthrow of the Egyptian government. One of those groups assassinated President Anwar al-Sadat in 1981 for what the assassin argued was betrayal of Islam. The Brotherhood itself remains in opposition and advocates a new moral order for the country. The official ulama, employees of the state, have sought to negotiate a middle ground in an effort to isolate radicals from moderate Muslims and to show the average Muslim that the state respects religion. The relationship between religion and politics remains unsettled.

The relationship remains unsettled in Israel, too, but there the temporary looks much more permanent than in Egypt. Without a formal constitution, the country has forged ahead on the basis of informal arrangements. The status quo letter provided assurances to the ultraorthodox to bring them toward support of the state. The state has provided progressively greater benefits to orthodox and ultraorthodox, as a result of the influence of these groups in the Knesset. Leftist, secular groups have resisted and called for radical reduction of religious influence, but they are playing politics within the system. The assassination of Yitzhak Rabin by an ultraorthodox yeshiva student from the West Bank, who declared that Rabin had violated religious law, shook the system momentarily but only solidified existing conventions in the long run. Secular law takes precedence over halakha. The state remains stable in its mix of religious and secular.

Turkey seems to be moving toward ever greater stability in the relationship between religion and politics. The long-term stability of that relationship under the Ottoman Empire came under pressure in the nineteenth century. Sultan Abdülhamid II played the Islamic card to shore up his empire. When those efforts failed, and a new Turkey emerged in the 1920s, the state under Atatürk committed itself to a complete reworking of that relationship. It sought monopolistic control of religion but failed in the long run to achieve it. Sufi orders, though prohibited from public meetings, lurked underground. Said Nursi cultivated a new religious sensibility. By relying on force to sustain its efforts at monopoly (which it termed "laiklik," or secularism), the state opted for apparent over genuine stability. As it moved toward multiparty competition after World War II, the parties that challenged the Republican People's Party, the party of Atatürk, sought to reintegrate the forces of religion. Then, after 1970, an Islamist movement arose to pursue that objective with greater intensity. Turkish democracy finally empowered Recep Tayyip

Erdoğan, a product of the Islamist movement, whose government appeared to be fashioning a sustainable equilibrium between religion and politics—one that both Islamists and the Turkish military were willing to accept.

Iran has veered from one sort of imbalance to another. Like Atatürk, Reza Shah tried the strong-armed approach to reducing the role of religion. His son, Muhammad Reza Shah, took greater care to cultivate religious authorities until the early 1960s. Then, rather than seeking accommodation of the strident complaints of Ayatollah Khomeini, who was concerned about Westernization and foreign privilege in the country, the shah reverted to the repressive tactics of his father. He exiled Khomeini, who settled in Iraq to study, teach, and preach. Khomeini ultimately convinced many of his fellow clerics that revising the relationship between religion and politics required revolution. Khomeini fashioned the forces of religion into a revisionist party.

Since the Iranian revolution, the tables have turned. The government led by clerics now seeks stability and, like the Pahlavi monarchs, has resorted to force to maintain it. Leading clerics who object to the new arrangements have been silenced by trial in special courts or, in the case of Ayatollah Ali Montazeri, once in line to become Khomeini's successor, placed under house arrest. Challenge to the notion of Islamic government would be unthinkable, but even those who pushed for reform within the Islamic model, the supporters of President Khatami, were harassed, imprisoned, or executed. Since the regime insists on cloaking its actions in religious language, every protest necessarily affects the relationship between religion and politics. While there is apparent stability in the relationship, appearances backed by repression often prove deceiving in the long run.

Instability

Instability in the relationship between religion and politics—defined as a situation in which either religious forces or the governing powers seek revision of the relationship—makes liberal democracy difficult to achieve. Hobbes understood the dangers of religious discontent and proposed radical separation as a solution. But his remedy of strict state control of religion under a "mortal god," subject only to review by the immortal God, did not hold up in the West.[4] He thought only an absolute sovereign could dominate religious passions and enforce an enduring settlement. But Locke, Rousseau, and Kant did not follow his solution. The liberal state came to depend on moral principles anchored in a universalistic religion that did not, however, require scriptural verification and therefore invite devastating strife. The "great separation" envisioned by Hobbes never occurred, although it remained the ideal of French secularism, or laicism. Judeo-Christian secularism of the sort practiced in England and especially in America sought instead to reconcile religious and secular values within institutions designed to prevent religious strife.[5] Religion became a bulwark of the state. Once in place, liberal democracies in Europe and America provided the mechanisms for "partisan mutual adjustment" in such a way that stability in the relationship between religion and politics could be maintained.[6]

Liberal democracy provides a set of formulas for stability. Nonliberal monarchies in many parts of the world have sought "settlement" in other ways. Some European monarchs claimed divine right to rule and depended upon the church for support of their claims. In the modern Middle East, several kings claim family ties to the clan of the Prophet and ally themselves closely with the ulama. The Saud family advances itself as the protector of the Holy Places (Mecca and Medina) and depends for its legitimacy on the corps of ulama, who in turn depend on the monarchy for support of the religious establishment. Jordan and Morocco have achieved considerable stability on the basis of relationships that bear some resemblance to the Saudi model. What Huntington defined as the "king's dilemma"—to promote modernity would be to undermine the notion of monarchy, but to not promote modernity would be to provoke revolt—has proved less daunting than he thought in 1968, perhaps because monarchs have often used religion effectively.[7]

Ibn Khaldun did not believe that there could be a permanent reconciliation of religion and politics. His cyclical theory of government presupposed periodic renewal by virtue of a process in which governments, established by military conquest and boldness, settle into a comfortable, debilitating lifestyle, lose their will to fight, neglect the dictates of their religion, and expose themselves to conquest by ferocious bedouins driven by puritanical religious fervor. His model served to explain much of Islamic history, and the history of North Africa in particular, but the Ottoman Empire, which was in its infancy when he wrote, far outlasted the five generations allotted it by the Khaldun model. The Ottomans achieved much greater stability than he imagined possible. The relationship they established between political and religious establishments, between bureaucrats and the corps of ulama, constitutes one secret of its success.

What causes stable formulas to erode? Ibn Khaldun blamed human nature. Regimes that establish themselves on piety fall prey to the soft life of city-based power. Contemporary modernization theorists argue that the process of social and economic modernization affects both politics and religion.

People are pulled from their villages toward increasing opportunities in the cities. They educate their children, who seek jobs in the modern economy and participate in modern organizations. Eventually they come to want to participate in political decisions. As Huntington observed, an increase of political participation via unions, associations, political parties, demonstrations, protest movements, etc., will likely produce political instability, unless there is institutional growth and adaptation to these new phenomena.[8]

Modernization theorists argue that this same set of changes produces a more secular society. Ronald Inglehart identifies a syndrome of traits that he calls "traditional" attitudes, many of them grounded in religion. Modernity means, he says, moving away from these attitudes and away from a number of religious beliefs. Some societies including the United States have not, however, moved in the predicted direction of secularism on this scale, even though the United States has clearly become a postindustrial society and scores high on a postmaterialist scale (emphasis on freedom and self-expression over materialism). Inglehart dismisses the United States as an anomaly. Western Europe best exemplifies his model by virtue of its ultramodernity (i.e., high degree of secularism) and postmaterialism.[9]

What Inglehart's surveys do not consider is how religion can change without ceasing to be religion. Several studies have linked Islamist movements to increasing literacy rates and the spread of higher education in Muslim countries. Contrary to modernization theory, more education seems to be producing more religious commitment, rather than less. Literate believers suddenly have direct access to the Quran and Quranic exegeses that have previously been inaccessible. Women's study groups abound. Religious publications have multiplied with the size of the literate audience. Sermons on cassette give even the illiterate access to interpretations they would likely never have heard. Religion has become a matter of choice, not just habit. Eickelman and Piscatori write about "objectification."[10] A believer who comes to reflect on religion, to see it as an object among other objects, who chooses one version of that object (political Islam?) over another is quite a different person than one who performs religious rituals to prolong the practices of ancestors.

The religious attitudes of a society can thus undergo change with the opportunities offered by modernizing societies. (To call this "secularization of religion" does not serve any useful purpose.) This change in religious consciousness can result in instability in the relationship between religion and politics. Egypt and Turkey bear testimony to the impact of the Islamist phenomenon. In both countries Islamist groups emerged to demand revision of the place of religion in politics.

In Iran the relationship between religion and politics eroded from both sides. On the one hand, rapid economic and social modernization, fueled by oil wealth, created new political demands that the monarchy found itself hard-pressed to satisfy. On the other hand, education created a growing elite that was receptive to the messages conveyed by Jalal Al-e Ahmad, Ali Shariati, and other dissident intellectuals who came to argue that Islam meant revolution. The Ayatollah Khomeini found a receptive audience for his Islamist appeal. Changes in the political and social environment thus affected both the political and religious spheres. The tenuous relationship achieved under the shah and maintained, in part, by repression became unstable.

Social change necessarily affects the relationship between religion and politics in a society, but instability may also result from exogenous political factors such as imperialism. The advent of nationalism in the Middle East constitutes another such factor. The great successes of socialism in the Soviet Union in the first fifty years of its existence constitute a third. Imperialism provoked a rallying to religion in a search for reasons why the lands of Islam were unable to defend themselves. The success of socialism probably encouraged the forces of secularism, but it was nationalism, itself a product of imperialism and a reaction to it, that required major readjustment of the older relationship between religion and politics.

Nationalism arrived in Egypt as a reaction against the Ottoman Empire and against European intervention. It came to Turkey as a revolt against the empire and against foreign domination. Iranian nationalism grew as a movement opposed to British and Russian imperialism, and subsequently as a parliamentary majority supporting Mussadiq in his move to nationalize Iranian oil. Nationalism in the Jewish community ultimately created a Jewish state where there had been none before. In each case, nationalism created change in the relationship between religion and politics.

Zionism represents the most dramatic example. In the Diaspora, Jews related to a variety of states in which they lived in one of two ways: assimilated into a state dominated by non-Jews or unassimilated as a ghettoized community with great internal coherence and organization but third-or fourth-class status in the society at large. In the case of assimilation, religion was irrelevant. In the case of ghettoization, it constituted a glue for the community, a reason for holding oneself apart and a manual for doing so. An assimilated Jew, Theodor Herzl, took the Dreyfus Affair in France as evidence that even Jewish citizens would never achieve genuine equality there. He revived the idea of a Jewish state, and while few of his fellow assimilated Jews responded to the appeal, the ghettoized communities of Eastern Europe responded with enthusiasm. The possibility of a state began to transform the relationship between Jews and the states of Europe, especially in the East; then came Hitler in Germany, whose persecution of Jews solidified efforts in Palestine to create an entirely new state, whose identity depended in part on religion. There was no precedent for establishing a relationship between religion and politics in this new entity.

The states included in this study have all experienced sharp changes in the relationship between religion and politics as a result of the forces of social mobilization and modernization and as a result of exogenous factors, especially nationalism. Building or rebuilding political stability necessarily entails revising the relationship between religion and politics in one or more of the four arenas where religion impinges on political life. If powerful religious organizations oppose political arrangements, political instability is a likely result. If an authoritarian government imposes its vision of religion on its citizens via proclamations, laws, institutions, and education, it generates hostility and potential instability. Establishing or reestablishing stability means achieving some sort of consensus on identity, ideology, institutions, and political culture.

Identity

Two of the four countries included in this study, Iran and Egypt, have long histories as states. These countries emerged from societies older than those of Europe, but they followed European states toward nationhood in the nineteenth and twentieth centuries. Because Arab Muslims conquered Egypt and Iran in the seventh century, Islam is an important element of national identity in those countries. Sixty percent of Iranians and 80 percent of Egyptians think of themselves first and foremost as Muslims.[11] Ninety percent of Iranians and 80 percent of Egyptians declare themselves "very proud" of their nationality. The comparable figures for Turkey and Israel are significantly lower: 54 percent and 65 percent. These differences between old states and new ones created in the twentieth century make sense.

The two venerable societies, Egypt and Iran, encountered nationalism in different ways than Turkey and Israel. For Egyptians, nationalism meant liberation from the French occupation launched by Napoleon Bonaparte and then from Ottoman rule. Later, after the occupation of Egypt by the British in 1881, nationalism came to mean genuine independence from imperialism—something not fully accomplished until 1952. Similarly, nationalism in Iran took the form of protest against the monarchy and its efforts to modernize the country by leasing its resources to Europeans. After World War II

Muhammad Mussadiq as prime minister led the forces of nationalism and challenged the shah by regaining control of Iranian oil. The shah himself invoked Iranian nationalism but came under attack for his dependence on the United States. Nationalism in these two countries thus assumed anti-imperial and anti-Western forms, even though the idea of nationalism itself is of European origin.

In both cases Islam emerged in stages as the principal source of alternative identity, even though other possibilities were available. Ulama provided indigenous leadership in Egypt when the French invaded. Muhammad Ali and his successors, themselves foreigners, tried to manipulate and control religion for their purposes as they sought to modernize the country. Meanwhile, the monarchy permitted foreigners to explore and even take home the ruins of ancient Egypt. The linkage of the pharaohs with the monarchy, foreigners, and absolutism pushed nationalists toward two other sources of identity. One was Arabism, pursued with special vigor by the regime of Gamal abd al-Nasir from 1952 to 1970, but Arabism led to quarrels with other Arab states and a disastrous war with Israel. The most successful effort to reformulate Egyptian identity in religious terms came with the creation of the Muslim Brotherhood in the 1920s. Its founder, Hasan al-Banna, saw himself as a nationalist opposed to the British and opposed eventually to the monarchy, which remained caught in British snares. The Brotherhood urged Egyptians to see themselves as Muslims and to become "good Muslims" by supporting Brotherhood activities, cultural, social, political, or even military. President Anwar al-Sadat sought to tip the country away from its Arab identity and toward Islam, but his assassins called him "pharaoh." Religion emerged as the badge of Egyptian authenticity for the Sadat and Hosni Mubarek regimes as well as for the Islamist opposition.

In Iran the story was similar. The ulama began to align themselves with the nationalist movement, first in the successful protest against the tobacco concession in 1891 and then in the Constitutional Revolution of 1906–1909. The ulama supported the creation of a new dynasty under Reza Shah Pahlavi in the belief that he represented the best chance for order and stability for Iran, free of foreign domination. A part of the clergy initially supported the nationalist government of Mussadiq, and a leading member of the ulama, the Ayatollah Khomeini, led protests in the 1960s against concessions to foreigners, particularly the grant of immunity from Iranian courts accorded to American military personnel in 1963. Muhammad Reza Pahlavi sought to bolster his legitimacy with references to ancient Persia. Such claims pushed the protest movement against the shah toward an alternative form of Iranian identity, the Islamic identity solidified by the Safavid dynasty's conversion of the country to Shii Islam after 1500. In both Egypt and Iran, Islamist movements extricated Islam from its reputation of antimodernism and fashioned it into a recipe for rescue of the "authentic" nation from foreign influence. In both cases, pre-Islamic identities suffered by association with previous regimes eager to assert their autonomy from the Islamic world and their solidarity with the West, but nothing precludes an eventual revival and further reworking of national identities, if ever the issues of foreign influence recede in prominence.

The "new" states of Turkey and Israel faced the problem of creating states and then national identities. Neither felt as much threat from foreign influence as did Egypt and Iran. The Young Turks fought off foreign domination to establish a new Turkey, but they saw their own past as a greater threat to legitimacy than foreign ideas. Mustafa Kemal Atatürk identified Islam with the Ottoman Empire and with antimodernism. He suppressed many religious organizations and subjected an official Islam to government supervision. Islam was to serve the interests of the secular state, which identified itself with "Turkism," even though the country included only a fraction of the Turkish-speaking population of the world and non-Turks constituted a substantial part of the new nation. The Kemalists pushed Turkey toward the French model of laïcité. Although circumstances have changed in Turkey since World War II, and Islam has reemerged as a factor in politics, the country seems increasingly capable of reintegrating Islam and even Ottoman history into its identity without giving up its commitment to modernism and even membership in the European Union. President Recep Tayyip Erdoğan has sought to recognize the overwhelming identification with Islam without downgrading the achievements of Atatürk or joining the anti-Western chorus.

Israel also emerged from a piece of the Ottoman Empire and, like Turkey, sought to dissociate itself from that element of its past. It depended for its creation on foreign, imperial forces, and while it eventually fought against British occupation, it turned to the West for further assistance once independence had been achieved. The agreement to accept reparations from Germany in exchange for friendly diplomatic relations illustrates that decision. The early settlers were predominantly secular Jews, who saw the Zionist movement as creating a refuge for Jews, a pioneering effort to establish a new community in a strange land, an experiment in social justice, and an opportunity to build a state. Identity flowed from those who committed themselves to that effort, who saw themselves as Jews. The Labor settlement movement, responsible for establishing democratic procedures for governing the incipient state, found itself obliged to accommodate religion for two reasons: Zionism as an idea doesn't make sense without some reference to historic Judaism, and the emerging state could not do without the cooperation and support of all Jews, whether they were secular, Orthodox, or ultraorthodox. Politics dictated inclusion of religion in the state's identity.

Israel resembles Iran in the centrality of religion to its official identity. Israel is a Jewish state, and Iran is an Islamic republic. To become something different, each country would have to rename itself. If Israel were to revert to the notion of a binational state, it would presumably become Israel-Palestine or a state of some other name. If Iran were to move toward an identity more inclusive of Iran's full history, it would presumably drop "Islamic" from its name. Both countries could diminish the role of religion in their identities, but this would be more difficult for Israel than for Iran. Without Zionism, Israel would not have come into being, and Zionism is not conceivable without Judaism, although it is not a necessary consequence of Judaism. The concept of Iran does not depend on Islam, whatever the current regime may think or proclaim.

In that sense Israel may be more dependent on religion for its political identity than even Iran, not to mention Egypt or Turkey, even though a much smaller portion of Israelis see themselves first as Jews (44 percent) than Egyptians, Turks, or Iranians see themselves as Muslims (61–80 percent). A plurality of Israelis see themselves first and foremost as Israelis, citizens of a state. An additional 12 percent see themselves simply as individuals, and about 20 percent identify themselves as Arabs, Muslims, Christians, or Druze.[12] Religion is thus central to Israeli identity not because its citizens are necessarily devout Jews but because the state itself owes much to religion for its coming into being. For a number of Israelis, religion has become an organizing tool for gaining political influence and protecting interests such as settlement in the West Bank, the definition of citizenship, the educational system, or the organization of religious institutions. It has been a factor in political opposition to the government, but more frequently the religious parties have participated in parliamentary majorities. Relations with the West also reinforce religious identity, not by virtue of "authenticity" as in Egypt and Iran, but because many in the West support Israel by virtue of its religious identity. Israel has transformed Judaism; many, and perhaps most, Jews worldwide now take Israel to be a central institution of the faith. Heightened religious identity and increasing pluralism in Israel may be producing a decrease in "Israeliness."[13]

Israel and modern Turkey congealed as states with elites who admired the West and took democratic ideas seriously. The timing of national independence/

autonomy gave these two states greater freedom to create national identities than either Egypt or Iran enjoyed. Both states enjoyed some discretion about who would be citizens. In Turkey, many Christians including Turkish speakers fled the new state for Greece. The Israeli government pursued a purposeful policy of reducing the Arab population of its new state. It drove out Arabs with force and fear and refused to permit their return.[14] Israel then depended upon voluntary immigration to grow the Jewish population and used war as a tool for refashioning its borders. Both states emerged as more coherent nations as a result of these adjustments, although neither managed to satisfactorily integrate remaining minorities: Kurds in Turkey, Arabs in Israel. Egypt and Iran bore the burdens of the past in the form of positive and negative associations with alternative visions of the nation. They sought to create nations in states that had long been together but largely by reason of geography or force. These states inherited multiple understandings of themselves, none of which has ever been entirely satisfactory to everyone. Much as they may try, they can never expunge the past. For now they have both tilted toward a greater identity with Islam, but history continues to offer other options. For now the "push of the desert" is stronger than the "pull of the Mediterranean" in Egypt, but the pattern could be reversed. Iran could conceivably reverse course and revive its recourse to pre-Islamic glories.

The authoritarian states of Egypt and Iran need to identify with Islam for political reasons but cannot stabilize that identity without opening their political systems to contestation. Syria, Tunisia, Libya, and Algeria, all ostensibly secular republics, find themselves in similar circumstances. All four have dealt with Islamist dissent. The Syrian government sent the army into Hama in 1982 to suppress Sunni Islamists; the Tunisians chased the principal Islamist leader out of the country and have kept him in exile, some of his followers in jail. The Algerian government fought a civil war for at least eight years against Islamist militants. Muammar al-Qadhdhafi, who seized power in Libya in 1969, proclaimed his regime Islamic and populist, but a distinguished Shii cleric from Lebanon, Musa al-Sadr, disappeared on a visit to Libya in the 1970s, presumably a victim of Qadhdhafi's regime.[15] Although civil war has ended in Algeria, it remains to be seen whether the country has achieved a stable understanding of the place of religion in national identity. All these countries have experienced instability in the past fifty years. None of them has achieved the stability that comes from the rule of law and democracy. In no case is political identity secure.

The monarchies of the Arab world have, unlike the republics, been remarkably stable, with two exceptions. Revolution ended a monarchy in

Yemen in 1962, and Qadhdhafi's coup ended the short-lived monarchy in Libya, a monarchy created by the United Nations Trusteeship Council in 1952. Otherwise, kings and shaykhs have done much better than Huntington predicted they would.[16] The kings of Morocco and Jordan both claim descent from the family of the Prophet. Morocco joined Saudi Arabia and Iran as creators of the Organization of the Islamic Conference, which regulates the pilgrimage. The Saudi monarchy leans heavily on its geographic centrality to the history of Islam and its role in hosting the pilgrimage. While all these monarchies have undergone some Islamist challenge, they have been able to defend themselves successfully. Identification of the state with Islam may help explain the political stability, but the formula does not come from Islam or even from Islamic history. These modernizing dynasties have nurtured their versions of religious identity for reasons of political survival.

None of these states is as venerable as Iran or Egypt. All except Saudi Arabia experienced imperial intervention. In Morocco the monarchy survived colonial control and emerged as a symbol of modern nationalism. In another, Jordan, the monarchy owes its control of the country to British indulgence. Starting in the eighteenth century and finishing in the twentieth, the Saudis managed to fight their way to power over an area largely beyond the interests of Europe and the control of the Ottoman Empire. In short, though these monarchies attribute their success to Islam, chance and politics have played a large role. Each monarchy has fashioned an Islam to suit its particular circumstances.

Ideology

Ideological stability in the relationship between religion and politics requires general consensus about the place of religious values and ideas in the political system. Such a consensus can be achieved at a level of either process or substance. Consensus on a decision-making process satisfactory to religious groups might mean protection, citizenship, and a measure of influence. Consensus might be substantive in the sense that the state might recognize religious holidays, follow a religious calendar, and require religious observance in public institutions without necessarily permitting religious access to the decision-making process. The stability achieved in Western Europe and the United States reflects both sorts of consensus, with process being the more fundamental. Religious groups have access to the system, reap concrete benefits, and forgo ideological opposition to liberal democracy.

All four states included in this study have struggled with ideological stability. In the three Muslim countries, the state assumed an aggressive, secular stance coupled with state control of religion. Mustafa Kemal pointed Turkey in that direction, Reza Shah Pahlavi followed his lead in Iran, and Gamal abd al-Nasir earned a secularist reputation by suppressing the Muslim Brotherhood, nationalizing Azhar University, venting hostility toward the conservative monarchies, and endorsing socialism. In the prestate period, the dominant political force in Israel, Labor Zionism, also waxed ideological against religion although it came to see, under David Ben-Gurion's leadership, the need to accommodate Orthodox Judaism.

All these states faced ideological opposition from religious groups. The Muslim Brotherhood, born as an expression of nationalism, became increasingly radical after the death of Hasan al-Banna and the rise to prominence of Sayyid Qutb. Groups with origins in the Brotherhood advocated revolution in the name of Islam in the 1970s. It was then that the National Outlook movement emerged in Turkey, turning its version of Islam into a political platform. The development of an Islamic protest movement arose in Iran at this same moment. In Israel, the victory of 1967 (which sparked despair and Islamic revival in neighboring countries) gave rise to a new ideology of settlement championed by the Gush Emunim, the Bloc of the Faithful. The Gush championed a Judaism that proclaimed Israeli achievements a step toward the millennium and incorporation of the holy places in the West Bank and Jerusalem as a religious duty. The assassin of Yitzhak Rabin pursued the basic premise of this thinking: Israel reflects God's will. Thus, Israeli policy and politicians must bow to religious revelation.

A state that seeks to control all religious institutions and observances can scarcely be called secular, but it will surely be regarded as secular by the religious groups it suppresses. Proponents took secularism to be an integral component of modernity. Marxist and anti-Marxist theorists of modernity viewed religion as an obstacle to progress. State control of religion was supposed to transform an obstacle into a tool. Religious doctrine and practice would be reshaped to suit political needs. Separation of church and state would have exposed the state to possible resistance from religious leaders invoking God's name against modernization policies.

Ideological secularism gave rise to ideological religious movements in all four countries. Secularism was destined to fail by (1) its fundamental inconsistencies and (2) its need for compulsion. Modernization meant education, literacy, communication, global awareness, individuality, and choice, all of which powered religious resurgence and undermined state-controlled religion. The inconsistencies became increasingly obvious and the compulsion increasingly repulsive. Ideological religious movements took up the complaint but doomed themselves to eventual failure because they, like the secularists, failed to command a consensus in the society. They, too, appeared inconsistent in their attitudes toward modernity and religious freedom. They evoked hopes among some who resented forcible secularization and fears among others that their triumph would result in forcible imposition of religious practices.

Resolution of the ideological dilemma cannot come from either complete separation of church and state or complete integration. The states that show the greatest progress toward resolution are Israel and Turkey, where relatively democratic political processes have helped to transform ideologies into candidates and issues. The Gush Emunim has succeeded in winning state approval for some settlements and de facto acceptance of others. It enjoys wide support in several political parties, but its ideology has not become the official ideology of the state. Recep Tayyip Erdoğan led his Justice and Development Party to electoral victory in Turkey because he abandoned the ideological Islamism characteristic of the early incarnations of the National Outlook movement. He has sought to blunt the ideological secularism of the Kemalists without breaking with the general Kemalist idea that religion ought not to dictate government policy. Secularist ideologues compete successfully for votes in both the Israeli and the Turkish systems, but they no longer dominate. Religious ideologues win offices and benefits but must give up antisystem ideology to do so. By playing the game they acknowledge the superiority of political logic over religious doctrine.

The question of religious law and its impact on secular law arises in Israel and Turkey. Many Turks voice their support of the sharia but few seem to want to see it implemented. Many seem to take the sharia as a concept that deserves to be honored, not a list of commands. A prime minister of Islamist conviction is hesitant to evoke the sharia in Turkey. Only some of the ultraorthodox in Israel might put the halakha above the law of the state, even though most Jews would acknowledge the importance of Jewish law. Secular courts struggle with the question of religious law in Israel. Debate in these countries thus turns not so much on whether religious law should be implemented but whether secular law should acknowledge the relevance of religious law in specific contexts. Debate over requirements for citizenship remains critical in Israel. Women's dress codes still concern Turks.

The ideological pressure for implementation of the sharia has been greater in Iran and Egypt than in Turkey and Israel. The reason in Egypt may be that the Muslim Brotherhood, chief element of the political opposition and advocate of greater implementation of the sharia, has not achieved a full stake in the government and has not been forced to take responsibility for its positions. It can afford to rail on the government for "violations" of the sharia, on the official ulama for sanctioning such "violations," and on the secular courts for failing to invoke it, without having to look at practical solutions to modern problems. It takes a position that the sharia is known, complete, unchanging, and clear, although it is possible to question all of those adjectives. The government pays homage to the sharia to placate its Islamist opposition and shore up its otherwise shaky legitimacy. Both government and opposition use ideology for their purposes.

In Iran the fact that Islamists control the government renders the situation different from Egypt, but authoritarianism makes the two cases similar. Because a specific institution, the Guardian Council, is entrusted with ensuring the compliance of all legislation with Islamic law, the sharia remains a subject of continual discussion in Iran. The president and the Majlis, charged with resolving practical problems, must invoke religious arguments to advance their legislation. They invoke the "interest of the community" to justify apparent deviations from the sharia or reversals of policies already proclaimed to be consistent with holy law. The Expediency Council speaks to the needs of practical action. An authoritarian regime founded upon Islamic legitimacy must continuously demonstrate its faithfulness to the sharia. It must defend itself not from secularists, who can be thrown in jail, but from critics working within the Islamic tradition, who must be treated with more care. Similarly, the authoritarian regime in Egypt, with its origins in a military coup, fears Islamist violence. It cannot afford to denounce the sharia and push moderate Muslims into the arms of the Muslim Brotherhood or extremism. The government must honor the sharia and court the official ulama with its rhetoric, if not its acts.

Ideology remains more important in authoritarian regimes than in parliamentary systems, such as those of Turkey and Israel. Both Iran and Egypt have constitutions. Both invoke the rule of law and the importance of elections, but political considerations determine the application of the law in these countries, and neither country meets commonly accepted standards of free, fair, competitive elections that are decisive for the governing process. Hence, both depend in some measure on ideological legitimacy—the very notion of velayat-e faqih comes from Khomeini's interpretation of Shii Islam. Mubarek's regime in Egypt resists the Brotherhood's calls for further implementation of the sharia, but it also engages in ideological propaganda to demonstrate its loyalty to Islam. It finds itself dependent on its dependents, the ulama, to defend its policies against the Brotherhood. It must make concessions.

The dependence on Islamic ideology, albeit of different sorts, renders the relationship between religion and politics less stable in Egypt and Iran than in

Turkey and Israel. In both Egypt and Iran, critics hammer away at the official ideologies. The Brotherhood criticizes the Mubarek regime for its authoritarianism and for its unwillingness to acknowledge the sharia as more than "a principal source of legislation." Critics such as Abdolkarim Soroush argue that the Iranian regime misinterprets the sharia. Such differences represent potential instability, because they betray underlying conflict about the nature of the sharia and its place in modern legislation. The conflict simmers, because political process does not require compromise of opposing views. Exclusion and repression prolong potential instability.

Institutions

Iran, Egypt, and the Ottoman Empire, ancestor to the modern states of both Egypt and Turkey, did not coincide with the classic image of "traditional societies" when they encountered the challenge of Europe. Religious institutions, distinct from political institutions, enjoyed differing degrees of autonomy. In Egypt, where before 1798 the Ottomans ruled but depended on Mamluk militias for military control, Egyptians retained control of religion. The ulama constituted a local elite, dependent on the Mamluk and Ottoman elites, but autonomous by virtue of function and powerful by virtue of their intimate connection to the Egyptian people. In Iran, at the outset of the nineteenth century, the ulama enjoyed greater autonomy than they had under Safavid rule, because the Qajars made no religious claims and were intrinsically weak. Similarly, regime weakness in the Ottoman Empire was both cause and effect of the debility of sultans by 1800. As sovereigns in all three of these places saw the need to defend themselves against imperial intervention by modernizing their societies, they sought to recuperate their authority by reducing the autonomy of frontier regions, far-flung provinces, military units (such as the janissaries) and militias, bureaucrats, and ulama. For these monarchies, modernization meant greater fusion of religion and politics, not separation. Separation meant autonomy, which translated into regime weakness.

This dynamic did not change with the fall of these monarchies. Campaigns to make religion and religious officials the servants of the state gained momentum in the nineteenth and twentieth centuries. Atatürk finished what the Ottoman sultans had begun. Nasir in Egypt finished the project begun by Muhammad Ali in 1800. Reza Shah won the support of the ulama and then proceeded to undermine their authority in more systematic fashion than the Qajars had ever dreamed possible. Ironically, the revolt of the clergy against the secularism of the Pahlavis led to a regime where religion and politics are more closely fused than ever before, although it is by no means certain that the clerics who dominate the state can effectively control the religious institutions, especially the madrasas in Qom that educate the clerical elite.

The development of the state of Israel confirms this same pattern: fusion of religion and politics, not separation, as predicted by the classic modernization model. At the invention of modern Zionism, Orthodox Judaism stood opposed. The Jewish community long resident in Palestine looked askance at the new endeavors. The founders tended to look at formal religion and religious leadership with some skepticism, but Ben-Gurion wanted to harness religion to the state. The status quo letter reflected his efforts to win religious support and tie the hands of religious leaders at the same time. Organized religion became utterly dependent on the Israeli state as a result of the accommodation it accepted. The political power of the religious parties, vastly augmented by the arrival of Jews from the Arab world, enriched the terms of accommodation over time: By participating in coalitions, the religious parties achieved access to government jobs, concessions on citizenship policy, and guarantees for religious education.

Complete separation of church and state is an unattainable ideal, because religious organizations, even if autonomous, must function within rules established by the state. To be sure, though a state ban on all but official religious groups of the sort implemented by Atatürk cannot abolish belief or even practice, it can make collective celebration virtually impossible. It may, as in the case of Soviet hostility to religion, result in an eventual reduction in religious belief among the population, but Sufism did not die in Turkey, and religion did not vanish in the Soviet Union. A perfect merger of church and state, which Machiavelli thought the early Romans had achieved, is not possible either, because the purposes of the two domains are quite different. The early caliphs of Islam discovered this fact. Quran reciters, the antecedents of ulama, quickly assumed a role in society distinct from the political and military role of the caliph.

These four countries all have official religious establishments. All tolerate nonofficial religions, but nowhere are members of nonofficial religions regarded as full citizens. Can one imagine a non-Muslim as prime minister of Turkey, Egypt, or Iran? A non-Jew as prime minister of Israel? Iran draws the line at permitting Bahais to enjoy even the rights accorded Christians and Jews. All these countries sponsor official religious establishments with somewhat limited tolerance for minorities within. For example, Conservative and Reformed congregations operate under handicap in Israel. The Shii elite in Iran accept Sunnis as full Muslims but conduct official ceremonies as if the country were entirely Shii. Similarly, in Turkey the Alevi minority regards the Islamist movement now controlling the government with suspicion, and the Directorate of Religious Affairs does not supervise Alevi ceremonies. Alevism does not fit into the official religion of Turkey.

This immixture of government in the organization and function of religion creates problems for democracy in every case. Citizens cannot all be equal if members of some religious organizations receive favored treatment over others. There cannot be equality before the law, if some religious groups are outlawed for religious reasons, as are the Bahais in Iran, or if there is effectively no place for atheists. These weaknesses exist in all four countries, three predominantly Muslim, one Jewish. They exist in the two countries that proclaim their religious character in their name, Israel and Iran, and they exist in two countries that like to think of themselves as more secular, Turkey and Egypt. The two countries with more democratic institutions, Turkey and Israel, struggle with this problem almost as much as the more authoritarian pair.

The strength of these four states depends in some measure on their identity with religion. The states have all sought to control religious institutions as they engaged in the process of state-building. Turkey and Israel have nonetheless moved rather decisively toward liberal democracy, while Iran and Egypt have made less progress in this direction. Somewhat greater separation of politics and religion would be helpful in promoting democracy in all cases, but to think that regimes will relinquish this sort of control without first making a much stronger commitment to democracy is unrealistic.

Some have argued that religious organizations such as the Muslim Brotherhood in Egypt constitute a part of civil society, and the growth of civil society can somehow force the hand of the regime in moving more quickly toward democracy. This study suggests the contrary sequence: Once a regime decides to democratize, it will permit more freedom for autonomous religious organization. This was the sequence in Turkey and Israel. Secular leadership, dedicated to creating democratic polities, saw that it needed the support of a religious public and needed to accord that public a legitimate place in the body politic. Democratic principles pushed these countries to permit freedom of association, the right to form political parties, the right to personal belief. Predominantly secular political organizations opened the way for greater religious influence in the system, without directly attacking the existence of an official religious establishment. The European dynamic was similar. Countries such as Britain maintained an established religion but gradually permitted equal access to other groups, even Catholics and atheists.

In none of the four countries does the government-managed religious establishment have a monopoly on religious organization. In Egypt new mosques appear and function without government knowledge or control. Dissident preachers manage to propagate their sermons. Sufi groups continue to meet within and without the establishment. And, of course, Coptic Christians maintain their own hierarchy of religious authority. The Muslim Brotherhood constitutes a loosely structured semipolitical, semireligious locus of activity. In Turkey the variety of religious activity is even greater, and the Directorate of Religious Affairs is more open in acknowledging the plurality. In Israel, even the hierarchy of the official establishment splits between Ashkenazi and Sephardim, each community with its own chief rabbi. But the ultraorthodox go their own way, Conservative and Reformed communities struggle for recognition, and the state recognizes fourteen non-Jewish groups. Not even in Iran can one speak of "monopoly" in describing state Shiism, even though control there may be tighter than in the other three states.

It is difficult to imagine an end to government endorsement of an established religion in these countries in any near future. Neither the American notion of separation nor the more radical French idea of laïcité seems relevant in these situations or even necessary for democratization. A progressive lessening of the monopolistic qualities of the religious establishments is both more realistic as an objective and more likely as a consequence of moves toward democratization. An organizational pluralism in the religious sphere is not so much a prerequisite but a natural outcome of the process by which all citizens acquire a larger stake and influence in government. The democratization of Turkey after 1950 eventually brought an end to Kemalist efforts to monopolize religious life. As democratic processes in Israel brought more and more Middle Eastern immigrants into political life, the religious establishment split to accommodate them. The victory of Likud in the "earthquake" election of 1977 opened the system to greater religious influence from groups such as the Gush Emunim and Shas, themselves outside the Ashkenazi establishment. Democratization in both countries led to a broadening of elites exercising state control over religion, and the broadening of elites led to a greater willingness to recognize religious pluralism.

The limiting factors in this process of moving toward institutional pluralism may be identity and ideology. To accord non-Jewish institutions fully equal status would be to compromise the Jewish character of the state of Israel. To permit state Shiism to be one religion among many in Iran would call into question the nature of the Islamic Republic. Ideology poses a further constraint on democratization insofar as religious officials insist upon a single, unerring interpretation of religious law. Some theoretical acceptance of religious pluralism must follow from the sort of democratic development sketched above, if the emerging configuration of plural institutions is to acquire legitimacy. Such an evolution of ideas may already be occurring within official religious establishments as the sociology of religion changes before their eyes. Witness the testimony of one *alim* at Azhar in Egypt: "We are not the only people who speak for Islam in this country!" Witness also the statement of the Turkish director of religious affairs: "Secularism does not call for the interpretation of religion by the state. Rather it provides freedom to individuals and to public institutions in the interpretation of religion and in the production and transmission of religious knowledge."[17] If there is movement in the domain of ideology, then identity may loom as the greatest obstacle to the achievement of genuine religious pluralism. Change of identity in Israel and Iran is difficult to conceive without revolution.

Political Culture

Modernization theory suggests that attitudes evolve as societies move from preindustrial to industrial and then to postindustrial stages of development. Inglehart proposes a global model of human development in which people first move away from traditional values, deeply anchored in religion, toward a quest for material well-being and security. Then, once a certain level of industrialization is achieved, they begin to shift their value priorities toward individual liberty and self-expression. Religious instincts come to be expressed differently. Inglehart does not insist on the inevitability of the process and is undismayed that some cases, such as the United States, do not confirm to his model countries. He believes that the grouping of countries on these two scales reflects "civilization." For him this is "political culture" at work.

Political culture appears to be an independent variable of some consequence in determining where countries now stand, but it is subject everywhere to the forces of economic and social development. Inglehart predicts that secularization will continue everywhere at different rates and in somewhat different patterns as a result of cultural differences. Muslim countries seem to be on a different path from that of former communist countries, which differs from that of African and West European states.

This study has included three predominantly Muslim countries, in which people show high levels of religiosity, and a Jewish state, where the percentage of highly religious respondents is small. But the three Muslim countries look radically dissimilar on many grounds, including that of political culture. It's

TABLE 7.1

Influences on Political Culture

	EGYPT	ISRAEL	TURKEY	IRAN
Imperialism	Occupation	Mandate	Defeat	Zones of Influence
Primary Religious Group	Sunni Muslim (90%)	Jewish (76%)	Sunni Muslim (85%?)	Shii Muslim (88%)
Principal Religious Minority	Christian (8–10%)	Muslim (16%)	Alevi (15%?)	Sunni (8%)
Language	Arabic (99%)	Hebrew (65%?)	Turkish (85%?)	Persian (51%)
Principal Minority Language	---	Arabic (20%)	Kurdish (15%?)	Turkish (25%)

Question marks denote author's estimate based on divergent sources. Many of these statistics have political significance. Minorities inevitably claim larger numbers than governments report. Governments tend to exaggerate the ethnic and religious dominance of the majority.

no surprise that the Israelis also appear unique. Rather, it is the similarities that surprise in looking at the relationship between religion and political culture in Israel and the Muslim states, because Israel has distanced itself from the others in socioeconomic development. Inglehart causes us to expect that Israel will be different, but he does not prepare us for the differences among Muslim states or the many similarities between Muslim states and Israel.

The underlying problem in all these countries is the creation or preservation of a political culture that is congruent with the identity of the state, the predominant political ideology, and the structure of political institutions. In Israel, for example, the political culture must support a state that identifies itself as Jewish, even though non-Jews constitute a significant portion of the body politic. The political culture must sustain a prevailing ethic of liberal democracy, even though some Jewish religious groups think identity questions and legislation in certain other areas ought not to be subject to democratic debate and decisions. The halakha should take precedence. The political culture must sustain a single unified state without destroying the religious pluralism that is a reality, and education is the state's principal tool for accomplishing these objectives. But the state has had to settle for four educational systems, which probably produce at least four different understandings of the relation between religion and politics, giving stability to the political conflict that has marked the state from independence. To unify education would jeopardize this stability.

Turkey seems headed for a similar sort of solution. After a long period in which state schools inculcated the Kemalist vision of secularism, the need to train imams led to the creation of a separate, government-controlled system of religious education. As the system became more democratic after 1950, the new political parties moved to strengthen religious education, and the products of religious education eventually made their way into government ministries to enhance and protect these changes. As everywhere else, a rise in literacy in Turkey, fostered in considerable measure by groups such as the Alevis and the Nurcus as well as Islamists, has contributed to a new understanding of religion and religious behavior as a matter of choice, and not just habit. Education reinforces the democratic proclivities of the body politic, and those proclivities make it impossible to turn the schools back toward the sort of civic education characteristic of the Kemalist era. Such politics also make it unlikely that Islamists can turn the public schools into a tool for eradicating Kemalism. The Erdoğan government disavows any such intent.

Important issues remain to be resolved. The place of Kurdish culture in the educational system is one. Scholarly treatment of the Armenian massacres of 1894–1895 and during World War I is another. The relationship of independent Turkey to its Ottoman past is a third, and the place of Mustafa Kemal Atatürk in Turkish history will surely be a part of the debate about the history curriculum. Will the schools be fully available to Muslim women who choose to cover their heads as a sign of piety? The effectiveness of any national government depends upon a supportive political culture. Every government wishes to enhance unity and patriotism, but, as the Turks discovered, trying to achieve that end by propaganda and an educational system hostile to religion produced the opposite result.

The battle for control of education goes on in both Egypt and Iran, albeit in authoritarian settings. Democracies depend upon compromise as a means of living with inconsistency and contradiction, but contradictions in Egypt and Iran are more difficult to resolve. Egypt provides separate schools to maintain Muslim and Christian cultures, even though it identifies itself as a Muslim state. The modern educational system of Egypt, begun under British rules, was supposed to train good Muslim citizens, but in fact it has also trained Islamist opponents, radical Muslims, and Coptic activists. The regime claims to be secular but makes concessions on all sides without apparent logic—not even the logic of democratic setting, where a majority carries the day. President Mubarek has never faced a seriously competitive election. Thus secularists, Islamists, Copts—all feel insecure. They fear that this regime, or a subsequent one, will seek radical change in the political culture of the country.

Those fears have afflicted Iran since the revolution. In a highly fragmented political culture on both ethnic and religious grounds, the regime has pushed hard on a Persian Shii version of the state, with greater emphasis on religion than on language. Thus, Azerbaijani Turks, who are predominantly Shii, are not considered a minority, but all non-Shii groups feel some threat from the regime's efforts at producing a single, homogenous political culture. The regime's focus on creating a single Islamic nation for all Muslims conflicts with the national reality. Efforts to create loyalty to the Supreme Leader, the faqih, conflict with the accepted notion that Iranians are free to select the Grand Ayatollah (marja), who will be their model for emulation, and with the broad acceptance of democratic principles in the political culture. Repression has thus far been the regime's primary response to dissidence in the political culture.

Stability in the political culture of these countries does not require secularism or even the disestablishment of religion. Forced secularization in Turkey did not produce a uniform, secular political culture, and it seems unlikely that the attempt to create uniform religiosity in Iran will create stability there, despite the efforts of the regime. Stability comes when government recognizes it has no interest in promoting or damaging particular religious groups, and religious groups themselves feel secure in their relationship to the government. They feel confident in their ability to perpetuate their unique communities. Almost everywhere this means some control over the education of their own progeny with necessary deference to state norms. Secularists must accept religious expression in the public sphere, and religious adherents must accept both secularists and other religious strains as legitimate and worthy of respect. In the Middle East, Israel, Turkey, and Lebanon have been leaders in this regard. The Saudi monarchy, with its attachment to the puritanical Wahhabi version of Islam and its intolerance for non-Muslims and even non-Wahhabi practices in school curricula, has lagged in moving toward toleration.

Any sort of stability evolves with domestic circumstances and international climate. A sharp increase in prosperity, as in Iran in the 1970s and in the Persian Gulf states since 1990, necessarily occasions readjustments. Economic stagnation and unemployment, characteristic of Egypt and Iran, produce readjustments of another sort. The wave of international opposition to U.S. policies in Palestine and Iraq has tipped the balance in a number of states.

Some governments have found the war on terrorism an excuse to further repress Islamist opposition. Tunisia would be an example. Others have found it harder to ally themselves with the United States on matters of local, regional, and international interest, for fear of provoking Islamist opposition. Saudi Arabia would be an example. One great advantage of democratic process is that it permits continual readjustment of policy and institutions. A measure of permanent flexibility ensures stability. Authoritarian regimes such as Tunisia and Saudi Arabia fear even the slightest tremor of primary instability, for lack of secondary stability in the system.

Hypotheses Revisited

The evidence collected from four case studies does not suffice to confirm any general hypothesis about religion and politics. I believe, however, that these case studies call into question a number of hypotheses set forth in chapter 2.

Hypothesis #1: A culture steeped in religion—committed to myth, to magic, to faith in God rather than faith in human effort—will be unable to produce subjects, much less citizens, of a modern state. Such a culture must be "secularized"—that is, "rationalized"—if genuine political development is to occur.

Mustafa Kemal Atatürk would have subscribed to this hypothesis, and even Inglehart seemed to accept it in early writings, but the statement is much too categorical. No state is fully secular. Many states combine liberal democracy or at least "genuine political development" (e.g., Israel and Turkey) with high commitment to religion.

Hypothesis #2: Because political development depends upon training subjects and then citizens, it ultimately depends upon education. The state must take from religious institutions the task of educating citizens; it has no responsibility for religious education and must avoid any involvement in particular sorts of religious education.

Most states have taken over much of the responsibility for public education from religious institutions, but a stable relationship between religious organizations and the state often depends upon the maintenance of plural educational systems, as in Europe and the United States. Israel maintains four tracks, and the other countries in this study all use two or three different systems to preserve religious sensibilities. Outright secularization of the educational system usually means teaching something about religion even if it does not mean teaching religion. Most states, even postindustrial states, seem to be involved "in particular sorts of religious education."

Hypothesis #3: Organized religion, where it takes hierarchical form, may obstruct political development by resisting state efforts to develop state authority and provide directly for the general welfare of citizens.

The Iranian example shows that religious hierarchy can also promote revolution. The late shah treated the religious establishment as an obstacle, and he lost a confrontation with it. It remains to be seen whether the religious establishment, still separate from government, will continue its support for the new regime in Iran or eventually undermine its position. Mostly, states have attempted to create religious hierarchy to enforce their own version of religion on the country. All four of these states have sought to create or subjugate religious hierarchies. In doing so they may strengthen state authority, but they also undermine the religious legitimacy of the hierarchies they create. They open the way for challenge from lay leaders.

Hypothesis #4: Only a state in which religion and politics are thoroughly separated can provide political development.

It is difficult to imagine what "thorough" separation would be. The French consider that they have achieved greater laïcité than any other European state, but the state's links with religious schools, religious holidays, and religious institutions (including a new Muslim council) make it difficult to talk about "thorough separation." In the United States, tax exemption for religious groups and ready use of religious language to support policies make even less apt the use of the term "thorough separation." Institutional separation takes priority in the United States. Separation in identity, ideology, and political culture is less clearly sought and achieved.

Hypothesis #5: Religious organizations and parties formed by groups intent upon imposing their version of God's will threaten the stability of any proto-democratic regime. To ensure its own development, a state must block the progress of such groups.

This hypothesis may be correct, but it is also true that drawing organizations into the political mix often changes the character and purpose of these groups. Turkey is the best example here. The New Outlook (Islamist) movement

Necmettin Erbakan founded and carried from one political organization to another became something quite different as a participant in the government of the Justice and Development Party headed by Erdoğan. The apparent intolerance of the Muslim Brotherhood blocks its progress toward democratic participation—or perhaps it serves the Egyptian regime with an excuse to prevent the Brotherhood from the sort of participation that might soften its ideological approach.

Hypothesis #6: Some religions, such as Roman Catholicism and Islam, are undemocratic in tendency. Others (varieties of Protestantism) seem to be linked to the growth of democratic institutions. Hence, some types of religion must give way or engage in reform if political development is to occur.

This study provides no means of testing this hypothesis. The differences in the nature of Islam among the three Muslim states studied here make one instinctively skeptical, however, of characterizing Islam as necessarily democratic or undemocratic in tendency. Israel and Turkey would seem to be examples where politics have led to changes in the nature of religion. Religious reform may follow political reform rather than vice versa.

Hypothesis #7: Religious ideology has no place in the public forum, because liberal-democratic development requires its progressive elimination. Reasoned argument susceptible to challenge must be the basis for the legitimacy of regimes and policies in a liberal-democratic setting, whereas arguments based in religious doctrine and conviction cannot be debated. Thus, one might argue against abortion on the grounds that a fetus is already a person worthy of defense, but one cannot simply say, "I am against abortion because God says it is wrong."

Such an argument makes no sense in the contexts of the Middle Eastern countries studied here. Religious arguments necessarily figure in public debate. Turkey held to this line for the first twenty-five years of independence but has been forced by political realities to move away from such a rigorous notion of secularism.

Hypothesis #8: The transformation of religious doctrine into contemporary political ideology cannot serve the purposes of political development (or the purposes of religion, for that matter). D. E. Smith called the politicization of religion a "short-lived process characteristic of the

*politics of transitional societies."[18] Inglehart refers to the Islamic revival
in the Middle East as a short-term exception to the pattern of secularization characteristic of modernization.*

A century from now, history will tell us whether the Islamic revival was a short-term or long-term phenomenon. The modern effort to make Islam into a political ideology is now more than a century old. In an age when other ideologies (Nazism, Marxism) have largely disappeared, it is tempting to think that Islamism will eventually lose its appeal, as well. In Israel and Turkey, conflict over religious ideology may have diminished.

Hypothesis #9: Religious identities, when not congruent with a state's boundaries, may prevent the formation of strong polities capable of ensuring peace and liberty for its citizens.

In none of these four states is there congruence between religious and political boundaries. Does such congruence exist anywhere in the world? Israel has made a virtue of its relationship to the larger world of Judaism. Iran has thus far been less successful in identifying itself with Islam as a whole. Egypt and Turkey have not sought to do so.

Hypothesis #10: Strong religious identities tend to spill over boundaries and cause groups to identify with religious cohorts elsewhere. Conflicts grounded in economic inequality, social injustice, or political struggle come to be regarded as religious confrontations and even elevated into a clash of civilizations.

These four cases confirm the importance of the nation-state. Iran hoped that its revolution would carry into other Muslim states, but it did not happen. What has happened in Turkey apparently has not affected Egypt, but Hamas, originally a spinoff of the Muslim Brotherhood in Egypt, might be an example of a religiously oriented spillover becoming identified with a political struggle previously seen as secular by most Palestinians. Egyptians who went to work in Algeria as teachers after independence, some of them loyal to the Brotherhood, contributed to the growth of a militant Islamist movement there.[19] Al-Qaida has sought to transform conflicts between North and South, East and West, into a clash of civilizations.

Hypothesis #11: Political development means weaning people from magic and superstition, but it also means winning the support of the

rural masses for the political system. Religion constitutes the point of con-
tact. Hence, the state must use religion to reach the masses and wean
them from magic and superstition. It must foster a version of religion
that is friendly to state authority, liberalism, tolerance, and democracy.

Said Nursi set out to do something like this in Turkey against the wishes of
the regime. Once the single party gave way to multipartism after World War
II, the new parties won support among the rural masses in part because of
their greater friendliness toward religion of all sorts. Jenny White's book
about "vernacular politics" in Turkey emphasizes just this point. She argues
that the Islamist movement has contributed to the development of Turkish
democracy.[20]

Hypothesis #12: "Rational" types of religion may trigger individual ini-
tiative, encourage the spread of education, and spur economic growth.
Economic prosperity will in turn make available resources vital to the
construction of a modern nation-state, and an increasingly educated, ra-
tional political culture will support liberalization and democratization.

The Nur movement and its successors started Turkey down this road. The
Alevis have played a somewhat similar role, as have some Sufi brotherhoods.
A new economy has emerged to support publications, associations, tourist facilities, shops, and even political parties. The Muslim Brotherhood has served
something of this purpose in Egypt.

Hypothesis #13: A state united in religious belief may enjoy higher lev-
els of mutual trust among citizens and rulers. Rulers may come to iden-
tify their own well-being with the state's strength and prosperity, and
subjects may be willing to sacrifice short-term well-being for the long-
term strength of public institutions.

Atatürk promoted Islam for that reason in the early days of Turkish independence. Islam served then, as it does now, as a bridge to the Kurdish population, in particular. But, however true the hypothesis, none of the four states
disposes of perfect religious unity. Judaism helps pull together Jewish citizens of
Israel but divides them from Arabs. Islam unites most Egyptians, but when
government emphasizes Islam, Copts feel excluded. Iran trumpets its Shii identity and downplays its non-Shii and non-Muslim minorities. As the hypothesis
suggests, religious unity would be advantageous but it may be unrealizable.

Hypothesis #14: At a basic level, religion and state are inseparable. Every state reflects a moral (or immoral) purpose, whether that be mere personal aggrandizement of the rulers, the rather modest objective of keeping the peace, or some combination of more ambitious objectives, such as justice, liberty, and social justice. To enjoy any semblance of legitimacy, the state must champion objectives grounded in the predominant understanding of morality.

These four cases support this hypothesis. The leadership of these four states has held to this position, as have others in the Middle East. The Soviet Union and its Eastern European puppet states sought to deny this proposition, as have some other Marxist regimes.

Hypothesis #15: The progressive exclusion of religion from the body politic would undermine the state's legitimacy. The most fundamental principles of liberal-democratic government cannot be reduced to empirical propositions. It is impossible to show empirically that people are equal. That proposition, like others, requires a leap of faith or a normative judgment. Religion can help nurture faith in democracy.

None of these states or others in the Middle East provide good data to test this proposition. None of these states has sought "progressive exclusion of religion from the body politic." The successor states of Eastern Europe constitute a better sample. Surveys suggest that Marxism did render these states more secular in attitude than other countries at their level of development.

Hypothesis #16: The separation of religion and politics deprives the state of a moral critique vital for its renewal. To exclude religious language from the public place and to insist on the complete assimilation of conservative religious groups is to weaken the state by alienating citizens for whom religion necessarily defines every political project.

This is a corollary of hypotheses 14 and 15, and the same comments apply. This hypothesis seems most problematic in the postindustrial democracies of Western Europe, not in the United States or the Middle East.

Hypothesis #17: Religious organizations engaged in projects promoting the common welfare—education, medical care, child care, etc.—can help generate a set of nongovernmental institutions that train citizens and open the way to a stronger, more inclusive state. They can contribute to the construction of civil society.

Some studies of Middle Eastern societies have taken the view that civil society can open the way toward a "stronger, more inclusive state." Civil society leads to democracy. The problem is that the state regulates civil society. Without authorization and autonomy, organizations cannot create the sort of dynamic civil society that would produce change. In Egypt and Iran the authorities block the sort of civil organizations that might threaten them. Political change appears to be a prerequisite for the development of the civil society that is supposed to produce the political change. Turkey and Israel provide models of that sequence.

Hypothesis #18: Harnessing the organizational power of religion can enhance the state's reach, giving it the strength to push ahead with economic and social development. Alternatively, the organizational capacity of religion can overturn a state otherwise incapable of galvanizing the support of the masses, as in Iran.

Iran may be exceptional for the hierarchical organization of the religious establishment that enabled Ayatollah Khomeini to lead a revolution. It remains to be seen whether any group of Sunni ulama could act against a state, or whether a lay Islamist group such as the Muslim Brotherhood could carry out a revolution.

Hypothesis #19: Politicization of religion produces a pluralization of religious groups that may eventually contribute to pluralism in the political arena.

Israel might be an example here, although political pluralism has existed from the prestate days of the Yishuv. Politicization of religion in Turkey under Atatürk, who sought to control all religious expression, did spark the creation of new, underground religious groups that ultimately resurfaced and contributed to politics. Regimes politicize religion in an aim to preserve or create a monopoly. Pluralism may sometimes be an unintended and undesired consequence of such policies.

Hypothesis #20: When organized religion decides to enter the democratic fray by sponsoring (or tolerating) political parties bearing the name of religion, the result is often tantamount to accepting democratic rule. In-

corporating religious groups strengthens the state and constitutes a step toward political development

The participation of Orthodox (National Religious Party) and ultraorthodox (Shas) political parties complicated political life in the new state of Israel. One or more of the religious parties have almost always been a vital element in Israeli coalitions. Could the state have survived without their support? Those rejecting the state out of religious conviction have remained a tiny minority. Because the religious parties have normally drawn 15 percent to 20 percent of the vote in Israel, one can imagine as much as a fifth of the electorate alienated from the state, if Orthodox and ultraorthodox leaders had not seen fit to collaborate.

Hypothesis #21: Modernization has generated the problem of identity by pulling people closer together, making them aware of differences, causing them to think about others and therefore about themselves. The spread of literacy enabled people to read for themselves the texts that defined their faith and to think about religion as a separable aspect of self. Identity then becomes a question, rather than an unreflected given. Political development requires an answer to that question, and religion can help provide such an answer.

This hypothesis calls attention to religion as a modern response to a modern question: the identity of a nation-state. All four of the states included in this study have committed or recommitted themselves to religion as an element of national identity in the past half century. Turkey moved in this direction in the 1960s and then more decisively in the 1980s. Egypt changed course under Anwar al-Sadat. Israel reaffirmed its commitment to Judaism with the election of Menachem Begin in 1977. Iran underwent religious revolution. While every country claims to evoke an eternal identity with religion, these changes all reflect modern needs and modern circumstances.

Hypothesis #22: A state built upon religious identity and reflecting major elements of national history may be able to construct institutions seen as indigenous in origin, capable of generating a loyalty among subjects and citizens that other governments do not enjoy.

This is the claim of authenticity. The monarchies have specialized in it. Some have not succeeded (Libya and Yemen, for instance) but others survive despite "the king's dilemma" observed by Huntington. The World Values

Survey has turned up strong evidence of a relationship between religiosity and nationalism, but it is not certain that a state can generate greater religiosity and thereby enhance nationalist feeling. Iran has tried to do just that. Egyptian, Turkish, and Israeli leaders have not cultivated religiosity as much as they have sought to exploit it for national purposes. Patriotism runs high in all these states.

Hypothesis #23: Building a strong state means developing a strong resource base, and to do that a state must grant productive forces sufficient autonomy and liberty to generate wealth. Once a state achieves a certain level of prosperity, the new, prosperous middle class will demand inclusion in the political system. Neither element of political development (institutional strength, inclusiveness) depends on religion.

The logic is compelling but these cases offer no empirical support for the proposition.

Hypothesis #24: Politics shapes religion much more than religion shapes politics. Religion should thus be understood as a dependent variable, not a causative factor for political development

That is the fundamental hypothesis of this study. One cannot understand the shape of religion in any of these four countries without understanding the political context in which religion has evolved. What can one predict from the nature of Judaism about the political contours of Israel? What can one derive from Islam about Turkey, Egypt, or Iran? If Islam were a principal factor in the politics of these countries, how could they be so different? Even if one studied Twelver Shiism and its development in Iran after 1500 and through 1960, one could scarcely project the political structure and processes of contemporary Iran. Politics made Shii Islam what it is today in Iran. Israel recreated contemporary Judaism, within its borders and beyond. Mustafa Kemal Atatürk is arguably the principal architect of modern Islam in Turkey, ironic as that may seem.

Hypothesis #25: Where there is sharp competition among religious sects and groups, religious organizations will tend to be stronger than in countries where a state-sponsored church dominates religious life.

These cases do not afford a test of this hypothesis. In all these cases the state dominates the religious establishment, but the states (in their current form) are not yet old enough for religious organization to ossify. Religion remains an important element of national identity, a factor in ideology, and a determining force in political culture.

These cases all demonstrate the importance of religion in political life. The identity claims, the ideological foundations, the institutions, and the political culture—all reflect religious texts, doctrines, history, and practices. Religious organizations exert influence on political life in all these countries, but they do so within limits established by the state. When religious organizations attain genuine political power, they offer the best testimony to the primacy of politics. Religious leadership can only defend itself, its organization, its resources, and its principles by political activity. Of course, religious organizations can choose to shun politics, but they can do so only if the state permits them to do so. When Turkey banned religious brotherhoods, it politicized them. Secret meetings became political acts of defiance.

The question then is not whether religion will become democratic in the Middle East, as in Western Europe and the United States. The question is whether democratizing states will compel religious groups to accept and participate in democratic politics. It is whether states will themselves abandon the hope of monopolizing religious organization and observance, accepting plurality, even if they maintain an established religion. It is whether they compel all religious groups to accept plurality in return for the right to a realm of autonomy, including some control over religious education.

These actions presume the existence of a strong state, bolstered by the allegiance of key religious groups. A state that wins allegiance by opening the political process to greater inclusiveness will in the long run be stronger than those who seek to impose an exclusive religion and compel allegiance. The state needs religious support, but religion needs the state even more.

Notes

1. See Zachary Lockman, *Contending Visions of the Middle East: The History and Politics of Orientalism* (Cambridge, UK: Cambridge University Press, 2004), for a judicious discussion of the debate about Orientalism.

2. See John C. Green, *The Faith Factor: How Religion Influences American Elections* (Westport, CT: Praeger, 2007).

3. See Elizabeth Shakman Hurd, *The Politics of Secularism in International Relations* (Princeton, NJ: Princeton University Press, 2008), 12. She writes: "Secularism refers to a public settlement of the relationship between politics and religion."

4. See Mark Lilla, *The Stillborn God* (New York: Alfred A. Knopf, 2007), for a superb discussion of Hobbes and those who have wrestled with this problem since he wrote.

5. Hurd, *The Politics of Secularism*, 26ff.

6. Charles E. Lindblom, *The Intelligence of Democracy: Decision Making Through Mutual Adjustment* (New York: Free Press, 1965).

7. Samuel P. Huntington, *Political Order in Changing Societies* (New Haven, CT: Yale University Press, 1967), chapter 2.

8. Huntington, *Political Order,* chapter 1.

9. Ronald Inglehart and Christian Weizel, *Modernization, Cultural Change, and Democracy: The Human Development Sequence* (Cambridge, UK: Cambridge University Press, 2005).

10. Dale Eickelman and James Piscatori, *Muslim Politics* (Princeton, NJ: Princeton University Press, 1996).

11. World Values Survey, WVS 9062000, G015, "Which of the following best describes you?" Online computation. Surveys of Egypt, Iran in 2000. Israel and Turkey in 2001.

12. World Values Survey, "Which of the following best describes you?"

13. Baruch Kimmerling, *The Invention and Decline of Israeliness* (Berkeley: University of California Press, 2001).

14. Kimmerling, *The Invention and Decline,* 39–40. For a detailed discussion of Israeli historiography of the period, see Sylvain Cypel, *Walled: Israeli Society at an Impasse* (New York: Other Press, 2006), chapter 1.

15. Fouad Ajami, *The Vanished Imam: Musa al-Sadr and the Shi'a of Lebanon* (Ithaca, NY: Cornell University Press, 1986).

16. The reference is to Samuel P. Huntington's formulation of the "king's dilemma." See Huntington's *Political Order in Changing Societies* (New Haven, CT: Yale University Press, 1967), chapter 3.

17. Ali Bardakoğlu, "'Moderate Perception of Islam' and the Turkish Model of the Diyanet: The President's Statement," *Journal of Muslim Minority Affairs* 24, no. 2 (October 2004): 369.

18. D. E. Smith, *Religion and Political Development* (Boston: Little, Brown, 1970), 125.

19. See, for example, Martin Evans and John Phillips, *Algeria: Anger of the Dispossessed* (New Haven, CT: Yale University Press, 2007), 77, 86–87.

20. Jenny White, *Islamist Mobilization in Turkey: A Study in Vernacular Politics* (Seattle: University of Washington Press, 2002).

Glossary

aliya (pl. aliyot) "Ascension" to Israel. Ingathering of Jews. Often used to designate a particular period of immigration, as, for example, the "second aliya," which brought many of the country's founders to Palestine.

Anatolia Peninsula containing the Asian provinces of modern Turkey.

Ashkenazi Israelis of European origin.

ayatollah Literally, "sign of God." Title assigned to Iranian ulama who have achieved a high level of religious learning.

Bahais Religious group founded by Bahaullah in nineteenth-century Iran. He was a follower of the Bab, who scandalized ulama by claiming to be the "gate" to the Hidden Imam. Iran regards Bahais as heretics.

bazaari(s) Merchants. The bazaar is the central market in an Iranian city.

cadi (qadi) Judge. One who applies the law of Islam, the sharia.

Coptic Christians One of the earliest Christian communities, host to some of the earliest Christian monasticism, distinguished in part by their attachment to the monophysite position on the nature of Christ.

dar al-Ifta Office of the mufti, source of religious opinions called fatwas.

dar al-Islam The "house of Islam," or that territory governed by Muslims.

dati Orthodox Jews. Those who follow most Jewish traditions and support Zionism.

devshirme A levy imposed by the Ottoman Empire on the Christian provinces, by which young Christian boys were inducted into the imperial service. Converted to Islam and educated as soldiers and bureaucrats, they became "slaves" of the sultan.

dhikr Routine by which Sufis (Muslim mystics) commune with God. A dhikr may include chanting the names of God, singing, dancing, or other acts.

dhimmi Protected minorities of the Ottoman Empire. "Religions of the book," such as Christianity and Judaism, enjoyed *dhimmi* status.

état laïc French term for a secular state.

faqih (pl. fuqaha') Jurisprudent. One who practices fiqh, which is the science of law.

fatwa A religious opinion.

fiqh Jurisprudence. The science of law.

ghazi (gazi) Raider on behalf of the faith; holy warrior

hadith (pl. ahadith) Saying or tradition attributed to the Prophet, known to subsequent generations by oral transmission. Legal scholars examined the whole body of hadith and compiled those they regarded as authentic.

hajj Pilgrimage to Mecca. One of the five pillars of Islam.

halakha Jewish religious law.

haredim Ultraorthodox Jews, many of whom reject the legitimacy of the state of Israel.

hijab (hejab) Scarf covering the head and shoulders. Some Muslims insist women must wear one when they are in a public place.

hijra The movement of the fledgling Muslim community from Mecca to Yathrib (which became Medina, the city of the Prophet) in 622 ce. That is the starting point for the traditional Muslim calendar.

hisba State of conforming to God's will by doing right and forbidding or avoiding wrong.

hojjatoleslam A title accorded to graduates of theological seminaries.

ijtihad Interpretation of sharia by qualified jurists. Legitimate at certain times and under certain conditions, according to some schools of thought.

imam Prayer leader. Also, in the Shii tradition, one of the legitimate line of successors to the Prophet.

Islamist A person or group who argues for the political relevance of Islam. In general, one who seeks the modern implementation of the sharia, or at least parts of it.

jahiliyya Ignorance. Hence, the age before the coming of Islam. Also applied by some radicals (Qutb, bin Laden) to the contemporary age.

javanmard An Iranian conception of the ideal man.

jihad Effort, striving on behalf of one's faith. May include the legitimate use of violence under some circumstances.

kahal (kehilla) Traditional Jewish community in the Diaspora.

kashrut Jewish dietary rules.

kibbutz (pl. kibbutzim) An egalitarian community in Israel originally dedicated to agricultural production on the basis of rotating responsibilities linked to the Labor Settlement Movement.

Knesset The Israeli parliament, a single-house legislature that exercises full sovereignty.

kufr Nonbeliever, heretic.

laïc Secular (French). Thoroughly separate from religion.

laïcité Secularism of a rather extreme form (French).

madrasa (medrese) Higher-level school for Islamic learning.

Majlis Parliament in Iran.

marja-e taqlid Shii cleric regarded by his peers as a model worthy of emulation.

marja-e taqlid matlaq Shii cleric regarded by peers as the sole model of emulation in his generation.

maslahat Public interest. Muslim jurists may seek to set aside provisions of the sharia to accommodate such interests.

masorti "Traditional" Jews. Tend to observe generally accepted traditions as well as customs from Middle Eastern and North African settings that do not figure in Ashkenazi Orthodoxy (dati).

millet A non-Muslim religious community enjoying some autonomy and protection (*dhimmi* status) in the Ottoman Empire.

Mizrachi (pl. Mizrachim) Israeli Jews of Middle Eastern and North African origin. (Also the name of an early Orthodox political movement that became the National Religious Party.) Such immigrants are also called Sephardim (as opposed to Ashkenazim) and Oriental (as opposed to Western) Jews.

mufti A high religious official, source of religious opinions.

mujtahid A Muslim jurist who engages in ijtihad, that is, exercises some independent judgment in interpreting the sharia.

mullah Common word for a cleric in Iran. *Ulama* is a more formal (Arabic) term for the clerical class.

NGO Nongovernmental organization, national or international.

niqab An extreme form of modest dress in which women cover themselves head to toe. A veil may cover all but the eyes.

Orientalism The study of the Middle East and North Africa as it developed in Europe in the nineteenth and early twentieth centuries. Marked by an emphasis on language and the analysis of texts.

Pahlavi Family name taken by Reza Khan when he took the throne in Iran in 1925 His son Muhammad Reza ruled as king until the revolution of 1978–1979.

pays réel French term for "real country," meaning that which lies beyond parliament.

Qajar Ruling family in Iran from the late eighteenth until the early twentieth century.

Quran (Qur'an) Holy scripture of Islam. Also spelled Coran or Koran.

sadr al-'ulama' Cleric appointed by the monarch in an effort to control the ulama in Iran.

Safavids Ruling family of Iran from 1501 until the early eighteenth century.

salafi (salafiyya) Pious ancestors and, by extension, those modern Muslims who seek to follow the path of the pious ancestors.

sharia (shari'a) The law constructed by Muslim scholars working from the Qur'an and the sunna of the Prophet in the centuries after his death.

shaykh A "white head," a leader, a tribal chief, or a mystic thought to have special abilities to commune with God.

Shaykh al-Azhar Government-appointed head of Azhar Mosque/University in Egypt. Regarded by some as the principal religious authority in the country.

shaykh al-Islam Principal religious authority in the Ottoman Empire.

Shia (Shi'a) "Party." Has come to refer to the "party of Ali," those who supported him as the legitimate heir of Muhammad and who regard his descendents as the rightful rulers of early Islam.

Shii (Shi'i) One who belongs to the "party of Ali." Also an adjective referring to that which pertains to the Shia. Also written Shiite.

Sufi A Muslim mystic, one who seeks spiritual purity in ways that go beyond adherence to the sharia.

sunna What was done in the time of the Prophet. Initially known by oral transmission and by tradition. Later known principally through the hadith literature, which recorded acts and sayings of the Prophet and his companions.

Sunni Mainstream Muslims, non-Shia. They constitute more than 90 percent of all Muslims in the world. Also an adjective used for those things pertaining to Sunnis and Sunnism.

tariqa (tarikat) Sufi orders or brotherhoods, headed by a shaykh and often named from a founding shaykh. Tariqa in Arabic. Tarikat in Turkish.

tekkes Meeting places of the Sufi brotherhoods in Turkey.

Twelvers One strain of Shi'i Islam, a strain that predominates in Islam. Ismailis are Seveners. Zaidis are Fivers. Twelvers believe that the twelfth in a line of designated successors to the Prophet disappeared in the ninth century and will reappear some day.

ulama (sing. *alim*) Scholars of Islam. Includes people who act in various religious capacities—preachers, prayer leaders, teachers—some much more scholarly than others. Also written "ulema."

umma The community of Muslim believers.

velayat-e faqih Persian for "rule of the supreme jurisprudent." A theory put forth by Ayatollah Khomeini and implemented in the Iranian constitution.

Wahhabi A school of puritanical Islam that came to dominate in Saudi Arabia. Looks to Ibn Abd al-Wahhab, an eighteenth-century scholar, as its founding authority.

waqf (pl. *awqaf*) Pious foundation for the support of Islamic institutions. *Vaqf* (*evqaf*) is the Turkish form. The concept seems to date from the twelfth century. Most governments have taken over the pious foundations.

yeshiva Ultraorthodox school for training pupils in the religious tradition. Little emphasis on modern subjects.

Yishuv The Jewish community in Palestine before 1948, when it declared its independence as the state of Israel.

Bibliography

General

Ahmed, Leila. *Women and Gender in Islam.* New Haven, CT: Yale University Press, 1992.

Ajami, Fouad. *The Vanished Imam: Musa al-Sadr and the Shi'a of Lebanon.* Ithaca, NY: Cornell University Press, 1986.

Almond, Gabriel A., and Sidney Verba, eds. *The Civic Culture Revisited.* Newbury Park, CA: Sage Publications, c1989.

———. *The Civic Culture: Political Attitudes and Democracy in Five Nations.* Princeton, NJ: Princeton University Press, 1963.

Anderson, Benedict. *Imagined Communities: Reflections on the Origin and Spread of Nationalism,* rev. ed. London: Verso, 1991.

Antonius, George. *The Arab Awakening: The Story of the Arab National Movement.* New York : G. P. Putnam's Sons, 1946.

Arkoun, Mohammed. *Humanisme et islam: combats et propositions.* Paris: Vrin, 2005.

———. *Rethinking Islam,* ed. and trans. Robert D. Lee. Boulder, CO: Westview, 1994.

———. "Positivisme et tradition dans une perspective islamique: Le cas du kémalisme." *Diogène* 127 (July–September 1984).

Asad, Talal. *Formations of the Secular: Christianity, Islam, Modernity.* Stanford, CA: Stanford University Press, 2003.

Audi, Robert. *Religious Commitment and Secular Reason.* Cambridge, UK: Cambridge University Press, 2000.

Ayoob, Mohammed. *The Many Faces of Political Islam: Religion and Politics in the Muslim World.* Ann Arbor: University of Michigan Press, 2008.

Azmeh, Aziz al-. *Muslim Kingship: Power and the Sacred in Muslim, Christian and Pagan Polities.* London: I. B. Tauris, 1995.

Banfield, Edward C. *The Moral Basis of a Backward Society.* New York: Free Press, 1958.

Barbier, Maurice. *La Laïcité.* Paris: Editions L'Harmattan, 1995.

Barnett, Michael N. *Dialogues in Arab Politics.* New York: Columbia University Press, 1998.

Bates, Robert H. *Prosperity and Violence: The Political Economy of Development.* New York: Norton, 2001.

Baudoin, Jean, and Philippe Portier, eds. *La laïcité, une valeur d'aujuourd'hui? Contestations et negotiations du modèle français.* Paris: Presses universitaires de France, 2001.

Bayat, Asef. *Making Islam Democratic: Social Movements and the Post-Islamist Turn.* Stanford, CA: Stanford University Press, 2007.

Bedouelle, Greg, and Jean-Paul Costa. *Les laïcités à la française.* Paris: Presses universitaries de France, 1998.

Bencheikh, Saheif. *Marianne et le prophète: l'Islam dans la France laïque.* Paris: Bernard Grasset, 1998.

Berger, Peter. *The Sacred Canopy: Elements of a Sociological Theory of Religion.* Garden City, NY: Doubleday, 1967.

Binder, Leonard. "The Crisis of Political Development," in Binder et al., *Crises and Sequences in Political Development.* Princeton, NJ: Princeton University Press, 1971.

Brown, Nathan J. "Shari'a and State in the Modern Muslim Middle East." *International Journal of Middle East Studies* 29, no. 3 (August 1997): 359–376.

Burgat, François. *Face to Face with Political Islam.* London: I. B. Tauris, 2003, trans. from the French, *Islamisme en face.* Paris: Editions La Découverte, 1996.

Carter, Stephen. *The Culture of Disbelief.* New York: Basic Books, 1993.

Casanova, José. *Public Religions in the Modern World.* Chicago: University of Chicago Press, 1994.

Cesari, Jocelyne. *Musulmans et républicaines; les jeunes, l'islam, et la France.* Paris: Editions Complexe, 1998.

Chadwick, Owen. *The Secularization of the European Mind in the Nineteenth Century.* Cambridge, UK: Cambridge University Press, 1975.

Chatterjee, Partha. *Nationalist Thought and the Colonial World.* London: Zed, 1986.

Coq, Guy. *Laïcité et République: Le lien nécessaire.* Paris: Editions du Félin, 1995.

Demerath, N. J. III. "Religious Capital and Capital Religions: Cross-Cultural and Non-Legal Factors in the Separation of Church and State." *Daedalus* 120, no. 3 (Summer 1991): 21–40.

Dobbelaere, Karel. "The Secularization of Society? Some Methodological Suggestions," in Jeffrey K. Hadden and Anson Shupe, eds., *Secularizaion and Fundamentalism Reconsidered: Religion and the Political Order, Vol. III.* New York: Paragon House, 1986.

Durkheim, Emile. "The Elementary Forms of Religious Life," in W. S. F. Pickering, ed., *Durkheim on Religion.* Atlanta: Scholars Press, 1994.

Eickelman, Dale F., and James Piscatori. *Muslim Politics.* Princeton, NJ: Princeton University Press, 1996.

Eisenach, Eldon J. *The Next Religious Establishment: National Identity and Political Theology in Post-Protestant America.* Lanham, MD: Rowman & Littlefield, 2000.

Ertman, Thomas. *Birth of the Leviathan: Building State and Regimes in Medieval and Early Modern Europe.* Cambridge, UK: Cambridge University Press, 1997.

Etienne, Bruno. *La France et l'islam.* Paris: Hachette, 1989.

Evans, Martin, and John Phillips. *Algeria: Anger of the Dispossessed.* New Haven, CT: Yale University Press, 2007.

Fortin, Ernest L. *Human Rights, Virtue and the Common Good: Untimely Meditations on Religion and Politics,* ed. J. Brian Benested. Lanham, MD: Rowman & Littlefield, 1996.

Gauchet, Marcel. *La religion dans la démocratie.* Paris: Gallimard, 1998.

————. *The Disenchantment of the World: A Political History of Religion.* Trans. Oscar Burge. Princeton, NJ: Princeton University Press, 1997.

Gibson, William. *The Church of England, 1688–1832: Unity and Accord.* London: Routledge, 2001.

Green, John C. *The Faith Factor: How Religion Influences American Elections.* Westport, CT: Praeger, 2007.

Hadden, Jeffrey K. "Desacralizing Secularization Theory," in Hadden and Anson Shupe, eds., *Secularization and Fundamentalism Reconsidered: Religion and the Political Order, Vol. III.* New York: Paragon House, 1986.

Haim, Sylvia, ed. *Arab Nationalism: An Anthology.* Berkeley: University of California Press, 1964.

Halpern, Manfred. *The Politics of Social Change in the Middle East and North Africa.* Princeton, NJ: Princeton University Press, 1963.

Hanson, Eric O. *Religion and Politics in the International System Today.* Cambridge, UK: Cambridge University Press, 2006.

Harris, Frederick C. "Something Within: Religion as a Mobilizer of African-American Political Activism." *Journal of Politics* 56, no. 1 (February 1994): 42–68.

Hefner, Robert W. *Civil Islam: Muslims and Democratization in Indonesia.* Princeton, NJ: Princeton University Press, 2000.

Hefner, Robert W., and Mohammad Qasim Zaman, eds. *Schooling Islam: The Culture and Politics of Modern Muslim Education.* Princeton, NJ: Princeton University Press, 2007.

Henry, Clement M., and Robert Springborg. *Globalization and the Politics of Development in the Middle East.* Cambridge, UK: Cambridge University Press, 2001.

Hodgson, Marshall. *The Venture of Islam,* vol. I,. Chicago: University of Chicago, 1961.

Huntington, Samuel P. *American Politics: The Promise of Disharmony.* Cambridge, MA: Belknap Press, 1981.

————. *The Clash of Civilizations and the Remaking of World Culture.* New York: Simon & Schuster, 1996.

Hurd, Elizabeth Shakman. *The Politics of Secularism in International Relations.* Princeton, NJ: Princeton University Press, 2008.

Inglehart, Ronald. *Modernization and Postmodernization: Cultural Economic and Political Change in 43 Societies.* Princeton, NJ: Princeton University Press, 1997.

Inglehart, Ronald, and Christian Weizel. *Modernization, Cultural Change, and Democracy: The Human Development Sequence.* Cambridge, UK: Cambridge University Press, 2005.

Kalyvas, Stathis N. "Democracy and Religious Politics." *Comparative Political Studies* 31, no. 3 (June 1998): 292–230.

Kaufman, Peter Iver. *Redeeming Politics*. Princeton, NJ: Princeton University Press, 1990.

Keddie, Nikki. *An Islamic Response to Imperialism: Political and Religious Writings of Sayyid Jamal al-Din "al-Afghani."* Berkeley: University of California Press, 1983.

Kedourie, Elie. *Nationalism*. London: Hutchinson, 1960.

———. *Afghani and Abduh: An Essay on Religious Unbelief and Political Activism in Islam*. New York: Humanities Press, 1966.

———. *Democracy and Arab Political Culture*. Washington, DC: Washington Institute for Near East Policy, 1991.

Kepel, Gilles, *Jihad: Expansion et déclin de l'islamisme*. Paris: Gallimard, 2000.

———. *Jihad: The Trail of Political Islam*, trans. Anthony F. Roberts. Cambridge, MA: Harvard University Press, 2002.

Kerr, Malcolm. *Islamic Reform: The Political and Legal Theories of Muhammad Abduh and Rashid Rida*. Berkeley: University of California Press, 1966.

———. *The Arab Cold War*. London: Oxford University Press, 1967.

Kopstein, Jeffrey, and Sven Steinmo, eds. *Growing Apart?: America and Europe in the Twenty-First Century*. Cambridge, UK: Cambridge University Press, 2008.

Lamchichi, Abderrahim. *Islam et musulmans de France*. Paris: L'Harmattan, 1999.

Lee, Robert D. *Overcoming Tradition and Modernity: The Search for Islamic Authenticity*. Boulder, CO: Westview Press, 1997.

Leege, David C. "Toward a Mental Measure of Religiosity in Research on Religion and Politics," in Ted G. Jelen, ed., *Religion and Political Behavior in the United States*. New York: Praeger, 1989.

Lewis, Bernard, ed. and trans. *Islam from the Prophet Muhammad to the Capture of Constantinople*, vol. I. New York: Harper, 1974.

Lilla, Mark. *The Stillborn God*. New York: Alfred A. Knopf, 2007.

Lindblom, Charles E. *The Intelligence of Democracy: Decision Making through Mutual Adjustment*. New York: Free Press, 1965.

Lockman, Zachary. *Contending Visions of the Middle East: The History and Politics of Orientalism*. Cambridge, UK: Cambridge University Press, 2004.

Margalit, Avishai. "Sectarianism." *Dissent* 55, no. 1 (Winter 2008): 37–46.

Martin, David. *A General Theory of Secularization*. Oxford, UK: Blackwell, 1978.

Martinez, Luis. *La guerre civile en Algérie, 1990–1998*. Paris: Editions Karthala, 1998.

Nasr, Seyyed Vali Reza. *Islamic Leviathan: Islam and the Making of State Power*. Oxford, UK: Oxford University Press, 2001.

Nicholls, David. *God and Government in an "Age of Reason."* London: Routledge, 1995.

Norton, Augustus Richard, ed. *Civil Society in the Middle East*, 2 vol. Leiden, Netherlands: Brill, 1995–1996.

Norris, Pippa, and Ronald Inglehart. *Sacred and Secular: Religion and Politics Worldwide*. Cambridge, UK: Cambridge University Press, 2004.

Pecora, Vincent P. *Secularization and Cultural Criticism: Religion, Nation, and Modernity*. Chicago: University of Chicago Press, 2006.

Redissi, Hamadi. *Le pacte de Nadjd: ou comment l'islam sectaire est devenue l'islam.* Paris: Seuil, 2007.

Rodinson, Maxime. *Mohammed,* trans. Anne Carter. New York: Viking, 1974.

Roy, Olivier. *La Sainte Ignorance: Le Temps de la Religion Sans Culture.* Paris: Seuil, 2008.

Said, Edward. *Orientalism.* New York: Pantheon Books, 1978.

Scott, David, and Charles Hirschkind, eds. *Power of the Secular Modern: Talal Asad and His Interlocutors.* Stanford, CA: Stanford University Press, 2006.

Shaban, M. A. *Islamic History: A New Interpretation,* 2 vol. Cambridge, UK: Cambridge University Press, 1976.

Smidt, Corwin. "Religion and Civic Engagement: A Comparative Analysis." *Annals of the American Academy of Political and Social Science* 565 (September 1999): 176–192.

Smith, Donald Eugene *Religion and Political Development.* Boston: Little, Brown, 1970.

Smith, Steven B. *Spinoza, Liberalism, and the Question of Jewish Identity.* New Haven, CT: Yale University Press, 1997.

Spinner-Halev, Jeff. *Surviving Diversity: Religion and Democratic Citizenship.* Baltimore: Johns Hopkins University Press, 2000.

Tessler, Mark, and Jodi Nachtwey. "Religion and International Conflict: An Individual-Level Analysis," in Tessler, ed., *Area Studies and Social Science: Strategies for Understanding Middle East Politics.* Bloomington: Indiana University Press, 1999.

Waldner, David. *State Building and Late Development.* Ithaca, NY: Cornell University Press, 1998.

Willaime, Jean-Paul. "Unification européene et religions," in Jean Baudoin and Philippe Portier, eds., *La laïcité, une valeur d'aujourd'hui? Contestations et negotiations du modèle français.* Paris: Presses universitaires de France, 2001.

Wolfart, Johannes C. *Religion, Government and Political Culture in Early Modern Germany: Lindau, 1520–1628.* New York: Palgrave, 2002.

Wuthnow, Robert. *Communities of Discourse: Ideology and Social Structure in the Enlightenment, and European Socialism.* Cambridge, MA: Harvard University Press, 1989.

Egypt

Abed-Kotob, Sana. "The Accommodationists Speak: Goals and Strategies of the Muslim Brotherhood of Egypt." *International Journal of Middle East Studies* 27 (August 1995): 321–339.

Al-Ali, Nadje. *Secularism, Gender and the State in the Middle East.* Cambridge, UK: Cambridge University Press, 2000.

Ben Néfissa, Sarah. "Citoyenneté et participation en Egypte: l'Action vertueuse selon la Gami'iyya Shari'iyya." *Monde Arabe Maghreb Machrek* 167 (January–March 2000): 14–24.

Berger, Maurits S. "Apostasy and Public Policy in Contemporary Egypt: An Evaluation of Recent Cases from Egypt's Highest Courts." *Human Rights Quarterly* 25 (2003).

Bowie, Robert R. *Suez, 1956*. New York: Oxford University Press, 1974.

Cook, Bradley J. "Islam and Egyptian Higher Education: Student Attitudes." *Comparative Education Review* 45, no. 3 (August 2001): 379–409.

Crecelius, Daniel. "The Course of Secularization in Modern Egypt," in *Islam and Development*, ed. John L. Esposito. Syracuse, NY: Syracuse University Press, 1980.

———. "The Ulama and the State in Modern Egypt." PhD dissertation, Princeton University, May 1967.

Dupret, Baudouin. "Justice égyptienne, moralité publique et pouvoir politique." *Monde Arabe Maghreb Machrek* 167 (January–March 2000): 25–31.

Fandy, Mamoun. "Egypt's Islamic Group: Regional Revenge?" *Middle East Journal* 48, no. 4 (Autumn 1994): 611–625.

Faraj, Muhammad Abd al-Salam. *The Neglected Duty: The Creed of Sadat's Assassins and the Creed of the Islamic Resurgence in the Middle East*, ed. and trans. Johannes J. G. Jansen. New York: Macmillan, 1986.

Ferrié, Jean-Noël, and Saâida Radi. "Consensus national et identité morale: le sida comme analyzeur de la société égyptienne." *Monde Arabe Maghreb Machrek* 167 (January–March 2000): 6–13.

Gershoni, Israel, and James P. Jankowski. *Redefining the Egyptian Nation, 1930–1945*. Cambridge, UK: Cambridge University Press, 1995.

Haawwa, Saeed. *The Muslim Brotherhood*, trans. Abdul Karim Shaikh. Kuwait: Al Faisal Islamic Press, 1985.

Hatina, Meir. "On the Margins of Consensus: The Call to Separate Religion and State in Modern Egypt." *Middle Eastern Studies* 36, no. 1 (January 2000): 35–67.

Hirschkind, Charles. "The Ethics of Listening: Cassette-sermon Audition in Contemporary Egypt." *American Ethnologist* 28, no. 3 (August 2001): 623–649.

Hirschl, Ran. "Constitutional Courts vs. Religious Fundamentalism: Three Middle Eastern Tales." *Texas Law Review* 82, no. 7 (June 2004): 1819–1870.

Ibrahim, Saad Eddin. *Egypt, Islam and Democracy: Critical Essays*. Cairo: American University in Cairo, 1996.

Jabarti, Abd al-Rahman al-. *Napoleon in Egypt: Al-Jabartî's Chronicle of the First Seven Months of the French Occupation, 1798*, trans. Smuel Moreh. Princeton, NJ: M. Wiener, c1993.

Johansen, Baber. "Apostasy as Objective and Depersonalized Fact: Two Recent Egyptian Court Judgments." *Social Research* 70, no. 3 (Fall 2003): 687–710.

Khatab, Sayed. "Al-Hudaybi's Influence on the Development of Islamist Movements in Egypt." *Muslim World* 91, no. 3/4 (Fall 2001): 451–479.

Levy, Guenter. "Nasserism and Islam: A Revolution in Search of Ideology," in Donald Eugene Smith, ed., *Religion and Political Modernization*. New Haven, CT: Yale, 1974, 280, quoting from P. J. Vatkiotis.

Mahmood, Saba. "Feminist Theory, Embodiment, and the Docile Agent: Some Reflections on the Egyptian Islamic Revival." *Cultural Anthropology* 16, no. 2 (May 2001): 202–236.

Mitchell, Richard P. *The Society of Muslim Brothers*. New York: Oxford University Press, 1993.

Qutb, Sayyid. *Milestones*, rev. trans. Indianapolis: American Trust Publications, 1990.
———. *A Child from the Village*, ed. and trans. by John Calvert and William Shepard. Syracuse, NY: Syracuse University Press, 2004.
Sedra, Paul. "Class Cleavages and Ethnic Conflict: Coptic Christian Communities in Modern Egypt." *Islam and Christian-Muslim Relations* 10, no. 2 (July 1999): 219–235.
Shahin, Emad El-Din. "Political Islam in Egypt." CEPS Working Document #266 (May 2007).
Shehata, Samer, and Joshua Stacher. "The Brotherhood Goes to Parliament." *Middle East Report* (240).
Shepard, William E. "Sayyid Qutb's Doctrine of Jāhiliyya." *International Journal of Middle East Studies* 35, no. 4 (November 2003): 521–545.
———. "Muhammad Said al-Ashmawi and the Application of the Shari'a in Egypt." *International Journal of Middle East Studies* 28, no. 4 (February 1996): 39–58.
Skovgaard-Petersen, Jakob. *Defining Islam for the Egyptian State: Muftis and Fatwas of the Dār al-Iftā*. Leiden, Netherlands: Brill, 1997.
Starrett, Gregory. *Putting Islam to Work: Education, Politics and Religious Transformation in Egypt*. Berkeley: University of California Press, 1998.
Sullivan, Denis J., and Sana Abed-Kotob. *Islam in Contemporary Egypt: Civil Society vs. the State*. Boulder, CO: Lynne Rienner, 1999.
Zeghal, Malika. *Gardiens de l'Islam: Les oulémas d'Alzhar dans l'Egypte contemporaine*. Paris: Fondation nationale des sciences politiques, 1996.
Zeidan, David. "The Copts—Equal, Protected or Persecuted? The Impact of Islamization on Muslim-Christian Relations in Modern Egypt." *Islam and Christian-Muslim Relations* 10, no. 1 (March 1999): 53–67.

Israel

Arian, Asher. *The Second Republic: Politics in Israel*. Chatham, NJ: Chatham House, 1998.
Avishai, Bernard. *The Tragedy of Zionism: Revolution and Democracy in the Land of Israel*. New York: Farrar, Straus, Giroux, 1985.
Ben Zadok, Efraim. "State-Religion Relations in Israel: The Subtle Issue Underlying the Rabin Assassination," in Efraim Karsh, ed., *Israeli Politics and Society Since 1948: Problems of Collective Identity*. London: Frank Cass, 2002.
Bar-Lev, Mordechai. "Politicization and Depoliticization of Jewish Religious Education in Israel." *Religious Education* 86, no. 4 (Fall 1991): 608–618.
Bick, Etta. "A Party in Decline: Shas in Israel's 2003 Elections." *Israel Affairs* 10, no. 4 (Summer 2004): 98–129.
Cohen-Almagor, Raphael. "Vigilant Jewish Fundamentalism: From the JDL to Kach (or 'Shalom Jews, Shalom Dogs')." *Terrorism and Political Violence* 4, no. 1 (Spring 1992): 44–66.
Dominguez, Virginia. *People as Subject, People as Object: Selfhood and Peoplehood in Contemporary Israel*. Madison: University of Wisconsin Press, 1989.

Dowty, Alan. *The Jewish State: A Century Later.* Berkeley: University of California Press, 1998.

Edelman, Martin. "A Portion of Animosity: The Politics of the Disestablishment of Religion in Israel." *Israel Studies* 5, no. 1 (Spring 2000): 204–227.

Gross, Zehavit, "State-Religious Education in Israel: Between Religion and Modernity." *Prospects* 33, no. 2 (June 2003): 149–164.

Harrison, Jo-Ann. "School Ceremonies for Yitzhak Rabin: Social Construction of Civil Religion in Israeli Schools." *Israel Studies* 6, no. 3 (Fall 2001): 113–134.

Hirschl, Ran. "Constitutional Courts vs. Religious Fundamentalism: Three Middle Eastern Tales." *Texas Law Review* 82, no. 7 (June 2004): 1819–1870.

Isaac, Rael Jean. *Israel Divided: Ideological Politics in the Jewish State.* Baltimore: Johns Hopkins University Press, 1976.

Leibowitz, Yeshayahu. *Judaism, Human Values, and the Jewish State*, ed. Eliezer Goldman. Cambridge, MA: Harvard University Press, 1992.

Lerner, Hanna. "Democracy, Constitutionalism, and Identity: The Anomaly of the Israeli Case." *Constellations* 11, no. 2 (June 2004): 237–257.

Liebman, Charles S., and Eliezer Don-Yehiya. *Religion and Politics in Israel.* Bloomington: Indiana University Press, 1984.

Liebman, Charles S., and Elihu Katz, eds. *The Jewishness of Israelis: Responses to the Guttman Report.* Albany: State University of New York Press, 1997.

Lockard, Joe. "Israeli Utopianism Today: Interview with Adi Ophir." *Tikkun* 19, no. 6 (November–December 2004): 18–21.

Mirsky, Yehudah. "Inner Life of Religious Zionism." *New Leader* 78, no. 9 (December 4, 1995): 10–14.

Neuberger, [Ralph] Benyamin. *Religion and Democracy in Israel*, trans. Deborah Lemmer. Jerusalem: Floersheimer Institute for Policy Studies, c1997.

Nyroos, Lari. "Religeopolitics: Dissident Geopolitics and the 'Fundamentalism' of Hamas and Kach." *Geopolitics* 6, no. 3 (Winter 2001).

Raday, Frances. "Women's Rights: Dichotomy between Religion and Secularism in Israel." *Israel Affairs* 11, no. 1 (January 2005): 78–94.

Ravitzky, Aviezer. "Is a Halakhic State Possible? The Paradox of Jewish Theocracy." *Israel Affairs* 11, no. 1 (January 2005): 137–164.

Sacks, Jonathan. *One People? Tradition, Modernity, and Jewish Unity.* London: Littman Library of Jewish Civilisation, 1993.

Segev, Tom. *1949: The First Israelis*, trans. Arlen Neal Weinstein. New York: Free Press, 1986.

Shafir, Gershon, and Yoav Peled. *Being Israeli: The Dynamics of Multiple Citizenship.* Cambridge, UK: Cambridge University Press, 2002.

Sharkansky, Ira. "Assessing Israel." *Shofar: An Interdisciplinary Journal of Jewish Studies* 18, no. 2 (Winter 2000): 1–18.

Sprinzak, Ehud. "Violence and Catastrophe in the Theology of Rabi Meir Kahane: the Ideologization of Mimetic Desire." *Terrorism and Political Violence* 3, no. 3 (Autumn 1991): 48–70.

Weissbrod, Lilly. "Shas: An Ethnic Religious Party." *Israel Affairs* 9, no. 4 (Summer 2003): 79–104.

Zucker, Norman L. *The Coming Crisis in Israel: Private Faith and Public Policy.* Cambridge, MA: MIT Press, 1973.

Turkey

Ahmad, Feroz. *Turkey: The Quest for Identity.* Oxford, UK: Oneworld Publications, 2003.

Aral, Berdal. "Dispensing with Tradition? Turkish Politics and International Society during the Özal Decade, 1983–93." *Middle Eastern Studies* 37, no. 1 (January 2001): 72–88.

Arat, Yeşim. *Rethinking Islam and Liberal Democracy: Islamist Women in Turkish Politics.* Albany: State University of New York Press, 2005.

Aydintaşbaş, Asli. "Murder on the Bosporous." *Middle East Quarterly*, (June 2000).

Bardakoğlu, Ali. "'Moderate Perception of Islam' and the Turkish Model of the Diyanet: The President's Statement." *Journal of Muslim Minority Affairs* 24, no. 2 (October 2004).

Barkey, Henry J. "The Struggles of a 'Strong' State." *Journal of International Affairs* 54, no. 1 (Fall 2000): 87–105.

Çinar, Alev. *Modernity, Islam, and Secularism in Turkey: Bodies, Places, and Time.* Minneapolis: University of Minnesota Press, 2005.

Daği, Ihsan D. "Transformation of Islamic Political Identity in Turkey: Rethinking the West and Westernization." *Turkish Studies* 6, no. 1 (March 2005): 21–37.

Deringil, Selim. "The Invention of Tradition as Public Image in the Late Ottoman Empire, 1808 to 1908." *Comparative Studies in Society and History* 35, no. 1 (January 1993): 3–29.

———. "'There Is No Compulsion in Religion': On Conversion and Apostasy in the Late Ottoman Empire: 1839–1856." *Comparative Studies in Society and History* 42, no. 3 (July 2000): 547–575.

Duran, Burhanettin. "Approaching the Kurdish Question via *Adil duzen*: An Islamist Formula of the Welfare Party for Ethnic Coexistence." *Journal of Muslim Minority Affairs* 18, no. 1 (April 1998): 111–128.

Erman, Tahire, and Emrah Göker. "Alevi Politics in Contemporary Turkey." *Middle Eastern Studies* 36, no. 4 (October 2000): 99–118.

Gaborieau, Marco, Alexandre Popovic, and Thierry Zarcone, eds. *Naqshbandis: cheminements et situation actuelle d'un ordre mystique musulman . . . : actes de la table ronde de Sèvres . . . 2–4 mai . . . 1985.* Istanbul: Isis Yayımcılık Ltd., 1990.

Göle, Nilüfer. "Snapshots of Islamic Modernities." *Daedalus* 129, no. 1 (Winter 2000): 91–117.

———. *The Forbidden Modern: Civilization and Veiling.* Ann Arbor: University of Michigan Press, 1996.

Gülalp, Haldun. "Whatever Happened to Secularization? The Multiple Islams of Turkey." *South Atlantic Quarterly* 102, no. 2/3 (Spring–Summer 2003): 381–395.

———. "Globalization and Political Islam: the Social Bases of Turkey's Welfare Party." *International Journal of Middle East Studies* 33, no. 3 (August 2001): 433–448.

———. "Enlightenment by Fiat: Secularization and Democracy in Turkey." *Middle Eastern Studies* 41, no. 3 (May 2005).

Gülen, Fethullah. *Advocate of Dialogue*. Fairfax, VA: The Fountain, 2000.

Herman, Rainer. "Political Islam in Secular Turkey." *Islam and Christian-Muslim Relations* 14, no. 3 (July 2003): 265–276.

Houston, Christopher. "Profane Intuitions: Kurdish Diaspora in the Turkish City." *Australian Journal of Anthropology* 12, no. 1 (April 2001): 15–31.

———. "Civilizing Islam, Islamist Civilizing? Turkey's Islamist Movement and the Problem of Ethnic Difference." *Thesis Eleven*, no. 58 (August 1999): 83–98.

Kalaycioğlu, Ersin. "The Mystery of the Türban: Participation or Revolt." *Turkish Studies* 6, no. 2 (June 2005): 233–251.

Kaya, Ibrahim. "Modernity and Veiled Women." *European Journal of Social Theory* 3, no. 2 (May 2000): 195–214.

Kinzer, Stephen. *Crescent and Star: Turkey Between Two Worlds*. New York: Farrar, Straus and Giroux, 2001.

Kosebalaban, Hasan. "The Impact of Globalization on Islamic Political Identity: The Case of Turkey." *World Affairs* 168, no. 1 (Summer 2005): 27–37.

Kushner, David. "Self-Perception and Identity in Contemporary Turkey." *Journal of Contemporary History* 32, no. 2 (April 1997): 219–233.

Lewis, Bernard. *The Emergence of Modern Turkey*. London: Oxford University Press, 1961.

Mardin, Serif. *Religion and Social Change in Modern Turkey: The Case of Bediüzzaman Said Nursi*. Albany: State University of New York Press, 1989.

———. "The Just and the Unjust." *Daedalus* 120, no. 3 (Summer 1991): 113–129.

———. "Turkish Islamic Exceptionalism Yesterday and Today: Continuity, Rupture and Reconstruction in Operational Codes." *Turkish Studies* 6, no. 2 (June 2005).

Mason, Whit. "The Future of Political Islam in Turkey." *World Policy Journal* 17, no. 2 (Summer 2000): 56–67.

Moaddel, Mansoor. *Islamic Modernism, Nationalism, and Fundamentalism: Episode and Discourse*. Chicago: University of Chicago Press, 2005.

Olsson, Tord, Elizabeth Ozdalga, and Catharina Randvere, eds. *Alevi Identity*. Istanbul: Swedish Research Institute in Istanbul, 1998.

Öniş, Ziya. "The Political Economy of Islamic Resurgence." *Third World Quarterly* 18, no. 4 (December 1997): 743–766.

Pamuk, Orhan. *Istanbul: Memories and the City*, trans. Maureen Freely. New York: Random House, 2006.

Payaslyoğlu, Arif, and Ahmet Içduygu. "Awareness Of and Support for Human Rights Among Turkish University Studies." *Human Rights Quarterly* 21, no. 2 (May 1999): 513–534.

Rahme, Joseph G. "Namik Kemal's Constitutional Ottomanism and Non-Muslims." *Islam and Christian-Muslim Relations* 10, no. 1 (1999): 23–39.

Rouleau, Eric. "Ce pouvoir si pesant des militaires turcs." *Le monde diplomatique* (September 2000): 8–9.

Sakallioğlu, Ümit Cizre. "Parameters and Strategies of Islam-State Interaction in Republican Turkey." *International Journal of Middle East Studies* 28, no. 2 (May 1996): 231–251.

Silverstein, Brian. "Islam and Modernity in Turkey: Power, Tradition and Historicity in the European Provinces of the Muslim World." *Anthropological Quarterly* 76, no. 3 (Summer 2003): 497–517.

Şimşek, Sefa. "New Social Movements in Turkey since 1980." *Turkish Studies* 5, no. 2 (Summer 2004): 111–139.

Tank, Pinar. "Political Islam in Turkey: A State of Controlled Secularity." *Turkish Studies* 6, no. 1 (March 2005): 3–19.

Turam, Berna. *Between Islam and the State.* Stanford, CA: Stanford University Press, 2007.

Vahide, Şükran. *Islam in Modern Turkey: An Intellectual Biography of Bediuzzaman Said Nursi.* Albany: State University of New York Press, 2005.

Ward, Robert E., and Dankwart Rustow, eds. *Political Modernization in Japan and Turkey.* Princeton, NJ: Princeton University Press, 1964.

Waxman, Dov. "Islam and Turkish National Identity: A Reappraisal." *Turkish Yearbook of International Relations* 30 (2000): 1–22.

White, Jenny. "State Feminism, Modernization and the Turkish Republican Woman." *NWSA Journal* 15, no. 3 (Fall 2003): 145–159.

———. *Islamist Mobilization in Turkey: A Study in Vernacular Politics.* Seattle: University of Washington Press, 2002.

Yavuz, M. Hakan. "Cleansing Islam from the Public Sphere." *Journal of International Affairs* 54, no. 1 (Fall 2000): 21–42.

———. *Islamic Political Identity in Turkey.* New York: Oxford University Press, 2003.

Iran

Abdo, Geneive. "Re-Thinking the Islamic Republic: A 'Conversation' with Ayatollah Hossein 'Ali Montazeri." *Middle East Journal* 55, no. 1 (Winter 2001): 9–22.

Abrahamian, Ervand. *Iran Between Two Revolutions.* Princeton, NJ: Princeton University Press, 1982.

———. *Khomeinism: Essays on the Islamic Republic.* Berkeley: University of California Press, 1993.

Adelkhah, Fariba. "Le ramadan comme négotiation entre le public et le privé: le cas de la République d'Iran," in Adelkhah et François Georgeon, eds., *Ramadan and politique.* Paris: CNRS, 2000.

———. *Being Modern in Iran,* trans. Jonathan Derrick. New York: Columbia University Press, 2000.

Ahmad, Jalal Al-i. *Occidentosis: A Plague from the West,* trans. R. Campbell, ed. Hamid Algar. Berkeley, CA: Mizan Press, 1984.

Akhavi, Shahrough. *Religion and Politics in Contemporary Iran: Clergy-State Relations in the Pahlavi Period.* Albany: State University of New York Press, 1980.

Algar, Hamid. *Religion and State in Iran, 1785–1906: The Role of the Ulama in the Qajar Period.* Berkeley: University of California Press, 1969.

Alinejad, Mahmoud. "Coming to Terms with Modernity: Iranian Intellectuals and the Emerging Public Sphere." *Islam and Christian-Muslim Relations* 13, no. 1 (January 2002): 25–47.

Amirpur, Katajun. "The Future of Iran's Reform Movement," in Amirpur and Walter Posch, eds., *Iranian Challenges*, Chaillot Paper #89. Paris: European Union Institute for Security Studies, 2006.

Arjomand, Saïd Amir. "The Rise and Fall of President Khatami and the Reform Movement in Iran." *Constellations* 12, no. 4 (December 2005): 502–520.

Ashraf, Ahmad. "Bazaar-Mosque Alliance: The Social Basis of Revolts and Revolutions." *International Journal of Politics, Culture and Society* 1, no. 4 (Summer 1988): 538–567.

Ashraf, Ahmad, and Ali Banuazizi. "Iran's Tortuous Path Toward 'Islamic Liberalism.'" *International Journal of Politics, Culture and Society* 15, no. 2 (Winter 2001): 237–256.

Bahramitash, Roksana. "Islamic Fundamentalism and Women's Economic Role: The Case of Iran." *International Journal of Politics, Culture and Society* 16, no. 4 (Summer 2003): 551–568.

Banuazizi, Ali. "Faltering Legitimacy: The Ruling Clerics and Civil Society in Contemporary Iran." *International Journal of Politics, Culture and Society* 8, no. 4 (Summer 1995): 237–256.

Berkey, Jonathan. *The Formation of Islam: Religion and Society in the Near East from 600–1800.* Cambridge, UK: Cambridge University Press, 2004.

Bill, James A. "The Cultural Underpinnings of Politics: Iran and the United States." *Mediterranean Quarterly* 17, no. 1 (Winter 2006): 22–33.

———. *The Politics of Iran: Groups, Classes and Modernization.* Columbus, OH: Merrill, 1972.

Brumberg, Daniel. *Reinventing Khomeini: The Struggle for Reform in Iran.* Chicago: University of Chicago Press, 2001.

———. "Dissonant Politics in Iran and Indonesia." *Political Science Quarterly* 116, no. 1 (2001): 381–411.

Buchta, Wilfried. *Who Rules Iran? The Structure of Power in the Islamic Republic.* Washington, DC: Washington Institute for Near East Policy, 2000.

Bulliet, Richard. *Conversion to Islam in the Middle Period: An Essay in Quantitative History.* Cambridge, MA: Harvard University Press, 1979.

Dabashi, Hamid. *The Theology of Discontent: The Ideological Foundations of the Islamic Revolution in Iran.* New York: New York University Press, 1993.

———. "The End of Islamic Ideology." *Social Research* 67, no. 2 (Summer 2000): 475–518.

———. *Iran: A People Interrupted.* New York: New Press, 2007.

Eshkevari, Hasan Yusefi. *Islam and Democracy in Iran: Eshkevari and the Quest for Reform*, eds. Ziba Mir-Hosseini and Richard Tapper. London: I. B. Tauris, 2006.

Friedl, Erika. *Children of Deh Koh.* Syracuse, NY: Syracuse University Press, 1997.

Gheissari, Ali, and Vali Nasr. "The Conservative Consolidation in Iran." *Survival* 47, no. 2 (Summer 2005): 175–190.

Ibn Khaldun. *The Muqaddima: An Introduction to History*, trans. Franz Rosenthal. Princeton, NJ: Princeton University Press, 1967.

Jahanbaksh, Forough. "Religious and Political Discourse in Iran: Moving Toward Post-Fundamentalism." *Brown Journal of World Affairs* 9, no. 2 (Winter–Spring 2003): 243–254.

Kadivar, Mohsen. "An Introduction to the Public and Private Debate in Islam." *Social Research* 70, no. 3 (Fall 2003).

Keddie, Nikki R. *Modern Iran: Roots and Results of Revolution.* New Haven, CT: Yale University Press, 2003.

Keshavarzian, Aran. "State Building and Religious Resources: An Institutional Theory of Church-State Relations in Iran and Mexico." *Politics and Society* 27, no. 3 (September 1999).

Khomeini, Ruhollah. *Islam and Revolution: Writings and Declarations of Imam Khomeini*, trans. Hamid Algar. Berkeley, CA: Mizan Press, 1981.

Kian, Azadeh. "Women and Politics in Post-Islamist Iran: The Gender Conscious Drive to Change." *British Journal of Middle Eastern Studies* 24, no. 1 (May 1997): 75–96.

Mayer, Ann Elizabeth. "The Islamic Law as a Cure for Political Law: The Withering of an Islamist Illusion." *Mediterranean Politics* 7, no. 3 (Autumn 2002): 117–142.

Mehran, Golnar. "Iran: A Shi'ite Curriculum to Serve the Islamic State," in Eleanor Abdella Doumato and Gregory Starrett, eds., *Teaching Islam: Textbooks and Religion in the Middle East.* Boulder, CO: Lynne Rienner, 2007.

Minoui, Delphine. "L'Iran des réformes: la société face au pouvoir." *Politique étrangère* 67, no. 1 (January–March 2002): 103–114.

Mir-Hosseini, Ziba. "*Divorce Iranian Style*," in Richard Tapper, ed., *The New Iranian Cinema: Politics, Representation and Identity.* London: I. B. Tauris, 2004.

———. "The Conservative-Reformist Conflict Over Women's Rights in Iran." *International Journal of Politics, Culture and Society* 16, no. 1 (Fall 2002): 37–53.

Mottahedeh, Roy. *The Mantle of the Prophet: Religion and Politics in Iran.* New York: Pantheon, 1985.

Nafisi, Azar. *Reading Lolita in Tehran: A Memoir in Books.* New York: Random House, 2003.

Naim, Abdullahi A. Al-. "Re-affirming Secularism for Islamic Societies." *New Perspectives Quarterly* 20, no. 3 (Summer 2003): 36–45.

Omid, Homa. "Theocracy or Democracy? The Critics of 'Westoxification' and the Politics of Fundamentalism, in Iran." *Third World Quarterly* 13, no. 4 (December 1992): 675–690.

———. *Islam and the Post-Revolutionary State in Iran.* New York: St. Martin's Press, 1994.

Paul, Ludwig. "'Iranian Nation' and Iranian-Islamic Revolutionary Ideology." *Die Welt des Islams* 39, no. 2 (July 1999): 183–217.

Roy, Olivier. "The Crisis of Religious Legitimacy in Iran." *Middle East Journal* 53, no. 2 (Spring 1999): 201–216.

Samii, A. William. "Iran's Guardians Council as an Obstacle to Democracy." *Middle East Journal* 55, no. 4 (Autumn 2001): 644–663.

Schirazi, Asghar. *The Constitution of Iran: Politics and the State in the Islamic Republic*, trans. John O'Kane. London: I. B. Tauris,1997.

Shaditalab, Jaleh. "Islamization and Gender in Iran: Is the Glass Half Full or Half Empty?" *Signs* 32, no. 1 (Autumn 2006): 14–21.

Shariati, Ali. *Marxism and Other Western Fallacies: an Islamic Critique*. Berkeley, CA: Mizan Press, 1980.

———. *Red Shi'ism*. Houston: Free Islamic Literatures, 1980.

———. *On the Sociology of Islam: Lectures*. Berkeley, CA: Mizan Press, 1979.

Tabari, Azar. "Shi'i Clergy in Iranian Politics," in Nikki Keddie. ed., *Religion and Politics in Iran*. New Haven, CT: Yale University Press, 1983.

Tabari, Keyvan. "The Rule of Law and the Politics of Reform in Post-Revolutionary Iran." *International Sociology* 18, no. 1 (March 2003): 96–113.

Vahdat, Farzin. *God and Juggernaut: Iran's Intellectual Encounter with Modernity*. Syracuse, NY: Syracuse University Press, 2002.

Watt, W. Montgomery. "The Significance of the Early States of Imami Shi'ism," in Nikki R. Keddie, ed., *Religion and Politics in Iran: Shi'ism from Quietism to Revolution*. New Haven, CT: Yale, 1983.

Zonis, Marvin. *The Political Elite of Iran*. Princeton, NJ: Princeton University Press, 1971.

Index